Contents

advanced skills

advano

Acknowledgements

To our families:

> Dorothy, Matthew and Teagan and
> Karen, Adrian and Ellena

for their love, support and understanding.

Picture credits

Paul Allister; Karen Andrews; Ricky Bond; Andrew Boyle; Catherine Dorsen; Zara Ellis; Andrew Elliot; Tamas Elliot; Samantha Everton; Shaun Guest; Orien Harvey; Itti Karuson; Anitra Keogh; Seok-Jin Lee; Anica Meehan, Benedikt Partenheimer; Raphael Ruz; Fabio Sarraff; Michael Wennrich; Amber Williams; Stuart Wilson.

Also our thanks go to www.ablestock.com for supporting this venture with the supply of various tutorial images.

All other images and illustrations by the authors.

Contents

foundation module

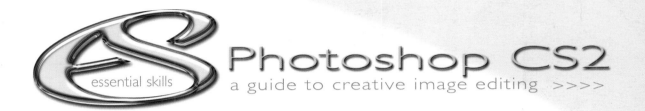

essential skills

Photoshop CS2
a guide to creative image editing >>>>

mark galer

philip andrews

ELSEVIER

AMSTERDAM · BOSTON · HEIDELBERG · LONDON · NEW YORK · OXFORD
PARIS · SAN DIEGO · SAN FRANCISCO · SINGAPORE · SYDNEY · TOKYO
Focal Press is an imprint of Elsevier

Focal
Press

Focal Press is an imprint of Elsevier
Linacre House, Jordan Hill, Oxford OX2 8DP, UK
30 Corporate Drive, Suite 400, Burlington, MA 01803, USA

First edition 2005
Reprinted 2006

British Library Cataloguing in Publication Data
A catalogue record for this book is available from the British Library

Library of Congress Cataloging-in-Publication Data
A catalog record for this book is available from the Library of Congress

ISBN–13: 978-0-240-52000-1
ISBN–10: 0-240-52000-9

For information on all Focal Press publications
visit our website at www.focalpress.com

Printed and bound in *Italy*

06 07 08 09 10   10 9 8 7 6 5 4 3 2

Working together to grow
libraries in developing countries

www.elsevier.com | www.bookaid.org | www.sabre.org

ELSEVIER   BOOK AID International   Sabre Foundation

Contents

advanced

Contents

imaging projects

imaging

Contents

projects

Introduction

Photoshop has helped revolutionize how photographers capture, edit and prepare their images for viewing. Most of what we now see in print has been edited and prepared using the Adobe software. The image editing process extends from basic retouching and sizing of images, to the highly manipulated and preconceived photographic montages that are commonly used by the advertising industry. This book is intended for photographers and designers who wish to use the 'digital darkroom' rather than the traditional darkroom for creative photographic illustration. The information, activities and assignments contained in this book provide the essential skills necessary for competent and creative image editing. The subject guides offer a comprehensive and highly structured learning approach, giving comprehensive support to guide Photoshop users through each editing process. An emphasis on useful (essential) practical advice and activities maximizes the opportunities for creative image production.

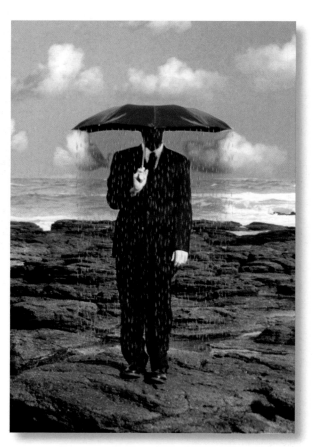

Anitra Keogh

Acquisition of skills

The first section of this book is a foundation module designed to help the user establish an effective working environment and act as a guide for successful navigation through the image-editing process from capture to print. Emphasis is placed on the essential techniques and skills whilst the terminology is kept as simple as possible using only those terms in common usage.

Advanced skills and projects

The subsequent modules extend and build on the basic skills to provide the user with the essential techniques to enable creative and skilful image editing. The guides explore creative applications including advanced retouching, toning, photomontage and special effects. Creative practical projects, using a fully illustrated and simple step-by-step approach, are undertaken in each of the guides to allow the user to explore the creative possibilities and potential for each of the skills being offered.

A structured learning approach

The study guides contained in this book offer a structured learning approach and an independent learning resource that will give the user a framework for the techniques of digital imaging as well as the essential skills for personal creativity and communication.

The skills

To acquire the essential skills to communicate effectively and creatively takes time and motivation. Those skills should be practised repeatedly so that they become practical working knowledge rather than just basic understanding. Become familiar with the skills introduced in one study guide and apply them to each of the following guides wherever appropriate.

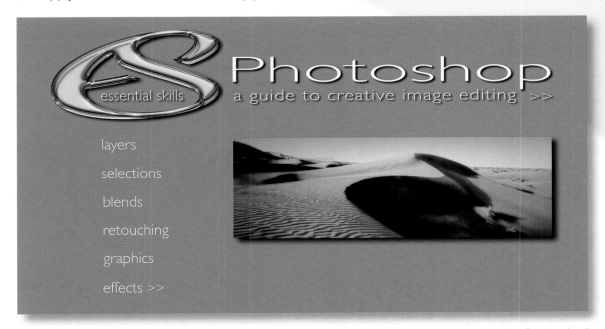

The web site associated with this book has images available for download

Supporting CD and web site

The supporting CD and the dedicated web site contain the images required to complete the projects within the study guides. QuickTime movies offer additional support with these projects. The address for the Internet web site is: **www.photoshopessentialskills.com**

Research and resources

You will only realize your full creative potential by looking at a variety of images from different sources. Artists and designers find inspiration in many different ways, but most find that they are influenced by other work they have seen and admired.

Essential information

The basic equipment required to complete this course is access to a computer with Adobe Photoshop CS2 (versions 7 and CS would suffice for most of the activities contained in the book). The photographic and design industries predominantly use Apple Macintosh computers but many people choose Windows-based PCs as a more cost-effective alternative. When Photoshop is open there are minor differences in the interface, but all of the features and tools are identical. It is possible to use this book with either Windows-based PCs or Apple Macintosh computers.

Storage

Due to the large file sizes involved with digital imaging it is advisable that you have a high capacity, removable storage device attached to the computer or use a CD writer to archive your images. Avoid bringing magnetic disks such as Zip disks into close contact with other magnetic devices such as can be found in mobile phones and portable music players – or even the speakers attached to your computer.

Commands

Computer commands which allow the user to modify digital files can be accessed via menus and submenus. The commands used in the study guides are listed as a hierarchy, with the main menu indicated first and the submenu or command second, e.g. Main menu > Command or Submenu > Command. For example, the command for opening the Image Size dialog box would be indicated as follows: Edit > Image Adjustments > Image Size.

Keyboard shortcuts

Many commands that can be accessed via the menus and submenus can also be accessed via keyboard '**shortcuts**'. A shortcut is the action of pressing two or more keys on the keyboard to carry out a command (rather than clicking a command or option in a menu). Shortcuts speed up digital image processing enormously and it is worth learning the examples given in the study guides. If in doubt use the menu (the shortcut will be indicated next to the command) until you become more familiar with the key combinations. See pages 359 and 360 for a list of the most frequently used shortcuts.

Note > **The keyboard shortcuts indicate both the Mac and PC equivalents.**

Example: The shortcut for pasting objects and text in most applications uses the key combination Command/Ctrl + V. The Macintosh requires the Command key (next to the spacebar) and the V key to be pressed in sequence whilst a PC requires the Control key (Ctrl) and the V key to be pressed.

the digital darkroom

photoshop photoshop photoshop photoshop photoshop photoshop phot

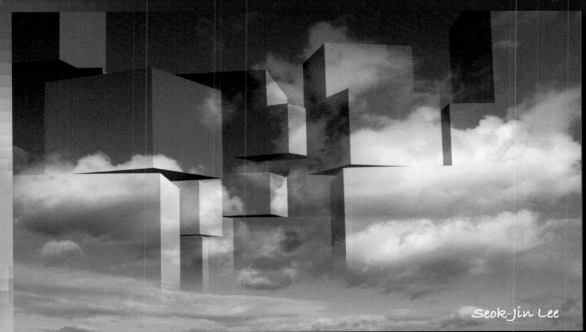

Seok-Jin Lee

photoshop photoshop photoshop photoshop photoshop photoshop phot

essential skills

~ Set up the computer, monitor and software preferences for effective digital image editing.

~ Create an effective image file management system.

~ Gain familiarity with the Photoshop interface.

~ Review Photoshop's basic tools and commands for navigating images on screen.

Digital setup

Photoshop is the professional's choice for digital image editing. Photoshop affords precise control over images that are destined to be viewed on screen and in print. In order to maximize this control it is necessary to spend some time setting up the software and hardware involved in the imaging process in order to create a predictable and efficient workflow.

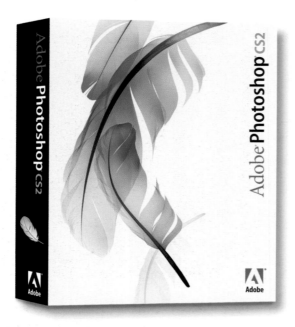

This chapter will act as a preflight checklist so that the user can create the best possible working environment for creative digital image editing. The degree of sophistication that Photoshop offers can appear daunting for the novice digital image-maker, but the time required setting up the software and hardware in the initial stages will pay huge dividends in the amount of time saved and the quality of the images produced.

Commands and shortcuts

This chapter will guide you to select various options from a list of menus on your computer. If a command or dialog box is to be found in a submenu which in turn is to be found in a main menu it will appear as follows: 'Main menu > Submenu > Command'. Many of the commands can be executed by pressing one or more of the keyboard keys (known as 'keyboard shortcuts').

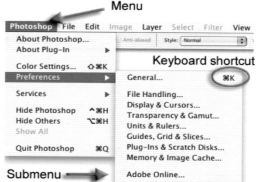

Keyboards: Mac and PC keyboards have different layouts. The 'Alt' key on a PC is the 'Option' key on a Mac. The functions assigned to the 'Control' key on a PC are assigned to the 'Command' key on a Mac (the key next to the spacebar with the apple on it). When the text lists a keyboard command such as 'Ctrl/⌘ Command + Spacebar' the PC user will press the Control key and the spacebar whilst the Mac user is directed to press only the Command key together with the spacebar.

Monitor settings

Resolution and colors

Set the monitor resolution to '1024 × 768' pixels or greater and the monitor colors to 'Millions'. If the 'Refresh Rate' is too low on a CRT monitor the monitor will appear to flicker. The best CRT monitors will enable a high resolution with a flicker-free or stable image. Monitor resolutions less than 1024 × 768 will result in excessively large palettes and a lack of 'screen real estate' or monitor space in which to display the image you are working on.

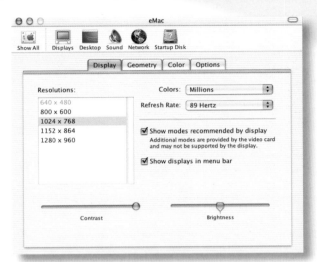 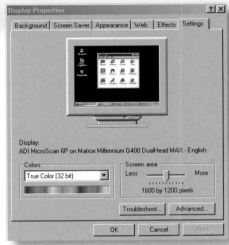

Color temperature – selecting a white point

The default 'color temperature' of a new monitor is most likely to be too bright and too blue for digital printing purposes (9300). Reset the 'Target White Point' (sometimes referred to as 'Hardware White Point' or 'Color Temperature') of your monitor to 'D65' or '6500', which is equivalent to daylight (the same light you will use to view your prints). Setting the white point is part of the 'calibration' process that ensures color accuracy and consistency.

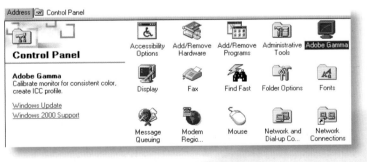 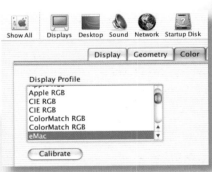

Calibration

Full monitor calibration is not recommended until a new monitor has had time to 'bed in' or 'settle down'. You should, however, select an appropriate color temperature for the monitor from the start. This can be adjusted using either the software 'Adobe Gamma' or 'Monitor Calibrator'.

Once a new monitor has had time to 'bed in' for a few days you should complete a full monitor calibration. Switch on the monitor and allow the image to stabilize for at least half an hour. Then set the brightness, contrast, gamma and color temperature of the monitor using calibration software. This will ensure that the appearance of an image on your screen will be the same on any other calibrated screen. Monitor calibration will also ensure that your prints will appear very similar to your screen image.

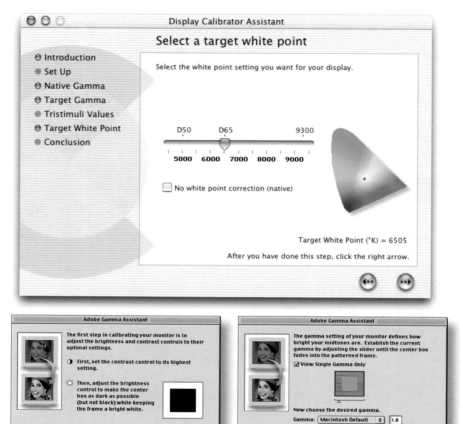

When using the Windows operating system open the software 'Adobe Gamma' (found in the 'control panel'). Alternatively go to 'System Preferences > Displays > Color > Calibrate' when using Macintosh OSX. This will launch the monitor calibrator software. Choose '6500' as the 'Target White Point' or the 'Hardware White Point' and 'Adjusted White Point' if using Adobe Gamma. The software will also guide the user to set the contrast, brightness and 'gamma' of the monitor. On completion of the calibration process you must save the newly calibrated monitor settings by giving it a profile name. It is advised that when you name this profile you include the date that you carried out the calibration. It is usual to check the calibration of a monitor every 6 months.

Note > When you choose 6500 as your target white point your monitor will initially appear dull and a little yellow compared to what you are used to seeing.

Desktop picture

Although images of tropical beaches and sunsets may look pretty relaxing, splashing them on your screen when editing digital images is not recommended. Any colors we see on the monitor – including the richly saturated colors of our desktop picture – will influence our subjective analysis of color, and our resulting image editing. It is therefore highly recommended to replace the desktop picture with a solid tone of gray. When using Mac OSX select Desktop from the System Preferences. See Screen modes in this chapter for an alternative approach.

Note > If you do not have a solid gray image in your 'Desktop Pictures' folder you can create one using the image-editing software.

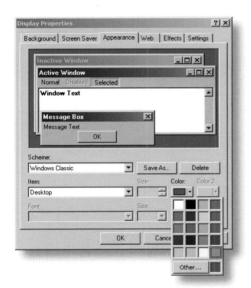

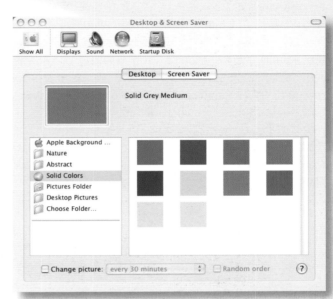

Desktop alias or shortcut

Create an alias or shortcut for Photoshop so that it is quick to launch from the desktop, Apple menu or 'Dock'. Open the Photoshop folder in the Applications folder to locate the Photoshop application icon. Select the Photoshop application icon and right-click in the destination you wish to create the shortcut. When using a Mac drag the application icon into the 'Dock' in OSX to automatically create an alias. To create an alias anywhere else on a Macintosh (such as the 'Apple Menu Items' in the 'System Folder' on OS9) simply hold down the Command and Option keys as you move the Photoshop icon. Dragging images onto the Photoshop alias/shortcut will automatically open them in the software.

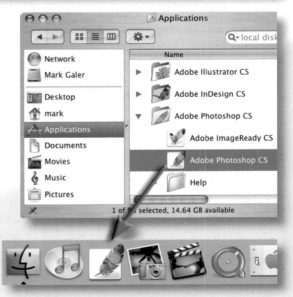

5

Managing your photos

There are many software applications available (such as 'Photoshop Album', 'iPhoto' and Adobe Bridge) to help catalog and index image files so they are quick to access, edit, output and archive.

Searching for an image file that is over a year old with a file name you can only begin to guess at is a task best avoided. The software enables 'Keywords' or 'Tags' to be assigned to the image so that a year down the track you can search for your images by date, name or content to simplify the task. Subsets of images can be displayed based on your search criteria. Some packages even provide the option of locating your images via a calendar display where the pictures are collated based on the date they were taken.

For the Mac OSX user it is advised that all images are stored in the 'Pictures' folder associated with each 'User'. For those readers with Windows machines it is good advice to save your pictures in the 'My Pictures' folder. These folders are often set as the default images folder by the indexing or browser programs. Storing your pictures here will mean that the program will automatically retrieve, index and display images newly added to your system.

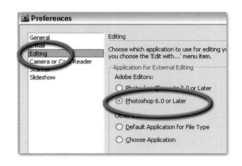

Many of the software packages available allow you to assign an image-editing program in the Preferences so that the image opens in this software when double-clicked. If you are provided with this option select Photoshop as your default image-editing program.

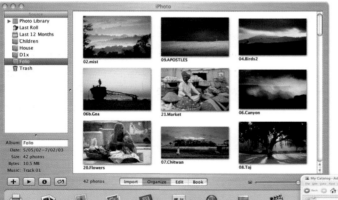

iPhoto for Macintosh

Organize your photographs according to date taken or content category

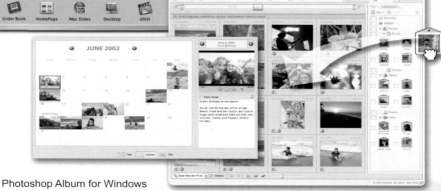

Photoshop Album for Windows

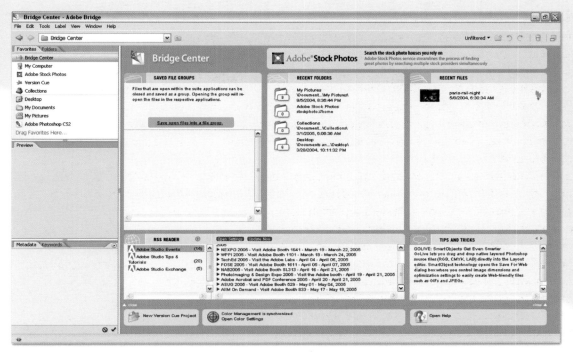

Adobe Bridge is a stand-alone super browser that ships with Photoshop CS2 and acts as the conduit between all applications in the Adobe Creative Suite.

Getting started with Photoshop

The interface of Photoshop is highly organized and presents the user with an effective interface offering maximum control over the process of image editing. If all of the information and control relating to a single image were on display there would be no room left on a standard monitor for the image itself. Most of the features of the editing software therefore are hidden from view but can be quickly accessed once the user starts to understand how the software is organized. The Photoshop interface consists of the:

- Menu
- Toolbox
- Options bar
- Image window
- Palettes
- Palette well

Note > Adobe Photoshop is available for both the Macintosh and Windows platforms. The interface for each system is very similar, with the only differences being the result of the underlying operating system of each computer. Once inside the program items like the menu structure and palette design are exactly the same irrespective of the computer platform you are working with. In practical terms the main difference between the two systems is that Windows and Macintosh use different key stroke combinations for shortcuts and most Macintosh systems use a single button mouse.

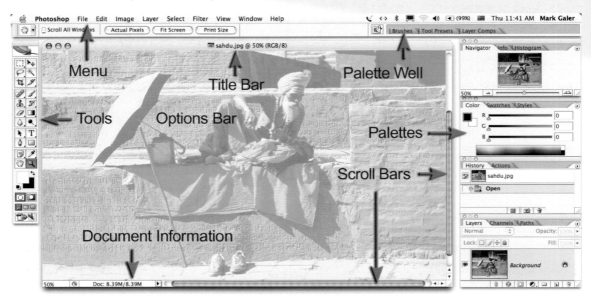

The menu

The menu at the top of the screen gives you access to the main commands. The menu is subdivided into main categories. Clicking on each menu category gives you access to the commands in this section. A command may have a submenu for selecting different options or for launching various 'dialog boxes'. Many of the commands can be accessed without using the menu at all by simply pressing a key combination on the keyboard called a 'shortcut'. Menu items can now be modified (hidden or color coded) by going to the Edit menu and selecting Menus. This is a useful way of rationalizing the menus or highlighting the key commands if you are a newcomer to Photoshop. A basic menus preset is available on the support CD in the resources section.

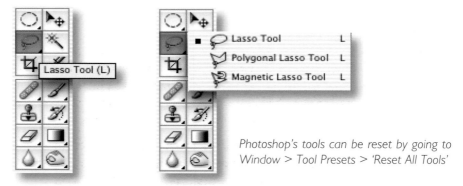

Photoshop's tools can be reset by going to Window > Tool Presets > 'Reset All Tools'

The toolbox

To select a tool to work on your image you simply click on it in the toolbox. If you leave your mouse cursor over the tool Photoshop will indicate the name of the tool and the keyboard shortcut to access the tool. Some of the tools are stacked in groups of tools. A small black arrow in the bottom right corner of the tool indicates additional tools are stacked behind. To access any of the tools in this stack hold the mouse clicker down on the uppermost tool for a second.

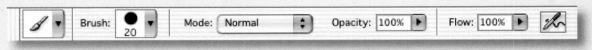

The Options bar

The 'Options' bar gives you access to the controls or specifications that affect the behavior of the tool selected. The options available vary as different tools are selected.

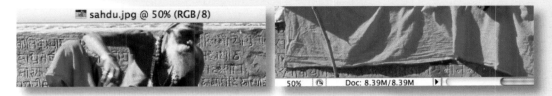

The image window

The file name, magnification, color mode and document size are all indicated by the image window. If the image is larger than the open window the scroll bars can control the section of the image that is visible.

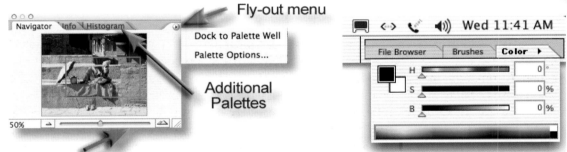

The palettes

The palettes provide essential information and control over the image editing process. They can be arranged in stacks and moved around the screen. Icons at the base of each palette provide access to frequently used commands whilst additional options are available from the palette fly-out menu. Double-clicking the palette tabs or title bars will collapse the palettes to save additional screen real estate. Pressing the 'Tab' key will temporarily hide the palettes. If you want to open a palette that has been closed it can be launched from the 'Window' menu.

Note > Pressing the 'Tab' key will hide the palettes and toolbox from view. Pressing the Tab key again returns the palettes and toolbox. Holding down the Shift key whilst pressing the Tab key will hide all the palettes but keep the toolbox on the screen.

The palette well

Palettes can be dragged to the 'palette well' so that maximum screen space is available for the image window. Clicking on a tab in the palette will temporarily open the palette. Clicking away from the palette will automatically collapse the palette back into the well.

Settings and preferences

Before you start working with an image in Photoshop it is important to select the 'Color Settings' and 'Preferences' in Photoshop. This will not only optimize Photoshop for your individual computer but also ensure that you optimize images to meet the requirements of your intended output device (monitor or print). These settings are accessed through either the 'Photoshop' menu or 'Edit' menu from the main menu at the top of the screen.

```
                              Preferences

  ┌ Memory & Image Cache        ▲▼ ┐                        ( OK )
  │ ┌─ Cache Settings ─────────────────────────────────┐    ( Cancel )
  │ │           Cache Levels: 6                         │
  │ │                                                   │    ( Prev )
  │ └───────────────────────────────────────────────────┘
  │ ┌─ Memory Usage ───────────────────────────────────┐    ( Next )
  │ │        Available RAM: 979MB                       │
  │ │ Maximum Used by Photoshop: 80  ▶ % = 783MB        │
  │ └───────────────────────────────────────────────────┘
  │        (!)  Changes will take effect the next
  │             time you start Photoshop.
```

Memory (the need for speed)

If you have a plentiful supply of RAM (512 MB RAM or greater) you have to give permission for Photoshop to tap into these RAM reserves to a greater or lesser extent when using Mac OSX. Seventy-five percent of the available RAM will automatically be assigned to Photoshop when using a PC. The best advice is to close all non-essential software when you are using Photoshop and allocate more RAM from the 'Memory & Image Cache' preferences (70% is a good starting point). You will need to restart Photoshop for the software to take advantage of the new memory allocation.

Image cache

The image cache setting controls the speed of the screen redraw (how long it takes an image to reappear on the screen after an adjustment is made). If you are working with very high-resolution images and you notice the redraw is very slow you can increase the redraw speed by raising the image cache setting (it can be raised from the default setting of 4 up to 8 depending on the speed required). The drawback of raising this setting is that the redraw is less accurate on screen images that are not displayed at 100%.

> **Allocation of RAM:** Allocate as much RAM to Photoshop as possible if you intend to edit large images. The computer's operating system requires a proportion of the available RAM. Photoshop CS2 now supports a maximum of 4 gigabytes of RAM compared to the previous maximum of 2 gigabytes of RAM with Photoshop CS.

Scratch disks

As well as using RAM, Photoshop also requires a plentiful amount of free memory on the hard drive to use as its 'scratch disk' (a secondary memory resource). To avoid memory problems when using Photoshop it is best to avoid eating into the last gigabyte of your hard drive space. As soon as you see the space dwindling it should be the signal for you to back up your work or consider the installation of a second hard drive. If you have a second hard drive installed you can select this as your 'Second Scratch Disk' by going to 'Preferences > Plug-ins and Scratch Disks'.

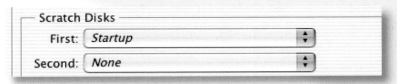

Note > If you are intending to work on a very large image file it is recommended that the scratch disk and image file location are using separate drives.

Efficient use of memory

When you have set up your memory specifications you can check how efficiently Photoshop is working as you are editing an image. Clicking to the right of the document size information (at the base of the image window) will reveal that additional information is available. Choosing the 'Scratch Sizes' option will display how much RAM and how much memory from the scratch disk are being used to process the image.

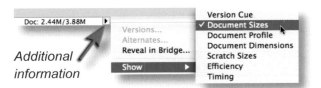

Additional information

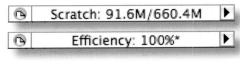

Choosing 'Efficiency' will display whether Photoshop is using the scratch disk to perform the image editing tasks. Values less than 100% indicate that if more RAM were made available to Photoshop the operations would be faster. Simply closing software or images not being used can often increase efficiency.

Photoshop's 'Color Settings'

The most appropriate color setting for image-makers who wish to output to print is Adobe RGB (1998). If Photoshop is open this can be changed in the RGB drop-down menu by going to the 'Color Settings' command, found in the 'Edit' menu. Choose a Prepress setting or go to the Working Spaces and choose Adobe RGB (1998) from the RGB menu.

Color Settings

> ⚠ For more information on color settings, search for "setting up color management" in Help. This term is searchable from any Creative Suite application.

Settings: North America Prepress 2

Working Spaces
RGB: Adobe RGB (1998)
CMYK: U.S. Web Coated (SWOP) v2
Gray: Dot Gain 20%
Spot: Dot Gain 20%

Default settings

It is possible to reset all of the software preferences to their default settings at the time of opening. Press and hold Alt + Control + Shift (Windows) or Option + Command + Shift (Mac OS) as the software is launching. A screen prompt will invite you to delete the current settings. This is useful when using a shared computer so that each tool behaves as you would expect it to. Return the working space to its default setting when the application is already open by going to 'Window > Workspace > Reset Palette Locations'.

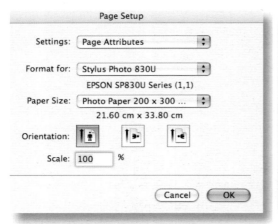 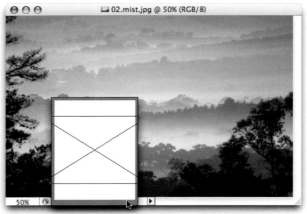

Page Setup

Select the paper size and orientation (vertical or horizontal) by going to File > Page Setup. When you have chosen the paper size you can quickly gain an idea of how large your image will be printed by holding down the Alt/Option key and clicking on the document size at the base of the image window. The window that springs open shows the relationship between the paper and the image (represented by a rectangle with a large cross).

Note > A shaded area around the edge of the paper indicates the portion of the paper that cannot be printed (older style printers).

Opening images

Double-clicking an image on the desktop should automatically open the file into image-editing software. If the file does not open into the image-editing software you can launch it by going to the 'File > Open' menu in the software program. If you prefer your Adobe software to handle all of your image files you should select it as the default image-editing software in your system preferences. In OSX click once to select a file that would normally be opened in software other than Adobe, e.g. QuickTime. Then select 'Get Info' from the 'File' menu of the 'Operating System' menu. Choose the Adobe software program in the 'Open with' submenu. Then select the 'Change All' button for all future documents of a similar format and file type to be opened by Adobe automatically.

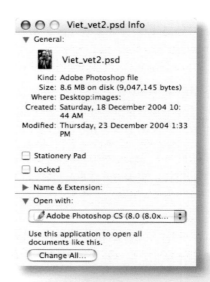

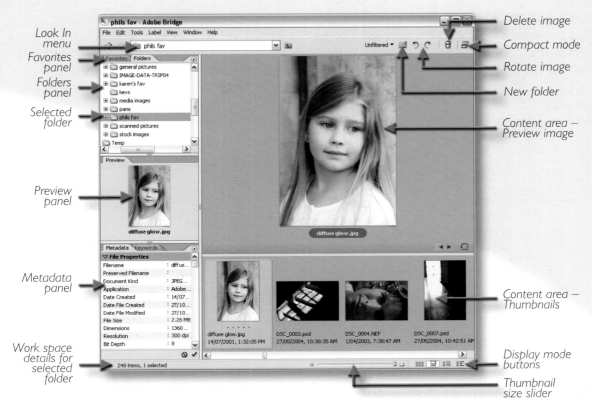

Look In menu

Favorites panel

Folders panel

Selected folder

Preview panel

Metadata panel

Work space details for selected folder

Delete image

Compact mode

Rotate image

New folder

Content area – Preview image

Content area – Thumbnails

Display mode buttons

Thumbnail size slider

Bridge – the new super browser

The Bridge feature, Adobe's new super browser, replaces the standard file browser option found in previous versions of Photoshop. Selecting File > Browse displays Bridge and the fastest way to open a file from your picture library is to search for, and select, the file from within bridge and then press Ctrl/Cmd + O or if Photoshop is not the default program used for opening the file, select File > Open With > Photoshop. Multi-selected files in the browser can also be opened in this way. Bridge is a separate application to Photoshop (stand-alone), has its own memory management system and can be opened and used to organize and manage your photo files without needing to have Photoshop running at the same time.

Using Bridge

To locate files – Files can be located by selecting the folder in which they are contained using either the Favorites or Folders panel or the Look In menu. Alternatively, the Edit > Find command can be used to search for pictures based on filename, file size, keywords, date, rating, label, metadata or comment.

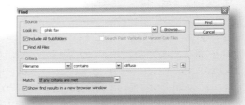

To manage files – Bridge is more than just a file browser, it is also a utility that can be used for sorting and categorizing your photos. Using the options listed under the Label menu, individual or groups of photos can be rated (with a star rating) or labeled (with a colored label) and these tags

PHOTOSHOP CS2 >>>   >>> essential skills >>>

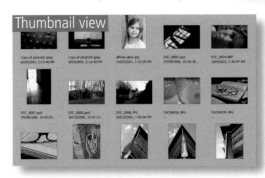

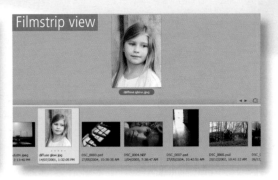

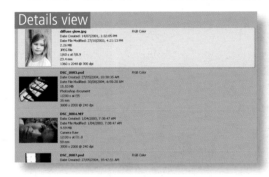

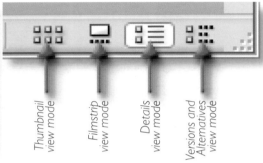

Bridge contains a range of ways to view the thumbnails in the work space. Switch between view modes using the buttons at the bottom right of the Bridge window.

can be used as a way to sort and display the best images from those taken at a large photo-shoot or grouped together in a folder. Labels and ratings are applied by selecting (or multi-selecting) the thumbnail in the Bridge work space and then choosing the tag from the Label menu. Shortcut keys can also be used to quickly attach tags to selected files.

Viewing thumbnails – One of the real bonuses of the Bridge is the multitude of ways that the thumbnails can be viewed in the work space. Two different controls alter the way that Bridge appears – Workspace and View.

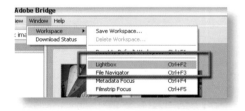

Workspace controls the overall look of the Bridge window and the Window > Workspace menu provides a variety of preset spaces that you can choose as well as allowing you to save your own design.

View options are specifically used to alter the way that the thumbnails are displayed in the Bridge work space (see above). Photoshop provides four basic view modes (Thumbnails, Filmstrip, Details, and Versions and Alternatives), all of which are available via the View menu or in button form at the bottom right of the Bridge window.

Tools used in Bridge – Although no real editing or enhancement options are available in the Bridge feature it is possible to use the browser as a starting point for many of the operations normally carried out in Photoshop. For instance, photos selected in the work space can be batch renamed, printed online, used to create a Photomerge panorama, compiled into a contact sheet or combined into a PDF-based presentation, all via options under the Tools menu. Some of these choices will open Photoshop before completing the requested task whereas others are completed without leaving the browser work space.

Processing RAW inside Bridge – One of the real bonuses of Bridge is the ability to open, edit and save RAW files from inside the browser work space. Now there is no need to open the files to process via Photoshop. The conversions to DNG, TIFF, JPEG or PSD files can be handled directly from the browsing work space by selecting (or multi-selecting) the files and then choosing File > Open in Camera Raw.

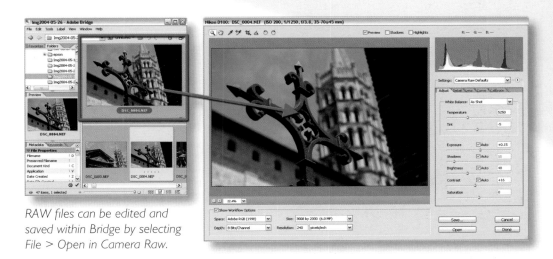

RAW files can be edited and saved within Bridge by selecting File > Open in Camera Raw.

Navigation and viewing modes

When viewing a high-resolution image suitable for printing it is usual to zoom in to check the image quality and gain more control over the editing process. There are numerous ways to move around an image and each user has their preferred methods to speed up the navigation process.

The Navigator palette

The Navigator palette is simple and effective to use. You can use it to both zoom in and out of the image and move quickly to new locations within the enlarged image. The rectangle that appears in the image shows the area visible inside the image window. This rectangle can be dragged to a new location within the image. Using the slider directly underneath the preview window or clicking on the icons either side of the slider controls magnification. It is also possible to type in a specific magnification and then press the Enter/Return key.

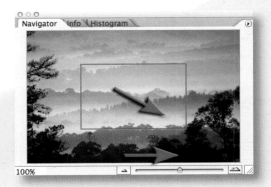

The 'Zoom' and 'Hand' Tools

These tools offer some advantages over the Navigator palette. They can be selected from within the toolbox or can be accessed via keyboard shortcuts. Clicking on the image with the Zoom Tool selected zooms into the image around the point that was clicked. The Zoom Tool options can be selected from the Options bar beneath the main menu. Dragging the Zoom Tool over an area of the image zooms into that area with just the one action (there is no need to click repeatedly).

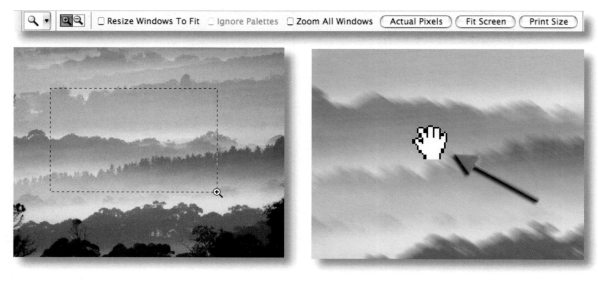

When you are zoomed into an area you can move the view with the 'Hand' Tool. Dragging the image with the Hand Tool selected moves the image within the image window (a little like using the scroll bars). The real advantage of these tools is that they can be selected via shortcuts. The Spacebar temporarily accesses the Hand Tool no matter what other tool is selected at the time (no need to return the cursor to the toolbox). The Zoom Tool can be accessed by pressing the Control/Command + Spacebar to zoom in or the Alt/Option + Spacebar to zoom out.

Note > When you are making image adjustments and a dialog box is open, the keyboard shortcuts are the only way of accessing the zoom and move features.

Additional shortcuts

Going to the View menu in the main menu will reveal the keyboard shortcuts for zooming in and out. You will also find the more useful shortcuts for 'Fit on Screen' and 'Actual Pixels' (100% magnification). These very useful commands can also be accessed via the toolbox by either double-clicking on the Hand Tool (Fit on Screen) or double-clicking the Zoom Tool (Actual Pixels) in the toolbox itself.

Screen modes

The screen can begin to look very cluttered when several applications or windows are open at the same time. A quick way to simplify the view is to switch to 'Full Screen Mode with Menu Bar'.

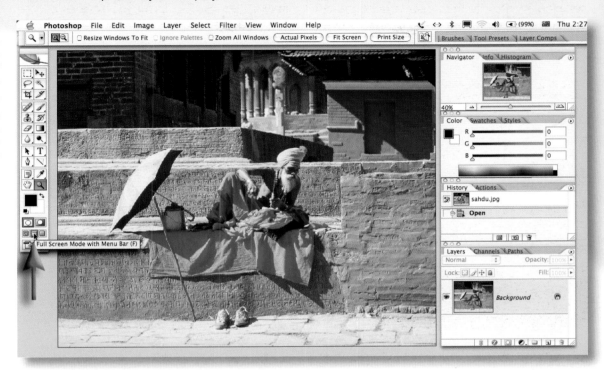

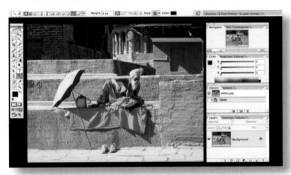
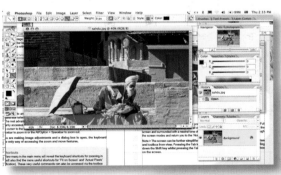

Press the icon located in the toolbox or press the letter 'F' on the keyboard to access the 'Full Screen Mode'. This will temporarily hide all other windows. The open image will be centered on the screen and surrounded with a neutral tone of gray. Continuing to press the F key will cycle through the screen modes and return you to the 'Normal View'.

Note > The screen can be further simplified by pressing the 'Tab' key. This hides the palettes and toolbox from view. Pressing the Tab key again returns the palettes and toolbox. Holding down the Shift key whilst pressing the Tab key will hide all the palettes but keep the toolbox on the screen.

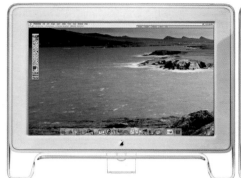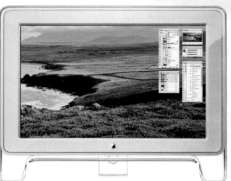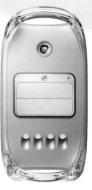

Side-by-side screens

For the ultimate in work space luxury some professionals use specially configured video cards to drive two screens that are placed side by side. In this setup Photoshop's tools and palettes can be spread over both monitors and the mouse moves freely from one screen to the other.

Tidy screen tips

No matter what size screen you have, or even if you have two side by side, it always seems that there is never enough space to arrange the various palettes and images needed for editing work. Here are a few tips that will help you make the most out of the 'screen property' that you do have.

Docking – Docking is a feature that allows several palettes or dialog boxes to be positioned together in the one space. Photoshop provides the option to dock all open palettes in a special docking well provided for this purpose in the Options bar at the top of the screen. Alternatively several palettes can be docked together in one palette group.

Roll-ups – Photoshop allows users to roll up large palettes so that the details of the box are hidden behind a thinner heading bar. This way the full box is rolled out only when needed.

Resizing the work window – If you have a small screen then it is still possible to work on fine detail within an image by zooming in to the precise area that you wish to work. For this reason it is worth learning the keyboard shortcuts for 'zooming in' and 'out'. This function is a little like viewing your enlargement under a focus scope.

Save your work space – Once you are satisfied with your work space arranging, save your setup by selecting Window > Workspace > Save Workspace. Now whenever you want to revert to this way of organizing your screen you can selected your setup from the Window > Workspace submenu.

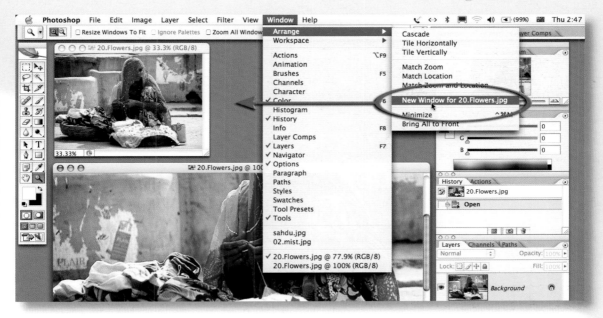

New Window

It is possible to have the same image open in two windows. This allows the user to zoom in to work on detail in one window and see the overall impact of these changes without having to constantly zoom in and out. Any changes made in one window will automatically appear in the other window.

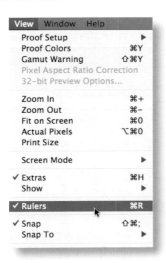

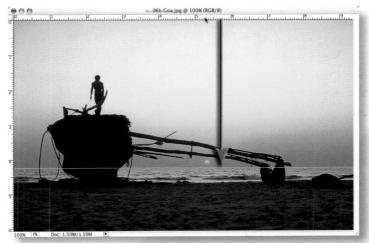

Rulers and guides

Guides can help you to align horizontals and verticals within the image area. Select 'Rulers' from the 'View' menu and then click on either the horizontal or vertical ruler and drag the guide into the image area. Guides can be temporarily hidden from view by selecting 'Extras' from the 'View' menu. Drag a guide back to the ruler using the Move tool to delete it or remove all the guides by selecting 'Clear Guides' from the 'View' menu.

Storage for digital photographs

It didn't take much time before digital photographers realized that high quality pictures use a lot of storage space. Very quickly manufacturers became aware of the need for big capacity portable storage solutions for archiving and transporting large picture files. A few systems have come and gone but the range of devices that we now have are bigger, faster and cheaper than ever before.

Zip disk

The Zip revolution started in 1995 when Iomega first released the 100MB removable cartridge and drive. Featuring a disk not much bigger than the old 1.4MB floppy disk, this storage option quickly became the media of choice with photographers and graphic designers worldwide. The latest incarnation of the drive is not only smaller than its predecessor but the new cartridge is now capable of storing 750MB of your precious pictures. What's more the new drive can still read and write the old cartridges. Unlike most CD-based storage, Zip drives work in a very similar way to your hard drive, allowing files to be read, written and overwritten with ease.

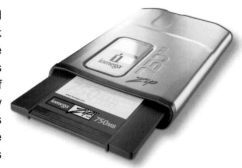

CD-ROM

The CD is a stable and familiar format that is used universally for storing massive amounts of data cheaply. As recently as seven years ago CD readers were an expensive add-on to your computer system. Now writers, and sometimes even rewriters, are thrown in as part of system package deals. The CD has become the floppy of the new millennium and unlike the Zip storage option the majority of all current computers have a CD drive.

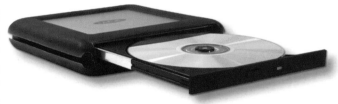

Drives and media are available in two formats. 'Write once, read many' or Worm drives (CD-R) are the cheapest option and allow the user to write data to a disk which can then be read as often as required. Once a portion of the disk is used it cannot be overwritten.

The advanced version of this system (CD-RW) allows the disk to be rewritten many times. In this way it is similar to a hard drive; however, the writing times are much longer. Most drives can read, write and rewrite all in one unit.

Portable hard drive

A new category in portable storage is the range of portable digital hard drives available for photographers. These devices operate with mains or battery power and usually contain a media slot that

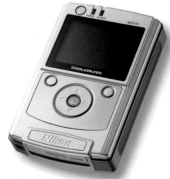

accepts one or more of the memory cards used in digital cameras. Options include Apple's very popular iPod and iPod Photo, both of which can be mounted as hard drives to your computer, and the Nixvue Vista and Nikon's own Coolwalker.

Designed to be used on the road, pictures are transferred from your camera's memory card to the device, freeing up space and allowing you to continue shooting. Back at the desktop the images are downloaded to your computer via a fast cable setup such as Firewire or USB 2.0.

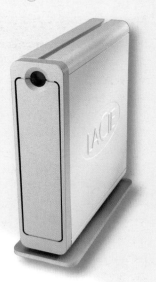

External hard drives

With the ever increasing need for storage and the desire of many users to be able to move their image archives from one machine to another, companies like Iomega are developing more and more sophisticated external hard drive options. Their latest offerings include capacities from 20 to 200GB and the choice of Firewire or USB 2.0 connection. When connected these devices act like another drive in your machine.

DVD

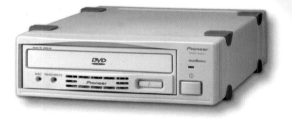

DVD is fast becoming the storage medium of choice for the professional image-maker. Capable of storing between 4.7 and a staggering 9.4GB of picture files DVD is perfect for archiving and sharing the vast amount of information that is collected daily as part of a professional photographic practice.

The technology comes in a variety of formats with different manufacturing companies supporting specific formats. This lack of a common or universal format initially reduced the attractiveness of this storage option, but now the best DVD drives can read and write more than one disk type, making these models the best option when looking for a DVD storage solution. As drive and disk prices continue to fall this technology is set to replace the CD as the digital photographer's main storage medium.

USB mini drives

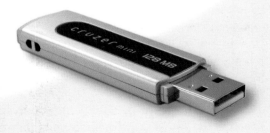

Also called Flash or pen drives, this is a comparatively new option in the portable storage market. These tiny devices plug directly into the USB port of your computer or laptop. Once recognized by your system they can be used just like any other drive in your computer. The fast transfer speed and 'hot-swappable' capabilities of the USB 2.0 connection mean that large files are quickly saved and can be transferred to other machines by disconnecting the drive from one computer and then plugging into another. The drives have no moving parts and are available in various sizes ranging from 64MB to 1GB.

Mouse or graphics tablet?

Much of the time spent working on digital images will be via the mouse or graphics tablet stylus. These devices are electronic extensions of your hand, allowing you to manipulate your images in virtual space. The question of whether to use a mouse or stylus is a personal one. The stylus does, however, provide pressure-sensitive options not available with a mouse-only system. Wacom, the company foremost in the production of graphics tablets for digital imaging use, has recently produced a cordless mouse and stylus combination that allows the user to select either pointer device at will.

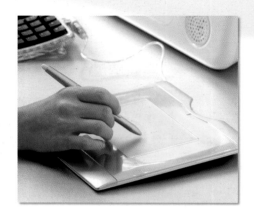

Mac or PC?

Photoshop was originally written as a Macintosh-only application back in 1990 and became available for PC with the release of version 2.5. Photoshop now happily works out of either platform. Many commercial image-makers who have to deal with the printing industry still use Apple Macintosh computers. Macs have traditionally been used by the publishing industry but they are not necessarily any better than PCs at image-making tasks. Commercial image-makers tend to purchase them because their colleagues within the industry are using them. It is really just a communication issue. Macs and PCs can talk to each other if required, e.g. Photoshop operating on either platform can open the same image file. The bottom line, however, is that small, but annoying,

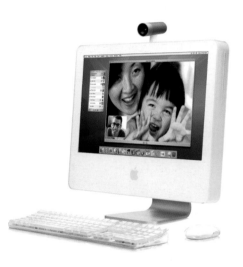

communication issues can often arise when files are passed 'between' the two platforms. Image-makers who are thinking of choosing the PC platform need to think carefully how, if at all, these communication issues will impact upon them. The biggest communication problem that exists to date is the formatting of CDs.

Use-by date

When choosing a computer for commercial digital imaging it is worth noting that most systems are usually past their use-by date before three years have expired. This may continue to be the case although the whole issue of speed is largely becoming academic for stills image editing. The days of waiting for extended periods whilst Photoshop completed a command are largely over, even using an entry-level computer. The question of speed, however, is still very much an issue for creators of DVD (digital video) where disk write speeds are still slow and file sizes are measured in gigabytes instead of megabytes.

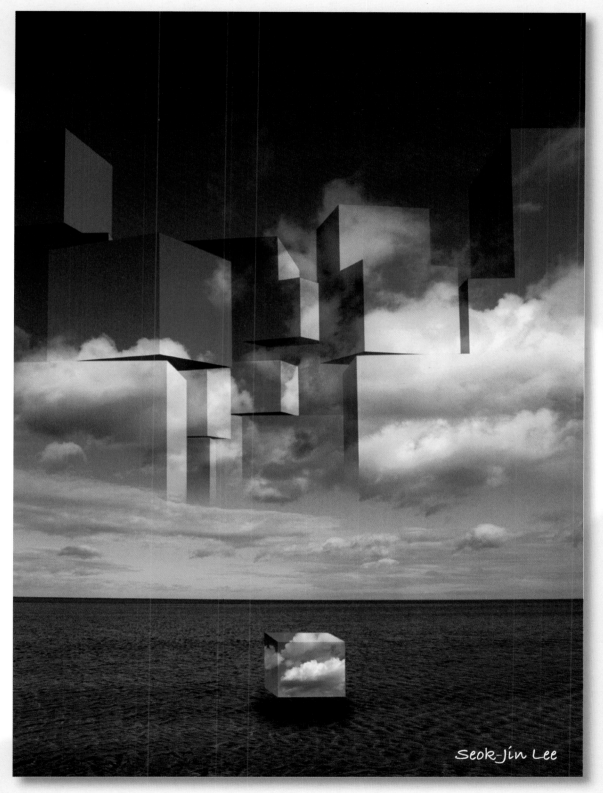

Seok-Jin Lee

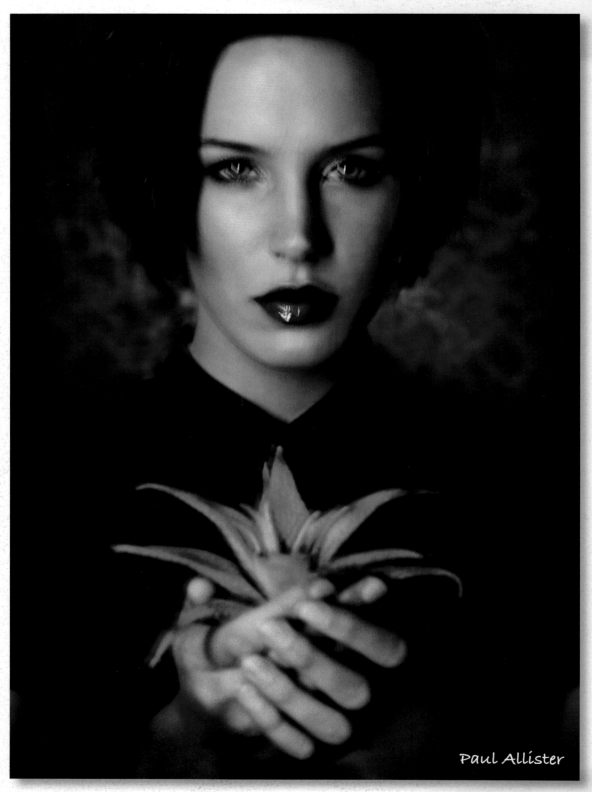

Paul Allister

digital basics

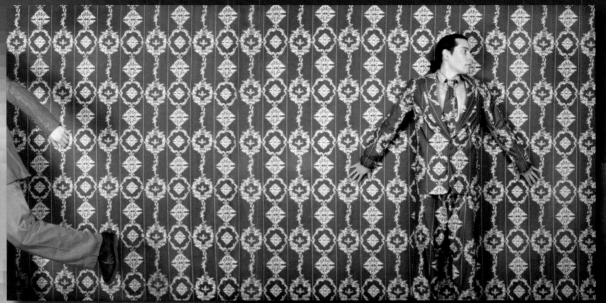

Sam Everton

essential skills

~ Gain a working knowledge of digital image structure.

~ Understand file size, bit depth, image modes, channels, file format and resolution.

~ Understand color theory and color perception.

Introduction

Digital imaging is now revolutionizing not only the process of photography but also the way we view photography as a visual communications medium. This new photographic medium affords the individual greater scope for creative expression, image enhancement and manipulation.

Before we rush into making changes to our digital files in order to create great art, or turn a warty old frog into a handsome prince, it makes sense to slow down and take time out to understand the structure of the digital image file. In this way the technical terms used to identify, quantify and specify the digital file as a whole, or the component parts of the digital file, serve to clarify rather than bamboozle our overloaded gray matter.

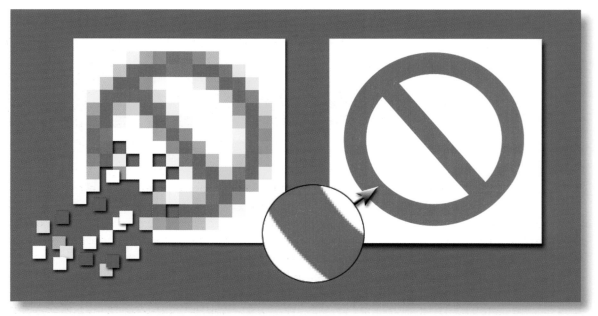

Anti-aliasing and small pixels ensure that a staircase of pixels is rendered as a smooth arc

Pixels

The basic building block of the digital image is the humble pixel (picture element). Pixels for digital imaging are square and positioned in rows horizontally and vertically to form a grid or mosaic. Each pixel in the grid is the same size and is uniform in color and brightness, i.e. the color does not vary from one side of the pixel to the other. If we fully zoom in on the pixels of a digital image, using image-editing software, we will see how smooth flowing shapes can be convincingly constructed out of rectangular building blocks (with not a curved pixel in sight). There are two processes used to create the illusion of curved lines in our photographs. The first is a process called anti-aliasing where some of the edge pixels adopt a transitional (in-between) color to help create a smoother join between two different adjacent colors or tones. This process helps camouflage the staircase or 'shark's teeth' that may become noticeable. The most convincing way to render a smooth flowing line, however, is to simply display the pixels so small that we cannot make them out to be square using the naked eye.

Channels and modes

All the colors of the rainbow when mixed together create white light (a prism is often used to split white light into its component colors to demonstrate the connection between light and color). All the colors of the rainbow can be created by mixing just three of these colors – **Red**, **Green** and **Blue** light (called the **primary** colors of light) – in differing amounts. Using these simple scientific principles all the variations of color in our multicolored world can be captured and stored in three separate component parts of our digital image file. These component parts are called the Red, Green and Blue '**Channels**'. An image that uses this process to store the color data is called an RGB image. RGB is one type of '**Image Mode**'.

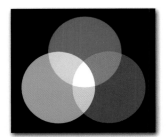 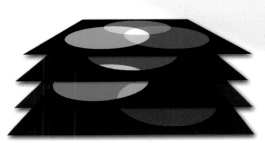 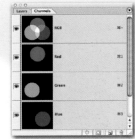

The primary colors of light (stored in three separate channels) create the secondary colors when mixed

In Adobe Photoshop CS2 the colored channels are working behind the scenes to create multicolored images by providing three sets of information regarding color, i.e. the amount of red, green and blue present in each pixel location. When the color from only one channel is present a primary color is created in the image window. When information from two channels is present a secondary color is displayed. These secondary colors (created by mixing two primaries) are called Cyan, Magenta and Yellow. When there is an absence of any color from the three channels the pixel location appears black (no illumination). Mixing all three channels together creates white light or gray if the brightness value from each of the three channels is lowered (see 'Levels'). Color information about the image can also be stored using the secondary colors (mixing two secondary colors creates a primary) plus black. Images using this system or **Mode** are called **CMYK** images. Photoshop users can view the information stored in the component channels by clicking on the Channels palette tab.

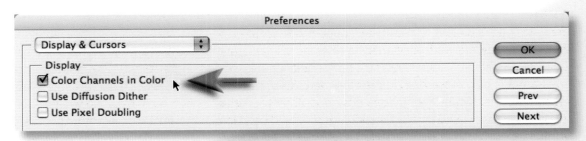

Note > You can view the information in each channel with or without color (Preferences > Display & Cursors). It is usually beneficial to view the information in the channels without color when conducting advanced post-production editing but for the purposes of understanding what is actually happening, color is a distinct advantage.

Levels

We have seen how mixing primary colors of light can create the secondary colors. In the previous illustration, where three colored circles were overlapped, the color in each of the three channels is either 'on' or 'off'. In this way six colors are created from three channels. The three channels can, however, house a greater range of information about color than simply 'yes' (fully on) or 'no' (fully off) in any one pixel location. The capture devices are capable of measuring '**how much**' color is present in any one given location. In a standard RGB image, 256 different levels of color can be assigned to each pixel location. The channels operate very much like a mixing desk, mixing varying amounts of color from each of the three color channels to create the full color spectrum.

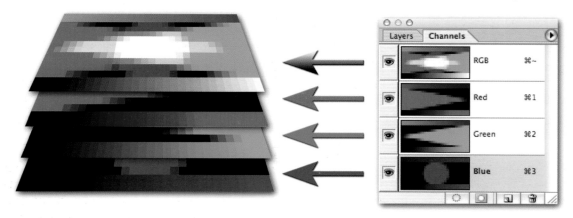

In a standard RGB digital image each pixel can be assigned one of 256 different '**levels**' of color from each of the three color channels, from 0 (no color in that pixel location) to 255 (full color present in that pixel location). If the three channels are mixed in equal proportions what we see is a series of tonal steps from black (0 in all three channels) to white (255 in all channels).

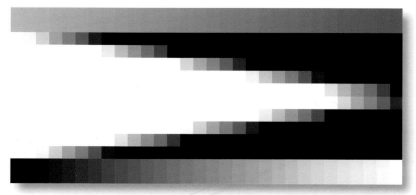

256 levels of tone are reduced to 30 so the steps can be clearly seen

256 separate tones are sufficient to create a smooth transition from dark to light with no visible steps. If the pixels are sufficiently small when printed out, the viewer of the image cannot see either the individual pixels or the steps in tone, and the illusion of '**continuous tone**' or '**photographic quality**' is achieved.

Hue, Saturation and Brightness

Equally high levels in each of the three color channels creates not only a bright or light toned pixel but may also indicate a bright level of illumination in the scene that has been captured. This can be attributed to the pixel being a record of a bright light, or the reflected light off a brightly illuminated subject, but it may alternatively be due to possible overexposure during the capture process, i.e. the sensor being exposed to the light source for too long.

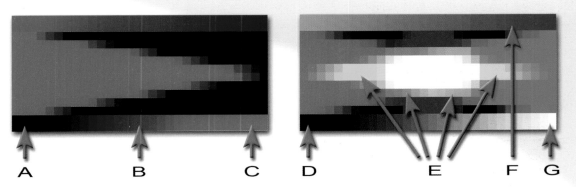

The illustration above shows the enormous variety of tones that can be achieved by combining 256 levels of information from the three color channels. Given that each channel can vary its level of information, independently of the other two, it is possible to create a single pixel with one of a possible 16.7 million different values (256 × 256 × 256). To describe the nature of a particular color value without resorting to numbers, Adobe has adopted a system where the characteristics of the color can be described in three ways. These descriptive categories are:

Hue – as dictated by the dominant primary or secondary color, e.g. red, yellow, blue, etc.
Saturation – the strength of the color, e.g. when one or two of the channels registers 0 the resulting color is fully saturated, i.e. no level of gray or white is weakening the purity of the color.
Brightness – from 0 (black – all channels 0) to 255 (at least one channel registering 255).

Using a common language of Hue, Saturation and Brightness (HSB) we can identify the colors indicated by letters in the illustration above, in terms that can be readily understood by the broader community that are neither mathematicians nor Photoshop nerds.

A to C are levels of brightness from black to fully saturated bright red. The levels from the other two channels are not influencing the overall color or brightness of any of the pixels (all Green and Blue values are set to level 0).

D and G are levels of brightness from black to white. When all channels read the same level the resulting tones are fully desaturated.

E indicates fully saturated secondary colors created by mixing two primary channels at level 255.

F indicates colors of lower saturation as information from the three channels is unequal (therefore creating a gray component to the color's characteristic).

Color Picker

As we have discussed previously it is essential when describing and analyzing color in the digital domain to use the appropriate terminology. A greater understanding of the characteristics of Hue, Saturation and Brightness (HSB) can be gained by viewing colors in the Adobe Color Picker. Click on the foreground swatch in the Tools palette to open the Color Picker.

> **Hue** – All colors can be assigned a location and a number (a degree between 0° and 360°). A vertical colored bar in the Color Picker allows the user to click anywhere on the bar to view the range of colors associated with that particular hue. Note the number in the top field next to the 'H' radio button. Each of the six primary and secondary colors are positioned 60° apart, e.g. Red at 0°, Yellow at 60°, Green at 120°, etc.

> **Saturation and Brightness** – Click in the large square box to the left of the bar to choose a Saturation and Brightness value for the selected Hue. Saturation increases when the selection circle is moved to the right side of the box and decreases when moved to the left. Brightness increases towards the top of the box and decreases towards the bottom of the box.

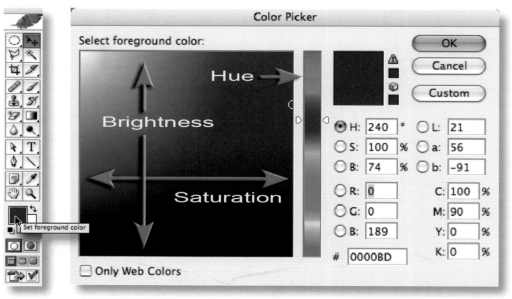

The 'foreground swatch' and 'Color Picker (CS version)'

Creating and sampling color from an image

If the mouse cursor is moved out of the Color Picker dialog box and into the image window the mouse cursor icon turns into the eyedropper icon, regardless of what tool was selected in the Tools palette when the Color Picker was opened. Pressing the Caps Lock key on the keyboard turns this icon into a target for precise selection of a color or tone. Clicking in an area of the image window will sample the color and reveal its characteristics in the Color Picker dialog box. The sample size can be changed from a single pixel to a '3 by 3 Average' or '5 by 5 Average' by right-clicking (PC) or Control-clicking (Mac) in the image window to reveal the context menu for the eyedropper tool.

Color and light overview

Additive color

The additive primary colors of light are Red, Green and Blue or RGB. Mixing any two of these primary colors creates one of the three secondary colors Magenta, Cyan or Yellow.

Note > Mixing all three primary colors of light in equal proportions creates white light.

Subtractive color

The three subtractive secondary colors are Cyan, Magenta and Yellow or CMY. Mixing any two of these secondary colors creates one of the three primary colors Red, Green or Blue. Mixing all three secondary colors in equal proportions in a CMYK file creates black or an absence of light (CS only).

ACTIVITY 1

Open the files RGB.jpg and CMYK.jpg (CS users only) from the supporting CD and look at the channels to see how they were created using Photoshop. Use the information palette to measure the color values.

Hue, Saturation and Brightness

Although most of the digital images are captured in RGB it is sometimes a difficult or awkward color model for some aspects of color editing. Photoshop CS allows the color information of a digital image to be edited using the HSB model.

Hue, Saturation and Brightness or HSB is an alternative model for image editing which allows the user to edit either the Hue, Saturation or Brightness independently of the other two.

ACTIVITY 2

Open the image Hue.jpg, Saturation.jpg and Brightness.jpg. Use the Color Picker to analyze the color values of each bar.

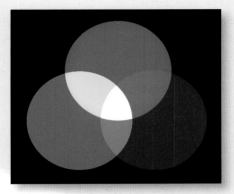

RGB – additive color

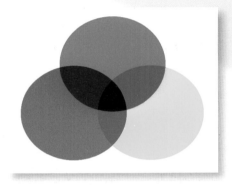

CMY – subtractive color

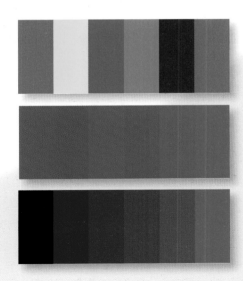

HSB – Hue, Saturation and Brightness

Color perception

Our perception of color changes and is dependent on many factors. We perceive color differently when viewing conditions change. Depending on the tones that surround the tone we are assessing, we may see it darker or lighter. Our perception of a particular hue is also dependent on both the lighting conditions and the colors or tones that are adjacent to the color we are assessing.

ACTIVITY 3

Evaluate the tones and colors in the image opposite. Describe the gray squares at the top of the image in terms of tonality. Describe the red bars at the bottom of the image in terms of hue, saturation and brightness. Open the supporting file and check the differences in tone and color.

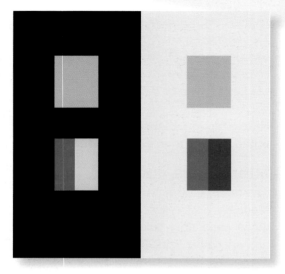

Color perception

Color gamut

Color gamut varies, depending on the quality of paper and colorants used (inks, toners and dyes, etc.). Printed images have a smaller color gamut than transparency film or monitors and this needs to be considered when printing. In the image opposite the out of gamut colors are masked by a gray tone (CS only). These colors are not able to be printed using the default Photoshop CMYK ink values.

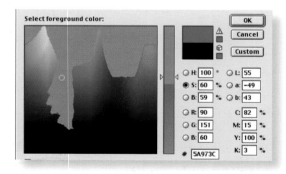

Out of gamut colors

Color management issues

The issue of obtaining consistent color – from original, to its display on a monitor, through to its reproduction in print – is considerable. The variety of devices and materials used to capture, display and reproduce color in print all have a profound effect on the end result (see Color Management).

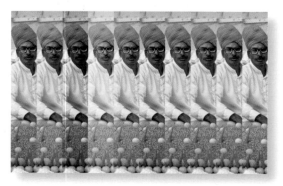

Color management ensures consistent colors

ACTIVITY 4

 1. Double-click the Hand Tool in the Tools palette to resize the image to fit the monitor.

 2. Click on the '**Zoom Tool**' in the Tools palette to select the tool (double-clicking the Zoom Tool in the Tools palette will set the image at 100% magnification).

3. Click on an area within the image window containing detail that you wish to magnify. Keep clicking to increase the magnification (note the current magnification both in the title bar of the image window and in the bottom left-hand corner of the image window).

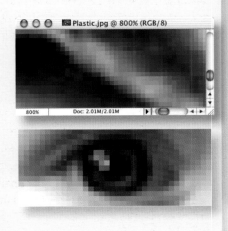

4. At a magnification of 400% you should be able to see the pixel structure of the image. Increase the magnification to 1200% (to decrease the magnification you should click the image with the Zoom Tool whilst holding down the Option/Alt key on the keyboard).

 5. Click on the hand in the Tools palette and then drag inside the image window to move the image to an area of interest (pixel variety).

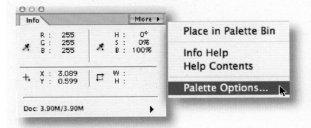 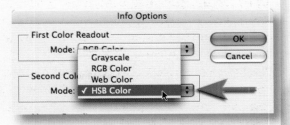

6. Open the Info palette from the Windows menu in your Adobe image-editing software. From the Palette Options choose 'HSB Color' as the 'Second Color Readout'.

 7. Click on the eyedropper in the Tools palette to sample the color information (note how the color of the selected pixel is displayed in the foreground swatch in the Tools palette).

8. View the color information in the Information palette in terms of its RGB numbers and its Hue, Saturation and Brightness values. Try to find the brightest, darkest, most saturated, least saturated areas within your selected image.

Bit depth and mode

As discussed earlier in 'Levels' each pixel in a single channel of a standard RGB image is described in one of a possible 256 tones or levels. The computer memory required to calculate and store this color data is '8 bits', a bit (binary digit) being the basic unit of the computer's memory. The amount of bits dedicated to describing and recording tonal or color variations is called the '**bit depth**'. If only tonal information is required (no color) a single channel 8-bit image is sufficient to create a good quality black and white image, reproducing all of the tonal variations needed to produce 'continuous tone'. An 8-bit image that handles only tonal variations is more commonly referred to as a **Grayscale** image.

When 8 bits are needed for each of the three channels of an RGB image this results in what is often referred to as a 24-bit image (3 × 8). Adobe, however, does not refer to an RGB image as a 24-bit image but rather as an RGB Color and lists the bit depth of each channel rather than the entire image, e.g. 8 Bits/Channel. Images with a higher '**bit depth**' have a greater potential for color or tonal accuracy although this sometimes cannot be viewed because of the limitations of the output device. Images with a higher bit depth, however, require more data or memory to be stored in the image file (Grayscale images are a third of the size of RGB images with the same pixel dimensions and print size). Adobe offers support for 16 Bits/Channel images.

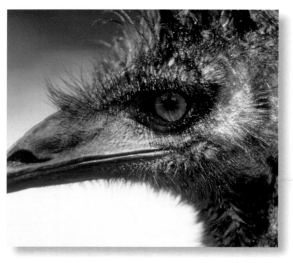
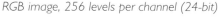
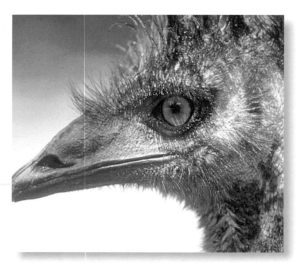

RGB image, 256 levels per channel (24-bit)   *256 levels (8-bit)*

Capturing and editing at bit depths exceeding 8 bits per channel

Sophisticated 'prosumer' digital cameras and digital SLRs (DSLRs) are able to export files in the 'RAW' format in bit depths higher than 8 bits per channel to the computer. Higher quality scanners are able to scan and export files at 16 bits per channel (48-bit). In Photoshop CS2 it is possible to edit an image using 16 bits per channel or 8 bits per channel. The file size of the 16-bit per channel image is double that of an 8-bit per channel file of the same pixel dimensions. Image editing in this mode is used by professionals for high quality retouching. When extensive tonal or color corrections are required it is recommended to work in 16 bits per channel whenever possible. It is, however, important to note that not all of the Adobe editing tools function in 16-bit mode.

File size

Digital images are data hungry (this data being required to record the extensive variations in color and/or tone of the original image or subject). The simple binary language of computers and the visual complexities of a photographic image lead to large '**file sizes**'. This data can require large amounts of computer memory to display, print or store the image. The text file for this entire book would only be a small fraction of the memory required for the cover image (10 megabytes).

Units of memory

8 bits	=	1 byte
1024 bytes	=	1 kilobyte
1024 kilobytes	=	1 megabyte
1024 megabytes	=	1 gigabyte

Storage capacity of disks and drives

Flash/USB pen	=	64 megabytes – 1 gigabyte
CD	=	700 – 800 megabytes
DVD	=	4.7 – gigabytes
iPod	=	512 megabytes to 60 gigabytes

Fortunately files can be '**compressed**' (reduced in memory size) when closing the file for storage or uploading over the Internet. Portable hard drives (such as Apple's 'iPod' or the smaller 'USB' or 'Flash' drives) are now commonly used for storing and transferring large image files conveniently and quickly. A 5 megapixel digital image can be saved as a 10 megabyte RAW file or a 1 megabyte JPEG file using a high quality compression setting in the camera. The same file opens up to a 14.1 megabyte file in Photoshop. When talking about file size it helps to know whether you are talking about an open or closed file and whether any image compression has been used.

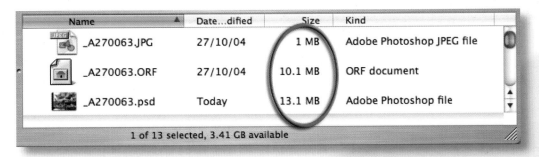

ACTIVITY 5

Find one digital image file and identify its file size when the image is closed. Open the same digital image using image editing software and identify its file size when open (go to the 'document sizes' underneath the image window or choose 'Image Size' from the 'Image' menu).

File formats

When an image is captured by a camera or scanning device it has to be 'saved' or memorized in a 'file format'. If the binary information is seen as the communication, the file format can be likened to the language or vehicle for this communication. The information can only be read and understood if the software recognizes the format. Images can be stored in numerous different formats. The four dominant formats in most common usage are:

- RAW (.dng) – Camera RAW and Digital Negative
- JPEG (.jpg, jpf and jpx) – Joint Photographic Experts Group
- TIFF (.tif) – Tagged Image File Format
- Photoshop (.psd) – Photoshop Document

Camera RAW and Digital Negatives – Unlike the other file formats, RAW is not an acronym for a much longer name. Selecting the RAW format in the camera instead of JPEG or TIFF stops the camera from processing the color data collected from the sensor. The RAW data is what the sensor 'saw' before the camera processes the image, and many photographers have started to refer to this file as the 'digital negative'. The unprocessed RAW has to be converted into a usable image file format using image editing software supplied by the camera manufacturer or built into software packages such as Adobe Photoshop CS2 and can be compressed and archived as a 'Digital Negative'.

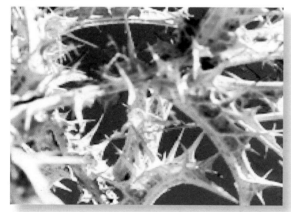
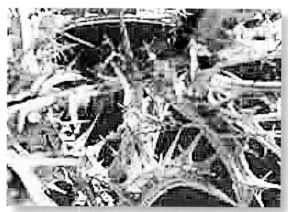

A close-up detail of an image file that has been compressed using maximum image quality in the JPEG options box

A close-up detail of an image file that has been compressed using low image quality in the JPEG options box. Notice the artifacts that appear as blocks

JPEG (Joint Photographic Experts Group) – Industry standard for compressing continuous tone photographic images destined for the World Wide Web (www) or for storage when space is limited. JPEG compression uses a 'lossy compression' (image data and quality are sacrificed for smaller file sizes when the image files are closed). The user is able to control the amount of compression. A high level of compression leads to a lower quality image and a smaller file size. A low level of compression results in a higher quality image but a larger file size. It is recommended that you only use the JPEG file format after you have completed your image editing and always keep a master Photoshop document for archival purposes.

PHOTOSHOP CS2 >>>

File formats

Format	Compression	Color modes	Layers	Transparency	Uses
RAW	No	Unprocessed	No	No	Master file
JPEG	Yes	RGB, CMYK, Grayscale	No	No	Internet and camera format (compressed)
JPEG2000	Yes	RGB, CMYK, Grayscale	No	No	Internet and archival
Photoshop	No	RGB, CMYK, Grayscale, Indexed color	Yes	Yes	Master file (modified)
TIFF	Yes	RGB, CMYK, Grayscale	Yes	Yes	Commercial printing and generic camera format (lossless)
GIF	Yes	Indexed color	No	Yes	Internet graphics and animations
DNG	Yes	Unprocessed	No	No	Archival format for storing original RAW and metadata

>>> essential skills >>>

JPEG2000 – The original JPEG format is over a decade old and despite its continued popularity it is beginning to show its age. This latest version of the format, JPEG200, supports 16 Bits/Channel and alpha channels and produces less image artifacts than the standard JPEG compression but uses a more complex list of saving options than the standard JPEG format. Photoshop CS supports the file format but it is not available as part of the 'Save for Web' options.

PSD (Photoshop Document) – This is the default format used by the Adobe image-editing software. A Photoshop document is usually kept as the master file from which all other files are produced depending on the requirements of the output device. The PSB format is another version of PSD and is designed specificaly for creating documents larger than 2GB.

TIFF (Tagged Image File Format) – This has been the industry standard for images destined for publishing (magazines and books, etc.). TIFF uses a 'lossless' compression (no loss of image data or quality) called '**LZW compression**'. Although preserving the quality of the image, LZW compression is only capable of compressing images by a small amount. TIFF files now support layers and transparency that can be read by other Adobe software products such as InDesign.

GIF (Graphics Interchange Format) – This format is used for logos and images with a small number of colors and is very popular with web professionals. It is capable of storing up to 256 colors, animation and areas of transparency. It is not generally used for photographic images.

DNG (Digital Negative Format) - The DNG format is a new archival file format that stores both the RAW picture data as well as the metadata saved by the camera at the time of shooting.

TOP TIPS FOR CROSS-PLATFORM SAVING

Many work and education environments contain a mix of Windows and Macintosh machines. Though both systems are far better at reading each other's files than they used to be, there are still occasions when you will have trouble when sharing files between the two platforms. Use these tips to ensure that work that you save is available for use in both environments.

1. Make sure that you always append your file names.
This means add the three-letter abbreviation of the file format you are using after the name. So if you were saving a file named 'Image1' as a TIFF the saved file would be 'Image1.tif', a JPEG version would be 'Image1.jpg' and a Photoshop file would be 'Image1.psd'. Macintosh Photoshop users can force the program to 'Always Append' by selecting this option in the 'Saving Files' section of Preferences.

2. Save TIFF files in the IBM version.
When saving TIFF files you are prompted to choose which platform you prefer to work with; choose IBM if you want to share files. Macintosh machines can generally read IBM (Windows) TIFFs, but the same is not true the other way around.

3. Macintosh users save images to be shared on Windows formatted disks.
If you are sharing images on a portable storage disk such as a Zip drive always use media that are formatted for Windows. Macintosh drives can usually read the Windows disks but Windows machines can't read the Macintosh versions.

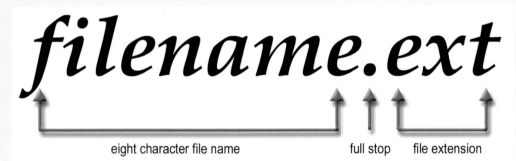

eight character file name   full stop   file extension

4. Try to keep file names to eight characters or less.
Older Windows machines and some web servers have difficulty reading file names longer than eight characters. So just in case you happen to be trying to share with a cantankerous old machine get into the habit of using short names – and always appended of course.

Image compression

Imaging files are huge. This is especially noticeable when you compare them with other digital files such as those used for word processing. A text document that is 100 pages long can easily be less than 1% the size of a file that contains a single 10 × 8 inch digital photograph. With files this large it soon became obvious to the industry that some form of compression was needed to help alleviate the need for us photographers to be continuously buying bigger and bigger hard drives.

What has emerged over the last few years is two different ways to compress pictures. Each enables you to squeeze large image files into smaller spaces but one system does this with no loss of picture quality – *lossless* compression – whereas the other enables greater space savings with the price of losing some of your image's detail – *lossy* compression.

What is compression?

All digital picture files store information about the color, brightness and position of the pixels that make up the image. Compression systems reorder and rationalize the way in which this information is stored. The result is a file that is optimized and therefore reduced in size. Large space savings can be made by identifying patterns of color, texture and brightness within images and storing these patterns once, and then simply referencing them for the rest of the image. This pattern recognition and file optimization is known as compression.

The compression and decompression process, or CODEC, contains three stages.
1. The original image is compressed using an algorithm to optimize the file.
2. This version of the file becomes the one that is stored on your hard drive or web site.
3. The compressed file is decompressed ready for viewing or editing.

If the decompressed file is exactly the same as the original after decompression, then the process is called 'lossless'. If some image information is lost along the way then it is said to be 'lossy'. Lossless systems typically can reduce files to about 60% of their original size, whereas lossy compression can reduce images to less than 1%.

There is no doubt that if you want to save space and maintain the absolute quality of the image then the only choice is the lossless system. A good example of this would be photographers, or illustrators, archiving original pictures. The integrity of the image in this circumstance is more important than the extra space it takes to store it.

On the other hand (no matter how much it goes against the grain), sometimes the circumstances dictate the need for smaller file sizes even if some image quality is lost along the way. Initially you might think that any system that degrades the image is not worth using, and in most circumstances, I would have to agree with you. But sometimes the image quality and the file size have to be balanced. In the case of images on the web they need to be incredibly small so that they can be transmitted quickly over slow telephone lines. Here some loss in quality is preferable to images that take 4 or 5 minutes to appear on the page. This said, I always store images in a lossless format on my own computer and only use a lossy format when it is absolutely crucial to do so.

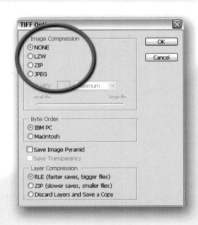

Unlike other imaging packages Photoshop CS2 provides a range of compression options when saving your pictures in the TIFF format

Balancing compression and image quality

One of the by-products of the tiny files produced using lossy compression systems is the inclusion of image artifacts or errors in the compressed file. These errors are a direct result of the lossy compression process and their appearance becomes more apparent as file sizes become smaller. One of the key tasks of any image-maker who regularly needs to compress their files is to judge what level of compression produces an acceptable level of artifacts whilst maintaining usable file sizes. Photoshop CS2 provides two visual tools to aid in this process. Both provide previews of how the picture will look after compression plus a prediction of its reduced file size. The 'Save for Web' option has quickly become a favorite with desktop compressors everywhere.

When Adobe initially included support for the JPEG format in its flagship image editing software the process was based around a simple dialog with a slider used to determine the amount of compression applied to the image file. The 'Save for Web' option is a much clearer and more visual approach and provides live

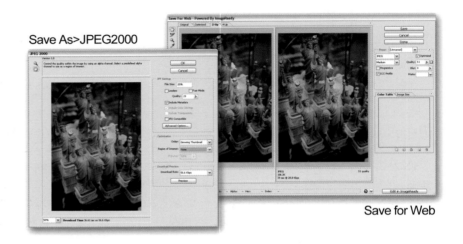

Save As>JPEG2000

Save for Web

previews of the compressed file, giving the user the chance to balance file size and image quality with all the artifact 'cards clearly on the table'. In addition to JPEG, GIF and PNG files can be saved using the Save for Web feature as well.

New for CS is the option to save your picture in the JPEG2000 format. The option is accessed not as you would expect in the Save for Web feature, but rather via the File > Save As dialog. Selecting JPEG2000 as your file type displays the JPEG2000 dialog, which includes a post-compression preview, compression amount control and a file size prediction. Adobe has also made use of the extra features built into the JPEG2000 algorithm to provide a 'lossless' option.

JPEG2000

The last few years has seen a lot of development work in the area of image compression. In the year 2000 the specifications for a new version of JPEG were released with the first commercial programs using this technology hitting the market a few months later. The revision, called JPEG2000, uses wavelet technology to produce smaller and sharper files than traditional JPEG. The standard also includes options to use different compression settings and color depths on selections within the image itself. It is also possible to save images in a lossless form. CS was the first Photoshop version with the ability to save pictures as a JPEG2000 file built in.

Compression amounts

Format	Compression amount	Original file size	Compressed file size	Lossy/ Lossless
JPEG	Minimum		0.14MB	Lossy
JPEG	Maximum		2.86MB	Lossy
JPEG2000	Minimum		0.07MB	Lossy
JPEG2000	Maximum		2.54MB	Lossy
JPEG2000	–	20.0MB (PSD file)	5.40MB	Lossless
TIFF	LZW		10.30MB	Lossless
TIFF	Zip		10.10MB	Lossless
TIFF	None		27.30MB	Lossless
PSD	–		20.00MB	Lossless

How lossy is lossy?

The term lossy means that some of the image's quality is lost in the compression process. The amount and type of compression used determines the look of the end result. Standard JPEG and JPEG2000 display different types of 'artifacts' or areas where compression is apparent. The level of acceptable artifacts and practical file sizes will depend on the required outcome for the picture.

To help ensure that you have the best balance of file size and image quality make sure that you:

• Use the Save for Web and Save As > JPEG2000 features as these both contain a post-compression preview option.
• Always examine the compressed image at a magnification of 100% or greater so that unacceptable artifacts will be obvious.

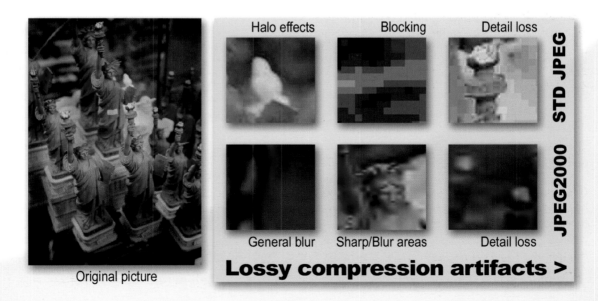

Original picture

Halo effects   Blocking   Detail loss

General blur   Sharp/Blur areas   Detail loss

STD JPEG

JPEG2000

Lossy compression artifacts >

Resolution

Resolution is a term that is used to specify the size of a pixel, a dot of colored light on a monitor or a dot of ink on the printed page. There are usually two resolutions at play at any one time – the resolution of the digital file and that of the output device. We can talk about capture size, image resolution, monitor resolution and printer resolution. They are all different, but they all come into play when handling a single digital image that is to be printed. Various resolutions can be quoted as we move through the chain of processes involved in creating a digital print (in the example below the total number of pixels remains constant throughout the chain of events).

Image sensor

The sensor to the right creates an image file with 5 million pixels or 5 megapixels (2560 × 1920 pixels). The resolution assigned to the image file by the capture device may be a print or monitor resolution. Either way it has no bearing on the file size, which is determined by the total number of pixels.

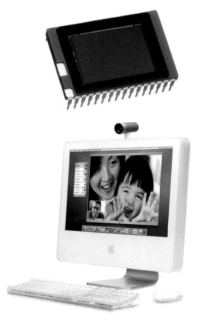

Digital file displayed on screen

The monitor resolution (the size of its display pixels) is defined by its resolution setting (approximately 100 pixels for every linear inch or 10,000 pixels for every square inch in a high definition TFT display). The image pixels (different to the display pixels) can be viewed in a variety of sizes by zooming in and out of the image using image-editing software.

Digital file adjusted in Photoshop

The resolution of the digital file is adjusted to 256 pixels per inch (ppi). Each pixel is allocated a size of 1/256th of an inch. Because the digital file is 2560 pixels wide this will create a print that is 10 inches wide if printed (256 × 10 = 2560).

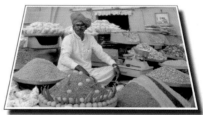

Note > Increasing the document size further will start to lower the resolution below the level which is recommended by commercial output devices (the pixels will be large enough to see with the naked eye).

The image is printed

The image is printed on an inkjet printer using a printing resolution of 1440 dots per inch. Many colored dots of ink are used to render a single image pixel.

Overview

The image is captured at a resolution of over 3000ppi and displayed at 100ppi on a high resolution monitor. Using image-editing software the image resolution is lowered to 256ppi (the pixel dimensions remain the same). The image is then printed using an inkjet printer with a printer resolution of 1440dpi. The different resolutions associated with this chain of events are:

Capture size > Display resolution > Image resolution > Output device resolution

Understanding resolution

Resolution is perhaps the most important, and the most confusing, subject in digital imaging. It is important because it is linked to quality. It is confusing because the term 'resolution' is used to describe at what quality the image is captured, displayed or output through various devices.

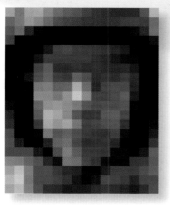
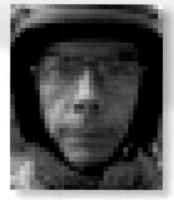
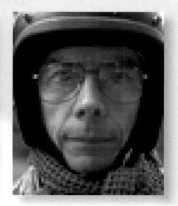

| 10 pixels per inch | 20 pixels per inch | 40 pixels per inch |

Resolution determines image quality and size

Increasing the total number of pixels in an image at the capture or scanning stage increases both the quality of the image and its file size. It is 'resolution' that determines how large or small the pixels appear in the final printed image. The greater the image resolution the smaller the pixels, and the greater the apparent sharpness of the image. Resolution is stated in 'pixels per inch' or 'ppi'.

Note > With the USA dominating digital photography, measurements in inches rather than centimeters are commonly used – 1 inch equals exactly 2.54 centimeters.

The images to the right have the same pixel dimensions (300 × 300) but different resolutions. The large image has a resolution half that of the small one. A digital image can be made to appear bigger or smaller without changing the total number of pixels, e.g. a small print or a big poster. This is because a pixel has no fixed size. The pixel size can be modified by the image-editing software to change the document size. Increasing the resolution of the image file decreases the size of the pixels and therefore the output size of the file.

Note > When talking about the 'size' of a digital image it is important to clarify whether it is the pixel dimensions or the document size (measured in inches or centimeters) that are being referred to.

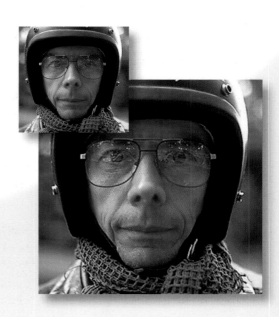

Dpi and ppi

If manufacturers of software and hardware were to agree that dots were round and pixels were square it might help users differentiate between the various resolutions that are often quoted. If this was the case the resolution of a digital image file would always be quoted in 'pixels per inch', but this is not the case.

At the scanning stage some manufacturers use the term dpi instead of 'ppi'. When scanning, 'ppi' and 'dpi' are essentially the same and the terms are interchangeable, e.g. if you scan at 300dpi you get an image that is 300ppi.

When working in Photoshop CS2 image resolution is always stated in ppi. You will usually only encounter dpi again when discussing the monitor or printer resolution. The resolutions used to capture, display or print the image are usually different to the image resolution itself.

Note > Just in case you thought this differentiation between ppi and dpi is entirely logical – it isn't. The industry uses the two terms to describe resolution, 'pixels per inch' (ppi) and 'dots per inch' (dpi), indiscriminately. Sometimes even the manufacturers of the software and hardware can't make up their minds which of the two they should be using, e.g. Adobe refer to image resolution as ppi in Photoshop and dpi in InDesign – such is the non-standardized nomenclature that remains in digital imaging.

File size and resolution

When we use the measurement 'ppi' or 'pixels per inch' we are referring to a linear inch, not a square inch (ignore the surface area and look at the length).

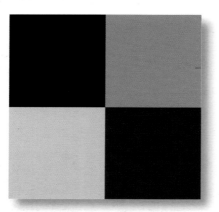
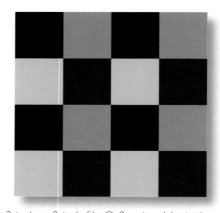

2 inch × 2inch file @ 1 ppi = 4 pixels   *2 inch × 2 inch file @ 2 ppi = 16 pixels*

File size, however, is directly linked to the **total** number of pixels covering the entire surface area of the digital image. Doubling the image output dimensions or image resolution quadruples the total number of pixels and the associated file size in kilobytes or megabytes.

Note > Handling files with excessive pixel dimensions for your output needs will slow down every stage of your digital image process including scanning, saving, opening, editing and printing. Extra pixels above and beyond what your output device needs will not lead to extra quality. Quality is limited or 'capped' by the capability of the output device.

PHOTOSHOP CS2 >>>

Calculating a suitable file size and scanning resolution

Scanning resolution is rarely the same as the resolution you require to print out your image. If you are going to create a print larger than the original you are scanning, the scanning resolution will be greater than the output resolution, e.g. a 35mm negative would have to be scanned at 1200ppi if a 6 × 4 inch commerical print is required. If the print you require is smaller than the original the scanning resolution will be smaller than the output resolution.

The smaller the original the higher the scanning resolution.

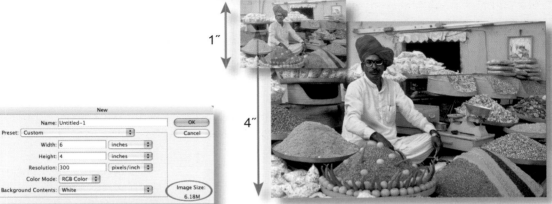

Magnification × output resolution = scanning resolution
scanning resolution = 4 × 300ppi = 1200ppi

To calculate the correct file size and scanning resolution for the job in hand you can:

1. Go to 'File > New' in Photoshop, type in the document size, resolution and mode you require and then make a note of the number of megabytes you require from the scanning process. Then adjust the scanning resolution until the required number of megabytes is captured.

2. Multiply the magnification factor (original size to output size) by the output resolution (as dictated by the output device) to find the scanning resolution (not so difficult as it sounds!).

essential skills >>> >>>

Size & mode	Output device resolution		
	100ppi screen	240ppi inkjet	300ppi commercial
8 × 10 RGB	2.29MB	13.20MB	20.60MB
8 × 10 Grayscale	781K	4.39MB	6.87MB
5 × 7 RGB	1.00MB	5.77MB	9.01MB
5 × 7 Grayscale	342K	1.92MB	3.00MB
4 × 6 RGB	703K	3.96MB	6.18MB
4 × 6 Grayscale	234K	1.32MB	2.06MB

File size

Image size

Before you adjust the size of the image you have to know how to deternine the size you need. Six and eight megapixel digital cameras are currently the affordable 'end' of professional digital capture. The image resolution produced by these digital cameras is not directly comparable to 35mm film capture but the images produced can satisfy most of the requirements associated with professional 35mm image capture. DSLRs using full frame sensors can match medium format film cameras for quality.

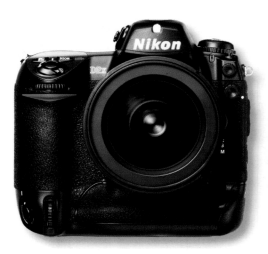 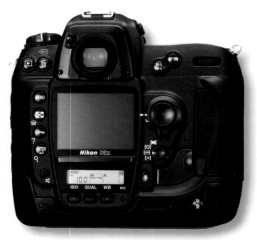

Six megapixel cameras capture images with pixel dimensions of around 3000 × 2000 (6 million pixels or 6 'megapixels'). The resulting file size of around 17MB (1 megapixel translates to nearly 3 megabytes of data) is suitable for commercial print quality (300ppi) to illustrate a single page in a magazine. Digital capture is now an affordable reality for all professional photographers.

Useful specifications to remember

- Typical high-resolution monitor: 1024 × 768 pixels
- Typical full-page magazine illustration: 3000 × 2000 (6 million pixels)
- High-resolution TFT monitor: 100ppi
- High quality inkjet print: 240ppi
- Magazine quality printing requirements: 300ppi
- Full-screen image: 2.25MB (1024 × 768)
- Postcard-sized inkjet print: 4MB
- 10 × 8 inch inkjet print: 13.2MB
- Full-page magazine image at commercial resolution: 20MB

Note > Remember to double the above file sizes if you intend to edit in 16-bit per channel mode.

A 20MB file will usually suffice if you are not sure of the intended use of the digital file. Thirty-five millimeter film scanned with a scanning resolution of **2300** will produce a 20.3MB file (2173 pixels × 3260 pixels).

Pixel dimensions, document size and resolution

Before retouching and enhancement takes place the '**image size**' should be scaled for the intended output (the capture resolution will probably require changing to output resolution). Choose Image > Image Size in Photoshop. This will ensure that optimum image quality and computer operating speed is maintained. Image size is described in three ways:

- Pixel dimensions (the number of pixels determines the file size in terms of kilobytes).
- Print size (output dimensions in inches or centimeters).
- Resolution (measured in pixels per inch or ppi).

If one is altered it will affect or impact on one or both of the others, e.g. increasing the print size must either lower the resolution or increase the pixel dimensions and file size. The image size is usually changed for the following reasons:

- Resolution is changed to match the requirements of the print output device.
- Print output dimensions are changed to match display requirements.

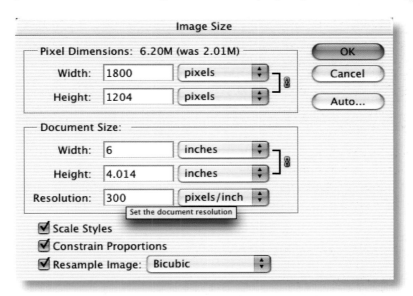

Image size options

When changing an image's size a decision can be made to retain the proportions of the image and/or the pixel dimensions. These are controlled by the following:

- If '**Constrain Proportions**' is selected the proportional dimensions between image width and image height are linked. If either one is altered the other is adjusted automatically and proportionally. If this is not selected the width or height can be adjusted independently of the other and may lead to a distorted image.

- If '**Resample Image**' is selected adjusting the dimensions or resolution of the image will allow the file size to be increased or decreased to accommodate the changes. Pixels are either removed or added. If deselected the print size and resolution are linked. Changing width, height or resolution will change the other two. Pixel dimensions and file size remain constant.

Resampling

An image is 'resampled' when its pixel dimensions (and resulting file size) are changed. It is possible to change the output size or resolution without affecting the pixel dimensions (see 'Understanding resolution'). Resampling usually takes place when the pixel dimensions of the original capture or scan do not precisely match the requirements for output (size and resolution). Downsampling decreases the number of pixels and information is deleted from the image. Increasing the total number of pixels or resampling up requires new pixels to be added to the file. The new pixels use information based on color values of the existing pixels in the image file.

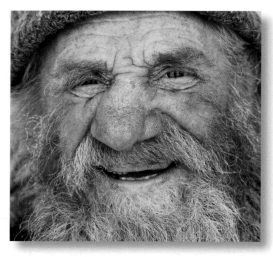 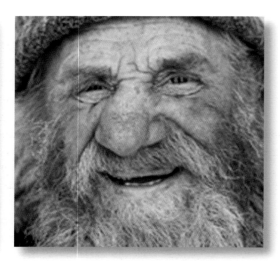

Image scanned at correct resolution   *Effects of excessive resampling*

Excessive resampling up can result in poor image quality (the image will start to appear blurry). Avoid the need for resampling to enlarge the file size, if at all possible, by capturing at a high enough resolution or by limiting the output size. If you have to resample due to the limitations of your capture device (not enough megapixels) then files that resample best are those that have been captured from a digital camera using a low ISO setting and have not previously been sharpened.

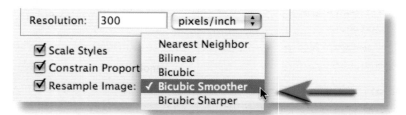

When resampling an image to create a larger file, choose the 'Bicubic Smoother' from the Interpolation options in the Image Size dialog box. Use 'Bicubic Sharper' when decreasing the size of the file. Bilinear and Nearest Neighbor are used for hard-edged graphics and are rarely used for the Interpolation of photographs. If you have already sharpened your image prior to resampling (best avoided) you will need to reapply the Unsharp Mask or Smart Sharpen to regain the sharp quality of the image.

Interpolation

Well it seems that in recent years a small revolution in refinement has been happening in the area of interpolation technologies. The algorithms and processes used to apply them have been continuously increasing in quality until now they are at such a point that the old adages such as

Sensor dimension/output resolution = maximum print size

don't always apply. Using either software or hardware versions of the latest algorithms it is now possible to take comparatively small files and produce truly large prints of good quality.

Resampling techniques

Bicubic – All resampling techniques in Photoshop use the best interpolation settings of Bicubic, Bicubic Sharper or Bicubic Smoother in conjunction with the Image > Image Size feature. The standard approach uses a 4 × 4 sampling scheme of the original pixels as a way of generating new image data. With the Resample and Constrain Properties options selected, the new picture dimensions are entered into the 'width' and 'height' areas of the dialog. Clicking OK will then increase the number of pixels in the original.

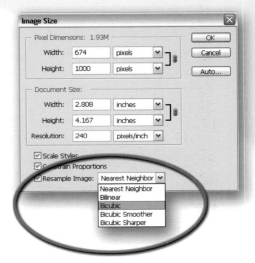

Use the Unsharp Mask after resampling rather than before and restrict the amount of resampling that is performed on a single image. If the software allows the user to crop, resize and rotate the image at the same time, this function should be utilized whenever possible.

Bicubic via LAB – In this technique the mode of the picture is changed from RGB to LAB first using the Image > Mode > Lab command. The two color channels (A and B) are then hidden in the channels palette and the bicubic interpolation is applied to just the lightness (L) channel. The color channels are then switched back on. The theory behind this approach is that by only interpolating the lightness channel the enlarged image will suffer less deterioration overall.

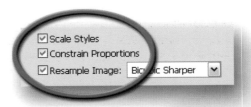

Stair interpolation – There is a growing school of thought that states that increasing the size of an image by several smaller steps will produce a sharper, more detailed result than making the upscale enlargement in a single jump. Most professionals who use this approach increase the size of their images by 10% each time until they reach the desired pixel dimensions.

The advances in the algorithms and procedures used to create large images have dramatically improved over the last few years. I still cringe saying it, but it is now possible to break the 'I must never interpolate my images rule' in order to produce more print area for the pixels I have available.

Resampling guidelines:

When resampling keep in mind the following guidelines for ensuring the best results:

1. Images captured with the correct number of pixels for the required print job will always produce better results than those that have been interpolated.

2. The softening effect that results from high levels of interpolation is less noticeable in general, landscape or portrait images and more apparent in images with sharp-edged elements.

3. The more detail and pixels in the original file the better the interpolated results will be.

4. A well-exposed, sharply focused original file that is saved in a lossless format such as TIFF is the best candidate image for upsizing.

What is interpolation anyway?

Interpolation is a process by which extra pixels are generated in a low resolution image so that it can be printed at a larger size than its original dimensions would normally allow. Interpolation, or as it is sometimes called, upsizing, can be implemented via software products such as the Image Size > Resample option in Photoshop or by using the resize options in the printer's hardware.

Both approaches work by sampling a group of pixels (a 4 × 4 matrix in the case of bicubic interpolation) and using this information together with a special algorithm as a basis for generating the values for newly created pixels that will be added to the image. The sophistication of the algorithm and the size of the sampling set determine the quality of the interpolated results.

Printer-based resampling

An alternative approach to using Photoshop to resample your picture is to make use of the 'scaling' options in your printer driver dialog. Most desktop and high-end laboratory digital printers are capable of the interpolation necessary to produce big prints.

When outsourcing to a professional printer the file is kept to its original pixel dimensions and the resolution is reduced so that the print size will equal the required print dimensions. The digital printer is then instructed to interpolate the file as it was printing to its optimum resolution of the machine. On the desktop a similar process is used with the digital photographer selecting a scale value in the print driver dialog that is greater than 100%.

Letting the output device perform the interpolation of the image has the following advantages – the process does not require the photographer to change the original file in any way and it removes an extra processing step from the file preparation process.

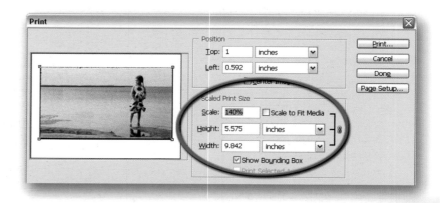

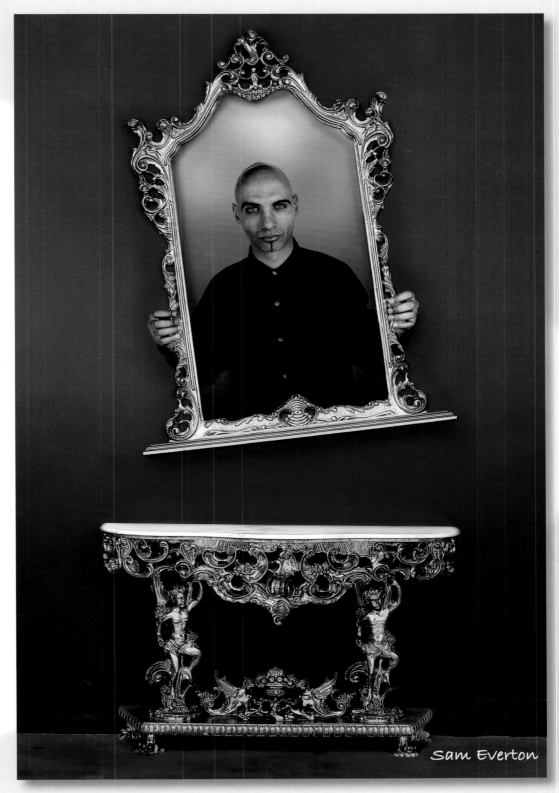

Sam Everton

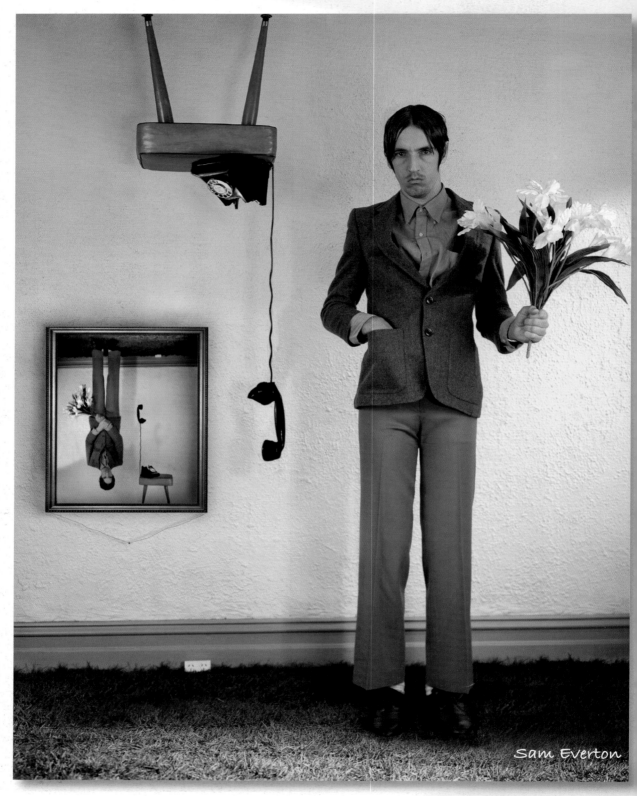

Sam Everton

capture and enhance

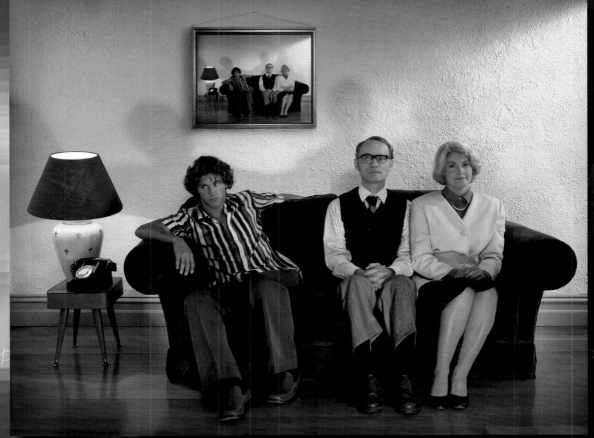

Sam Everton

op *p* *photos*

essential skills

- ~ Capture high quality digital images for image editing.
- ~ Gain control over the color, tonality and sharpness of a digital image.
- ~ Duplicate, optimize and save image files for print and for web.

Introduction

Every digital image that has been captured can be enhanced further so that it may be viewed in its optimum state for the intended output device. Whether images are destined to be viewed in print or via a monitor screen, the image usually needs to be re-sized, cropped, retouched, color-corrected, sharpened and saved in an appropriate file format. The original capture will usually possess pixel dimensions that do not exactly match the requirements of the output device. In order for this to be corrected the user must address the issues of '**Image Size**', '**Resampling**' and '**Cropping**'.

To end up with high quality output you must start with the optimum levels of information that the capture device is capable of providing. The factors that greatly enhance final quality are:

- A 'subject brightness range' that does not exceed the exposure latitude of the capture medium (the contrast is not too high for the film or image sensor).
- Using a low ISO setting or fine grain film to capture the original image.
- The availability of 16 bits per channel scanning or RAW camera file import.

Optimizing image quality

This chapter focuses its attentions on the standard adjustments made to all images when optimum quality is required without using any advanced techniques. Standard image adjustments usually include the process of optimizing the color, tonality and sharpness of the image. With the exception of dust or blemish removal, these adjustments are applied globally (to all the pixels). Most of the adjustments in this chapter are 'objective' rather than 'subjective' adjustments and are tackled as a logical progression of tasks. Automated features are available for some of these tasks but these do not ensure optimum quality is achieved for all images. The chapter uses a 'hands-on' project to guide you through the steps required to achieve optimum quality.

Save, save and save

Good working habits will prevent the frustration and the heartache that are often associated with the inevitable '**crash**' (all computers crash or '**freeze**' periodically). As you work on an image file you should get into the habit of saving the work in progress and not wait until the image editing is complete. It is recommended that you use the 'Save As' command and continually rename the file as an updated version. Unless computer storage space is an issue the Photoshop (PSD) file format should be used for work in progress. Before the computer is shut down, the files should be saved to a removable storage device or burnt to a CD/DVD. In short, save often, save different versions and save back-ups.

Stepping back

Digital image editing allows the user to make mistakes. There are several ways of undoing a mistake before resorting to the '**Revert** ' command from the File menu or opening a previously saved version. Photoshop allows the user to jump to the previous state via the Edit > Undo command (Command/ Ctrl + Z) whilst '**Histories**' allows access to any previous state in the Histories palette without going through a linear sequence of undos. Alternatively the user can 'Step Backward' by using the keyboard shortcut Ctrl+Alt+Z (PC) or Command+Option+Z (Mac).

Advantages and disadvantages of 16-bit editing

When the highest quality images are required there are major advantages to be gained by starting off the editing process in '16 Bits/Channel' mode. In 16 bits per channel there are trillions, instead of millions, of possible values for each pixel. Spikes or comb lines, that are quick to occur whilst editing in 8 bits per channel, rarely occur when editing in 16 bits per channel mode. The disadvantages of editing in 16 bits per channel are:

- Not all digital cameras are capable of saving in the RAW format.
- The size of file is doubled when compared to an 8 bits per channel image of the same output size and resolution.
- Some editing features (including many filters) do not work in 16 bits per channel mode.
- Only a small selection of file formats support the use of 16 bits per channel.

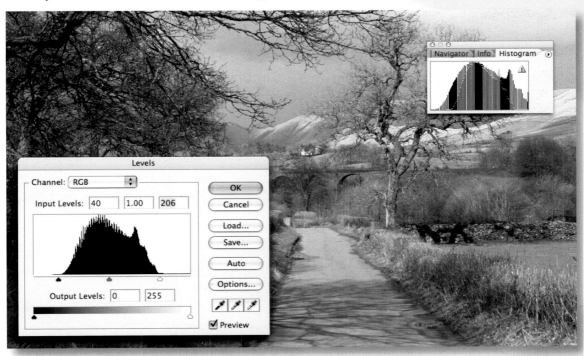

Comb lines that appear in the histogram will usually disappear if editing in 16 bits per channel

Choosing your bit depth

It is still preferable to make major changes in tonality or color in 16-bit mode before converting the file to 8-bit mode. Images can be converted from 8-bit (Image > Mode > 16 Bits/Channel) or captured in 16-bit (the preferred choice). Most of the better scanners that are now available (flatbed and film) now support 16 bits per channel image capture. Many scanners refer to 16 bits per channel scanning as 48-bit RGB scanning. Some scanners offer 14 bits per channel scanning but deliver a 48-bit image to Photoshop. Remember, you need twice as many megabytes as the equivalent 8-bit image, e.g. if you typically capture 13.2 megabytes for an 8 × 10 @ 240ppi you will require 26.4 megabytes when scanning in 16 bits per channel.

Foundations project I

Follow the seven steps over the following pages in order to create one image optimized for print and one file optimized for web viewing.

Image capture – *Step I*

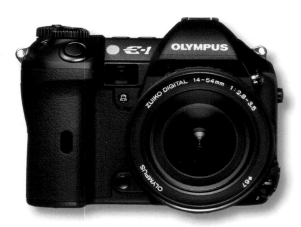

Select or create a softly lit color portrait image (diffused sunlight or window lighting would be ideal). The image selected should have detail in both the highlights and shadows and should have a range of colors and tones. An image with high contrast and missing detail in the highlights or shadows is not suitable for testing the effectiveness of the capture or output device.

Digital capture via a digital camera

Images can be transferred directly to the computer from a digital camera or from a card reader if the card has been removed from the camera. Images are usually saved on the camera's storage media as JPEG, RAW or TIFF files. If using the JPEG file format to capture images you should choose the high or maximum quality setting whenever possible. If using the TIFF or JPEG file formats, it is important to select low levels of image sharpening, saturation and contrast in the camera's settings to ensure optimum quality and editing flexibility in the image-editing software. If the camera has the option to choose Adobe RGB instead of sRGB as the color space this should also be selected.

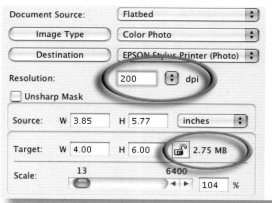

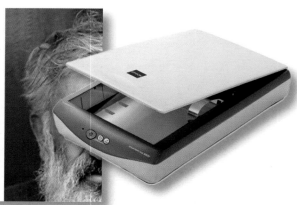

Digital capture via a scanning device

Ensure the media to be scanned is free from dust and grease marks. Gloss photographic paper offers the best surface for flatbed scanning. The scanning device can usually be accessed directly from the Adobe software via the 'Import' command. Ensure that you scan the image at an appropriate resolution for your image-editing needs (see 'Digital Basics > Calculating file size and scanning resolution').

Cropping an image – *Step 2*

When sizing an image for the intended output it is important to select the width and height in pixels for screen or web viewing and in centimeters or inches for printing. Typing in 'px', 'in' or 'cm' after each measurement will tell Photoshop to crop using these units. If no measurement is entered in the field then Adobe will choose the default unit measurement entered in the Preferences (Preferences > Units & Rulers'). The preference can be quickly changed by Control-clicking on either ruler (select 'View > Rulers' if they are not currently selected).

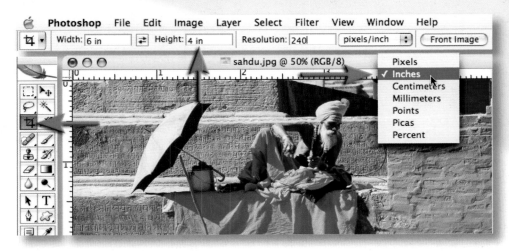

Select the 'Front Image' option to select the current measurements of a selected image. This option is useful when you are matching the size of a new image to an existing one that has already been prepared. Select the 'Clear' option to quickly delete all of the existing units that may already be entered in the fields from a previous crop. The action of entering measurements and resolution at the time of cropping ensures that the image is sized and cropped or 'shaped' as one action. Entering the size at the time of cropping ensures the format of the final image will match the printing paper, photo frame or screen where the image will finally be output.

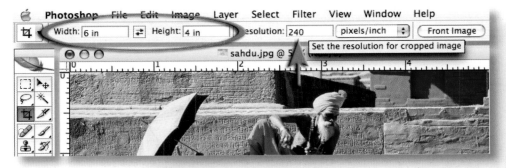

Note > If both a width and a height measurement are entered into the fields the proportions of the final crop will be locked and may prevent you from selecting parts of the image if the capture and output formats are different, e.g. if you have entered the same measurement in both the width and height fields the final crop proportions are constrained to a square.

Perfecting the crop

If the image is crooked you can rotate the cropping marquee by moving the mouse cursor to a position just outside a corner handle of the cropping marquee. A curved arrow should appear, allowing you to drag the image straight.

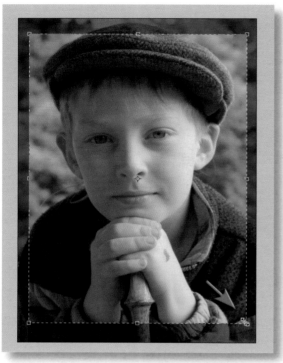 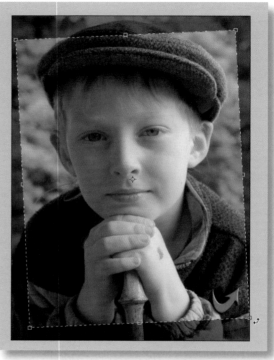

Click and drag the corner handle to extend the image window to check if there are any remaining border pixels that are not part of the image. Press the 'Return/Enter' key on the keyboard to complete the cropping action. Alternatively press the 'Esc' key on the keyboard to cancel the crop.

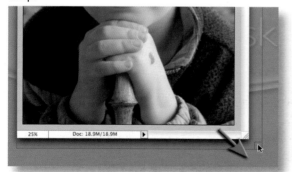 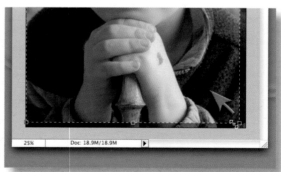

The marquee tool is programmed to snap to the edges of the document as if they were magnetized. This can make it difficult to remove a narrow border of unwanted pixels. To overcome this problem you will need to go to the 'View' menu and switch off the 'Snap To' option.

Note > See 'Image Enhancements – Project 1' for more information on cropping images.

Tonal adjustments – *Step 3*

The color information in a 24-bit RGB digital image file is separated into three 'channels' (8 bits per channel). Each color channel is capable of storing 256 levels of brightness between black (level 0) and white (level 255). When viewing all three color channels simultaneously each pixel is able to be rendered in any one of 16.7 million colors (256 × 256 × 256).

These brightness levels can often be displayed as a simple graph or histogram in both the capture device and the image-editing software. The horizontal axis displays the brightness values from left (darkest) to right (lightest). The vertical axis of the graph shows how much of the image is found at any particular brightness level. If the subject contrast or 'brightness range' exceeds the latitude of the capture device or the exposure is either too high or too low, then tonality will be 'clipped' (shadow or highlight detail will be lost).

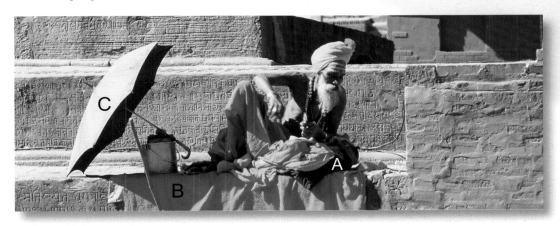

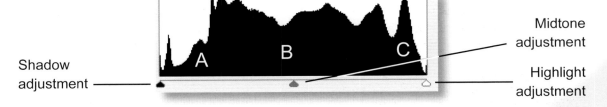

Shadow adjustment

Midtone adjustment

Highlight adjustment

Histograms

During the capture stage it is usually possible to check how the device has handled or interpreted the tonality and color of the subject. This useful information can often be displayed as a 'histogram' on the LCD screen of high quality digital cameras immediately after capture, or in the scanning software during the scanning process. The histogram displayed shows the brightness range of the subject in relation to the latitude or 'dynamic range' of your capture device's image sensor. Most digital camera sensors have a dynamic range similar to color transparency film (around five stops) when capturing in JPEG or TIFF. This may be expanded beyond seven stops when the RAW data is processed manually.

Note > You should attempt to modify the brightness, contrast and color balance at the capture stage to obtain the best possible histogram before editing begins in the software.

Optimizing tonality

In a good histogram, one where a broad tonal range with full detail in the shadows and highlights is present, the information will extend all the way from the left to the right side of the histogram. The histogram below indicates missing information in the highlights (on the right) and a small amount of 'clipping' or loss of information in the shadows (on the left).

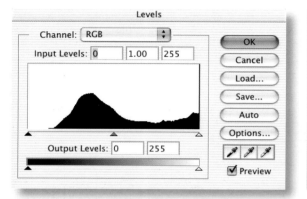 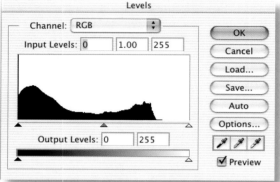

Histograms indicating image is either too light or too dark

Brightness

If the digital file is too light a tall peak will be seen to rise on the right side (level 255) of the histogram. If the digital file is too dark a tall peak will be seen to rise on the left side (level 0) of the histogram.

Solution: Decrease or increase the exposure/brightness in the capture device.

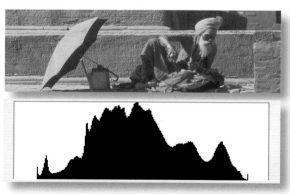 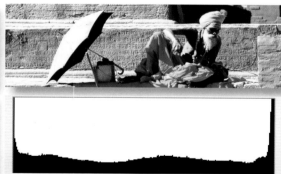

Histograms indicating image either has too much contrast or not enough

Contrast

If the contrast is too low the histogram will not extend to meet the sliders at either end.
If the contrast is too high a tall peak will be evident at both extremes of the histogram.

Solution: Increase or decrease the contrast of the light source used to light the subject or the contrast setting of the capture device. Using diffused lighting rather than direct sunlight or using fill-flash and/or reflectors will ensure that you start with an image with full detail.

Optimizing a histogram after capture

The final histogram should show that pixels have been allocated to most, if not all, of the 256 levels. If the histogram indicates large gaps between the ends of the histogram and the sliders (indicating either a low-contrast scan or low-contrast subject photographed in flat lighting) the subject or original image should usually be re-captured a second time.

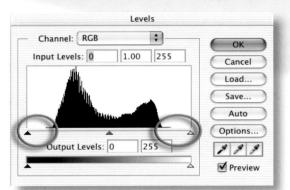 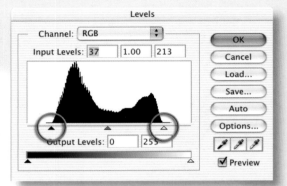

Small gaps at either end of the histogram can, however, be corrected by dragging the sliders to the start of the tonal information. Holding down the Alt/Option key when dragging these sliders will indicate what, if any, information is being clipped. Note how the sliders have been moved beyond the short thin horizontal line at either end of the histogram. These low levels of pixel data are often not representative of the broader areas of shadows and highlights within the image and can usually be clipped (moved to 0 or 255).

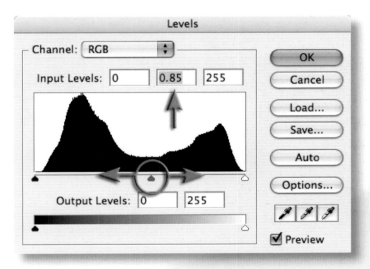

Moving the 'Gamma' slider can modify the brightness of the midtones. After correcting the tonal range using the sliders, click 'OK' in the top right-hand corner of the Levels dialog box.

Note > Use the Levels for all initial brightness and contrast adjustments. The Brightness/ Contrast adjustment feature in Photoshop CS should be avoided as this will upset the work performed using Levels and can result in a loss of information.

Shadows and highlights

When the tonality has been optimized using the Levels dialog box the shadow and highlight values may require further work. One of the limitations of the Levels adjustment feature is that it cannot focus its attention on only the shadows or the highlights, e.g. when the slider is moved to the left both the highlights and the shadows are made brighter.

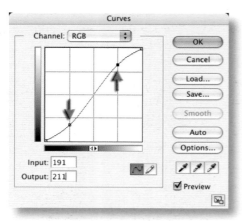 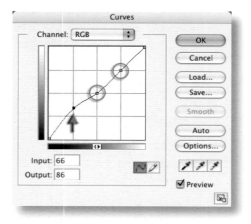

Targeted adjustments can be achieved using the Curves adjustment feature. Curves allows the user to target tones within the image and move them independently of other tones within the image, e.g. the user can decide to make only the darker tones lighter whilst preserving the value of both the midtones and the highlights. It is also possible with a powerful editing feature such as Curves to move the shadows in one direction and the highlights in another. In this way the contrast of the image could be increased without losing valuable detail in either the shadows or the highlights. See 'Advanced Retouching – Projects 1 and 2' for more information on Curves.

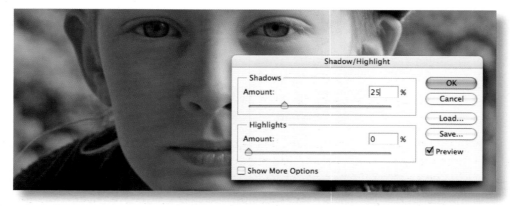

The Shadow/Highlight adjustment feature offers an alternative. This targets and adjusts tonality in a non-destructive way and in many ways offers superior control than the Curves adjustment feature (midtone contrast) in a user friendly interface. The disadvantage is that the adjustment is not available as an adjustment layer. See 'Advanced retouching' for more information.

Note > See 'Retouching Projects – Project 5' for more information on shadow and highlight control.

Target values – using the eyedroppers

To make sure the highlights do not 'blow out' and the shadows do not print too dark it is possible to target, or set specific tonal values, for the highlight and shadow tones within the image using the eyedroppers (found in the Levels and Curves dialog boxes). The tones that should be targeted are the lightest and darkest areas in the image with detail. The default settings of these eyedroppers are set to 0 (black) and 255 (white). These settings are only useful for targeting the white paper or black film edge. After establishing the darkest and lightest tones that will print using a step wedge (see 'Digital Printing', page 87) these target levels can be assigned to the eyedroppers.

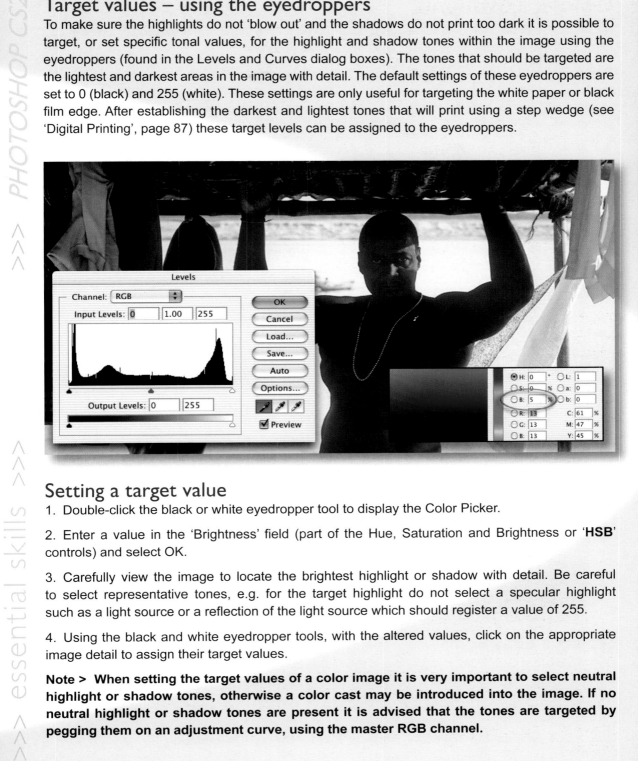

Setting a target value

1. Double-click the black or white eyedropper tool to display the Color Picker.

2. Enter a value in the 'Brightness' field (part of the Hue, Saturation and Brightness or '**HSB**' controls) and select OK.

3. Carefully view the image to locate the brightest highlight or shadow with detail. Be careful to select representative tones, e.g. for the target highlight do not select a specular highlight such as a light source or a reflection of the light source which should register a value of 255.

4. Using the black and white eyedropper tools, with the altered values, click on the appropriate image detail to assign their target values.

Note > When setting the target values of a color image it is very important to select neutral highlight or shadow tones, otherwise a color cast may be introduced into the image. If no neutral highlight or shadow tones are present it is advised that the tones are targeted by pegging them on an adjustment curve, using the master RGB channel.

Color adjustments – *Step 4*

Neutral tones in the image should appear desaturated on the monitor. If a color cast is present try to remove it at the time of capture or scanning if at all possible.

Solution: Control color casts by using either the white balance on the camera (digital), shoot using the RAW file format or by using an 80A or 80B color conversion filter when using tungsten light with daylight film. Use the available color controls on the scanning device to correct the color cast and/or saturation.

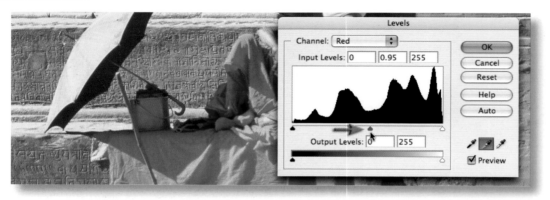

Color correction using Levels

If you select a Red, Green or Blue channel (from the channel's pull-down menu) prior to moving the Gamma slider you can remove a color cast present in the image. For those unfamiliar with color correction the adjustment feature 'Variations' in Photoshop gives a quick and easy solution to the problem.

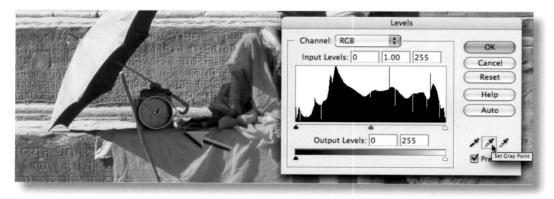

Setting a Gray Point

Click on the 'Set Gray Point' eyedropper in the Levels dialog box and then click on any neutral tone present in the image to remove a color cast. Introducing a near white card or gray card into the first image of a shoot can aid in subsequent color corrections for all images shot using the same light source.

Note > See 'Retouching Projects – Projects 2 and 3' for more information.

Variations (not available when editing 16-bit files)

The 'Variations' command allows the adjustment of color balance, contrast and saturation to the whole image or just those pixels that are part of a selection. For individuals that find correcting color by using the more professional color correction adjustment features intimidating, variations offers a comparativley user friendly interface. By simply clicking on the alternative thumbnail that looks better the changes are applied automatically. The adjustments can be concentrated on the highlights, midtones or shadows by checking the appropriate box. The degree of change can be controlled by the Fine/Coarse slider.

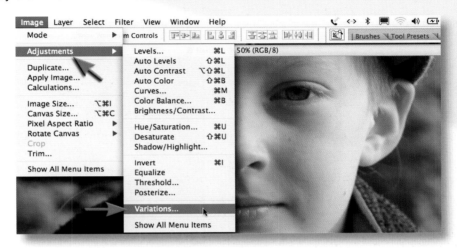

Variations can be accessed from the the Adjustments submenu in the Image menu. Start by selecting the 'Midtones' radio button and then adjust the intensity until you can see a thumbnail that looks about right, and then click on the one you like. Then click 'OK'.

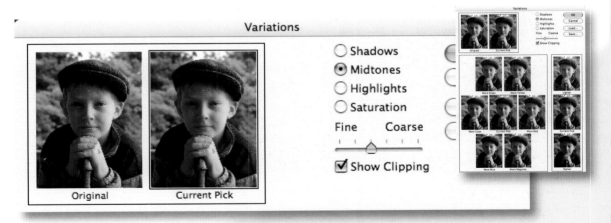

Note > Editing with the highlights, shadows or saturation button checked can lead to a loss of information in one or more of the channels. If the 'Show Clipping' is checked a neon warning shows areas in the image that have been adjusted to 255 or 0. Clipping does not, however, occur when the adjustment is restricted to the midtones only.

Cleaning an image – *Step 5*

The primary tools for removing blemishes, dust and scratches are the 'Clone Stamp Tool', the 'Healing Brush Tool' and the new 'Spot Healing Brush Tool'. The Clone Stamp is able to paint with pixels selected or 'sampled' from another part of the image. The Healing Brush is a sophisticated version of the Clone Stamp Tool that not only paints with the sampled pixels but then 'sucks in' the color and tonal characteristics of the pixels surrounding the damage. The Spot Healing Brush Tool requires no prior sampling and is usually the first port of call for most repairs. The following procedures should be taken when working with the Spot Healing Brush Tool or Healing Brush Tool.

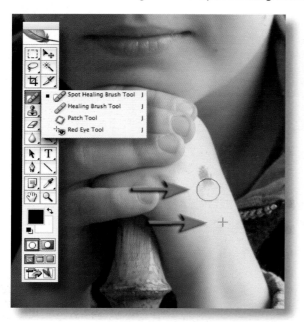
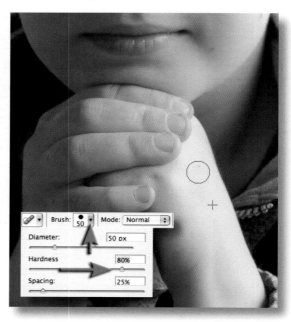

- Select the Spot Healing Brush Tool from the Tools palette.
- Zoom in to take a close look at the damage that needs to be repaired.
- Choose an appropriate size, soft-edged brush from the brushes palette that just covers the width of the blemish, dust or scratch to be repaired.
- Move the mouse cursor to the area of damage.
- Click and drag the tool over the area that requires repair.
- Increase the hardness of the brush if the repair area becomes contaminated with adjacent tones, colors or detail that does not match the repair area.
- For areas proving difficult for the Spot Healing Brush to repair switch to either the Healing Brush Tool or the Clone Stamp Tool. Select a sampling point by pressing the Alt or Option key and then clicking on an undamaged area of the image (similar in tone and color to the damaged area). Click and drag the tool over the area to paint with the sampled pixels to conceal the damaged area (a cross hair marks the sampling point and will move as you paint).

Note > If a large area is to be repaired with the Clone Stamp Tool it is advisable to take samples from a number of different points with a reduced opacity brush to prevent the repairs becoming obvious.

Sharpening an image – *Step 6*

Sharpening the image is the last step of the editing process. Many images benefit from some sharpening even if they were captured with sharp focus. The 'Unsharp Mask' and the new 'Smart Sharpen' filters from the 'Sharpen' group of filters are the most sophisticated and controllable of the sharpening filters. They are used to sharpen the edges by increasing the contrast where different tones meet.

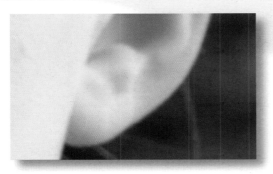 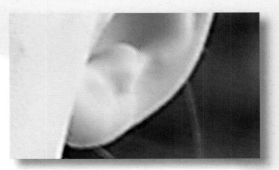

The pixels along the edge on the lighter side are made lighter and the pixels along the edge on the darker side are made darker. Before you use the Unsharp Mask go to 'View > Actual Pixels' to adjust the screen view to 100%. To access the Unsharp Mask (the slightly simpler of the two sophisticated sharpening filters) go to 'Filter > Sharpen > Unsharp Mask'. Start with an average setting of 100% for 'Amount', a 1 to 1.5 pixel 'Radius' and a 'Threshold' of 3. The effects of the Unsharp Mask filter are more noticeable on-screen than in print. For final evaluation always check the final print and adjust if necessary by returning to the saved version from the previous stage. The three sliders control:

Amount – This controls how much darker or lighter the pixels are adjusted. Eighty to 180% is normal.

Radius – Controls the width of the adjustment occurring at the edges. There is usually no need to exceed 1 pixel if the image is to be printed no larger than A4/US letter. A rule of thumb is to divide the image resolution by 200 to determine the radius amount, e.g. 200ppi ÷ 200 = 1.00.

Threshold – Controls where the effect takes place. A zero threshold affects all pixels whereas a high threshold affects only edges with a high tonal difference. The threshold is usually kept very low (0 to 2) for images from digital cameras and medium or large format film. The threshold is usually set at 3 for images from 35mm. Threshold is increased to avoid accentuating noise, especially in skin tones.

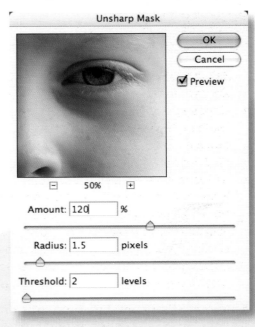

Note > See 'Retouching Projects – Project 6' for more information on sharpening images.

Saving a modified file – *Step 7*

Go to the 'File' menu and select 'Save As'. Name the file, select 'TIFF' or 'Photoshop' as the file format and the destination 'Where' the file is being saved. Check the 'Embed Color Profile' box and click 'Save'. Keep the file name short using only the standard characters from the alphabet. Use a dash or underscore to separate words rather than leaving a space and always add or 'append' your file name after a full stop with the appropriate three- or four-letter file extension (.psd or .tif). This will ensure your files can be read by all and can be safely uploaded to web servers if required. Always keep a back-up of your work on a remote storage device if possible.

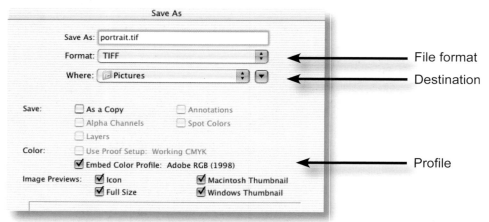

Resize for screen viewing

Duplicate your file by going to 'Image > Duplicate Image'. Rename the file and select OK. Go to 'Image > Image Size'. Check the 'Constrain Proportions' and 'Resample Image' boxes. Type in approximately 600 pixels in the 'Height' box (anything larger may not fully display in a browser window of a monitor set to 1024 × 768 pixels without the viewer having to use the scroll or navigation bars). Use the Bicubic Sharper option when reducing the file size for optimum quality.

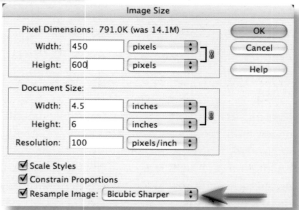

Using the Crop Tool (typing in the dimensions in pixels, e.g. 600px and 450px) will also resize the image quickly and effectively. This technique does not, however, make use of Bicubic Sharper and images may require sharpening a second time using the Unsharp Mask.

Note > Internet browsers do not respect the resolution and document size assigned to the image by image-editing software – image size is dictated by the resolution of the individual viewer's monitor. Two images that have the same pixel dimensions but different resolutions will appear the same size when displayed in a web browser. A typical screen resolution is often stated as being 72ppi but actual monitor resolutions vary enormously.

JPEG format options

After resizing the duplicate image you should set the image size on screen to 100% or 'Actual Pixels' from the View menu (this is the size of the image as it will appear in a web browser on a monitor of the same resolution). Go to 'File' menu and select 'Save As'. Select JPEG from the Format menu. Label the file with a short name with no gaps or punctuation marks (use an underscore if you have to separate two words) and finally ensure the file carries the extension .jpg (e.g. portrait_one.jpg). Click 'OK' and select a compression/quality setting from the 'JPEG Options' dialog box. With the Preview box checked you can check to see if there is excessive or minimal loss of quality at different compression/quality settings in the main image window.

Note > Double-clicking the Zoom Tool in the Tools palette will set the image to actual pixels or 100% magnification.

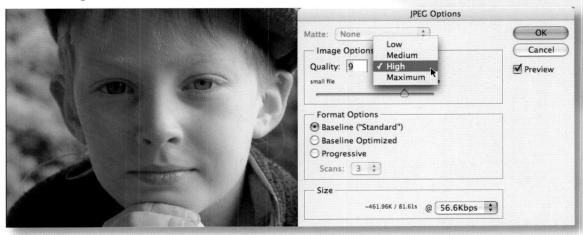

Choose a compression setting that will balance quality with file size (download time). High compression (low quality) leads to image artifacts, lowering the overall quality of the image. There is usually no need to zoom in to see the image artifacts as most browsers and screen presentation software do not allow this option.

Image Options: The quality difference on screen at 100% between the High and Maximum quality settings may not be easily discernible. The savings in file size can, however, be enormous, thereby enabling much faster uploading and downloading via the Internet.

Format Options: Selecting the 'Progressive' option from the Format Options enables the image to be displayed in increasing degrees of sharpness as it is is downloading to a web page, rather than waiting to be fully downloaded before being displayed by the web browser.

Size: The open file size is not changed by saving the file in the JPEG file format as this is dictated by the total number of pixels in the file. The closed file size is of interest when using the JPEG Options dialog box as it is this size that dictates the speed at which the file can be uploaded and downloaded via the Internet. The quality and size of the file is a balancing act if speed is an issue due to slow modem speeds.

Save for Web

The Save for Web command from the File menu offers the user an alternative option to resizing, optimizing and previewing the image prior to saving the file in the JPEG format. Access the Save for Web feature from the File menu. Click on the 2-up tab to see a before and after version of your image. Click on the second image and from the 'Preview Menu'; choose either the Mac or Windows options. This will enable you to anticipate how your image may be viewed in software that cannot read the ICC profile that Photoshop normally embeds as part of the color management process, e.g. most web browsers.

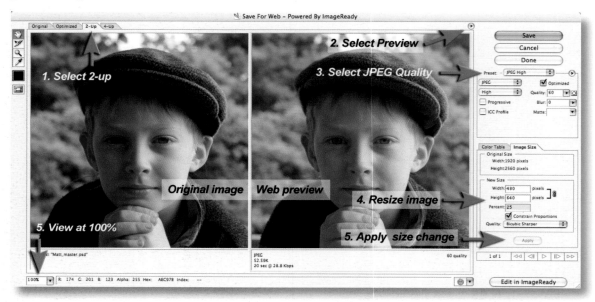

To adjust the color or tone prior to saving as a JPEG exit the Save for Web feature and go to View > Proof Setup and then choose either Macintosh RGB or Windows RGB depending on the intended monitor that the image will be viewed on. With the Proof Setup switched on, adjustments may be required to both image brightness and saturation in order to return the appearance of the image to 'normal'. Brightness should be controlled via the 'Gamma' slider in the 'Levels' adjustment feature and color saturation via the 'Hue/Saturation' adjustment feature.

Capture and enhance overview

1. Capture an image with sufficient pixels for the intended output device.
2. Resize and crop the image to the intended output size.
3. Optimize the histogram using the Levels dialog box.
4. Adjust the tonality and color.
5. Clean the image using the Spot Healing Brush Tool.
6. Apply the Unsharp Mask or Smart Sharpen filter.
7. Save the adjusted image as a Photoshop file (PSD).
8. Duplicate the file and resize for uploading to the web if required.
9. Save the file as a JPEG with a suitable compression/quality setting.

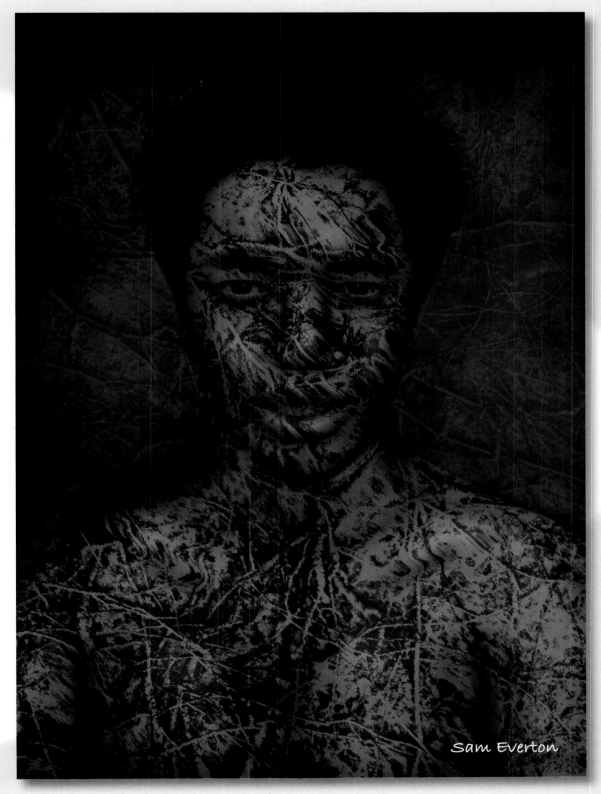

Sam Everton

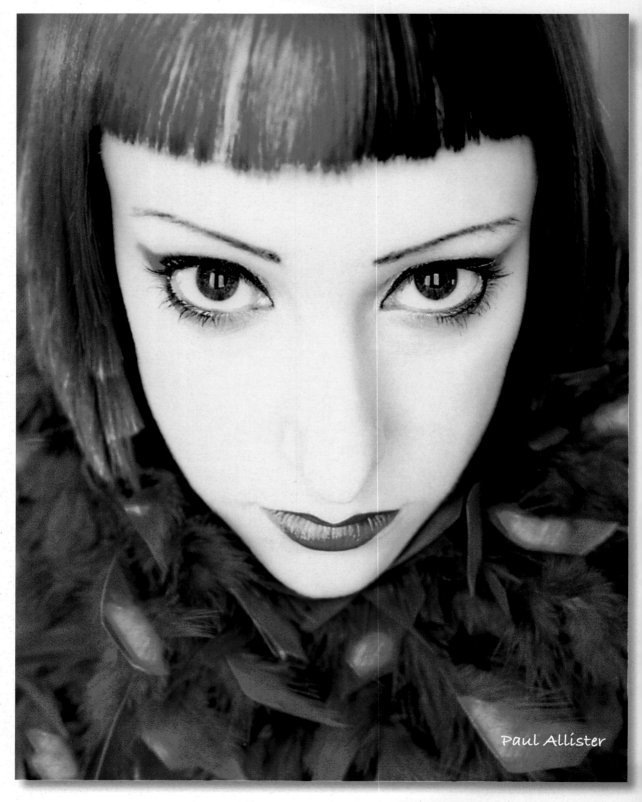

Paul Allister

digital negatives

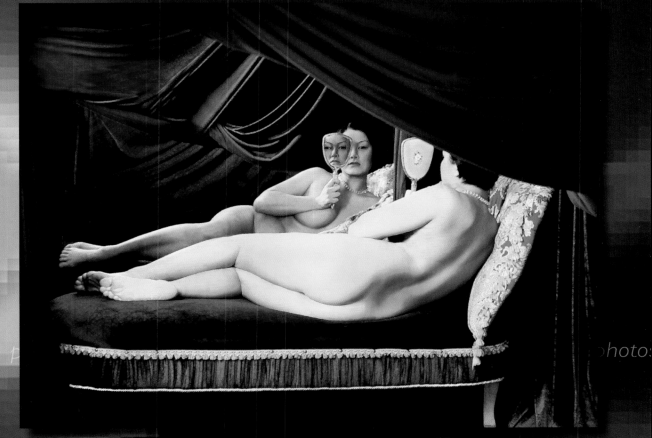

Sam Everton

essential skills

~ Capture high quality digital images as camera RAW files.

~ Process a camera RAW file to optimize color, tonality and sharpness.

~ Use camera RAW settings to batch process images for print and web viewing.

~ Convert RAW files to digital negatives for archival storage.

Introduction

One of the big topics of conversation since the release of Photoshop CS has been the subject of 'RAW' files and 'Digital Negatives'. This chapter guides you through the advantages of choosing the RAW format and the steps you need to take to process a RAW file from your camera in order to optimize it for final editing in Photoshop CS2.

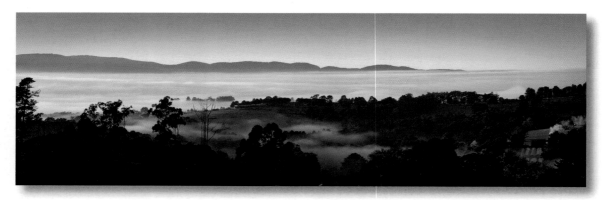

All digital cameras capture in RAW but only Digital SLRs and the medium- to high-end 'Prosumer' cameras offer the user the option of saving the images in this RAW format. Selecting the RAW format in the camera instead of JPEG or TIFF stops the camera from processing the color data collected from the sensor. Digital cameras typically process the data collected by the sensor by applying the white balance, sharpening and contrast settings set by the user in the camera's menus. The camera then compresses the bit depth of the color data from 12 to 8 bits per channel before saving the file as a JPEG or TIFF file. Selecting the RAW format prevents this image processing taking place. The RAW data is what the sensor 'saw' before the camera processes the image, and many photographers have started to refer to this file as the 'digital negative'.

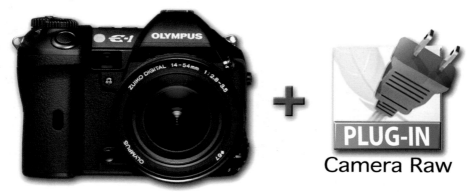

The sceptical amongst us would now start to juggle with the concept of paying for a 'state-of-the-art' camera to collect and process the data from the image sensor, only to stop the high-tech image processor from completing its 'raison d'être'. If you have to process the data some time to create a digital image why not do it in the camera? The idea of delaying certain decisions until they can be handled in the image-editing software is appealing to many photographers, but the real reason for choosing to shoot in camera RAW is QUALITY.

Processing RAW data

The unprocessed RAW data can be converted into a usable image file format by the latest image-editing software from Adobe. Variables such as bit depth, white balance, brightness, contrast, saturation and sharpness can all be assigned as part of the conversion process. Performing these image-editing tasks on the full high-bit RAW data (rather than making these changes after the file has been processed by the camera) enables the user to achieve a higher quality end-result. Double-clicking a RAW file, or selecting 'Open in Camera Raw' in Bridge, opens the camera RAW dialog box, where the user can prepare and optimize the file for final processing in the normal image-editing interface. If the user selects the 16 Bits/Channel option, the 12 bits per channel data from the image sensor is rounded up – each channel now capable of supporting 32,769 levels instead of the 256 we are used to working with in 8 bits per channel. Choosing the 16 Bits/Channel option enables even more manipulation in the main editing space without the risk of degrading the image quality. When the file is opened into the image-editing work space of your Adobe software the RAW file closes and remains in its RAW state, i.e. unaffected by the processing procedure.

RAW processing projects – images on supporting CD

Although the camera RAW dialog box appears a little daunting at first sight, it is reasonably intuitive and easy to master, and then RAW image processing is a quick and relatively painless procedure. The dialog box has been cleverly organized by Adobe so the user starts with the top slider and works their way down to the bottom control slider. If the image you are processing is one of a group of images shot in the same location, and with the same lighting, the settings used can be applied to the rest of the images as an automated procedure.

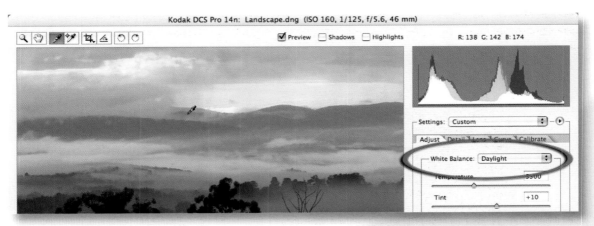

White balance – Step 1

The first task is to set the white balance by choosing one of the presets from the drop-down menu. If a white balance was performed in the camera the 'As Shot' option can be selected. If none of the presets adjust the color to your satisfaction you can manually adjust the 'Temperature' and 'Tint' sliders to remove any color cast present in the image. The 'Temperature' slider controls the blue/yellow color balance whilst the 'Tint' slider controls the green/magenta balance. Moving both the sliders in the same direction controls the red/cyan balance.

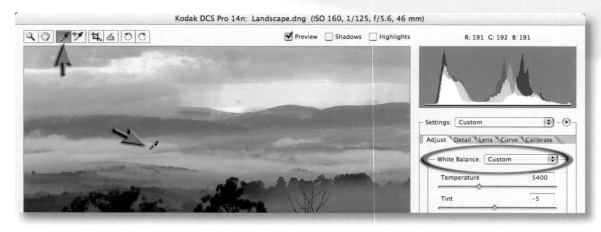

Alternatively you can click on the 'White Balance' eyedropper in the small tools palette (top left-hand corner of the dialog box) and then click on any neutral tone you can find in the image.

Note > Although it is a 'White Balance' you actually need to click on a tone that is not too bright. Clicking on a light or mid gray is preferable. A photographer looking to save a little time later may introduce a 'gray card' in the first frame of a shoot to simplify this task.

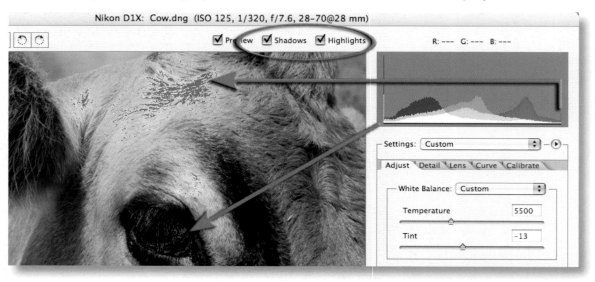

Tonal adjustments — *Step 2*

Set the tonal range of the image using the 'Exposure', 'Shadows' and 'Brightness' sliders. These sliders behave like the input sliders in the 'Levels' dialog box and will set the black and white points within the image. The 'Brightness' slider adjusts the midtone values in a similar way to the 'Gamma' slider when using 'Levels' dialog. When tall peaks appear at either end of the histogram you will lose shadow, highlight or color detail when you export the file to the main editing software. Careful adjustment of these sliders will allow you to get the best out of the dynamic range of your imaging sensor, thereby creating a tonally rich image with full detail.

Clipping information

Hold down the 'Alt/Option' key when adjusting either the 'Exposure' or 'Shadows' slider to view the point at which highlight or shadow clipping begins to occur (the point at which pixels lose detail in one or more channels). You can check the 'Shadows' and 'Highlights' boxes above the main image window instead of holding down the Alt or Option key.

Note > If you hold down the 'Alt' or 'Option' key to view the clipping, the color that appears in the image window indicates the channel or channels where clipping is occurring (this only applies to the Alt/Option key technique). Color Saturation as well as overly dark shadows and overly bright highlights will also influence the amount of clipping that occurs. Clipping in a single channel (indicated by the Red, Green or Blue warning colors) will not always lead to a loss of detail in the final image. When the secondary colors appear, however (Cyan, Magenta and Yellow), you need to take note, as loss of information in two channels starts to get a little more serious. Loss of information in all three channels (indicated by black when adjusting the shadows and white when adjusting the exposure) should be avoided at all costs.

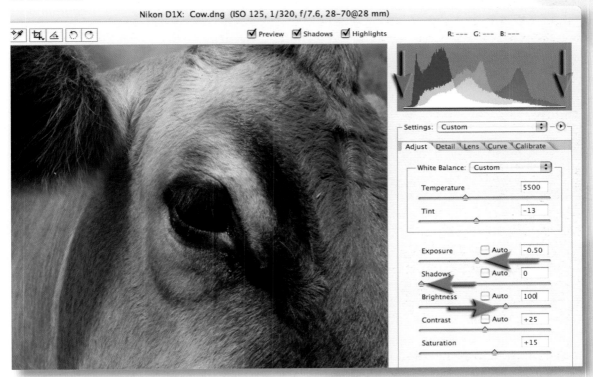

Example > By moving the Exposure and Shadows sliders to the left, information is restored to the blue and red channels. The image is then made brighter using the Brightness slider.

Note > Large adjustments to the 'Brightness', 'Contrast' or 'Saturation' sliders may necessitate further tweaking of the 'Exposure' and 'Shadows'.

Adjusting tonality in RAW using the Tone Curve

It is possible to fine-tune the tonality in camera RAW using the 'Curve' editor. This works in a similar way to the Curves adjustment feature in the main editing space of Photoshop. The user is able to choose one of the presets from the Tone Curve menu or choose 'Linear' from this menu and then place their own adjustment points on the curve. To place an adjustment point on the curve simply click on the line and then drag the adjustment point to a new position.

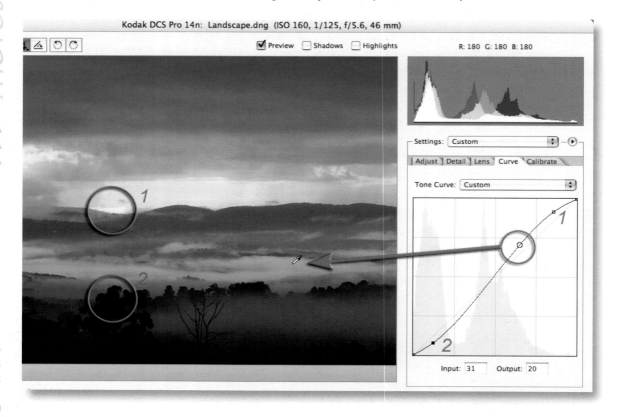

Selecting adjustment points from the image

It is possible to create an adjustment point by sampling a tone from the preview image. To select an adjustment point in this manner move the mouse cursor into the preview window. Hold down the Ctrl key (PC) or Command key (Mac) to access the sample tool. Note the small ring that appears on the tone curve in the relative position to the tone being sampled. Click the mouse whilst sampling a highlight tone, a midtone and a shadow tone to add adjustment points. Click on an adjustment point on the tone curve to make it the active adjustment point. Either drag the adjustment point to make the selected tonal range darker or lighter or enter a new value in the ouput field just below the tone curve. See 'Advanced Retouching' for more information on adjustment curves.

Note > The keyboard shortcut for cycling through the adjustment points (to make a different adjustment point active) is to hold down the Ctrl key and then press the Tab key (PC and Mac). Remove adjustment points by selecting an adjustment point and then pressing the Backspace key (PC) or Delete key (Mac).

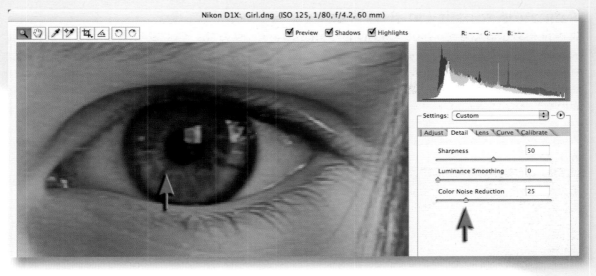

Noise reduction and sharpening – *Step 3*

If you intend to carry on enhancing or manipulating the image in the main editing space of Photoshop it is recommended that you only perform either a gentle amount of sharpening in the RAW dialog box (less than 25) or no sharpening at all (set the slider to 0). The Luminance Smoothing and Color Noise Reduction sliders (designed to tackle the camera noise that occurs when the image sensor's ISO is high) should only be raised from 0 if you notice image artifacts such as noise appearing in the image window.

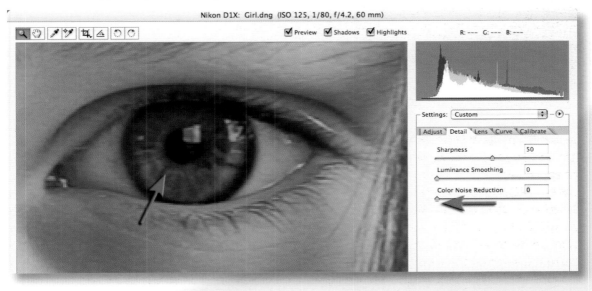

WARNING > The current default setting of 25 for the 'Color Noise Reduction' slider can remove important color detail that may go unnoticed if the photographer is not careful to pay attention to the effects of these sliders. Zoom in to take a closer look, and unless you can see either little white speckles or color artifacts set these sliders to 0.

Choosing a bit depth – *Step 4*

Select the 'Depth' in the lower left-hand corner of the dialog box and then click 'OK'. If the user selects the 16 Bits/Channel option, the 12 bits per channel data from the image sensor is rounded up – each channel is now capable of supporting 32,769 levels. In order to produce the best quality digital image, it is essential to preserve as much information about the tonality and color of the subject as possible. If the digital image is edited further in 8 bits per channel the final quality will be compromised. If the digital image has been corrected sufficiently for the requirements of the output device in the RAW dialog box the file can be edited in 8-bit mode with no apparent loss in quality. Sixteen-bit editing, however, is invaluable if maximum quality is required from an original image file that requires further or localized editing of tonality and color after leaving the camera RAW dialog box.

The problem with 8-bit editing

As an image file is edited extensively in 8 bits per channel mode (24-bit RGB) the histogram starts to 'break up', or become weaker. 'Spikes' or 'comb lines' may become evident in the resulting histogram after the file has been flattened.

Note > The least destructive 8-bit editing techniques make use of adjustment layers so that pixel values are altered only once, when the layers are flattened prior to printing.

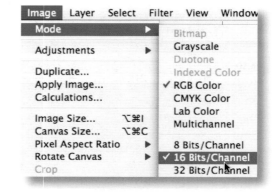

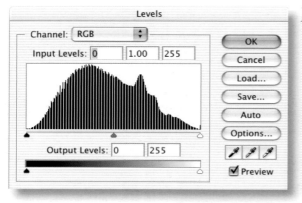
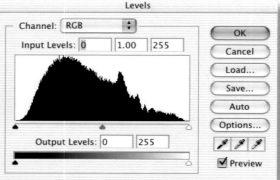

Final histograms after editing the same image in 8 and 16 bits per channel mode

The problem with editing extensively in 8-bit mode is that there are only 256 levels or tones per channel to describe the full color range of the image. This is usually sufficient if the histogram looks healthy (few gaps) when we begin the editing process and the amount of editing required is limited. If many gaps start to appear in the histogram as a result of extensive adjustment of pixel values this can result in 'banding'. The smooth change between dark and light, or one color and another, may no longer be possible with the data supplied from a weak histogram. The result is a transition between color or tone that is visible as a series of steps in the final image.

Crop and color space – *Step 5*

Select the cropping tool and crop to the required size before opening the file in Photoshop. The crop size is listed below the image as pixel dimensions and megapixels. The resolution can also be set prior to opening the image in Photoshop. You should also choose the profile that suits your current workflow, e.g. sRGB for Web and Adobe RGB (1998) for print.

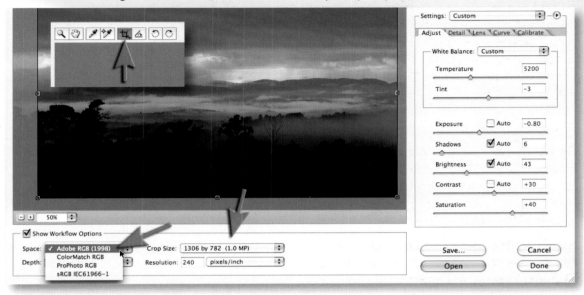

A new addition to the working space profiles is ProPhoto. This is a wide gamut color space and is the default editing space used by the camera RAW plug-in.

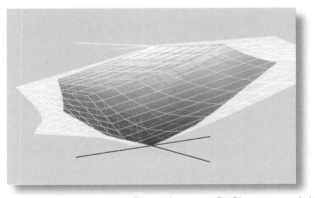
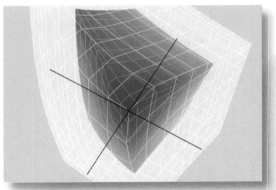

The wide gamut ProPhoto space (white) compared to the Adobe RGB 1998 space (color)

Note > The ProPhoto color space should only be selected if you have access to a print output device with a broad color gamut. The profile is suitable for users who are intending to stay in 16 Bits/Channel for the entire editing process and who have access to a print output device with a broader color gamut than traditional CMYK devices are capable of offering.

Additional information

Distribution of data

Most digital imaging sensors capture images using 12 bits of memory dedicated to each of the three color channels, resulting in 4096 tones between black and white. Most of the imaging sensors in digital cameras record a subject brightness range of approximately five to eight stops (five to eight f-stops between the brightest highlights with detail and the deepest shadow tones with detail).

Tonal distribution in 12-bit capture					
Darkest Shadows	- 4 stops	- 3 stops	- 2 stops	-1 stop	Brightest Highlights
128 Levels	256	512	1024	2048	4096 Levels

Distribution of levels

One would think that with all of this extra data the problem of banding or image posterization due to insufficient levels of data (a common problem with 8-bit image editing) would be consigned to history. Although this is the case with midtones and highlights, shadows can still be subject to this problem. The reason for this is that the distribution of levels assigned to recording the range of tones in the image is far from equitable. The brightest tones of the image (the highlights) use the lion's share of the 4096 levels available whilst the shadows are comparatively starved of information.

An example of posterization or banding

Shadow management

CCD and CMOS chips are, however, linear devices. This linear process means that when the amount of light is halved, the electrical stimulation to each photoreceptor on the sensor is also halved. Each f-stop reduction in light intensity halves the amount of light that falls onto the receptors compared to the previous f-stop. Fewer levels are allocated by this linear process to recording the darker tones. Shadows are 'level starved' in comparison to the highlights that have a wealth of information dedicated to the brighter end of the tonal spectrum. So rather than an equal amount of tonal values distributed evenly across the dynamic range, we actually have the effect as shown above. The deepest shadows rendered within the scene often have fewer than 128 allocated levels, and when these tones are manipulated in post-production Photoshop editing there is still the possibility of banding or posterization.

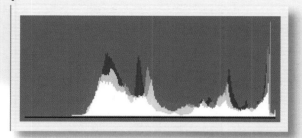 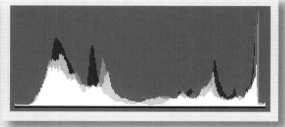

Expose right and adjust left

'Expose right' and multiple exposures

This inequitable distribution of levels has given rise to the idea of 'exposing right'. This work practice encourages the user seeking maximum quality to increase the exposure of the shadows (without clipping the highlights) so that more levels are afforded to the shadow tones. This approach to make the shadows 'information rich' involves increasing the amount of fill light or lighting with less contrast in a studio environment. If the camera RAW file is then opened in the camera RAW dialog box the shadow values can then be reassigned their darker values to expand the contrast before opening it as a 16 Bit/Channel file. When the resulting shadow tones are edited and printed, the risk of visible banding in the shadow tones is greatly reduced.

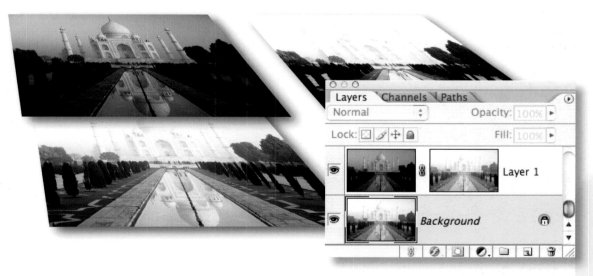

Separate exposures can be combined during the image-editing process

This approach is not possible when working with a subject with a fixed subject brightness range, e.g. a landscape, but in these instances there is often the option of bracketing the exposure and merging the highlights of one digital file with the shadows of a second. Choose 'Merge to HDR' (high dynamic range) from the File > Automate menu or use the manual approach outlined in 'Advanced Retouching'. The example above shows the use of a layer mask used to hide the darker shadows in order to access the bit-rich shadows of the underlying layer and regain the full tonal range of the scene.

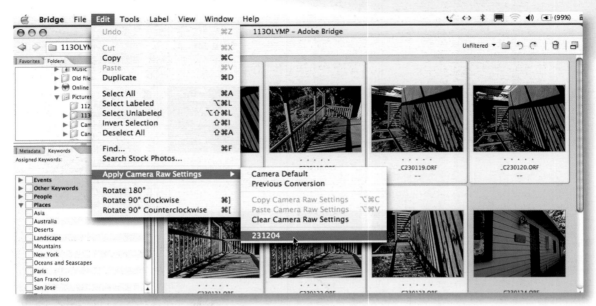

Batch processing

The settings you have used in the camera RAW dialog box can then be used for all the images captured in the same lighting using the automate option in the 'File Browser'. Hold down the Control key (Command key on a Mac) and click on each image you wish to adjust using these settings and then select 'Apply Camera Raw Settings' from the 'Automate' menu.

Archiving digital negatives

Working with camera RAW files is going to create some extra strain on the storage capacity found on a typical computer's hard drive. What to do with all of the extra gigabytes of RAW data is a subject that people are divided about. You can burn them to CD or DVD disks – but are the disks truly archival? You can back them up to a remote FireWire drive – but what if the hard drive fails? Some believe that digital tape offers the best track record for longevity and security. Why archive at all you may ask? Who can really tell what the image-editing software of the future will be capable of – who can say what information is locked up in the RAW data that future editions of the RAW editors will be able to access. Adobe has now created a universal RAW file format called DNG (Digital

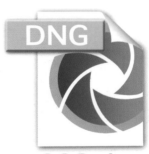

Negative) in an attempt to ensure that all camera RAW files (whichever camera they originate from) will be accessible in the future. The Digital Negative format also includes lossless compression to reduce the size of the RAW files. The Adobe DNG converter is available from the Adobe website or from the supporting CD. The converter will not only ensure that your files are archived in a format that will be understood in the future. Expect to see future models of many digital cameras using this DNG format as standard. One thing *is* for sure – RAW files are a valuable source of the rich visual data that many of us value – and so the format will be around for many years to come.

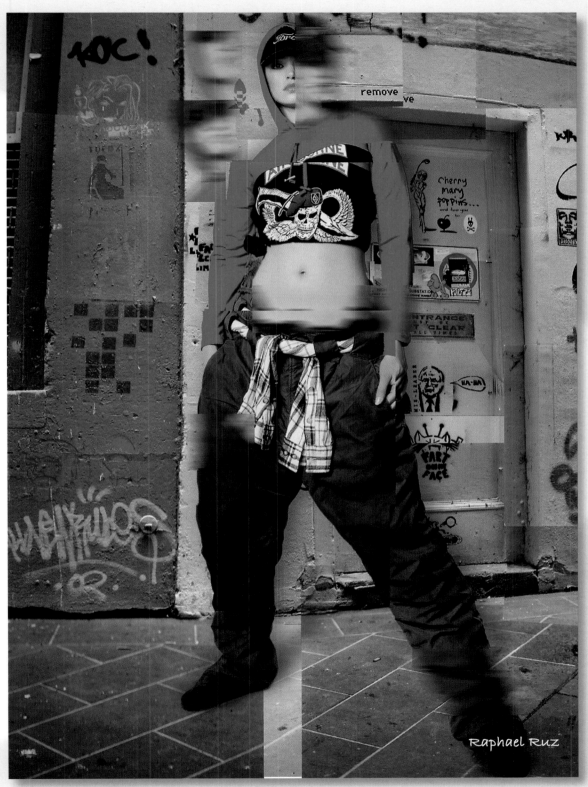

Raphael Ruz

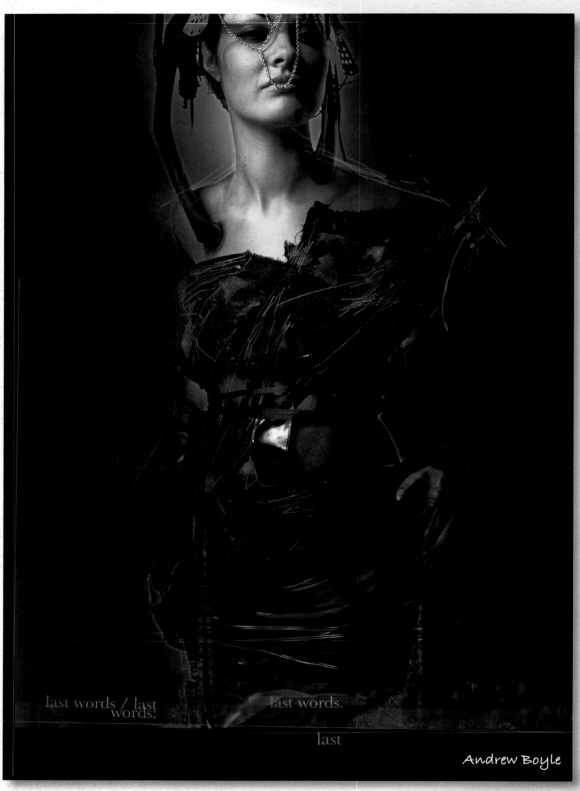

last words / last words:

last words.

last

Andrew Boyle

digital printing

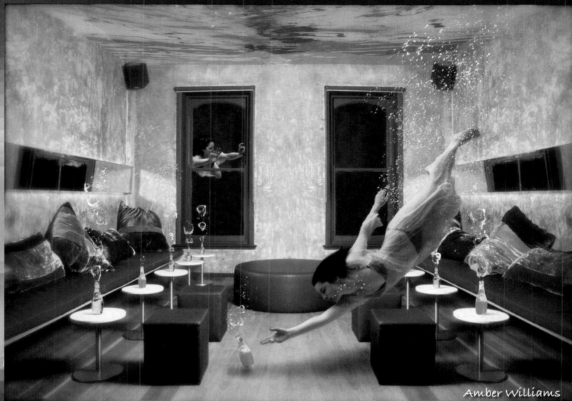

Amber Williams

essential skills

~ Control the color accuracy between monitor preview and print.

~ Understand the procedures involved with producing a digital print.

~ Print a color-managed digital image using a desktop inkjet printer.

~ Compensate for visual differences between the monitor preview and print.

Introduction

Creating high quality prints using desktop inkjet printers can be a mystifying, infuriating and costly experience. You can really only hope to get close to the quality of traditional photographic prints if you follow a color-managed workflow and print on digital 'Photo Paper' using a '6-ink' (minimum) rather than a '4-ink' inkjet printer. Using high quality photo papers ensures that the images you print will appear sharp and with richly saturated colors. Matching the colors of the print to those that appear on your monitor is, however, a mystifying experience for many. A little understanding of the issues involved will help you find a personal path to perfect prints.

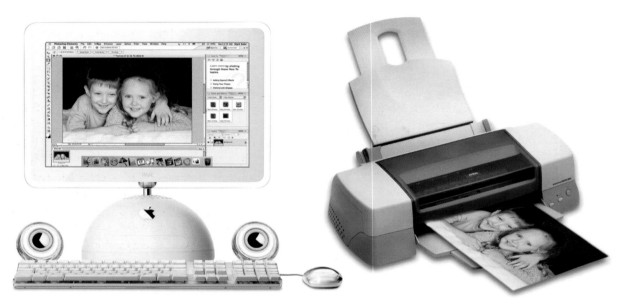

If you choose to print using a 4-ink inkjet printer, the lower quality is most noticeable in the highlights of the image. The addition of light cyan and light magenta inks to the normal 3-ink color cartridge ensures smooth photographic quality highlights (the ink dots are hard to see without a magnifying glass). Epson 6-ink printers retail under the 'Epson Stylus Photo' name, whilst Canon's 6-ink models are often referred to as 'bubble-jet' printers.

Color conversions

Color on a computer's monitor is created by mixing red, green and blue light (RGB) whilst the reflected light from cyan, magenta, yellow and black inks (CMYK) creates color on the printed page. A perfect match is therefore very difficult to achieve, as the range or 'gamut' of colors capable of being reproduced by each of the two display mediums is similar, but different. The colors present in a digital image file have to be translated or converted to fit the gamut or 'color space' of each output device or printer. Once you have achieved an accurate translation, however (a good looking print that resembles what you have pictured on your monitor), just changing the brand of printing paper can upset the apple cart if the translation process is not adjusted accordingly.

PHOTOSHOP CS2 >>>

essential skills >>>

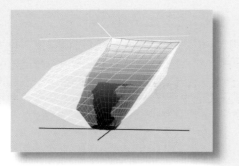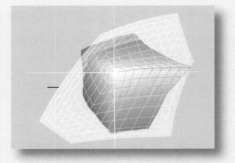

The range or 'gamut' of colors that each output device is capable of displaying can vary enormously. In the illustrations a CMYK printing space (shown in color) is contained by the much larger RGB monitor space (shown in white)

Profiles

The accuracy of color translation is made possible by the use of 'ICC profiles' such as 'sRGB' and 'Adobe RGB'. Profiles are tagged onto image files by digital cameras, scanners and image-editing programs as a way of recording not only the color numbers (the numerical values taken from the levels in each of the channels) but how the colors actually appear in terms of their relative hue, saturation and brightness. In a 'color-managed' workflow it is a 'color management engine' (such as Adobe's 'ACE' built into Photoshop) that will massage the numbers of the colors captured so that the actual appearance of the color is the same on your calibrated and profiled monitor. Your monitor has a distinctly different set of color characteristics to the capture device, and so the color management engine uses your monitor's profile to perform the task of color matching. Color accuracy is only possible, however, if you have calibrated and profiled your monitor.

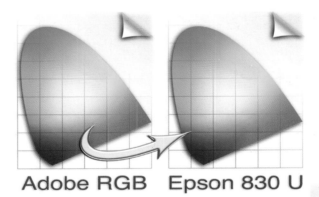

Adobe RGB   Epson 830 U

Colour profiles help to ensure that what you see is what you get

The completion of this color management process is where the colors we see on our monitor are then translated accurately into the colors that we can see reproduced by our chosen output device. With this final step there are however choices, as the computer's operating system, the Adobe software and the printer are all capable of managing this final step – and these choices typically lead to the confusion that often surrounds the printing procedure. Get the mix of choices wrong and the final result can look like the proverbial dog's dinner. Find the right route through the maze of options and color consistency is yours.

Monitor calibration and working color space

To ensure the level of visual consistency outlined earlier we must first check that our monitor's contrast, brightness and color are fairly standard, i.e. not on a 60s trip to the world of weird. Each monitor requires its own custom profile (not the canned one considerately installed by the factory). Standardizing the monitor's display is called 'monitor calibration'. When the monitor is calibrated we can save a profile for the monitor. In this way the precise colors captured by the camera can be interpreted by Photoshop and tweaked using the monitor profile so that the image can be displayed accurately on your unique screen (a case of 'what-you-see-is-really-what-you-get'). Reset the '**Target White Point**' (sometimes referred to as '**Adjusted White Point**') of the monitor to D65 or 6500, which is equivalent to daylight (the same light you will use to view your prints), using 'Adobe Gamma' (from the 'Control Panel/s' in Windows) or 'Display Calibrator' (from the 'Utilities' folder in Mac OSX).

Note > See '**The Digital Darkroom**' **for extended information on this important subject.**

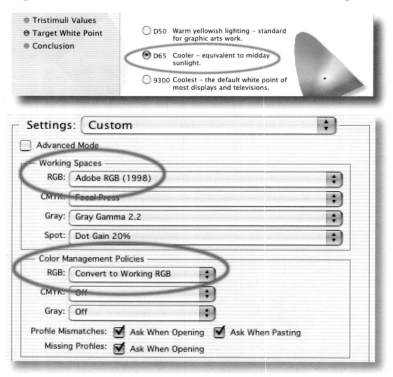

Select an appropriate color setting for the software

To create an on-screen preview of the image that will be eventually output by your printer, it is important to select a 'working space' for Photoshop that is sympathetic to the range of colors that can be achieved by your inkjet printer using good quality 'photo paper'. The most suitable working space currently available is called 'Adobe RGB (1998)'. To implement this working space choose 'Color Settings' in Photoshop and set the work space to 'Adobe RGB (1998)' from the RGB pull-down menu. In the 'Color Management Policies' section, select 'Convert to Working RGB' from the 'RGB' pull-down menu and check the 'Ask When Opening' boxes.

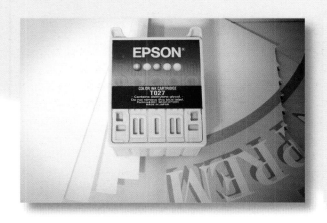

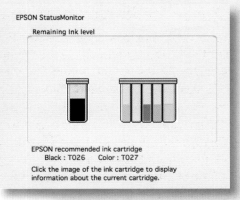

Pre-flight check list

In an attempt to make the first time not too memorable, for all the wrong reasons, check that your ink cartridges are not about to run out of ink and that you have a plentiful supply of good quality paper (same surface and same make). It is also worth starting to print when there are several hours of daylight left, as window light (without direct sun) is the best light to judge the color accuracy of the prints. If you are restricted to printing in the evening it may be worthwhile checking out 'daylight' globes that offer a more 'neutral' light source than tungsten globes or fluorescent tubes. It is also important to position the computer's monitor so that it is not reflecting any light source in the room (including the direct illumination from windows and skylights). If your monitor is reflecting a brightly colored wall or window then consider shifting your furniture.

Note > Refilling your ink cartridges and using cheap paper is not recommended for absolute quality and consistency.

Keeping a record

The settings of the translation process (all the buttons and options that will be outlined next), the choice of paper, the choice of ink and the lighting conditions used to view the print will all have enormous implications for the color that you see on the printed page. The objective when you have achieved a color match is to maintain consistency over the process and materials so that it can be repeated with each successive print. It is therefore important to keep a track of the settings and materials used.

Project	Portrait	Sept 22/04
Image File	TIFF	220 ppi
Paper	Epson	Matte HW
Inks	Epson	AUG 04
Colour Management	Adobe ☐	Printer ☑
Profiles	N/A	Same As Source
Printer Settings	Matte HW	Best Photo
Colour Controls	Photo-realistic	+4 Saturation

There is only one thing more infuriating than not being able to achieve accuracy, and that is achieving it once and not being sure of how you did it. Some words of advice – WRITE IT DOWN!

Note > A template for the print record sheet is available on the supporting CD.

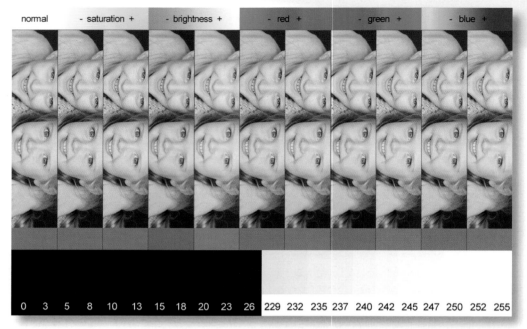

Use the test file to help you target the perfect color balance quickly and efficiently

Preparing a test print

Start the printing process by selecting 'Print with Preview' from the 'File' menu. As discussed previously there are several methods of printing. There is no one road. In order to discover a workflow that suits your own setup it is recommended that you use a test file that has a broad range of colors of varying saturations. Use a test file that incorporates a range of saturated colors, neutral grays and skin tones. If this file prints perfectly you can be confident that subsequent prints using the same media and settings will follow true to form. The test print file in the illustration above is available on the supporting CD. It will help you target your optimum shadow and highlight points and stop you from chasing what initially appears to be a color cast and in the end turns out to be a blocked ink jet.

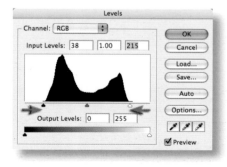
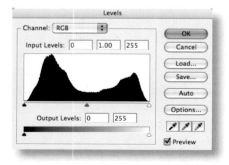

Note > There is an old saying, 'quality in – quality out'. Each image you print must be checked that it has been optimized for printing. The file's histogram should be optimized and any obvious color cast removed. See 'Capture and Enhance'.

Printer color management

The first path uses the Photoshop default settings in the 'Print' dialog box. This path allows the printer to manage the colors. Although Adobe has the industry standard color management engine it is only as effective as the profiles it is handed for the conversion job. The printer profiles shipped with the printer are again canned and may, or may not, bear any resemblance to the color characteristics of the actual printer you are using.

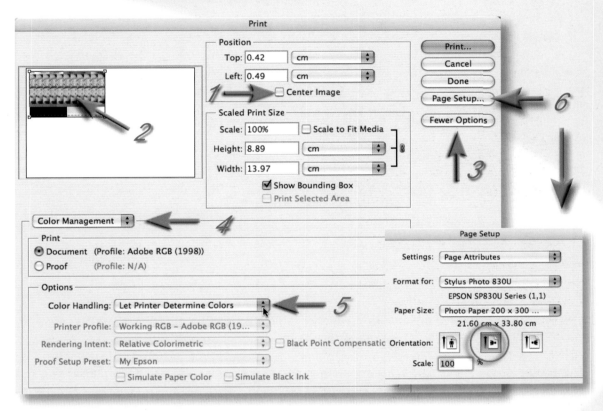

1. Deselect the 'Center Image' check box
2. Drag the image preview to a corner of the page to save printing paper
3. Click on the 'More/Fewer Options' box to expand the dialog box
4. Choose 'Color Management' from the options menu
5. Select the 'Let Printer Determine Colors' option in the Color Management section
6. Click on 'Page Setup' to select the paper size and orientation (horizontal or vertical).

Note > The default settings in the Adobe Print dialog box use a setting called 'Let Printer Determine Colors', which you can only see if you click on the 'More Options' button. This setting instructs the Adobe software to hand over the image to the printer without making any changes to the color numbers. When you click on the Print button in the Print dialog box you will be transported to the printer driver dialog box.

Printer driver

Look for the following options in your printer dialog box:

    1. Select the paper you are using from the 'Media Type' menu

    2. Select the 'Advanced' option (usually found in the 'Custom' menu on a PC)

    3. Select the maximum dpi from the 'Print Quality' menu or any option that indicates the 'Best Photo' quality option has been selected

    4. Select 'Color Controls' from the 'Color Management' menu (you should see the Magenta, Cyan and Yellow color sliders)

    5. Select 'Print'.

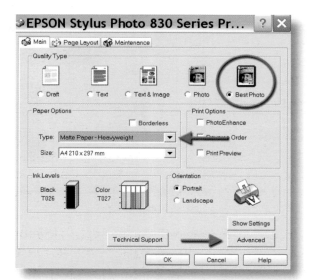 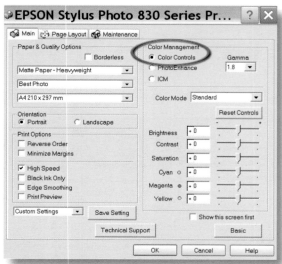

The options for 'Printer Color Management' in an Epson printer driver for a PC

The printer is now handling the color management. Once the test file has been printed you can make an assessment of what changes need to be made before printing a modified or 'tweaked' version. Be sure to let the test print dry for at least 10 to 15 minutes before making an asseesment of the color and tonal values as these may change quite dramatically. Subtle changes can continue to occur for several hours during the drying process. See 'Analyzing the test print' when assessing whether any changes need to be made to the first test print. To speed up and simplify the procedure for subsequent prints a 'custom setting' or 'preset' can be resaved in the printer driver once you have achieved accuracy by fine-tuning the color sliders. Name the custom setting incorporating the paper surface, e.g. Matte HW-PCM (printer color management).

Note > The precise wording of the options in the printer drivers may vary between different manufacturers and models of printer.

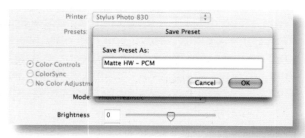

Adobe color management

The secret to success when using Adobe's color management is to select 'No Color Adjustment' from the 'Color Management' controls in the printer driver software (if using a Canon printer go to 'Color > Color Control > None').

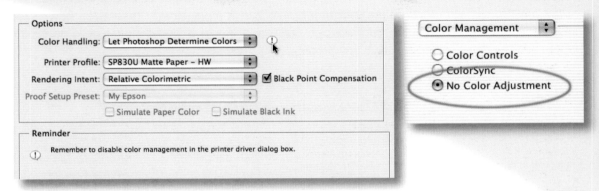

Select 'No Color Adjustment' in the printer driver when using Adobe to color-manage your printing

From the Color Management section of the print dialog box choose the 'Let Photoshop Determine Colors' option and choose the printer profile. Choose 'Relative Colorimetric' or 'Perceptual' as the rendering intent and check the 'Black Point Compensation' check box. When you select print and the printer driver opens it is now essential to cancel the printer's color management.

Note > You may have to hunt (sometimes in vain) for the 'No Color Adjustment' option in your own printer driver as this is not the most common printing method used by non-professionals. The bargain basement inkjet printers are designed to take the reins of the color management procedure as not all image-editing software is capable of handling the color management, Adobe being the exception to the rule.

Warning > The worst colors imaginable are produced by instructing Adobe to manage the color translation, and then NOT disabling the color management in the printer driver software. If in doubt follow the printer color management approach.

PHOTOSHOP COLOR MANAGEMENT WORKFLOW

Select the 'Media Type' and quality settings as in the previous path and then click 'Print'. The Adobe color management workflow is as follows:

1. Check the 'Show More Options' box in the corner of the print dialog box.
2. Select the profile for the printer and media type (if available) from the 'Print Space' menu.
3. The 'Source Space' indicates the current profile of the image you are about to print.
4. Choose 'Perceptual' or 'Relative Colorimetric' as the 'Intent'.
5. Choose the media type and highest dpi or 'Best Photo' print quality.
6. In the Color Management section choose 'No Color Management'.
7. Select 'Print'.

Soft proofing

Although the image that appears on your monitor has been standardized (after the calibration process and the implementation of the Adobe RGB working space), the printed image from this standardized view would appear different if printed through a variety of different inkjet printers onto different paper surfaces or 'media types'. In Photoshop it is possible to further alter the visual appearance of the image on your monitor so that it more closely resembles how it will actually appear when printed by your specific make and model of inkjet printer on a particular paper surface. This process is called 'soft proofing'.

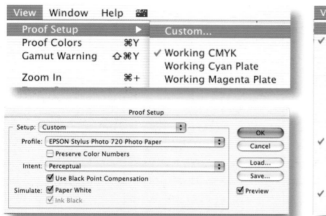
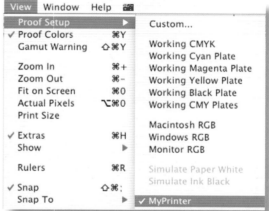

To set up the soft proof view go to View > Proof Setup > Custom. From the Profile menu select the profile of your printer and paper or 'media type'. Choose 'Perceptual' from the 'Intent' menu and check the 'Use Black Point Compensation' and 'Paper White' boxes. Save these settings so they can be accessed quickly the next time you need to soft proof to the same printer and media type.

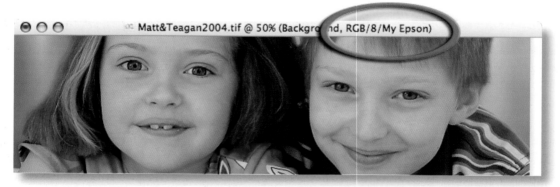

When you view your image with the soft proof preview the color and tonality will be modified to more closely resemble the output characteristics of your printer and choice of media.

The image should now be edited with the soft proof preview on, to achieve the desired tonality and color that you would like to see in print. It is recommended that you edit in 'Full Screen Mode' to remove distracting colors on your desktop and use adjustment layers to modify and fine-tune the image on screen. Avoid using 'Brightness and Contrast' that will result in a loss of highlight or shadow detail (use a 'Curves' adjustment instead).

Analyzing the test print

View the print using soft window light (not direct sunlight) when the print is dry, and try to ascertain any differences between the print and the screen image in terms of hue (color), saturation and brightness. Any differences may be attributed to inaccuracies in your initial monitor calibration and/or the profile that was shipped with your printer (Photoshop color management only).

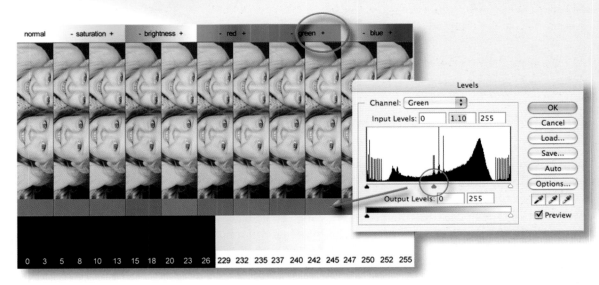

1. Check that the color swatches at the top of the image are saturated and printing without tracking marks or banding (there should be a gradual transition of color). If there is a problem with missing colors, tracking lines or saturation clean the printer heads using the printer guidelines.

2. View the skin tones to assess the appropriate level of saturation. The lower and higher saturation swatches have a −10 and +10 adjustment applied using Photoshop's Hue/Saturation adjustment.

3. View the gray tones directly beneath the images of the children to determine if there is a color cast present in the image. The five tones on the extreme left are desaturated in the image file. If these print as gray then no color correction is required. If, however, one of the gray tones to the right (which have color adjustments applied) appears to be gray then a color cast is present.

4. Find the tone that appears to be desaturated (the color cast corresponds with the color swatches at the top of the test file). Apply this color correction to the next print. For example, if the plus green strip appears to print with no color cast then a 1.1 gamma adjustment in the green channel is required (when using the Photoshop color management) for the next test print. A minus value will need to be entered in the Magenta slider in the 'Color Controls' when using 'Printer Color Management'.

Note > Each of the color strips in the test image has the same gamma adjustment applied using the RGB channels. The correction necessary can be made using the Levels dialog box by sliding the gamma slider to 0.9 or 1.1 in the corresponding color channel when using Photoshop color management.

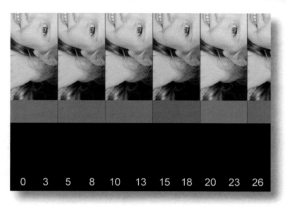
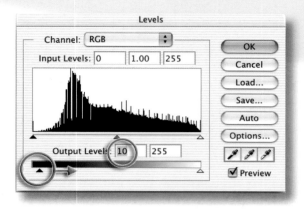

Maximizing shadow and highlight detail

Examine the base of the test strip to establish the optimum highlight and shadow levels that can be printed with the medium you have chosen to use. If the shadow tones between level 10 and level 20 are printing as black then you should establish a Levels adjustment layer to resolve the problem in your Adobe software. The bottom left-hand slider should be moved to the right to reduce the level of black ink being printed. This should allow dark shadow detail to be visible in the second print. A less common problem is highlight values around 245 not registering on the media. However, if this is a problem, the highlight slider can be moved to the left to encourage the printer to apply more ink.

Note > It is important to apply these output level adjustments to an adjustment layer only as these specific adjustments apply to only the output device you are currently testing.

PRINTING OVERVIEW

Materials
Start by using the printer manufacturer's recommended ink and paper.
Use premium grade 'Photo Paper' for maximum quality.

Monitor
Position your monitor so that it is clear of reflections.
Select a target white point or color temperature of 6500.
Set contrast, brightness and 'Gamma' using 'Adobe Gamma' or 'Monitor Calibrator'.

Adobe
Set the Color Settings of the Adobe software.
Select 'Same As Source' (Path One) or the profile of the 'Destination Space' (Path Two).

Printer
Use a 6-ink inkjet printer for maximum quality.
Select the 'Media Type' in the printer software dialog box.
Select highest dpi or 'Best Photo' quality setting.

Proofing
Allow print to dry and use daylight to assess color accuracy of print.

Creating a 'ringaround'

It is advisable to limit the variables once color consistency has been achieved. When changing an ink cartridge it is recommended that you run a test from the same image used to initiate the color consistency and then modify any settings if required.

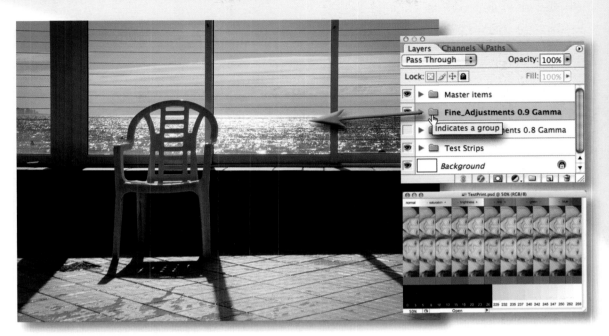

It is possible to use the adjustment layers used to create the 'ringaround' in the test print to monitor variations in color and saturation in additional images. This involves opening the test print PSD file on the supporting CD and dragging the layer group (the folder above the background layer in the Layers palette) into your image window. Use the Free Transform command from the Edit menu to resize the adjustment layers to fit your own image. If one of the adjustments hits the target switch off all of the other adjustment layers in the group and remove the layer mask of the correct adjustment layer (drag it to the trash can in the Layers palette or click the layer mask thumbnail whilst holding down the Shift key) and then proceed to print.

In conclusion

Although daunting at first, obtaining a color-managed workflow is reasonably quick and easy to use once the settings have been saved in the printer driver dialog box. It is probably worth mentioning that you should print out another test strip each time you change paper or inks just to ensure the print accuracy has not been upset by the change. It is also worth printing out a test strip if the printer has been idle for a number of weeks to ensure all the inks are printing as they should. This is not the entire color story but one of the two paths outlined in this tutorial should get you out of the maze that you may have found yourself in.

Printing using a professional laboratory

Professional photographic laboratory services are now expanding into the production of large and very large prints using the latest inkjet and piezo technology. Many are also capable of printing your digital files directly onto color photographic paper. In fact, outputting to color print paper via machines like the Durst Lambda and Fuji Frontier has quickly become the 'norm' for a lot of professional photographers. Adjusting of image files that print well on desktop inkjets so that they cater for the idiosyncrasies of these RA4 and large inkjet machines is an additional output skill that is really worth learning.

With improved quality, speed and competition in the area, the big players like Epson, Kodak, Durst, Fuji and Hewlett Packard are manufacturing units that are capable of producing images that are not only visually stunning, but also very, very big. Pictures up to 54 inches wide can be made

on some of the latest machines, with larger images possible by splicing two or more panels together. A photographer can now walk into a bureau with a CD containing a favorite image and walk out the same day with a spliced polyester poster printed with fade-resistant, all-weather inks the size of a billboard.

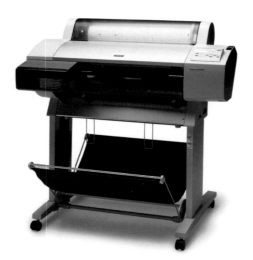

In addition to these dedicated bureau services, some professionals, whose day-to-day business revolves around the production of large prints, are actually investing in their own wide format piezojet or inkjet machines. The increased quality of pigment-based dye systems together with the choice of different media, or substrates as they are referred to in the business, provides them with more imaging and texture choices than are available via the RA4 route.

Before you start

Getting the setup right is even more critical with large format printing than when you are outputting to a desktop machine. A small mistake here can cause serious problems to both your 48 × 36 inch masterpiece as well as your wallet, so before you even turn on your computer, talk to a few professionals. Most output bureaus are happy to help prospective customers with advice and usually supply a series of guidelines that will help you set up your images to suit their printers. These instructions may be contained in a pack available with a calibration swatch over the counter, or might be downloadable from the company's web site.

Some of the directions will be general and might seem a little obvious, others can be very specific and might require you to change the CMYK settings of your image-editing program so that your final files will match the ink and media response of the printer. Some companies will check that your image meets their requirements before printing, others will dump the unopened file directly to the printer's RIP assuming that all is well. So make sure that you are aware of the way the bureau works before making your first print.

General Guidelines

The following guidelines have been compiled from the suggestions of several output bureaus. They constitute a good overview but cannot be seen as a substitute for talking to your own lab directly.

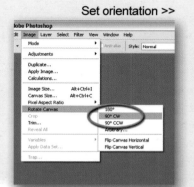

Set orientation >>

1. Ensure that the image is orientated correctly. Some printers are set up to work with a portrait or vertical image by default; trying to print a landscape picture on these devices will result in areas of white space above and below the picture and the edges being cropped.

2. Make sure the image is the same proportion as the paper stock. This is best achieved by making an image with the canvas the exact size required and then pasting your picture into this space.

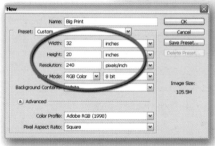

Set paper size >>

3. Don't use crop marks. Most printers will automatically mark where the print is to be cropped. Some bureaus will charge to remove your marks before printing.

4. Convert text to line or raster before submission. Some imaging and layout programs need the font files to be supplied together with the image at the time of printing. If the font is missing then the printer will automatically substitute a default typeface, which in most cases will not be a close match for the original. To avoid failing to supply a font needed, convert the type to line or raster before sending the image to the bureau.

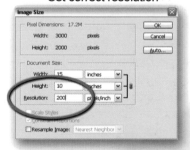

Set correct resolution >>

5. Use the resolution suggested by the lab. Most output devices work best with an optimal resolution; large format inkjet printers are no different. The lab technician will be able to give you details of the best resolution to supply your images in. Using a higher or lower setting than this will alter the size that your file prints so stick to what is recommended.

6. Keep file sizes under the rip maximum. The bigger the file the longer it takes to print. Most bureaus base their costings on a maximum file size. You will need to pay extra if your image is bigger than this value.

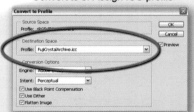

Convert to or Assign ICC profile >>

7. Use the color management system recommended by the lab. In setting up you should ensure that you use the same color settings as the bureau. This may mean that you need to manually input set values for CMYK or use an ICC profile downloaded from the company's web site.

Printing monochromes

To the eyes of experienced darkroom workers the difficulties of printing black and white photographs with a color printer are immediately apparent. Most photo quality inkjets use the five colored inks, as well as black, to produce monochromes. With dot sizes now being so small it is only under the closest scrutiny that the multi-colored matrix that lies beneath our black and white prints is revealed. Balancing the different colors so that the final appearance is neutral is a very tricky task. Too many dots of one color and a gray will appear blue, too few and it will contain a yellow hue.

With just this type of situation in mind several of the bigger third party ink manufacturers have produced dedicated monochrome cartridges and ink sets for all popular desktop and wide format inkjet printers. The system is simple – pure black and white can be achieved by removing all color from the print process. The manufacturers produce replacement cartridges containing three levels of gray instead of the usual cyan, yellow and magenta or five levels instead of cyan, light cyan, magenta, light magenta and yellow for five-color cartridges. All inks are derived from the same pigment base and so prints made with these cartridges contain no strange color casts.

Printing with dedicated monochrome ink sets is the closest thing to making finely crafted fiber-based prints that the digital world has to offer. Not only are your images cast free, but they also display an amazing range of grays. With pictures that have been carefully adjusted to spread image tones and retain shadow and highlight details, the Quad Black system produces unparalleled quality prints on a wide range of gloss, satin, matte and fine art stock.

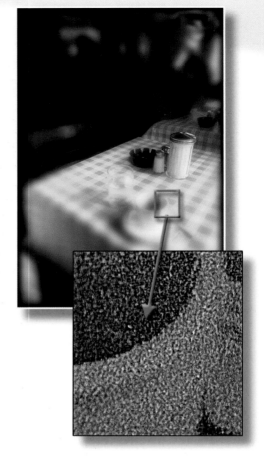

After the success of the initial Quad Black system, Lyson produced two more monochrome ink sets – Warm Tone, affectionately known as 'sepia', and Cool Tone, sometimes called 'selenium'. Though the nicknames are familiar don't be confused, there are no toning processes involved here. The whole procedure is still digital and the images

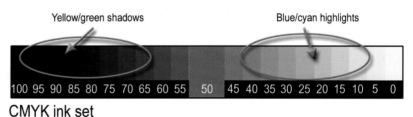

Yellow/green shadows · Blue/cyan highlights

100 95 90 85 80 75 70 65 60 55 | 50 | 45 40 35 30 25 20 15 10 5 0

CMYK ink set

100 95 90 85 80 75 70 65 60 55 | 50 | 45 40 35 30 25 20 15 10 5 0

Dedicated Quad Black Neutral ink set

are produced with ink on paper. Quad tone sets are available for a selected range of photo quality printers from Canon and Epson. This includes those models that have chip-based cartridges designed to restrict the user to installing the manufacturer's own inks.

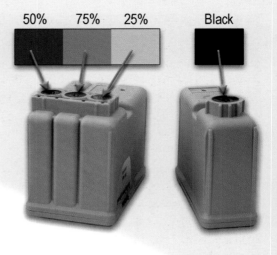

50%   75%   25%   Black

OK, what's the catch?

With such results, and options, you might be forgiven for thinking that all is now 'well with the world' and that 'peace amongst the nations' must be just around the corner, but be warned, it is not recommended that you continually swap between your old CMYK system and the monochrome options. Lyson has no qualms about suggesting that you dedicate a printer solely for Quad tone output. For most of us the purchase of one such machine is expensive enough, but two might just break the bank. You will also need to keep in mind that the hardware manufacturers don't support the use of non-genuine inks and, in some cases, will not uphold warranty claims made for machines using alternative inking systems.

Making your first Quad Black print

1. Download and decompress the Lyson ICC profile for your paper and ink set from www. lyson.com. Drag and drop the profiles into the 'Color' folder in your Mac or Windows system.

2. Restart Photoshop. Open a test image.

3. Adjust the picture to ensure a good spread of tones. Make sure that monochrome pictures are also stored in RGB mode.

4. With the image still open, select File > Page Setup. Select 'Properties'. Select 'Custom' and then 'Advanced'.

5. Select 'Photo Quality Gloss Film' as the Media Type, 'Photo-1440dpi' as the Print Quality, 'High Quality Half toning' and 'No Color Adjustment' from the Color Adjustment options. Click 'OK'.

6. Select File > Print with Preview. Ensure the 'Document' option is set to the 'Document' space. Select 'Let Photoshop Determine Colors', choose the Lyson profile as the 'Printer Profile' and then Choose 'Perceptual' as the rendering intent. Now click 'Print'.

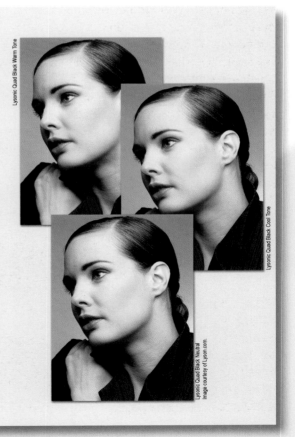

Lysonic Quad Black Warm Tone

Lysonic Quad Black Cool Tone

Lysonic Quad Black Neutral
Image courtesy of Lyson.com.

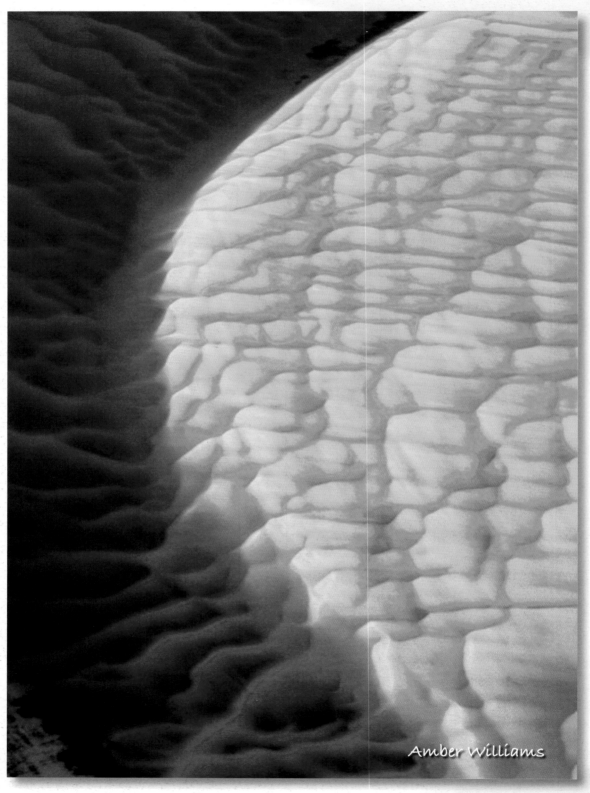

Amber Williams

layers and channels

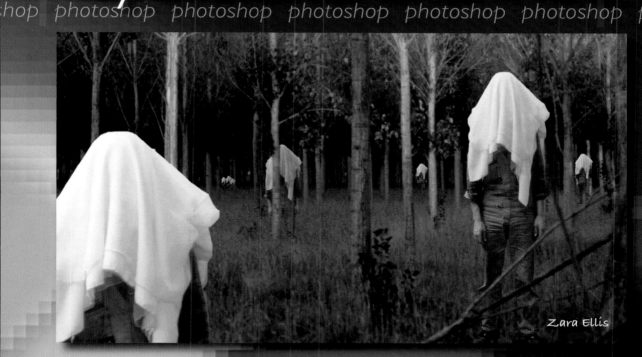

Zara Ellis

photoshop photoshop photoshop photoshop photoshop photo

essential skills

~ Learn the creative potential of layers, adjustment layers, channels and layer masks.

~ Develop skills and experience in the control and construction of digital montages.

Introduction

The traditional photograph contains all the picture elements in a single plane. Digital images captured by a camera or sourced from a scanner are similar in that they are also flat files. And for a lot of new digital photographers this is how their files remain – flat. All editing and enhancing work is conducted on the original picture but advanced techniques require things to be a little different.

Digital pictures are not always flat

Photoshop contains the ability to use layers with your pictures. This feature releases your images from having to keep all their information in a flat file. Different image parts, added text and certain enhancement tasks can all be kept on separate layers. The layers are kept in a stack and the image you see on screen in the work area is a composite of all the layers.

Sound confusing? Well try imagining, for example, that each of the image parts of a simple portrait photograph are stored on separate plastic sheets. These are your layers. The background sits at the bottom. The portrait is laid on top of the background and the text is placed on top. When viewed from above the solid part of each layer obscures the picture beneath. Whilst the picture parts are based on separate layers they can be moved, edited or enhanced independently of each other. If they are saved using a file format like Photoshop's PSD file (which is layer friendly) all the layers will be preserved and present next time the file is opened.

Layers and channels confusion

Another picture file feature that new users often confuse with layers is channels. The difference is best described as follows:

- Layers separate the image into picture, text, shapes and enhancement parts.
- Channels, on the other hand, separate the image into its primary base colors.

The Layers palette will display the layer stack with each part assembled on top of each other, whereas the Channels palette will show the photograph broken into its red, green and blue components (if it is an RGB image – but more on this later).

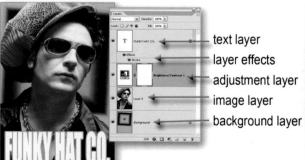

text layer
layer effects
adjustment layer
image layer
background layer

Example image showing the layer components

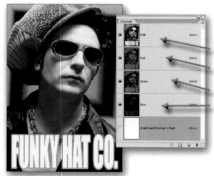

all channels
red channel
green channel
blue channel

Example image showing the channels

Layers overview

Being able to separate different components of a picture means that these pieces can be moved and edited independently. This is a big advantage compared to flat file editing where the changes are permanently made part of the picture and can't be edited at a later date. A special file type is needed if these edit features are to be maintained after a layered image is saved and reopened. In Photoshop, the PSD, PDF and PSB formats support all layer types and maintain their editability. It is important to note that other common file formats such as standard JPEG and TIFF don't generally support these features (although JPEG2000 and TIFF saved via Photoshop CS2 can support layers). They flatten the image layers whilst saving the file, making it impossible to edit individual image parts later.

The Layers palette is used to view the content of the different layers that make up a picture

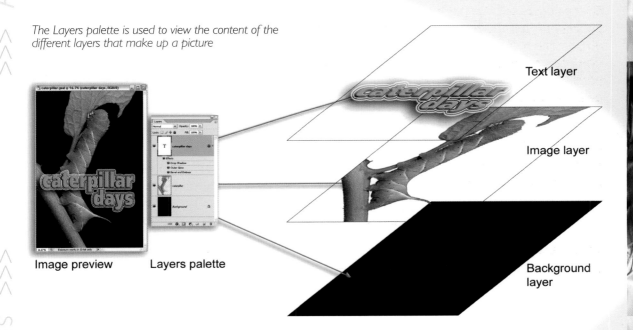

Image preview   Layers palette

Text layer

Image layer

Background layer

Adding layers

When a picture is first downloaded from your digital camera or imported into Photoshop it usually contains a single layer. It is a 'flat file'. By default the program classifies the picture as a background layer. You can add extra 'empty' layers to your picture by clicking the Create New Layer button at the bottom of the Layers dialog or choosing the Layer option from the New menu in the Layer heading (Layer > New > Layer). The new layer is positioned above the currently selected layer.

Some actions such as adding text with the Type Tool automatically or drawing a shape create a new layer for the content. This is also true when adding adjustment and fill layers to your image and when selecting, copying and pasting image parts.

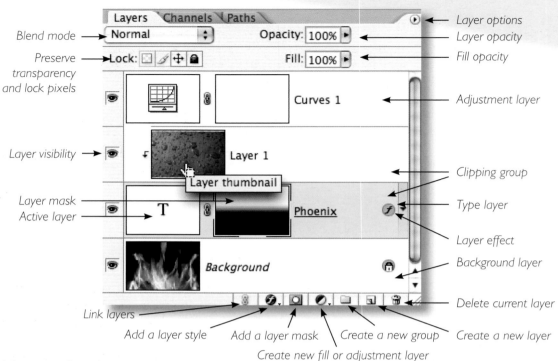

Blend mode → Normal — Opacity: 100% → Layer options / Layer opacity

Preserve transparency and lock pixels → Lock: — Fill: 100% → Fill opacity

Curves 1 → Adjustment layer

Layer visibility → Layer 1

Clipping group

Layer mask / Active layer → Layer thumbnail — Phoenix → Type layer

Layer effect

Background → Background layer

Link layers — Delete current layer

Add a layer style / Add a layer mask / Create a new group / Create a new layer

Create new fill or adjustment layer

Viewing layers

Photoshop's Layers palette displays all your layers and their settings in the one dialog box. If the palette isn't already on screen when opening the program, choose the option from the Window menu (Window > Layers). The individual layers are displayed, one on top of each other, in a 'layer stack'. The image is viewed from the top down through the layers. When looking at the picture on screen we see a preview of how the image looks when all the layers are combined. Each layer is represented by a thumbnail on the left and a name on the right. The size of the thumbnail can be changed, as can the name of the layer. By default each new layer is named sequentially (layer 1, layer 2, layer 3). This is fine when your image contains a few different picture parts, but for more complex illustrations it is helpful to rename the layers with titles that help to remind you of their content (portrait, sky, tree). Layers can be turned off by clicking the eye symbol on the far left of the layer so that it is no longer showing. This action removes the layer from view but not from the stack. You can turn the layer back on again by clicking the eye space.

Working with layers

You can only edit or enhance one layer at a time. To select the layer that you want to change you need to click on the layer. At this point the layer will change to a different color from the rest in the stack. This layer is now the 'selected layer' and can be edited in isolation from the others that make up the picture. It is common for new users to experience the problem of trying to edit pixels on a layer that has not been selected. Always check the correct layer has been selected prior to editing a multi-layered image.

Each layer in the same image must have the same resolution and image mode (a selection that is imported into another image will take on the host image's resolution and image mode). Increasing the size of any selection will lead to 'interpolation' which will degrade its quality.

Manipulating layers

Layers can be moved up and down the layer stack by click-dragging. Moving a layer upwards will mean that its picture content may obscure more of the details in the layers below. Moving downwards progressively positions the layer's details further behind the picture parts of the layers above. In this way you can reposition the content of any layers (except background layers) using the Move tool.

Two or more layers can be linked together so that when the content of one layer is moved the other details follow precisely. Simply multi-select the layers to link (hold down the Shift key and click onto each layer) and click the Link Layers button (chain icon) at the bottom of the palette. A chain symbol will appear on the right of the thumbnail to indicate that these layers are now linked. To unlink selected layers click on the Link Layers button again.

Unwanted layers can be deleted by dragging them to the dustbin icon at the bottom of the Layers palette or by selecting the layer and clicking the dustbin icon.

Layer styles

In earlier versions of Photoshop creating a drop shadow edge to a picture was a process that involved many steps; thankfully the latest version of the program includes this as one of the many built-in layer styles. Including other options such as inner shadow, outer glow, inner glow, bevel and emboss, satin, color overlay, gradient overlay and pattern overlay, these effects can be applied to the contents of any layer.

Users can add effects by clicking on the Layer Style button at the bottom of the Layers palette, by choosing Layer Style from the Layer menu or by dragging existing effects from one layer to another. The effects added are listed below the layer in the palette. You can turn effects on and off using the eye symbol and even edit effect settings by double-clicking on them in the palette.

Opacity

As well as layer styles, or effects, the opacity (how transparent a layer is) of each layer can be altered by dragging the opacity slider down from 100% to the desired level of translucency. The lower the number the more detail from the layers below will show through. The opacity slider is located at the top of the Layers palette and changes the selected layer only.

Blending modes

On the left of the opacity control is a drop-down menu containing a range of blending modes. The default selection is 'normal', which means that the detail in upper layers obscures the layers beneath.

Switching to a different blending mode will alter the way in which the layers interact.

Layer shortcuts

1. To display Layers palette – Choose Windows > Layers.

2. To access layers options – Click sideways triangle in the upper right-hand corner of the Layers palette.

3. To change the size of thumbnails – Choose Palette Options from the Layers palette menu and select a thumbnail size.

4. To make a new layer – Choose Layer > New > Layer.

5. To create a new adjustment layer – Choose Layer > New Adjustment Layer and then select the layer type.

6. To create a new layer set – Choose Layer > New > Layer Set.

7. To add a style to a layer – Select the layer and click on the Layer Styles button at the bottom of the palette.

Checking the 'preserve transparency' box confines any painting or editing to the areas containing pixels (transparent areas remain unaffected).

Layer groups (sets)

Layer groups are a collection of layers organized into a single 'folder'. Placing all the layers used to create a single picture part into a group makes these layers easier to manage and organize. Layers can be moved into the group by dragging them onto the group's heading.

To create a layer group click on the New Group button at the bottom of the palette or choose Layer > New > Group or multi-select the layers to include in the group and press Ctrl/Cmd+G. In previous versions of Photoshop this feature was referred to as Layer Sets.

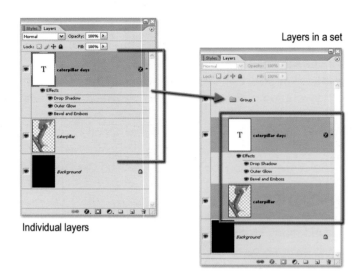

Layers in a set

Individual layers

Layer masks

A '**layer mask**' is attached to a layer and controls which pixels are concealed or revealed on that layer. Masks provide a way of protecting areas of a picture from enhancement or editing changes. In this way masks are the opposite to selections, which restrict the changes to the area selected. Masks are standard grayscale images and because of this they can be painted, edited and erased just like other pictures. Masks are displayed as a separate thumbnail to the right of the main layer thumbnail in the Layers palette. The black portion of the mask thumbnail is the protected area and the white section shows the area where the image can be edited and enhanced.

Photoshop provides a variety of ways to create masks but one of the easiest is to use the special Quick Mask mode.

Quick steps for making a Quick Mask

1. Click the Quick Mask mode button in the toolbox. The foreground and background colors automatically become black and white.

2. Select the layer to be masked and using the Brush tool paint a mask on the image. You will notice that the painted mask area is now ruby red. Painting with different levels of gray will create a semi-transparent mask.

3. Remove areas of the mask with the Eraser tool.

4. Switch back to the selection mode by clicking the Standard Mode button at the bottom of the toolbox. The non-masked area now becomes a selection ready for enhancement.

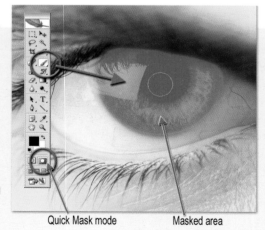

Quick Mask mode   Masked area

Layer types

Image layers: This is the most basic and common layer type containing any picture parts or image details. Background is a special type of image layer.

Text layers: Designed solely for text, these layers allow the user to edit and enhance the text after the layer has been made. It is possible to create '**editable text**' in Photoshop. If the text needs to be modified (font, style, spelling, color, etc.) the user can simply double-click the type layer. To filter the contents of a text layer it must be Rasterized (Layer > Rasterize) first. This coverts the text layer to a standard image layer and in the process loses the ability to edit the text.

Shape layers: Shape layers are designed to hold the shapes created with Photoshop's drawing tools (Rectangle, Ellipse, Polygon, Line and Custom Shape). Like text layers the content of these layers is 'vector' based and therefore can be scaled upwards or downwards without loss of quality.

Adjustment layers: These layers alter the layers that are arranged below them in the stack. Adjustment layers act as a filter through which the lower layers are viewed. They allow image adjustments to be made without permanently modifying the original pixels (if the adjustment layer is removed the pixels revert to their original value). You can use adjustment layers to perform many of the enhancement tasks that you would normally apply directly to an image layer without changing the image itself.

Background layers: An image can only have one background layer. It is the bottom-most layer in the stack. No other layers can be moved beneath this layer. You cannot adjust this layer's opacity or its blending mode. You can convert background layers to standard image layers by double-clicking the layer in the Layers palette, setting your desired layer options in the dialog provided and then clicking OK.

Saving an image with layers

The file formats that support layers are Photoshop's native Photoshop document (PSD) format, PDF, JPEG2000, PSB and Photoshop TIFF. The layers in a picture must always be flattened if the file is to be saved as a standard JPEG. It is recommended that a PSD with its layers is always held as the master copy.

It is possible to quickly flatten a multi-layered image and save it as a JPEG or TIFF file by choosing File > Save As and then selecting the required file format from the pull-down menu.

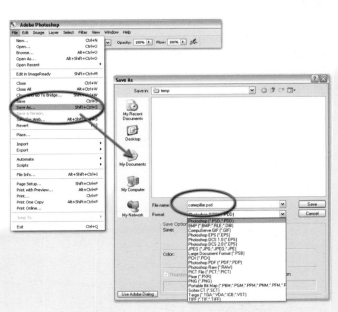

Quick Masks, selections and alpha channels

When first starting to use Photoshop it is easy to think of selections, masks and channels as all being completely separate program features, but in the reality of day-to-day image enhancement each of these tools is inextricably linked. As your skills develop most image-makers will develop their own preferred ways of working. Some use a workflow that is selection based, others switch easily between masking and selections and a third group concentrates all their efforts on creating masks only. No one way of working is right or wrong. In fact many of the techniques advocated by the members of each group often provide a different approach to solving the same problem. Selections isolate parts of a picture.

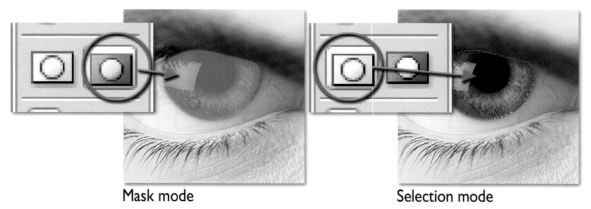

Mask mode   Selection mode

Switching between Mask and Selection modes

You can switch between Mask and Selection (also called 'Standard') modes by clicking on mode buttons positioned at the bottom of the toolbox. Any active selections will be converted to red shaded areas when selecting the Mask mode. Similarly active masks will be outlined with 'marching ants' when switching to Selection mode.

When you save a selection you create a grayscale alpha channel

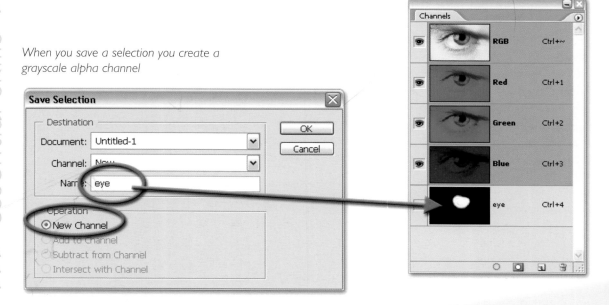

PHOTOSHOP CS2 >>>

>>> essential skills >>>

Saving selections

Photoshop provides users with the option to save their carefully created selections using the Select > Save Selection option. In this way the selection can be reloaded at a later date in the same session via the Select > Load Selection feature, or even after the document has been closed and reopened. Though not immediately obvious to the new user, the selection is actually saved with the picture as a special alpha channel and this is where the primary link between selections and masks occurs. Masks too are stored as alpha channels in your picture documents.

Alpha channels are essentially grayscale pictures where the black section of the image indicates the area where changes can be made, the white portion represents protected areas and gray values allow proportional levels of change.

Alpha channels can be viewed, selected and edited via the Channels palette.

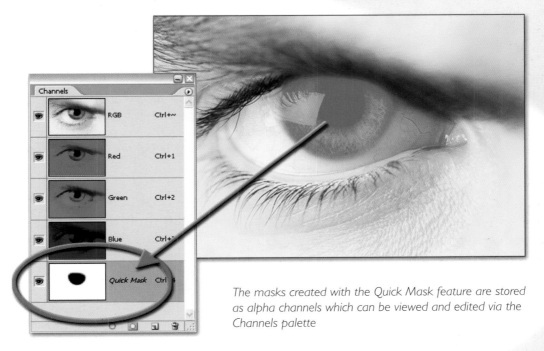

The masks created with the Quick Mask feature are stored as alpha channels which can be viewed and edited via the Channels palette

QUICK DEFINITIONS

Selections – A selection is an area of a picture that is isolated so that it can be edited and enhanced independently of the rest of the image. Selections are made with a range of Photoshop tools including the Marquee, Lasso and Magic Wand tools.

Masks – Masks also provide a means of restricting image changes to a section of the picture. Masks are created using standard painting tools whilst in the Quick Mask mode.

Alpha channels – Alpha channels are a special channel type that are separate to those used to define the base color of a picture such as Red, Green and Blue. Selections and masks are stored as alpha channels and can be viewed in the Channels palette. You can edit a selected alpha channel using painting and editing tools as well as filters.

Channels

As we have already seen, channels represent the way in which the base color in an image is represented. Most images that are created by digital cameras are made up of Red, Green and Blue (RGB) channels. In contrast, pictures that are destined for printing are created with Cyan, Magenta, Yellow and Black (CMYK) channels to match the printing inks. Sometimes the channels in an image are also referred to as the picture's 'color mode'.

Viewing channels

Many image-editing programs contain features designed for managing and viewing the color channels in your image. Photoshop uses a separate Channels palette (Window > Channels). Looking a little like the Layers palette, hence the source of much confusion, this palette breaks the full color picture into its various base color parts.

Changing color mode

Though most editing and enhancement work can be performed on the RGB file, sometimes the digital photographer may need to change the color mode of his or her file. There are a range of conversion options located under the Mode menu (Image > Mode) in Photoshop. When one of these options is selected your picture's color will be translated into the new set of channels. Changing the number of channels in an image also impacts on the file size of the picture. Four-channel CMYK images are bigger than three-channel RGB pictures, which in turn are roughly three times larger than single-channel grayscale photographs.

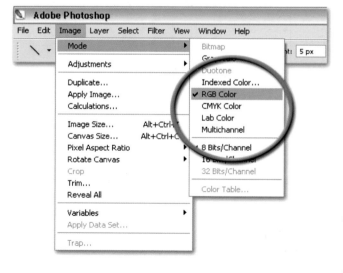

The type and number of color channels used to create the color in your pictures can be changed via the Mode option in the Image menu

When do I need to change channels?

For most image-editing and enhancement tasks RGB color mode is all you will ever need. Some high quality and printing-specific techniques do require changing modes, but this is generally the field of the 'hardened' professional. A question often asked is 'Given that my inkjet printer uses CMYK inks, should I change my photograph to CMYK before printing?' Logic says yes, but practically speaking this type of conversion is best handled by your printer's driver software. Most modern desktop printers are optimized for RGB output even if their ink set is CMYK.

Channel types

RGB: This is the most common color mode. Consisting of Red, Green and Blue channels, most digital camera and scanner output is supplied in this mode.

CMYK: Designed to replicate the ink sets used to print magazines and newspapers, this mode is made from Cyan, Magenta, Yellow and Black (K) channels.

LAB: Consisting of Lightness, A colors (green–red) and B colors (blue–yellow) channels, this mode is used by professional photographers when they want to enhance the details of an image without altering the color. By selecting the L channel and then performing their changes only the image details are affected.

Grayscale: Consisting of a single black channel, this mode is used for monochrome pictures.

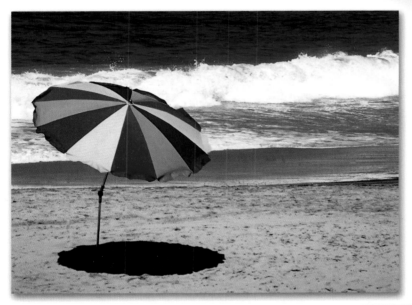

The most used color modes (channel types) are RGB, CMYK, LAB and Grayscale. Unless you are working in the publishing industry, or you want to use advanced image-editing techniques, you should keep your picture in RGB mode

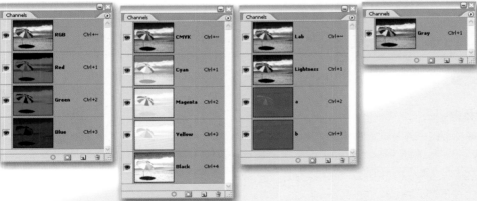

RGB mode   CMYK mode   LAB mode   Grayscale mode

Adjustment layers and editing quality

As introduced earlier, adjustment layers act as filters that modify the hue, saturation and brightness of the pixels on the layer or layers beneath. Using an adjustment layer instead of the 'Adjustments' from the 'Image' menu allows the user to make multiple and consecutive image adjustments without permanently modifying the original pixel values.

Non-destructive image editing

The manipulation of image quality using '**adjustment layers**' and '**layer masks**' is often termed 'non-destructive'. Using adjustment layers to manipulate images is preferable to working directly and repeatedly on the pixels themselves. Using the 'Adjustments' from the 'Image' menu, or the manipulation tools from the toolbox (Dodge, Burn and Sponge Tools), directly on pixel layers can eventually lead to a degradation of image quality. If adjustment layers are used, together with '**layer masks**' to limit their effect, the pixel values are physically changed only once when the image is flattened or the layers are merged. Retaining the integrity of your original file is essential for high quality output.

Note > With the release of CS2 it is also now possible to scale or 'transform' a layer or group of layers non-destructively by turning a layer, or layers, into a 'Smart Object'.

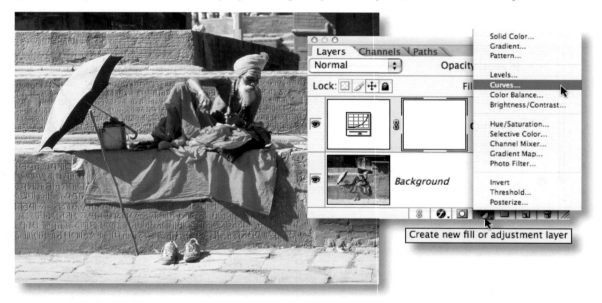

Retaining quality

The evidence of a file that has been degraded can be observed by viewing its histogram. If the resulting histogram displays excessive spikes or missing levels there is a high risk that a smooth transition between tones and color will not be possible in the resulting print. A tell-tale sign of poor scanning and image editing is the effect of '**banding**' that can be clearly observed in the final print. This is where the transition between colors or tones is no longer smooth, but can be observed as a series of steps, or bands, of tone and/or color. To avoid this it is essential that you start with a good scan (a broad histogram without gaps) and limit the number of changes to the original pixel values.

Layer masks and editing adjustments

The use of 'layer masks' is an essential skill for professional image retouching. Together with the Selection tools and 'adjustment layers' they form the key to effective and sophisticated image editing. A 'layer mask' can control which pixels are concealed or revealed on any image layer except the background layer. If the layer mask that has been used to conceal pixels is then discarded or switched off (Shift + click the layer mask thumbnail) the original pixels reappear. This non-destructive approach to retouching and photographic montage allows the user to make frequent changes. To attach a layer mask to any layer (except the background layer) simply click on the layer and then click on the 'Add layer mask' icon at the base of the Layers palette.

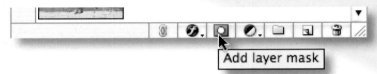

A layer mask is automatically attached to every adjustment layer. The effects of an adjustment layer can be limited to a localized area of the image by simply clicking on the adjustment layer's associated mask thumbnail in the Layers palette and then painting out the adjustment selectively using any of the painting tools whilst working in the main image window. The opacity and tone of the foreground color in the toolbox will control whether the adjustment is reduced or eliminated in the localized area of the painting action. Painting with a darker tone will conceal more than when painting with a lighter tone or a dark tone with a reduced opacity.

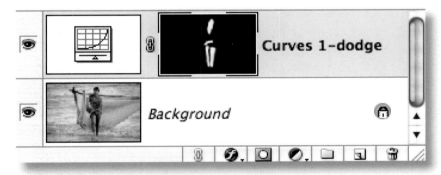

Painting with white will reveal the adjustment in the localized area of the painting action

Painting an adjustment

A layer mask can be filled with black to conceal the effects of the adjustment layer. Painting with white in the layer mask will then reveal the adjustment in the localized area of the painting action.

LAYER MASK SHORTCUTS

Disable/enable layer mask	Shift + Click layer mask thumbnail
Preview contents of layer mask	Opt/Alt + Click layer mask thumbnail
Preview layer mask and image	Opt/Alt + Shift + Click layer mask thumbnail

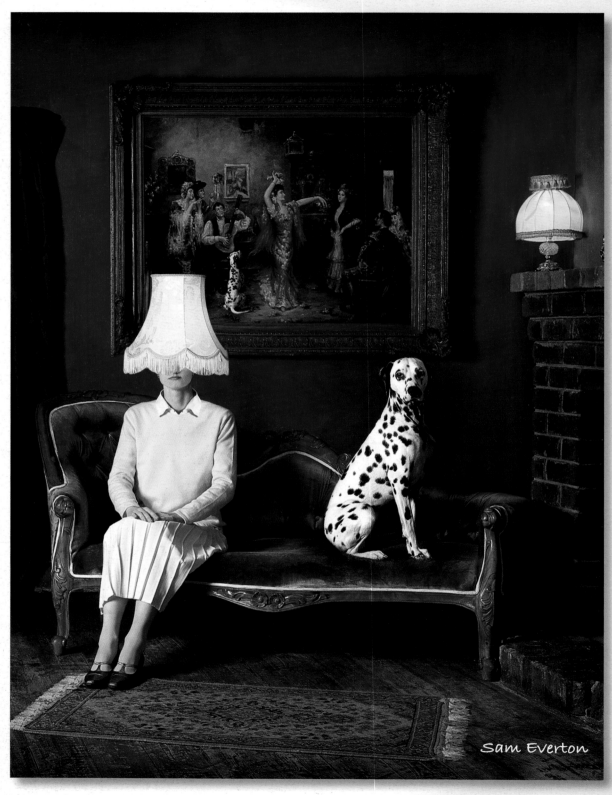

Sam Everton

selections

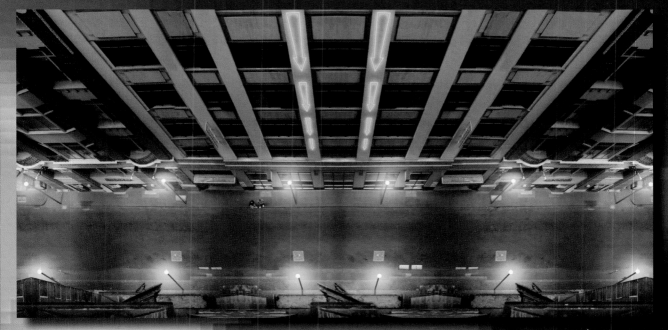

Stuart Wilson

essential skills

~ Develop skills in creating and modifying selections to isolate and mask image content.

~ Develop skills using the following tools and features:

– Selection Tools

– Quick Mask, alpha channels and layer masks

– Color Range and Extract filter

– Pen Tool.

Introduction

One of the most skilled areas of digital retouching and manipulation is the ability to make accurate selections of pixels for repositioning, modifying or exporting to another image. This skill allows localized retouching and image enhancement. Photoshop provides several different tools that allow the user to select the area to be changed. Called the 'Selection' Tools, using these features will fast become a regular part of your editing and retouching process. Photoshop marks the boundaries of a selected area using a flashing dotted line sometimes called 'marching ants'. Obvious distortions of photographic originals are common in the media but so are images where the retouching and manipulations are subtle and not detectable. Nearly every image in the printed media is retouched to some extent. Selections are made for a number of reasons:

- Making an adjustment or modification to a localized area, e.g. color, contrast, etc.
- Defining a subject within the overall image to mask, move or replicate.
- Defining an area where an image or group of pixels will be inserted ('paste into').

Selection Tools overview

Photoshop groups the Selection Tools based on how they isolate picture parts. These categories are:

- The '**Marquee Tools**' are used to draw regular-shaped selections such as rectangles or ellipses around an area within the image.

- The '**Lasso Tools**' use a more freehand drawing approach and are used to draw a selection by defining the edge between a subject and its background.

- The '**Magic Wand**' makes selections based on color and tone and is used to isolate groups of pixels by evaluating the similarity of the neighboring pixel values (hue, saturation and brightness) to the pixel that is selected.

Shape-based selections with the Marquee Tools

The Marquee Tools select by dragging with the mouse over the area required. Holding down the Shift key as you drag the selection will 'constrain' the selection to a square or circle rather than a rectangle or oval. Using the Alt (Windows) or Options (Mac) key will draw the selections from their centers. The Marquee Tools are great for isolating objects in your images that are regular in shape, but for less conventional shapes, you will need to use one of the Lasso Tools.

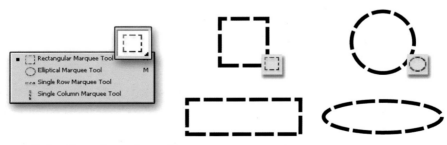

Selections based on shapes

Selections based on drawing

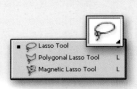
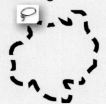
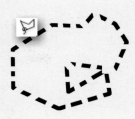

Drawn selections using the Lasso Tools

Select by encircling or drawing around the area you wish to select. The standard Lasso Tool works like a pencil, allowing the user to draw freehand shapes for selections. A large screen and a mouse in good condition (or a graphics tablet) are required to use the Freehand Lasso Tool effectively. In contrast, the Polygonal Lasso Tool draws straight-edge lines between mouse-click points. Either of these features can be used to outline and select irregular-shaped image parts.

A third tool, the Magnetic Lasso, helps with the drawing process by aligning the outline with the edge of objects automatically. It uses contrast in color and tone as a basis for determining the edge of an object. The accuracy of the 'magnetic' features of this tool is determined by three settings in the tool's Options bar. **Edge Contrast** is the value that a pixel has to differ from its neighbor to be considered an edge, **Width** is the number of pixels either side of the pointer that are sampled in the edge determination process and **Frequency** is the distance between fastening points in the outline.

Double-clicking the Polygonal Lasso Tool or Magnetic Lasso Tool automatically completes the selection using a straight line between the last selected point and the first.

Note > Remember the Magnetic Lasso Tool requires a tonal or color difference between the object and its background in order to work effectively.

Selections based on color and tone

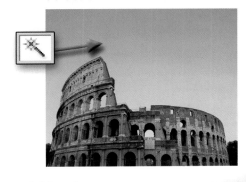
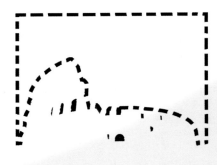

The Magic Wand

Unlike the Lasso and Marquee Tools the Magic Wand makes selections based on color and tone. It selects by relative pixel values. When the user clicks on an image with the Magic Wand Tool Photoshop searches the picture for pixels that have a similar color and tone. With large images this process can take a little time but the end result is a selection of all similar pixels across the whole picture.

Tolerance

How identical a pixel has to be to the original is determined by the **Tolerance** value in the Options bar. The higher the value, the less alike the two pixels need to be, whereas a lower setting will require a more exact match before a pixel is added to the selection. Turning on the **Contiguous** option will only include the pixels that are similar and adjacent to the original pixel in the selection.

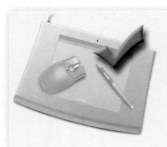

Better with a tablet:
Many professionals prefer to work with a stylus and tablet when creating complex selections.

Moving a selection

If the selection is not accurate it is possible to move the selection without moving any pixels. With the Selection Tool still active place the cursor inside your selection and drag the selection to reposition it. To move the pixels and the selection, use the Move Tool from the Tools palette. Press the Spacebar to realign a marquee selection before the selection is completed.

To remove a selection

Go to Select > Deselect or use the shortcut 'Command/Ctrl + D' to deselect a selection.

Modifying your selections

Basic selections of standard, or regular-shaped, picture parts can be easily made with one simple step – just click and drag. But you will quickly realize that most selection scenarios are often a little more complex. For this reason the thoughtful people at Adobe have provided several ways of allowing you to modifying your selections. The two most used methods provide the means to 'add to' or 'subtract from' existing selections. This, in conjunction with the range of Selection tools offered by the program, gives the user the power to select even the most complex picture parts. Skillful selecting takes practice and patience as well as the ability to choose which Selection tool will work best for a given task.

Photoshop provides two different ways to modify an existing selection.

1. The first uses keyboard shortcuts in conjunction with the Selection Tools to 'add to' and 'subtract from' the selection. Using this approach is fast and convenient and is the one preferred by most professionals.

2. The second uses the mode buttons located in a special portion of the tool's Options bar. This way of working is a great way to start changing your selections. The default mode is 'New Selection', which means that each selection you make replaces the last. Once another option is selected the mode remains active for the duration of the selection session. This is true even when you switch Selection Tools.

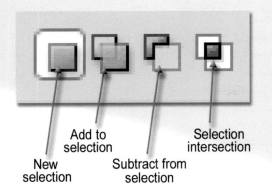

Add to
selection

Selection
intersection

New
selection

Subtract from
selection

Add to a selection

To add to an existing selection hold down the Shift key whilst selecting a new area. Notice that when the Shift key is held down the Selection Tool's cursor changes to include a '+' to indicate that you are in the 'add' mode. This addition mode works for all tools and you can change Selection Tools after each new selection is complete.

Subtract from a selection

To remove sections from an existing selection hold down the Alt key (Option – Macintosh) whilst selecting the part of the picture you do not wish to include in the selection. When in the subtract mode the cursor will change to include a '–'.

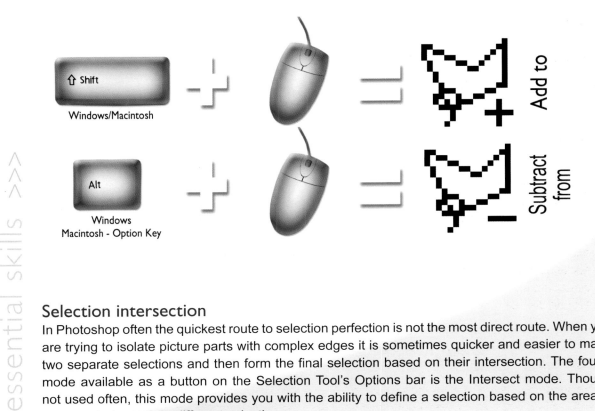

Selection intersection

In Photoshop often the quickest route to selection perfection is not the most direct route. When you are trying to isolate picture parts with complex edges it is sometimes quicker and easier to make two separate selections and then form the final selection based on their intersection. The fourth mode available as a button on the Selection Tool's Options bar is the Intersect mode. Though not used often, this mode provides you with the ability to define a selection based on the area in common between two different selections.

Inversing a selection

In a related technique, some users find it helpful to select what they don't want in a picture and then instruct Photoshop to select everything but this area. The Select > Inverse command inverts or reverses the current selection and is perfect for this approach. In this way foreground objects can be quickly selected in pictures with a smoothly graduated background of all one color (sky, snow or a wall space) by using the Magic Wand to select the background. Then the act of inversing the selection will isolate the foreground detail.

Professionals who know that the foreground will be extracted from the picture's surrounds often shoot their subjects against an evenly lit background of a consistent color to facilitate the application of this technique.

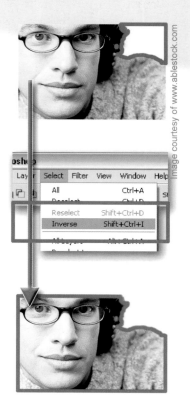

Saving and loading selections

The selections you make remain active whilst the image is open and until a new selection is made, but what if you want to store all your hard work to use on another occasion? As we have already seen in the previous chapter Photoshop provides the option to save your selections/masks as part of the picture file. Simply select Select > Save Selection and the existing selection will be stored with the picture.

To display a selection saved with a picture, open the file and choose Load Selection from the Select menu. In the Load Selection dialog click on the Channel drop-down menu and choose the selection you wish to reinstate. Choose the mode with which the selection will be added to your picture from the Operation section of the dialog. Click OK to finish.

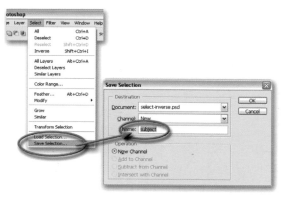

Save selection

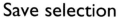

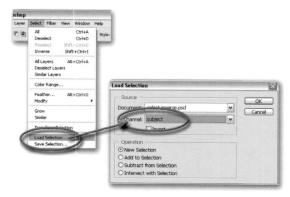

Load selection

Feather and anti-alias

The ability to create a composite image or '**photomontage**' that looks subtle, realistic and believable rests with whether or not the viewer is able to detect where one image starts and the other finishes. The edges of each selection can be modified so that it appears as if it belongs, or is related, to the surrounding pixels.

Options are available with most image-processing software to alter the appearance of the edges of a selection. Edges can appear sharp or soft (a gradual transition between the selection and the background). The options to effect these changes are:

- Feather
- Anti-aliasing.

Feather

When this option is chosen the pixels at the edges of the selection are blurred. The edges are softer and less harsh. This blurring may either create a more realistic montage or cause loss of detail at the edge of the selection.

You can choose feathering for the Marquee or Lasso Tools as you use them by entering a value in the tool options box, or you can add feathering to an existing selection (Select > Feather). The feathering effect only becomes apparent when you move or paste the selection to a new area.

Anti-aliasing

When this option is chosen the jagged edges of a selection are softened. A more gradual transition between the edge pixels and the background pixels is created. Only the edge pixels are changed so no detail is lost. Anti-aliasing must be chosen before the selection is made (it cannot be added afterwards). It is usual to have the anti-alias option selected for most selections. The anti-alias option also needs to be considered when using type in image-editing software. The anti-alias option may be deselected to improve the appearance of small type to avoid the appearance of blurred text.

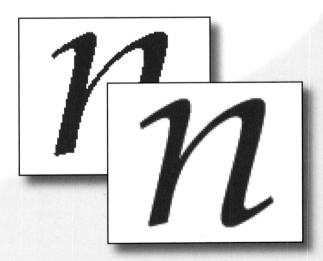

Defringe and Matting

When a selection has been made using the anti-alias option some of the pixels surrounding the selection are included. If these surrounding pixels are darker, lighter or a different color to the selection a fringe or halo may be seen. From the Layers menu choose Matting > Defringe to replace the different fringe pixels with pixels of a similar hue, saturation or brightness found within the selection area.

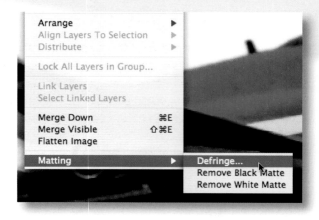

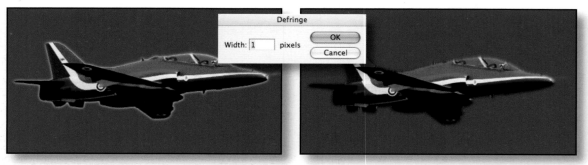

Fringe   Defringe

The user may have to experiment with the most appropriate method of removing a fringe. The alternative options of Remove White Matte and Remove Black Matte may provide the user with a better result. If a noticeable fringe still persists it is possible to contract the selection prior to moving it using the Modify > Contract option from the Select menu.

Saving a selection as an alpha channel

Selections can be permanently stored as '**alpha channels**'. The saved selections can be reloaded and/or modified even after the image has been closed and reopened. To save a selection as an alpha channel simply click the '**Save selection as channel**' icon at the base of the Channels palette. To load a selection either drag the alpha channel to the '**Load channel as selection**' icon in the Channels palette or Command/Ctrl-click the alpha channel.

It is possible to edit an alpha channel (and the resulting selection) by using the painting and editing tools. Painting with black will add to the alpha channel whilst painting with white will remove information. Painting with shades of gray will lower or increase the opacity of the alpha channel. The user can selectively soften a channel and resulting selection by applying a Gaussian Blur filter. Choose Blur > Gaussian Blur from the Filters menu.

Note > An image with saved selections (alpha chanels) cannot be saved in the standard JPEG format. Use the PSD, PDF or TIFF formats or JPEG2000 if storage space is tight.

The 'Magic Wand'

If you are new to the magic of the wand, enter the default setting of 32 in the Tolerance field of the Options bar (raising the value makes the ants increasingly frisky). Make sure the 'Anti-alias' box is checked as this smoothes the edge of the selection (to stop it looking like the mouth of 'Jaws'). Also check the 'Contiguous' box, as this will make sure your ants respect any boundaries and borders they encounter. Before attempting to make a selection decide which is easier – selecting the background around the object or selecting the object itself (choose the one with fewest colors). You can always 'Inverse' the selection when you are done (Select > Inverse). A careful selection of the background can quickly be turned into a selection of the subject in this way.

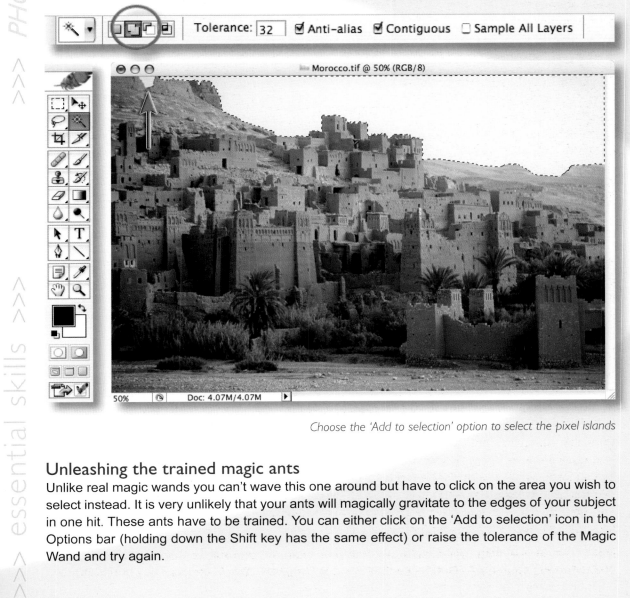

Choose the 'Add to selection' option to select the pixel islands

Unleashing the trained magic ants

Unlike real magic wands you can't wave this one around but have to click on the area you wish to select instead. It is very unlikely that your ants will magically gravitate to the edges of your subject in one hit. These ants have to be trained. You can either click on the 'Add to selection' icon in the Options bar (holding down the Shift key has the same effect) or raise the tolerance of the Magic Wand and try again.

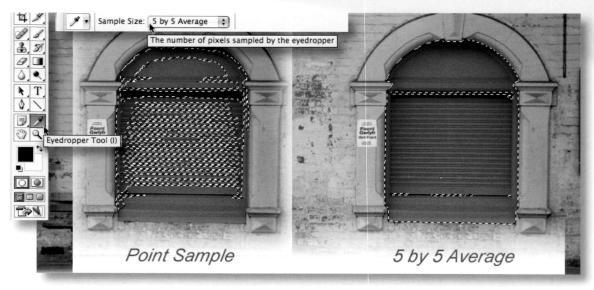

Point Sample   *5 by 5 Average*

If you raise the tolerance of the wand but the selection is either patchy or excessive go to 'Edit > Undo' and try the following. Raise the setting of the eyedropper tool from 'Point Sample' to '5 by 5 Average'. The wand usually becomes a little more stable and the ants just might be encouraged to make the selection you are looking for.

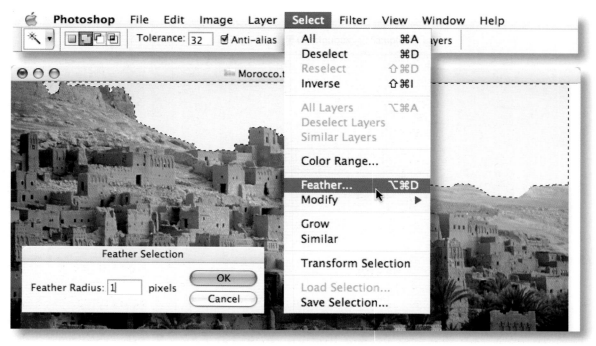

There is no feather option with the Magic Wand Tool so this important step is often overlooked. A small amount of feather is nearly always needed – even with seemingly sharp edges. One of the problems with the Magic Wand is that the magic ants have a fear of edges. They prefer to stand back and admire the view from a safe distance.

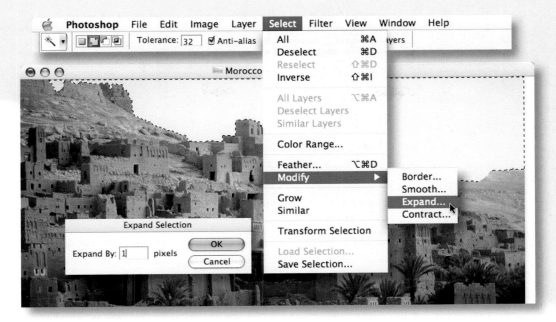

Move the reluctant ants closer to the edge by expanding the selection (Select > Modify > Expand). This will counteract the halo effect that is all too often seen with poor selection work.

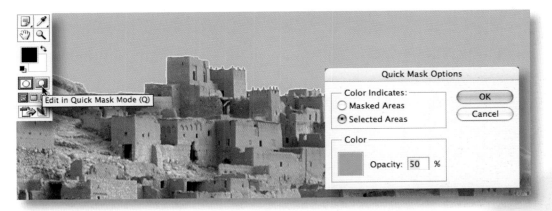

'Quick Mask'

The problem with feathering and modifying selections using the 'Select' menu items is that the ants give very poor feedback about what is actually going on at the edge. Viewing the selection as a 'Mask' in 'Quick Mask mode' allows you to view the quality and accuracy of your selection. Zoom in on an edge to take a closer look. Double-click the Quick Mask icon to change the mask color, opacity and to switch between 'Masked Areas' and 'Selected Areas'. If the mask is still falling short of the edge, expand the selection again. If the mask is over the edge you can contract the selection (also from the 'Select > Modify' menu). Alternatively give the Select menu the flick and proceed to work on the mask directly. A 'Levels' adjustment in Quick Mask mode provides a 'one-stop shop' for editing the mask, giving you the luxury of a preview as you modify the resulting selection.

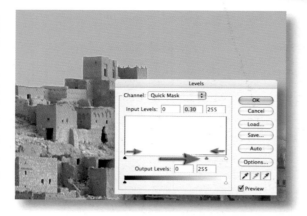
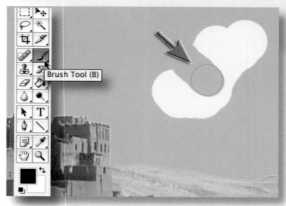

Using a 'Levels' adjustment (Image > Adjustments > Levels) in Quick Mask mode allows you to modify the edge quality if it is too soft and also reposition the edge so that it aligns closely with your subject. Dragging the shadow and highlight sliders in towards the center will reduce the softness of the mask whilst moving the midtone or 'Gamma' slider will move the edge itself.

Note > The selection must have been feathered prior to the application of the Levels adjustment for this to be effective.

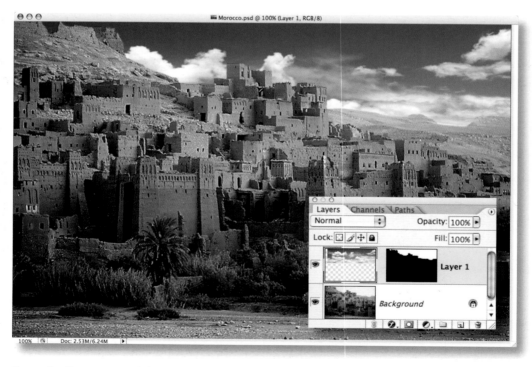

Save the selection as an alpha channel. This will ensure that your work is stored permanently in the file. If the file is closed and reopened the selection can be reloaded. Finish off the job in hand by modifying or replacing the selected pixels. If the Magic Wand is not working for you, you should explore the following alternatives.

'Color Range'

Photoshop has many alternative methods for creating selections. The 'Color Range' option from the 'Selection' menu should be considered next. This option is useful for selecting subjects that are defined by a limited color range (sufficiently different from those of the background colors). This option is especially useful when the selection is to be used for a hue adjustment.

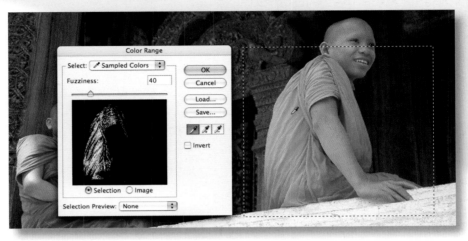

Use a Marquee Tool (from the Tools palette) to limit the selection area before you start using the Color Range option.

Note > The Color Range option can misbehave sometimes. If the selection does not seem to be restricted to your sampled color press the Alt/Option key and click on the reset option or close the dialog box and re-enter.

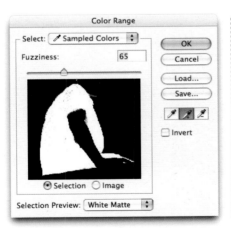
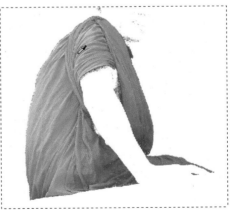

Use the 'Add to sample' eyedropper and drag the eyedropper over the subject area you wish to select. In the later stages you can choose a matte color to help the task of selection. Adjust the Fuzziness slider to perfect the selection. Very dark or light pixels can be left out of the selection if it is to be used for a hue adjustment only.

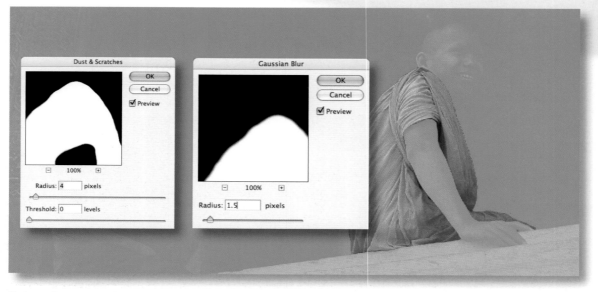

Select OK and view the selection in Quick Mask mode to gain an idea of the selection's suitability for the job in hand. The mask can be 'cleaned' using the Dust & Scratches filter and softened using a Gaussian Blur filter.

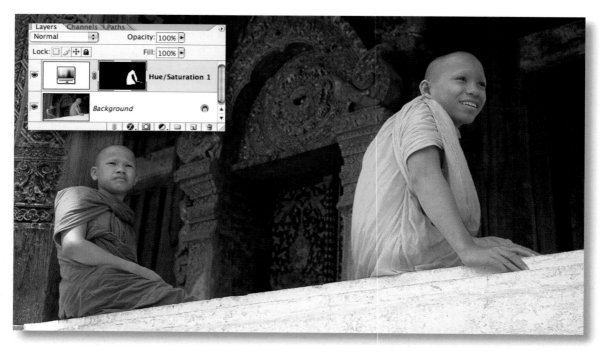

A selection prepared by the 'Color Range' command is ideal for making a hue adjustment. It is also recommended to view the individual channels to see if the subject you are trying to isolate is separated from the surrounding information. If this is the case a duplicate channel can act as a starting point for a selection.

Channel masking

An extremely quick and effective method for selecting a subject with reasonable color contrast to the surrounding pixels is to use the information from one of the channels to create a mask and then to load this mask as a selection.

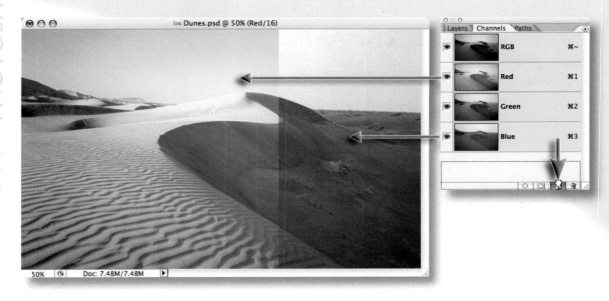

Click on each individual channel to see which channel offers the best contrast and then duplicate this channel by dragging it to the 'New Channel' icon.

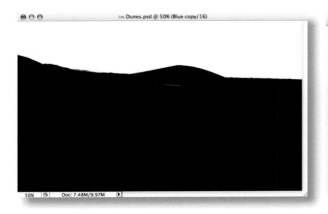

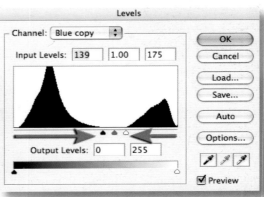

Apply a Levels adjustment to the duplicate channel to increase the contrast of the mask. Slide the shadow, midtone and highlight sliders until the required mask is achieved. The mask may still not be perfect but this can be modified using the painting tools.

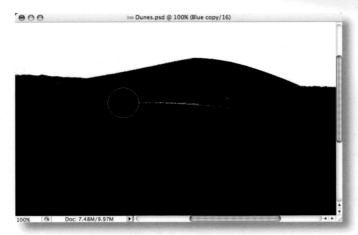

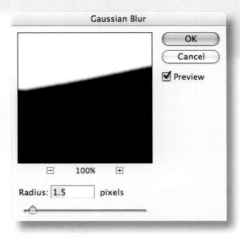

Select the default settings for the foreground and background colors in the Tools palette, choose a paintbrush, set the opacity to 100% in the Options bar and then paint to perfect the mask. Zoom in to make sure there are no holes in the mask before moving on. To soften the edge of the mask, apply a small amount of Gaussian Blur.

Note > Switch on the master channel visibility or Shift-click the RGB master to view the channel copy as a mask together with the RGB image. This will give you a preview so that you can see how much blur to apply and if further modifications are required.

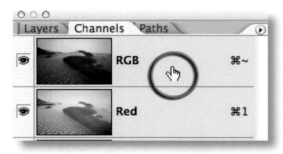

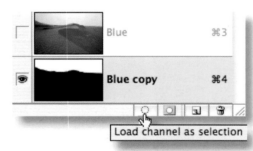

Click on the active duplicate channel or drag it to the 'Load channel as selection' icon. Click on the RGB master before returning to the Layers palette.

Channel masking may at first seem a little complex but it is surprisingly quick when the technique has been used a few times. This technique is very useful for photographers shooting products for catalogs and web sites. A small amount of color contrast between the subject and background is all that is required to make a quick and effective mask.

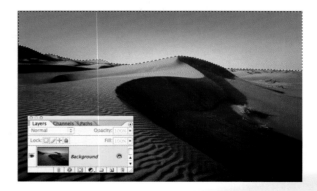

Extract filter

Photoshop's 'Extract filter' can be an indispensable tool for montage work. With a suitable edge the Extract filter works well, e.g. a sharp outline on a contrasting background. If the final montage is to be effective the new background also needs to complement the tone and color of the subject's edge pixels. Many of the problems encountered when trying to achieve effective and sophisticated extractions usually lie with the images chosen and not with the Extract filter itself. As soon as the edge is difficult for the filter to detect the results are often less than convincing. If unsuitable images are chosen a lot of patching, rebuilding or manual removal of the unwanted background pixels may follow.

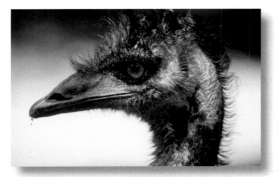 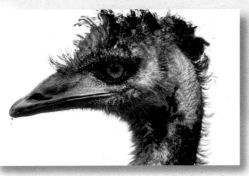

The filter has difficulty extracting a background where the edge contrast is low

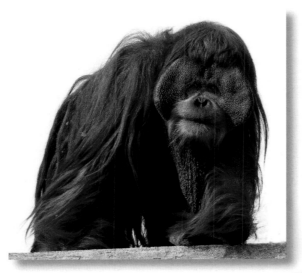 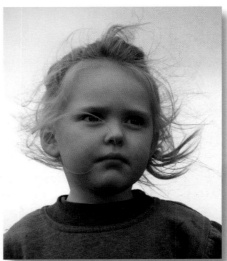

Simple and challenging images for extraction

A studio backdrop that is lit independently of the subject will make extraction easier. You may, however, not have access to a studio where the background illumination and content can be controlled so effectively. When on location the photographer can choose the least busy background and use shallow depth of field (wide aperture on a telephoto lens) to help delineate the edge of the subject clearly to help the Extract filter perform its task.

PHOTOSHOP CS2 >>>

The Extract filter is about as magic as the wand! It helps if the edge of the subject you are trying to isolate is clearly defined by an edge. The strength of the filter is its ability to select complex outlines with soft edges.

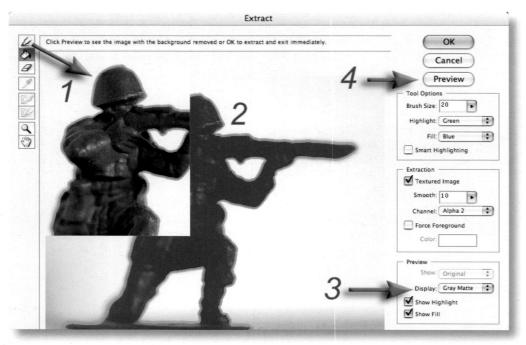

Duplicate the layer you are working before starting the extraction process as the extraction process removes rather than hides the pixels surplus to requirements. To start the process select the layer and go to 'Filter > Extract'. The next step is to use the Edge Highlighter Tool to define the edge of transition. The highlighter outline should be wider than the soft edge. The highlighter can extend broadly into the background but must not extend into the subject for any great distance. Smart highlighting adjusts the width as it goes. Alternatively an outline can be loaded from an alpha channel (first create a new channel, then stroke the selection and finally invert the channel).

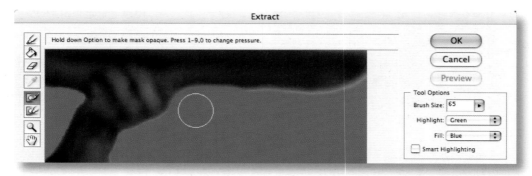

Unless the edge is sharp and clearly defined it is preferable to move to 'Preview' rather than hit 'OK'. From the Preview menu choose a suitable 'matte' color against which to view your extracted subject. The 'Cleanup' and 'Edge Touchup' Tools can help to perfect the edges.

essential skills >>>

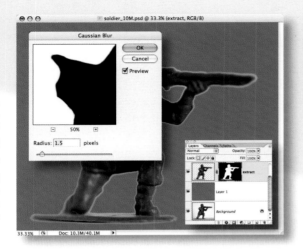
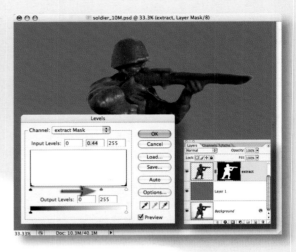

If the extraction is not perfect there are still a few options. Command/Ctrl-click the layer thumbnail to load the pixels on the layer as a selection and then click on the 'Add layer mask' icon. The mask can either be softened by applying the Gaussian Blur filter or shrunk using the 'Levels' adjustment feature (Image > Adjustments > Levels) to exclude any remaining halo present.

Overview

These selection techniques will never replace the need for the Lasso or Pen Tool completely but they do provide an insight into the range of tools that can be used to approach the business of separation. As knowledge of the tools available increases, the choice of background becomes an important issue for photographers who 'create' rather than 'capture' images for digital editing. And if you still can't grow to love the Lasso consider burying the mouse in the garden and invest in a 'graphics tablet'!

Selection shortcuts

Add to selection	Hold ⇧ key and select again
Subtract from selection	Hold ⌥/Alt key and select again
Copy	⌘/Ctrl + C
Cut	⌘/Ctrl + C
Paste	⌘/Ctrl + V
Paste Into	⌘/Ctrl ⇧ + V
Free Transform	⌘/Ctrl + T
Distort image in Free Transform	Hold ⌘ key + Move handle
Feather	⌘/Ctrl ⌥/Alt + D
Select All	⌘/Ctrl + A
Deselect	⌘/Ctrl + D
Inverse selection	⌘/Ctrl + I
Edit in Quick Mask mode	Q

Selections from paths

The Pen Tool is often used in the creation of sophisiticated smooth-edged selections, but strictly speaking it is not one of the selection tools. The Pen Tool creates vector paths instead of selections; these, however, can be converted into selections that in turn can be used to extract or mask groups of pixels. The Pen Tool has an unfortunate reputation – neglected by most, considered an awkward tool by those who have made just a passing acquaintance, and revered by just a select few who have taken a little time to get to know 'the one who sits next to Mr Blobby' (custom shape icon) in the Tools palette. Who exactly is this little fellow with the 'ye olde' ink nib icon and the awkward working persona? The Pen Tool was drafted into Photoshop from Adobe Illustrator. Although graphic designers are quite adept at using this tool, many Photographers the world over have been furiously waving magic wands and magnetic lassos at the megapixel army and putting graphics tablets on their shopping lists each year in an attempt to avoid recognizing the contribution that this unique tool has to offer.

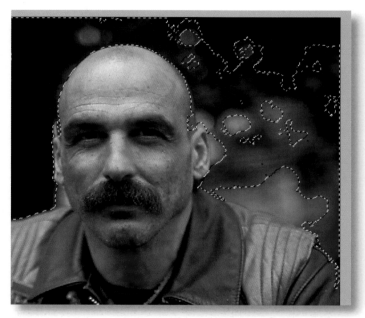 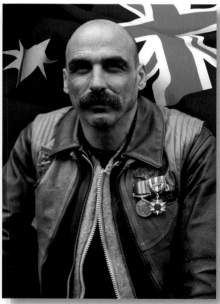

Not everything you can see with your eye can be selected easily with a selection technique based on color or tonal values. The resulting ragged selections can be fixed in Quick Mask mode, but sometimes not without a great deal of effort. The question then comes down to 'how much effort am I prepared to apply, and for how long?' Its about this time that many image-editors decide to better acquaint themselves with the Pen Tool. Mastering the Pen Tool in order to harness a selection prowess known to few mortals is not something you can do in a hurry – it falls into a certain skill acquisition category, along with such things as teaching a puppy not to pee in the house, called time-based reward, i.e. investing your time over a short period of time will pay you dividends over a longer period of time. The creation of silky smooth curvaceous lines (called paths) that can then be converted into staggeringly smooth curvaceous selections makes the effort of learning the Pen Tool all worthwhile.

Basic drawing skills

Vector lines and shapes are constructed from geographical markers (anchor points) connected by lines or curves. Many photographers have looked with curiosity at the vector tools in Photoshop's Tools palette for years but have dismissed them as 'not for me'. The reason for this is that drawing vector lines with the Pen Tool for the inexperienced image-editor is like reversing with a trailer for the inexperienced driver. It takes practice, and the practice can be initially frustrating.

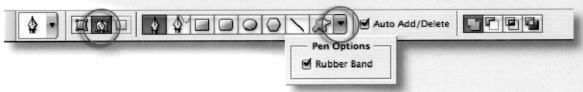

The pen can multi-task (just like most women and very few men that I know). The pen can draw a vector shape whilst filling it with a color and applying a layer style – all at the same time. Although tempting, this has nothing to do with selecting a bald man's head, so we must be sure to disarm this charming little function. We can also use the training wheels, otherwise known as the 'Rubber Band' option, by clicking on the menu options next to 'Mr Blobby'.

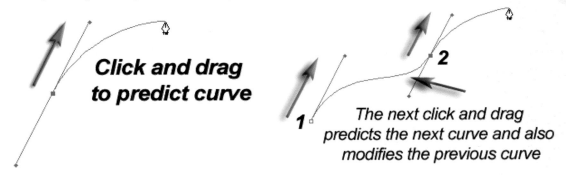

Click and drag to predict curve

1 **2** *The next click and drag predicts the next curve and also modifies the previous curve*

Basics Step 1 – Go to 'File > New' and create a new blank document. Choose 'White' as the 'Background Contents'. Size is not really important (no really – in this instance anything that can be zoomed to fill the screen will serve your purpose). Click on the Pen Tool (double-check the 'Paths' option, rather than the 'Shape layers' option, is selected in the Options bar) and then click and drag (hold down the mouse clicker as you drag your mouse) in the direction illustrated above. The little black square in the center of the radiating lines is called an anchor point. The lines extending either side of this anchor point are called direction lines, with a direction point on either end, and that thing waving around (courtesy of the Rubber Band option) is about to become the path with your very next click of the mouse.

Basics Step 2 – Make a second click and drag in the same direction. Notice how the dragging action modifies the shape of the previous curved line. Go the 'Edit' menu and select 'Undo'. Try clicking a second time and dragging in a different direction. Undo a third time and this time drag the direction point a different distance from the anchor point. The thing you must take with you from this second step is that a curve (sometimes referred to as a Bézier curve) is both a product of the relative position of the two anchor points either side of the curve, and the direction and length of the two direction lines (the distance and direction of the dragging action).

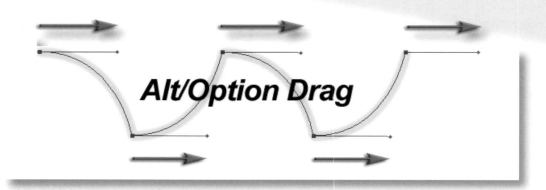

Basics Step 3 – Scenario one: Let us imagine that the first click and drag action has resulted in a perfect curve, the second dragging action is not required to perfect the curve but instead upsets the shape of this perfect curve – so how do we stop this from happening? Answer: Hold down the Alt key (PC) or Option key (Mac) and then drag away from the second anchor point to predict the shape of the next curve. This use of the Alt/Option key cancels the first direction line that would otherwise influence the previous curve.

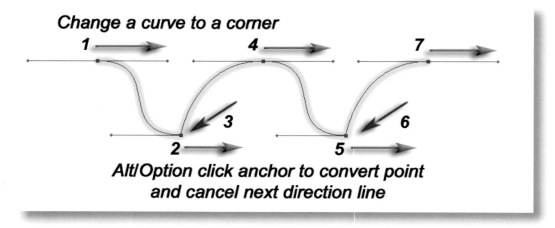

Scenario two: Let us imagine that we have created the first perfect curve using two normal click and drag actions (no use of a modifier key). The direction lines that are perfecting the first curve are, however, unsuitable for the next curve – so how do we draw the next curve whilst preserving the appearance of the first curve? Answer: The last anchor point can be clicked whilst holding down the Alt/Option key. This action converts the smooth anchor point to a corner anchor point, deleting the second direction line. The next curved shape can then be created without the interference of an inappropriate direction line.

Note > The information that you need to take from this third step is that sometimes direction lines can upset adjacent curves. The technique of cancelling one of the direction lines using a modifier key makes a series of perfect curves possible. These two techniques are especially useful for converting smooth points into corner points on a path.

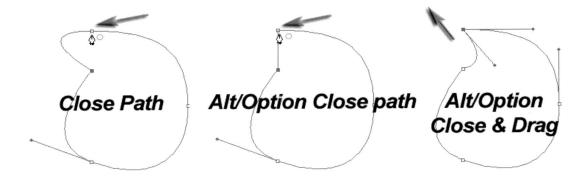

Alt/Option Drag handle to modify previous or next curve

Basics Step 4 – Just a few more steps and we can go out to play. It is possible to change direction quickly on a path without cancelling a direction line. It is possible to alter the position of a direction line by moving the direction point (at the end of the line) independently of the direction line on the other side of the anchor point. To achieve this simply position the mouse cursor over the direction point, and again using the Alt/Option key, click and drag the direction point to a new position.

Close Path   **Alt/Option Close path**   **Alt/Option Close & Drag**

Basics Step 5 – If this path is going to be useful as a selection, it is important to return to the start point. Clicking on the start point will close the path. As you move the cursor over the start point the Pen Tool will be accompanied by a small circle to indicate that closure is about to occur. You will also notice that the final curve is influenced by the first direction line of the starting anchor point. Hold down the Alt/Option key when closing the path to cancel this first direction line. Alternatively hold down the Alt/Option key and drag a new direction line to perfect the final curve.

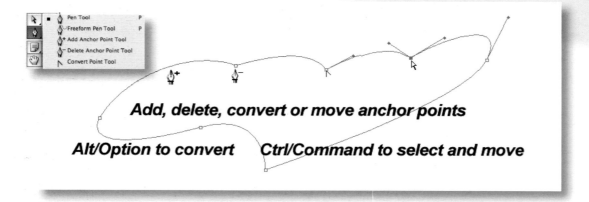

Basics Step 6 – When a path has been closed it is possible to add, delete, convert or move any point. Although these additional tools are available in the Tools palette they can all be accessed without moving your mouse away from the path in progress. If the Auto Add/Delete box has been checked in the Options bar you simply have to move the Pen Tool to a section of the path and click to add an additional point (the pen cursor sprouts a plus symbol). If the Pen Tool is moved over an existing anchor point you can simply click to delete it. Holding down the Ctrl key (PC) or Command Key (Mac) will enable you to access the Direct Selection Tool (this normally lives behind the Path Selection Tool). The Direct Selection Tool has a white arrow icon and can select and move a single anchor point (click and drag) or multiple points (by holding down the Shift key and clicking on subsequent points). The Path Selection Tool has to be selected from the Tools palette and is able to select the entire path.

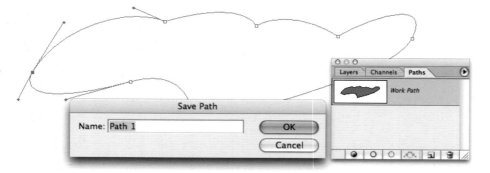

Basics Step 7 – The final step in the creation of a Path is to save it. All Paths, even Work Paths, are saved with the image file (PSD, PDF, PSB, JPEG or TIFF). If, however, a Work Path is not active (such as when the file is closed and re-opened) and then the Pen Tool is inadvertently used to draw a new Path, any previous Work Path that was not saved is deleted.

Click on the Paths palette tab and then double-click the Work Path. This will bring up the option to save and name the Work Path and ensure that it cannot be deleted accidentally. To start editing an existing Path click on the path in the Paths palette and then choose either the Direct Selection Tool or the Pen Tool in the Tools palette. Click near the Path with the Direct Selection Tool to view the handles and the Path.

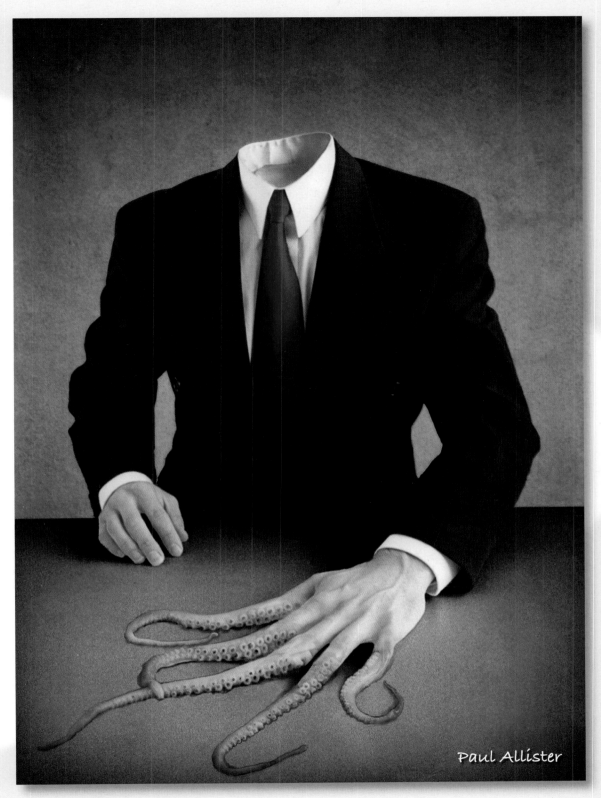

Paul Allister

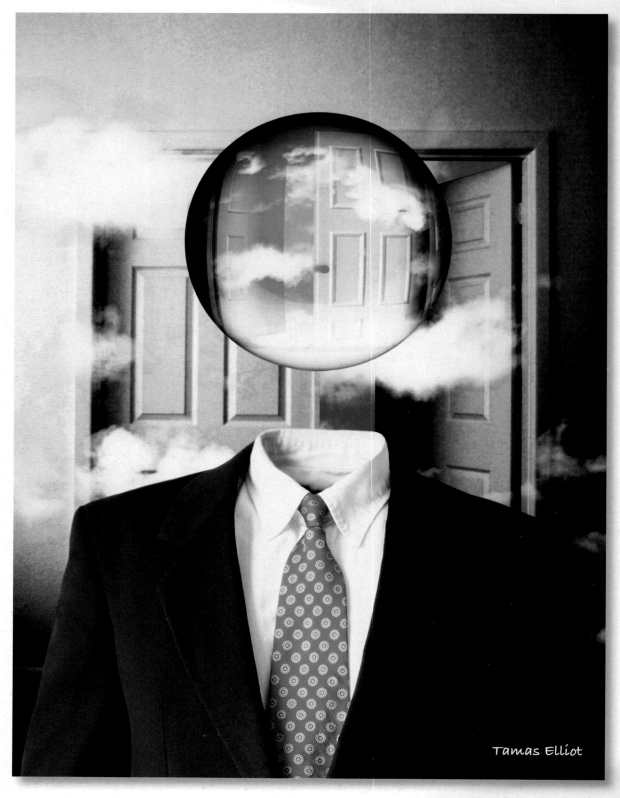

Tamas Elliot

layer blends

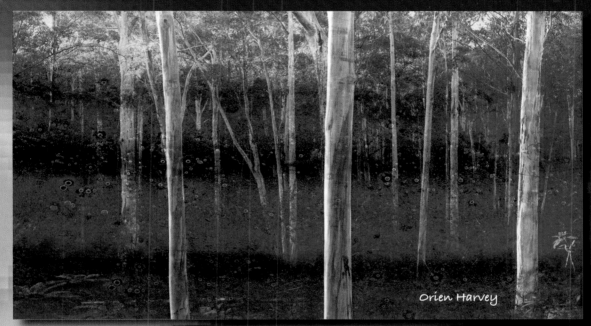

Orien Harvey

essential skills

~ Learn the practical applications of layer blend modes for image retouching and creative montage work.

~ Develop skills using the the following techniques:
- blend modes
- layers and channels
- layer masks.

Introduction

When an image, or part of an image, is placed on a separate layer above the background, creative decisions can be made as to how these layers interact with each other. Reducing the opacity of the top layer allows the underlying information to show through, but Photoshop has many other ways of mixing, combining or 'blending' the pixel values on different layers to achieve different visual outcomes. The different methods used by Photoshop to compare and adjust the hue, saturation and brightness of the pixels on the different layers are called 'blend modes'. Blend modes can be assigned to the painting tools from the Options bar but they are more commonly assigned to an entire layer when editing a multi-layered document. The layer blend modes are accessed from the 'blending mode' pull-down menu in the top left-hand corner of the Layers palette.

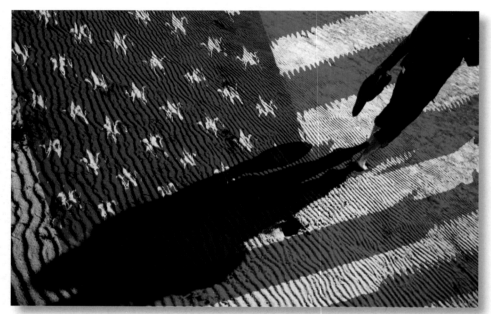

Orien Harvey

The major groupings

The blend modes are arranged in family groups of related effects or variations on a theme. Many users simply sample all the different blend modes until they achieve the effect they are looking for. This, however, can be a time-consuming operation and a little more understanding of what is actually happening can ease the task of choosing an appropriate blend mode for the job in hand. A few of the blend modes are commonly used in the routine compositing tasks, whilst others have very limited or specialized uses only. The five main groups of blend modes after Normal and Dissolve that are more commonly used for image-editing and montage work are:

- Darken
- Lighten
- Overlay
- Difference
- Hue.

Opacity and Dissolve

At 100% opacity the pixels on the top layer obscure the pixels underneath. As the opacity is reduced the pixels underneath become visible. The Dissolve blend mode only becomes apparent when the opacity of the layer is reduced. Random pixels are made transparent on the layer rather than reducing the transparency of all the pixels. The effect is very different to the reduced opacity of the 'Normal' blend mode and has commercial applications as a transition for fading one image into another, but the effect has very limited commercial applications for compositing and photomontage of stills image work.

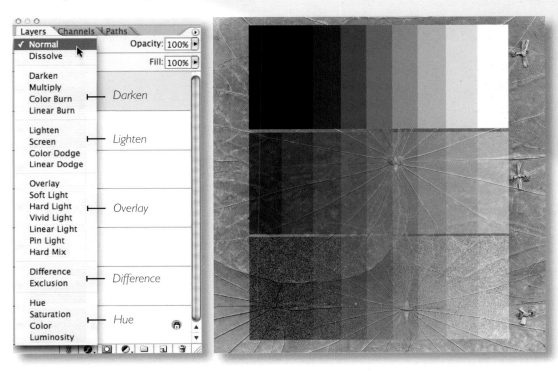

The groups of blend modes are listed using the name of the dominant effect. A step wedge is then used to demonstrate 'Normal' at 100% and 50% opacity and the 'Dissolve' blend mode with the layer set to 50% opacity

The 'Opacity' control for each layer, although not strictly considered as a blend mode, is an important element of any composite work. Some of the blend modes are quite pronounced or 'aggressive' in their resulting effect if applied at 100% opacity and could be overlooked if the user does not experiment with the combined effects of opacity and blend mode together.

SHORTCUTS

The blend modes can be applied to layers using keyboard shortcuts. Hold down the Shift key and press the '+' key to move down the list or the '−' key to move up the list. Alternatively you can press the Alt/Option key and the Shift key and key in the letter code for a particular blend mode. If a painting tool is selected the blend mode is applied to the painting tool instead of the layer. See Keyboard Shortcuts for more information.

The 'Darken' group

It's not too hard to figure out what this group of blend modes have in common. Although Darken leads the grouping, Multiply is perhaps the most used blend mode in the group.

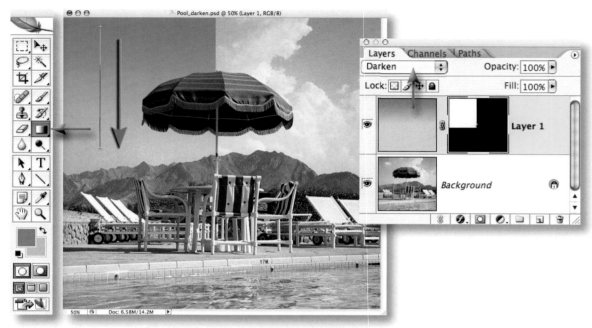

The Darken mode can be used to replace existing highlights whilst ignoring darker tones

Darken

The 'Darken' blend mode chooses pixels from either the blend layer or underlying layers to display at 100% opacity depending on their brightness value. Any underlying tone that is darker than the blend color remains unaffected by the blend mode, and any color that is lighter than the blend color is replaced rather than multiplied with the blend color. This blend mode is usually restricted to pasting a carefully chosen tone into the highlights of an image.

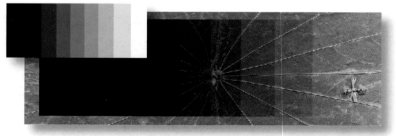

Multiply is a useful blend mode when overall darkening is required

Multiply

The 'Multiply' blend mode belongs to the 'Darken' family grouping. The brightness values of the pixels on the blend layer and underlying layer are multiplied to create darker tones. Only values that are multiplied with white (level 255) stay the same.

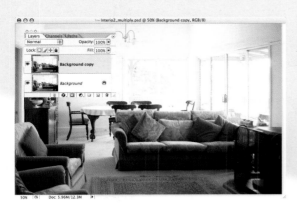 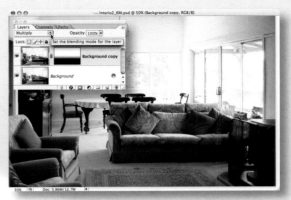

The Multiply blend mode is used to darken the top half of the image

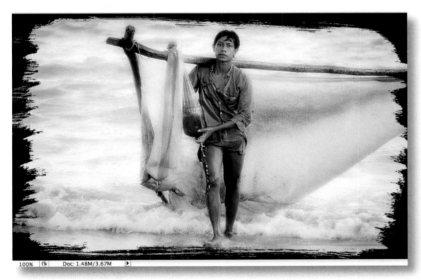 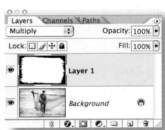

The Multiply blend mode is used to apply a dark edge to the image

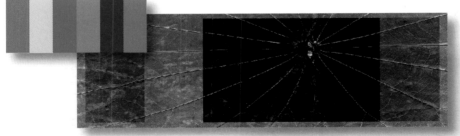

Color Burn

Color Burn and Linear Burn

The image is darkened to reflect the blend color. Color Burn increases the underlying contrast to do this whilst Linear Burn decreases the underlying brightness. This is a difficult blend mode to find a use for at 100% opacity. Saturation can become excessive and overall brightness, now heavily influenced by the underlying color, can 'fill in' (become black).

The 'Lighten' group

Everything that was mentioned with the Darken group is now reversed for this group of blend modes. The 'Screen' blend mode is often considered the firm favorite of this group.

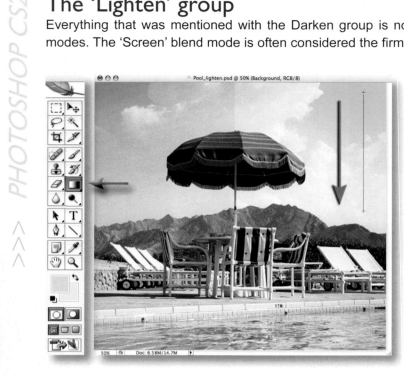

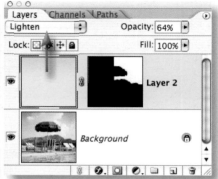

The 'Lighten' mode is used to replace the original dark sky color with a lighter color sampled from the pool. Note how the layer mask is used to protect the umbrella from the blend color

Lighten

The 'Lighten' blend mode chooses pixels from either the blend layer or underlying layers to display at 100% opacity depending on their brightness value. Any underlying tone that is lighter than the blend color remains unaffected by the blend mode, and any color that is darker than the blend color is replaced rather than multiplied with the blend color. This blend mode is usually restricted to blending a carefully chosen tone into the midtones or shadows of an image. This technique can be useful for replacing dark colored dust and scratches from light areas of continuous tone.

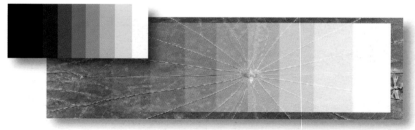

Screen is useful when overall lightening is required

Screen

The 'Screen' blend mode belongs to the 'Lighten' family grouping. The 'inverse' brightness values of the pixels on the blend layer and underlying layers are multiplied to create lighter tones (a brightness value of 80% is multiplied as if it was a value of 20%). Only values that are screened with black (level 0) stay the same.

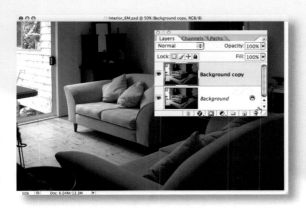 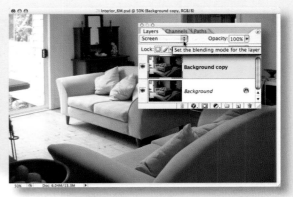

A background layer is duplicated and a Screen blend mode is applied to lighten all levels

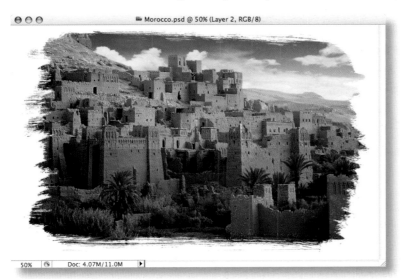 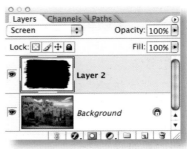

The Screen mode is used to apply a white border around an image

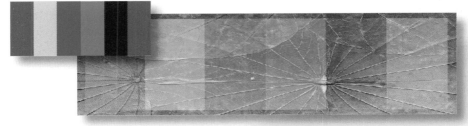

Color Dodge

Color Dodge and Linear Dodge

The image is lightened to reflect the blend color. Color Dodge decreases the underlying contrast to do this whilst Linear Dodge increases the underlying brightness. This again is a difficult blend mode to find a use for at 100% opacity. Saturation can become excessive and overall brightness, heavily influenced by the underlying color, can blow out (become white).

The 'Overlay' group

This is perhaps the most useful group of blend modes for photomontage work.

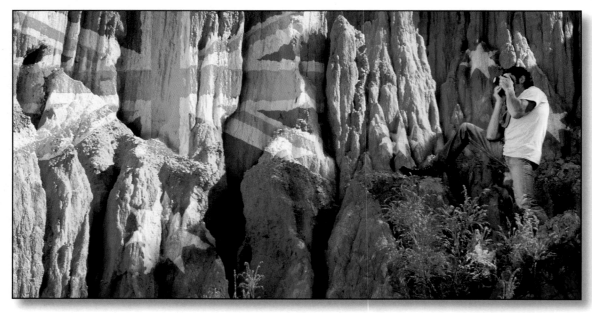

Applying the blend mode 'Overlay' to a texture or pattern layer will create an image where the form appears to be modeling the texture. Both the highlights and shadows of the underlying form are respected

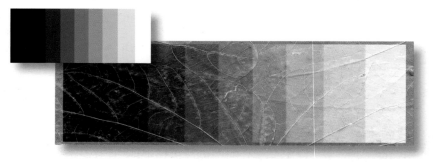

The 'Overlay' blend mode is useful for overlaying textures over 3D form

Overlay

The Overlay blend mode uses a combination of the Multiply and Screen blend modes whilst preserving the highlight and shadow tones of the underlying image. The Overlay mode multiplies or screens the colors, depending on whether the base color is darker or lighter than a midtone. The effect is extremely useful when overlaying a texture or color over a form modeled by light and shade. Excessive increases in saturation may become evident when overlaying white and black. The 'Soft' and 'Hard Light' blend modes produce variations on this overlay theme.

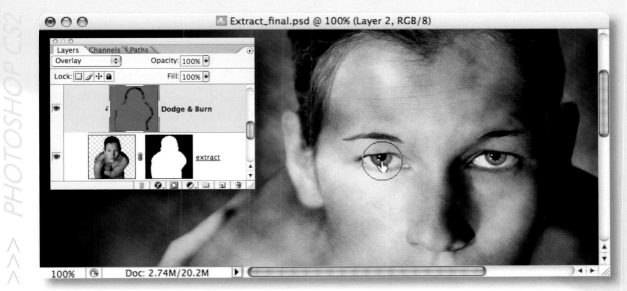

A 50% Gray layer set to Overlay mode is used to dodge and burn the underlying image

Note> A layer filled with 50% Gray is invisible in Overlay mode and, as a result, is commonly used as a 'non-destructive' dodging and burning layer.

Soft and Hard Light – variations on a theme

The Soft and Hard Light blend modes are variations on the 'Overlay' theme. Photoshop describes the difference in terms of lighting (diffused or harsh spotlight). If the Overlay blend mode is causing highlights or shadows to become overly bright or dark then the Soft Light blend mode will often resolve the problem. The Hard Light on the other hand increases the contrast – but care must be taken when choosing this option as blending dark or light tones can tip the underlying tones to black (level 0) or white (255).

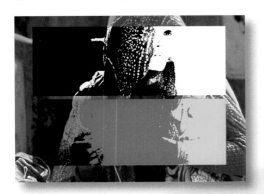 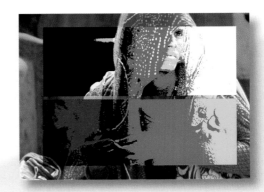

Hard Mix

The Hard Mix blend mode was new to Photoshop CS. It has a threshold effect when blending desaturated tones into a desaturated layer and a color posterization effect when blending saturated or desaturated tones with a color layer.

153

PHOTOSHOP CS2 >>>

Blend modes for tinting and toning

The Hue and Color blend modes are predominantly used for toning or tinting images whilst the Saturation blend mode offers more limited applications. Photoshop 8 also offers photo filters.

Hue

The 'Hue' blend mode modifies the image by using the hue value of the blend layer and the saturation value of the underlying layer. As a result the blend layer is invisible if you apply this blend mode to a fully desaturated image. Opacity levels of the blend layer can be explored to achieve the desired outcome.

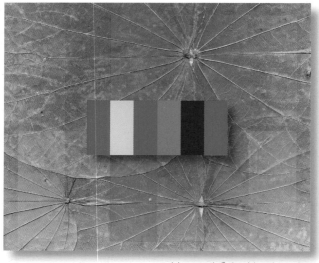

Color

The 'Color' blend mode is useful for toning desaturated or tinting colored images. The brightness value of the base color is blended with the hue and saturation of the blend color.

Hue and Color blend modes

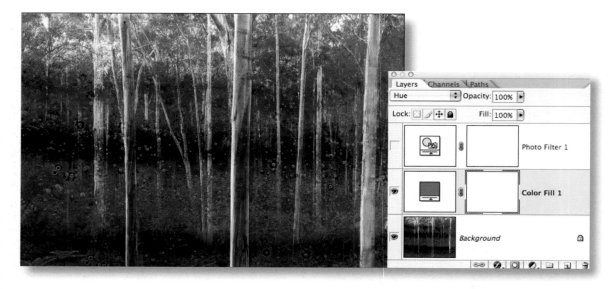

>>> essential skills >>>

Note > Color fills can be used to tint or tone images by setting them to Hue or Color mode. Photoshop's Photo Filter layers (introduced with CS) perform a similar task but without the need to set the layer to the Hue or Color mode.

Saturation

The brightness or 'luminance' of the underlying pixels is retained but the saturation is replaced with that of the blend layer.

Note > This blend mode has limited uses for traditional toning effects but can be used to locally desaturate colored images. To work with this blend mode try creating a new empty layer. Then either fill a selection with any desaturated tone or paint with black or white at a reduced opacity to gradually remove the color from the underlying image.

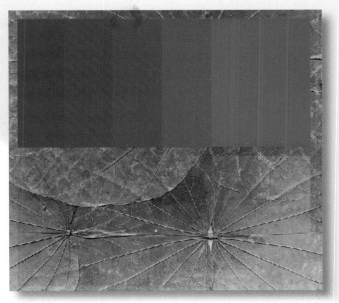

The Saturation blend mode

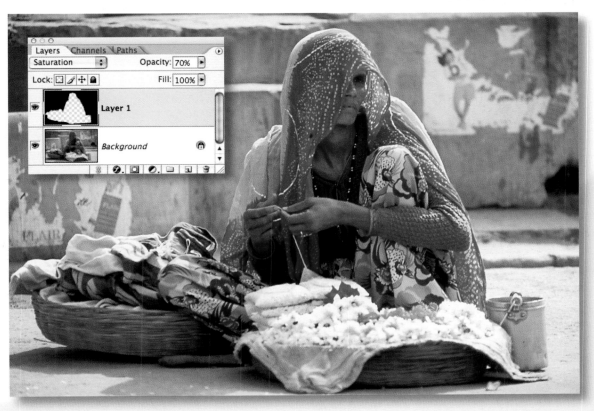

A Saturation layer is used to desaturate the underlying image

Luminosity

The 'Luminosity' blend mode creates the same result as the 'Color' mode if the layers are reversed, i.e. the color layer is underneath. The luminosity values within an RGB image have a number of very useful applications. The luminosity values can be extracted from an RGB image (from the Channels palette) and saved as an alpha channel, used as a layer mask or pasted as an independent layer above the background layer.

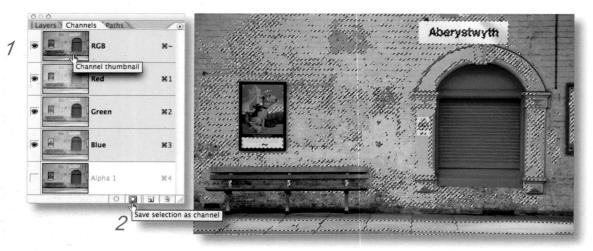

Creating a luminance channel

1. Command/Ctrl-click the master RGB channel to select the luminance values.
2. Click on the 'Save selection as channel' icon to create an alpha channel.

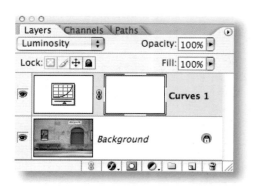

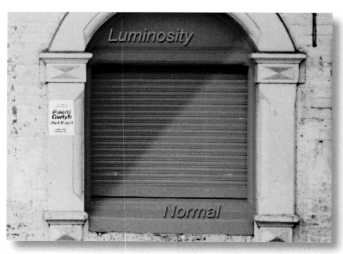

A Curves adjustment layer can be switched to Luminosity mode to eliminate shifts in saturation when contrast is increased. The example above demonstrates what happens when contrast is increased using a Curves layer in Luminance and Normal blend modes.

Difference and Exclusion

The Difference blend mode subtracts either the underlying color from the blend color or vice versa depending on which has the highest brightness value. A duplicated layer with a Difference blend applied will result in a totally black image. These blend modes can be useful for registering layers with the same content if they are accidentally put out of alignment during image editing (when realigned the layer pixels can be locked). The Exclusion blend mode works in the same way except where the blend color is white. In this instance the underlying color is inverted.

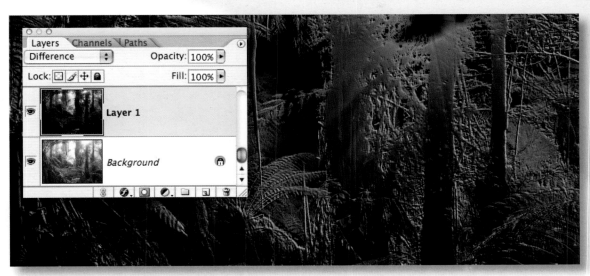

The Difference mode is used to align two images

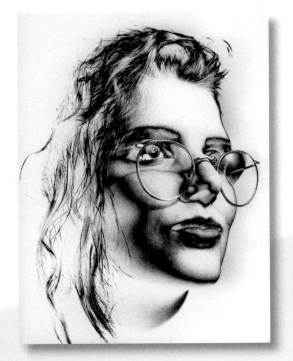

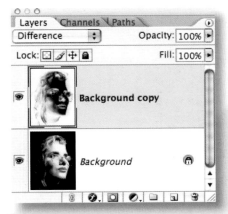

The Difference mode can also be used to create a quick 'sabattier' effect with a grayscale image. To create this effect duplicate the layer and go to Image > Adjustments > Invert. Apply the Difference blend mode to this copy layer.

157

Creating a simple blend

Blending two images in the computer is similar to creating a double exposure in the camera or sandwiching negatives in the darkroom. Photoshop allows a greater degree of control over the final outcome. This is achieved by controlling the specific blend mode, position and opacity of each layer. The use of '**layer masks**' can shield any area of the image that needs to be protected from the blend mode. The blending technique enables the texture or pattern from one image to be modeled by the form of a selected subject in another image (see Montage Projects > Projects 2 and 5).

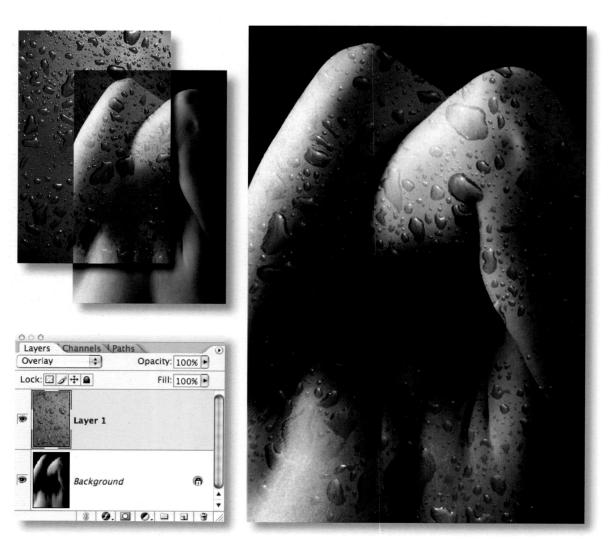

Note > In the montage above the image of the body has been blended with an image of raindrops on a car bonnet. The texture blended takes on the shadows and highlights of the underlying form but does not wrap itself around the contours or shape of the three-dimensional form.

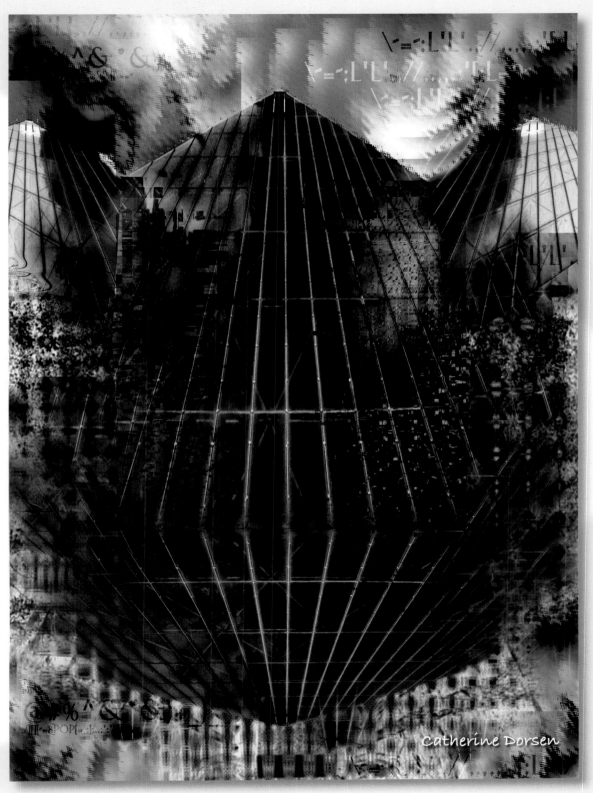

Catherine Dorsen

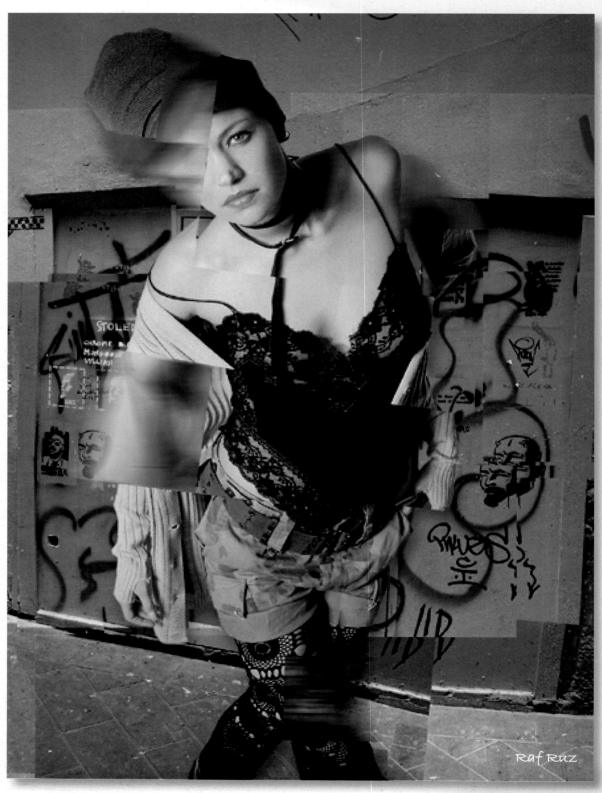

Raf Ruz

filters

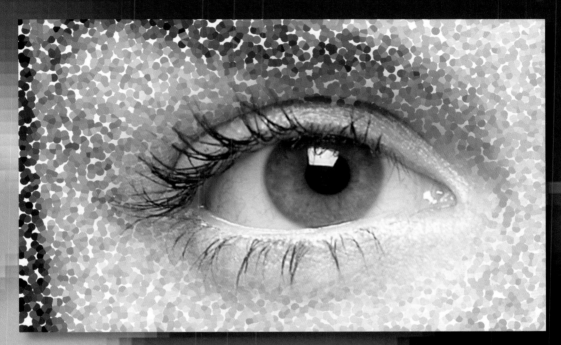

essential skills

~ Apply filter effects to a picture.

~ Use the Filter Gallery feature to apply several filters cumulatively.

~ Using filters with text and shape layers.

~ Filtering a section of a picture.

~ Painting with a filter effect.

~ Installing and using third party filters.

~ The great filter roundup.

~ The ten commandments for filter usage.

~ Filter DIY.

Filtering in Photoshop

Okay, hands up all of you who have a range of 'Cokin' filters in your camera kit bag. If your arm is raised in timid salute then you are not alone, I too admit to buying a few of these pieces of colored gelatine in an attempt to add drama and interest to my images. Ranging from the multi-image split prism to the keyhole mask for that all-important wedding shot, these photographic 'must haves' seem to be less popular now than they were in the eighties.

It's not that these handy 'end of lens add-ons' are essentially bad, it's just that I think that we have all seen too many hideous examples of their use to risk adding our own images to this infamous group. In fairness though, I still would not leave home without a good set of color correction filters, and I am sure that my landscape colleagues would argue strongly for the skillful use graduated filters to add theater to distant vistas.

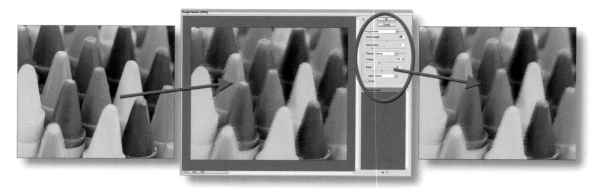

As much as anything the filter's decline can be attributed to changes in visual fashion and, just as we thought that 'flares' would never return to the streets, digital effects filters of the seventies have also made a comeback. This time they don't adorn the end of our lenses but are almost hidden from the unsuspecting user, sometimes in their hundreds, underneath the Filter menu of Photoshop.

I think just the association with days past and images best forgotten has caused most of us to overlook, no let's be honest, run away from, using any of the myriad of filters that are available. These memories coupled with a host of 'garish' and 'look at this effect' type examples in the weekly computing magazines have overshadowed the creative options available to any image-maker with the careful use of the digital filter.

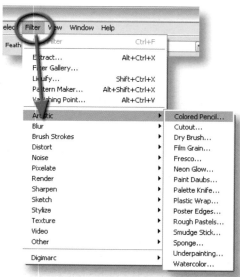

To encourage you to get started I have included a variety of examples from the range that comes free with Photoshop. I have not shown Gaussian Blur or all the sharpening filters as most people seem to have overcome their filter phobia and made use of these to enhance their imagery, but I have tried to sample a variety that, to date, you might not have considered using.

If you are unimpressed by the results of your first digital filter foray, try changing some of the variables. An effect that might seem outlandish at first glance could become usable after some simple adjustments of the in-built sliders contained in most filter dialog boxes.

The Filter Gallery

Most Photoshop filters can now be applied using the Filter Gallery feature. Designed to allow the user to apply several different filters to a single image it can also be used to apply the same filter several times. The dialog consists of a preview area, a collection of filters that can be used with the feature, a settings area with sliders to control the filter's effect and a list of filters that are currently being applied to the image. The gallery is faster and provides previews that are much

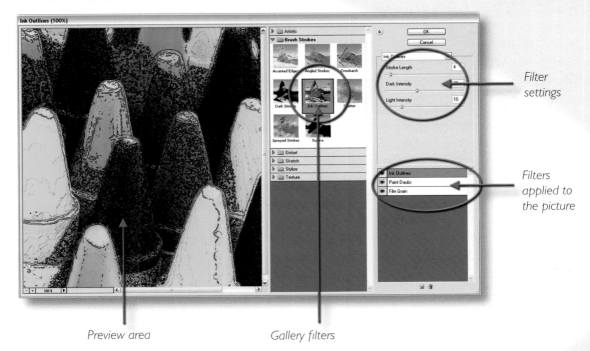

Filter settings

Filters applied to the picture

Preview area   *Gallery filters*

larger than those contained in individual filter dialogs. Filters are arranged in the sequence that they are applied. Filters can be moved to a different spot in the sequence by click-dragging up or down the stack. Click the 'eye' icon to hide the effect of the selected filter from preview. Filters can be deleted from the list by dragging them to the dustbin icon at the bottom of the dialog.

Most of the filters that can't be used with the Filter Gallery feature are either applied directly to the picture with no user settings or make use of a filter preview and settings dialog specific to that particular filter, and they generally cannot be used on 16-bit images.

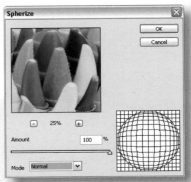

The Spherize filter does not work with the Filter Gallery but has its own preview and settings dialog

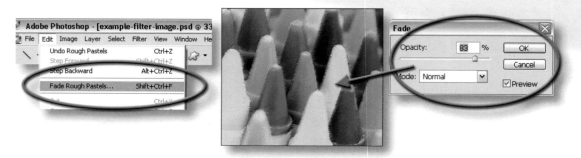

Fade Filter command

The opacity, or strength, of the filter effect can be controlled by selecting the Edit > Fade command when selected directly after the filter is applied. With a value of 0% the filter changes are not applied at all, whereas a setting of 100% will apply the changes fully. As well as controlling opacity the Fade dialog also provides the option to select a different blend mode for the filter changes.

Improving filter performance

A lot of filters make changes to the majority of the pixels in a picture. This level of activity can take considerable time, especially when working with high resolution pictures or underpowered computers. Use the following tips to increase the performance of applying such filters:

~   Free up memory by using the Edit > Purge command before filtering.
~   Allocate more memory to Photoshop via the Edit > Preferences > Memory and Image Cache option before filtering.
~   Try out the filter effect on a small selection before applying the filter to the whole picture.
~   Apply the filter to individual channels separately rather than the composite image.

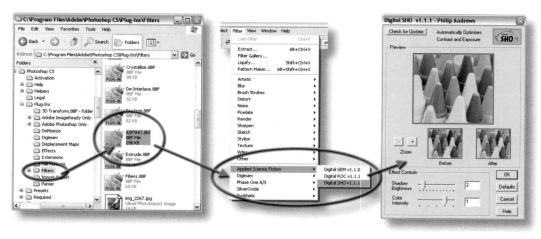

Third party filters are generally installed automatically into the Photoshop Plug-Ins > Filter folder. The program then attaches the extra plug-in to the bottom of the Filter menu the next time Photoshop is opened. Here the Applied Science Fiction Digital SHO filter is installed with other filters from the group's suite of enhancement filters

Installing and using third party filters

Ever since the early versions of Photoshop Adobe provided the opportunity for third party developers to create small pieces of specialist software that could plug into Photoshop. The modular format of the software means that Adobe and other software manufacturers can easily create extra filters that can be added to the program at any time. In fact, some of the plug-ins that have been released over the years have became so popular that Adobe themselves incorporated their functions into successive versions of Photoshop. This is how the Drop Shadow layer effect came into being.

Most plug-ins register themselves as extra options in the Filter menu where they can be accessed just like any other Photoshop feature. The Digital SHO filter from Applied Science Fiction is a great example of plug-in technology. Designed to automatically balance the contrast and enhance the shadow detail in digital photographs, when installed it becomes part of a suite of filters supplied by the company that are attached to the Filter menu. Other filters like those supplied by Pixel Genius Suite are automation filters and are therefore placed in the Automate folder.

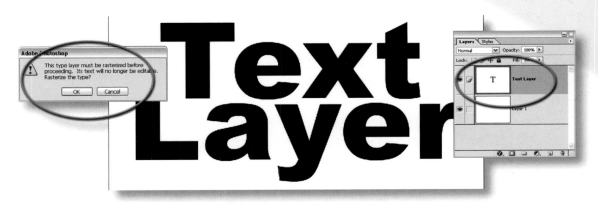

Filtering a shape or text (vector) layer

Filters only work with bitmap or pixel-based layers and pictures. As text, vector masks and custom shape layers are all created with vector graphics (non-pixel graphics), these layers need to be converted to bitmap (pixel based picture) before a filter effect can be applied to them. Photoshop uses a Rasterize function to make this conversion. Simply select the text or shape layer and then choose the Layer > Rasterize option.

Alternatively if you inadvertently try to filter a vector layer Photoshop will display a warning dialog that notifies you that the layer needs to be converted before filtering and offers to make the conversion before proceeding.

The great filter roundup

The filter examples on the next few pages are grouped according to the menu heading that they fall under in Photoshop. Effects of different filter options are compared using a common 'crayons' image and the associated dialog box for controlling these effects is displayed alongside. Not all the filters in each group are shown and specific examples are used for major filters such as Liquify, Extract, Lens Blur and the new Vanishing Point filter.

EXTRACT FILTER

The Extract filter was first included in Photoshop back in version 5.5 of the program. Here it was hidden away under the Image menu. Now the feature has pride of place in the first section of the Filter menu and provides users with a specialist selection tool that removes the background from the surrounds of an object.

The concept is simple: draw around the outside of the object you want to extract, making sure that the highlighter overlaps the edge between background and foreground and then fill in the middle. The program then analyses the edge section of the object using some clever fuzzy logic to determine what should be kept and what should be discarded, and 'Hey Presto' the background disappears.

The tool provides extracted objects faster than using the Lasso or Pen Tools as you don't need to be as accurate with your edge drawing, and it definitely handles wispy hair with greater finesse than most manual methods.

When previewing the results you can refine the edges left by the extraction process using the Cleanup and Edge Touchup Tools.

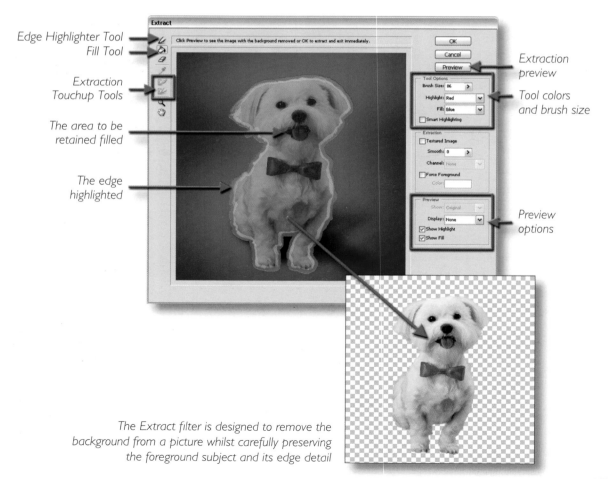

Edge Highlighter Tool
Fill Tool

Extraction
Touchup Tools

The area to be
retained filled

The edge
highlighted

Extraction
preview

Tool colors
and brush size

Preview
options

The Extract filter is designed to remove the background from a picture whilst carefully preserving the foreground subject and its edge detail

Usage summary:

1. Select the layer you wish to extract.
2. Choose Filter > Extract from the Photoshop menus.

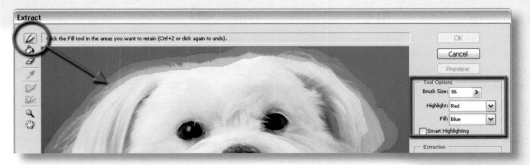

3. Use the Edge Highlighter Tool to draw around the edges of the object you wish to extract.

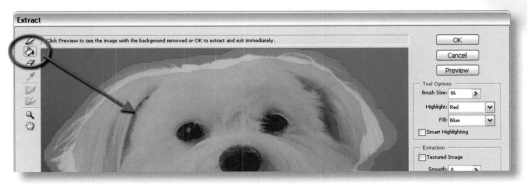

4. Select the Fill Tool and click inside the object to fill its interior.
5. Click Preview to check the extraction.
6. Click OK to apply the final extraction.

Extraction tips:

~ Make sure that the highlight slightly overlaps the object edges and its background.
~ For items such as hair, use a larger brush to encompass all strands.
~ Make sure that the highlight forms a complete and closed line around the object before filling.
~ Use the Smart Highlighting option to automatically locate the edge between foreground and background objects and to adjust the size of the highlighter to suit the clarity of the edge.

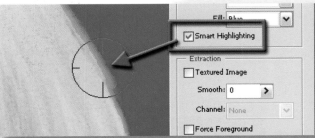

PHOTOSHOP CS2 >>>

LIQUIFY FILTER

The Liquify filter is a very powerful tool for warping and transforming your pictures. The feature contains its own sophisticated dialog box complete with a preview area and no less than ten different tools that can be used to twist, warp, push, pull and reflect your pictures with such ease that it is almost as if they were made of silly putty. In CS2 the filter now also works with 16-bit images. The effects obtained with this feature can be subtle or extreme depending on how the changes are applied. Stylus and tablet users have extra options and control based on pen pressure (in Photoshop only).

Liquify works by projecting the picture onto a grid or mesh. In an unaltered state, the grid is completely regular; when liquifying a photo the grid lines and spaces are intentionally distorted which in turn causes the picture to distort. As the mesh used to liquify a photo can be saved and reloaded, the distortion effects created in one picture can also be applied to an entirely different image.

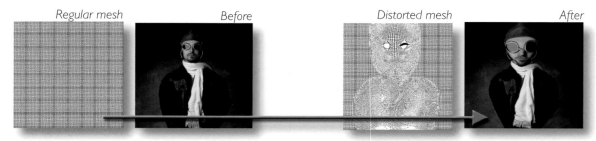

Regular mesh　　*Before*　　*Distorted mesh*　　*After*

The tools contained in the filter's toolbox are used to manipulate the underlying mesh and therefore distort the picture. Areas of the picture can be isolated from changes by applying a Freeze Mask to the picture part with the Freeze Mask Tool.

Whilst working inside the filter dialog it is possible to selectively reverse any changes made to the photo by applying the Reconstruct Tool. When applied to the surface of the image the distorted picture parts are gradually altered back to their original state (the mesh is returned to its regular form). Like the other tool options in the filter, the size of the area affected by the tool is based on the Brush Size setting and the strength of the change is determined by the Brush Pressure value.

essential skills >>>

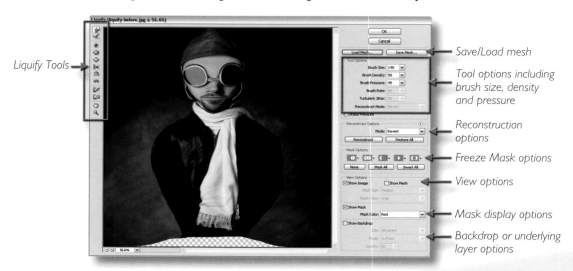

Liquify Tools

Save/Load mesh

Tool options including brush size, density and pressure

Reconstruction options

Freeze Mask options

View options

Mask display options

Backdrop or underlying layer options

Usage summary:

1. Open an example image and then the Liquify filter (Filter > Liquify). The dialog opens with a preview image in the center, tools to the left and tool options to the right. The Size, Pressure, Rate and Jitter options control the strength and look of the changes, whereas the individual tools alter the type of distortion applied. In order to create a caricature of the example picture we will exaggerate the perspective of the figure. Select the Pucker Tool and increase the size of the Brush to cover the entire bottom of the subject. Click to squeeze inwards the lower part of the subject.

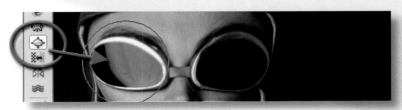

2. Now select the Bloat Tool and place it over the head, click to expand this area. If you are unhappy with any changes you can use the keyboard shortcuts for Edit > Undo (Ctrl + Z) to remove the last changes. Use a smaller brush size to bloat the goggles.

3. To finish the caricature switch to the Forward Warp Tool and push in the cheek areas. You can also use this tool to drag down the chin and lift the cheekbones.

4. The picture can be selectively restored at any point by choosing the Reconstruct Tool and painting over the changed area. Click OK to apply the distortion changes.

Liquify tools:

 Forward Warp Tool – is used to push pixels in the direction you drag the cursor across the picture surface.

 Reconstruct Tool – restores the picture and mesh back to its original appearance before any distortion was applied.

 Twirl Clockwise Tool – used for rotating pixels in a clockwise direction. Use with the Alt key to twirl in an anti-clockwise direction.

 Pucker Tool – is designed to suck or pinch the pixels towards the center of the brush.

 Bloat Tool – balloons the pixels away from the center of the brush towards the outside edges.

 Push Left Tool – is used to move the pixels to the left or to the right (Alt-drag) of the drag.

 Mirror Tool – is used to copy and reflect the pixels perpendicular to the direction of the stroke. Use Alt-drag to reflect the pixels in the opposite direction.

 Turbulence Tool – is used for creating clouds, fire and waves by smoothly scrambling pixels.

 Freeze Mask Tool – adds a mask that protects the masked area from liquify changes.

 Thaw Mask Tool – acts as an eraser for the Freeze Mask Tool.

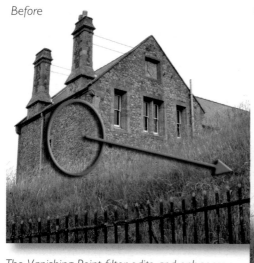

Before

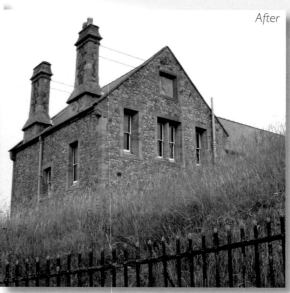

After

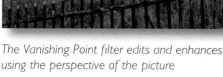

The Vanishing Point filter edits and enhances using the perspective of the picture

VANISHING POINT FILTER

The Vanishing Point filter is a new addition to the specialist filter line up that includes Extract, Lens Blur and Liquify. Like the others, the feature has its own dialog complete with preview image, toolbox and options bar. The filter allows the user to copy and paste and even Clone Stamp portions of a picture whilst maintaining the perspective of the original scene. Using the filter is a two-step process:

Step 1: Define perspective planes

To start, you must define the perspective planes in the photo. This is achieved by selecting the Create Plane Tool and marking each of the four corners of the rectangular-shaped feature that sits in perspective on the plane. A blue grid means that it is correct perspective, yellow that it is borderline, and red that it is mathematically impossible. In the example, the four corners of a window were used to define the plane of the building's front face. Next, a second plane that is linked to the first at an edge is dragged onto the surface of the left side wall.

Step 2: Copy and Paste or Stamp

With the planes established the Marquee Tool can be used to select image parts which can be copied, pasted and then dragged in perspective around an individual plane and even onto another linked plane. All the time the perspective of the copy will alter to suit the plane it is positioned on. The feature's Stamp Tool operates like a standard stamp tool except that the copied section is transformed to account for the perspective of the plane when it is applied to the base picture.

Usage summary:

1. Create a new layer above the image layer to be edited (Layer > New > Layer) and then choose the Vanishing Point filter from the Filter menu.

2. Select the Create Plane Tool and click on the top left corner of a rectangle that sits on the plane you wish to define. Locate and click on the top right, bottom right and bottom left corners. If the plane has been defined correctly the corner selection box will change to a perspective plane grid. In the example, the front face of the building was defined first.

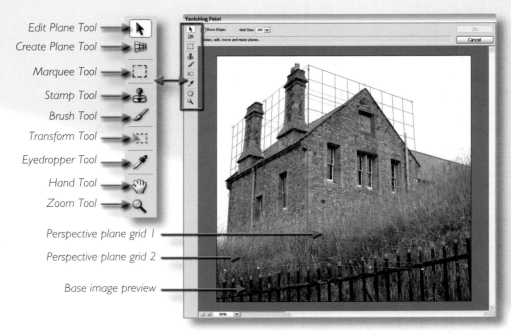

Edit Plane Tool
Create Plane Tool
Marquee Tool
Stamp Tool
Brush Tool
Transform Tool
Eyedropper Tool
Hand Tool
Zoom Tool

Perspective plane grid 1
Perspective plane grid 2

Base image preview

3. To create a second, linked, plane, Ctrl-click the middle handle of the existing plane and drag away from the edge. The left side of the building was defined using the second plane.

4. To copy the window from the building's front face, select the Marquee Tool first, set a small feather value to soften the edges and then outline the window to be copied. Choose Edit > Copy then Edit > Paste menu options. This pastes a copy of the window in the same position as the original marquee selection.

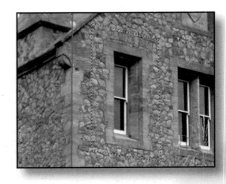

5. Click-drag the copy from the front face around to the side plane. The window (copied selection) will automatically snap to the new perspective plane and will reduce in size as it is moved further back in the plane. Position the window on the wall surface and choose Heal > Luminance from the Marquee options bar.

6. Press 'T' to enter the Transform mode and select Flip from the option bar to re-orientate the window so that the inside edge of the framework matches the other openings on the wall. Click OK to complete the process.

Vanishing Point tips:

~   Use the Edit Plane Tool to click and drag the corners of the grid if grid lines do not match up with the edges of the picture parts that are sitting on the perspective plane.

~   In order to copy and paste in full perspective the source plane and destination plane must be joined by a series of linked perspective planes.

~   Use the Heal option to help match tones of the copied parts and their new locations.

~   Grids can be output as layers, are 16-bit capable, text can be pasted into a grid and grids are auto-saved as part of the PSD file format.

ARTISTIC FILTERS

The artistic group of filters contains a varied assortment of effects ranging from those that simulate fine art techniques such as the Watercolor, Dry Brush, Colored Pencil and Palette Knife filters, to those that produce very graphic results such as Neon Glow and Cutout filters. One very unusual inclusion is the Plastic Wrap filter, which recreates the look of the picture being wrapped in a thin sheet of plastic.

All the filters in this group are applied via the Filter Gallery dialog.

Colored Pencil…
Cutout…
Dry Brush…
Film Grain…
Fresco…
Neon Glow…
Paint Daubs…
Palette Knife…
Plastic Wrap…
Poster Edges…
Rough Pastels…
Smudge Stick…
Sponge…
Underpainting…
Watercolor…

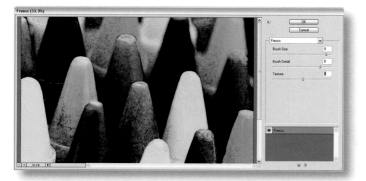

Fresco

Filter > Artistic > Fresco

Effect: Black edged painterly effect using splotches of color.

Variables: Brush Size, Brush Detail, Texture

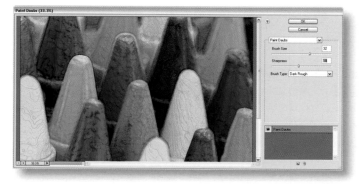

Paint Daubs

Filter > Artistic > Paint Daubs

Effect: Edges and tones defined with daubs of paint-like color.

Variables: Brush Size, Sharpness, Brush Type

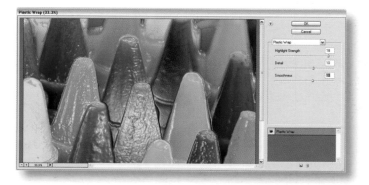

Plastic Wrap

Filter > Artistic > Plastic Wrap

Effect: Plastic-like wrap applied to the surface of the image area.

Variables: Highlight Strength, Detail, Smoothness

>>> PHOTOSHOP CS2

>>> essential skills >>>

BRUSH STROKES FILTERS

The filters in the Brush Strokes group generally add outlines and surface texture to the various picture elements in your image. The most familiar of these options is the Crosshatch filter, which recreates the picture's tone and color with a series of alternating and overlapping strokes. Controls usually include the stroke length, sharpness and strength and, where an edge is added, the width and intensity of this border.

All the filters in this group are applied via the Filter Gallery dialog.

Accented Edges...
Angled Strokes...
Crosshatch...
Dark Strokes...
Ink Outlines...
Spatter...
Sprayed Strokes...
Sumi-e...

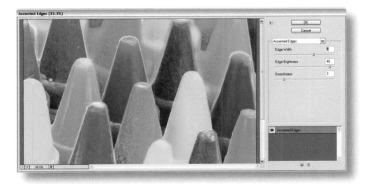

Accented Edges

Filter > Brush Strokes > Accented Edges

Effect: Image element edges are highlighted until they appear to glow.

Variables: Edge Width, Edge Brightness, Smoothness

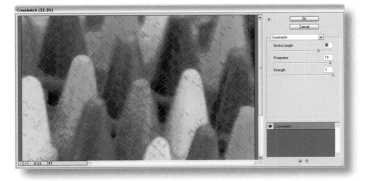

Crosshatch

Filter > Brush Strokes > Crosshatch

Effect: Colored sharp-ended, pencil-like crosshatching to indicate edges and tones.

Variables: Stroke Length, Sharpness, Strength

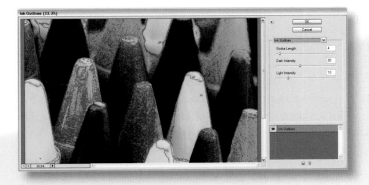

Ink Outlines

Filter > Brush Strokes > Ink Outlines

Effect: Black ink outlines and some surface texture laid over the top of the original tone and color.

Variables: Stroke Length, Dark Intensity, Light Intensity

PHOTOSHOP CS2 >>> >>> essential skills >>>

BLUR FILTERS

The Blur filters are designed to add a degree of softness to the photo. The most basic filters in this group are the Blur and Blur More options. These apply a set level of blur to your picture quickly and easily. For a more sophisticated and controllable blur filter try Gaussian Blur or the new Box, Shape, Smart and Surface Blur versions. They all contain controls that alter the style and strength of the effect.

Average
Blur
Blur More
Box Blur...
Gaussian Blur...
Lens Blur...
Motion Blur...
Radial Blur...
Shape Blur...
Smart Blur...
Surface Blur...

THE LENS BLUR FILTER

One popular application for the Blur filters is to recreate a shallow focus photo where the main subject is sharp and the rest of the picture is unsharp. By selecting the areas to blur and then applying a filter you can create a crude shallow focus result. This approach does create a simple in-focus and out-of-focus effect but it would be hard to say that the results are totally convincing. To achieve a depth of field (DOF) effect that is more realistic and believable, the basic idea of this technique needs to be coupled with the Lens Blur filter.

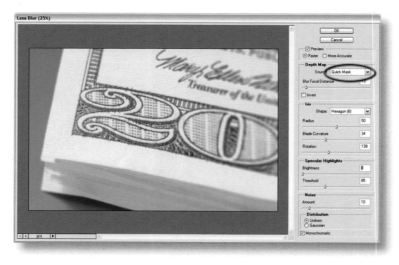

Photoshop's Lens Blur filter is a dedicated feature designed to create realistic DOF effects in your pictures. The feature is 16-bit capable in CS2

If realism is your goal then it is necessary to look a little closer at how camera-based DOF works, and more importantly, how it appears in our images. Imagine an image shot with a long lens using a large aperture. The main subject situated midway into the image is pin sharp. Upon examination it is possible to see that those picture elements closest to the main subject are not as 'unsharp' as those further away. In effect the greater the distance from the point of focus the more blurry the picture elements become.

This fact, simple though it is, is the key to a more realistic digital DOF effect. The application of a simple one-step blurring process does not reflect what happens with traditional camera-based techniques. The Lens Blur filter (Filter > Blur > Lens Blur) is designed specifically to help replicate this gradual change in sharpness. The filter uses selections or masks created before entering the feature to determine which parts of the picture will be blurred and which areas will remain sharp. In addition, if you use a mask that contains areas of graduated gray (rather than just black and white) the filter will adjust the degree of sharpness according to the level of gray in the mask.

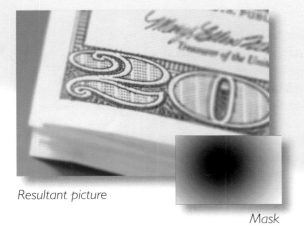

Resultant picture

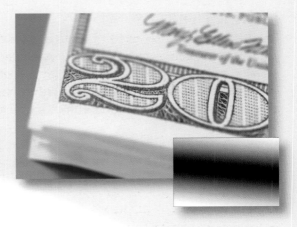

Mask

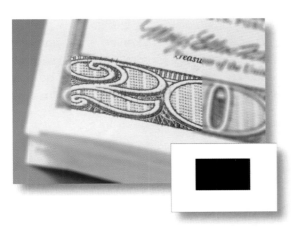

The Lens Blur filter uses a mask or selection to determine which parts of the picture will remain sharp and which areas will be blurred. In addition, the level of sharpness is directly related to the density of the mask. Graduated masks will produce graduated sharpness similar to that found in photographs with camera-based shallow DOF techniques. Image courtesy of www.ablestock.com

Lens Blur filter options >>

Preview – Faster to generate quicker previews. More accurate to display the final version of the image.

Iris Shape – Determines the way the blur appears. Iris shapes are controlled by the number of blades they contain.

Invert – Select this option to inverse the alpha channel mask or selection.

Gaussian or **Uniform** – Select one of these options to add noise to the picture to disguise the smoothing and loss of picture grain that is a by-product of applying the Lens Blur filter.

Depth Map Source - Select the mask or selection that you will use for the filter from the drop-down list.

DISTORT FILTERS

The Distort filters push, pull and twist the pixels within your pictures. Unlike other filter options, which recreate the image using different drawing or painting styles, the Distort filters deform the original image. The controls included are used to alter the strength of the distortion, sometimes the direction and often how to handle any areas of the image that are left blank by the filter's action.

Generally the filters in this group are not applied via the Filter Gallery dialog but rather have their own specific dialog containing both controls and preview.

| Diffuse Glow... |
| Displace... |
| Glass... |
| Lens Correction... |
| Ocean Ripple... |
| Pinch... |
| Polar Coordinates... |
| Ripple... |
| Shear... |
| Spherize... |
| Twirl... |
| Wave... |
| ZigZag... |

Distort filters in action – Correcting lens distortion

New to Photoshop CS2 is the sophisticated Lens Correction filter (Filter > Distort > Lens Correction). The feature is specifically designed to correct the imaging problems that can occur when shooting with different lenses. Apart from correcting barrel and pincushion distortion, the filter can also fix the color fringing (color outlines around subject edges) and vignetting (darkening of the corners) problems that can also occur as a result of poor lens construction. Controls for changing the perspective of the picture (great for eliminating the issue of converging verticals) as well as how to handle the vacant areas of the canvas that are created after distortion correction are also included.

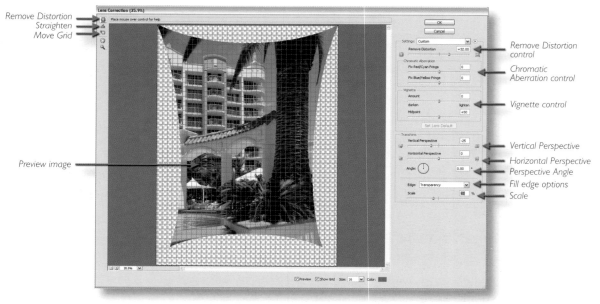

The symptoms of lens distortion

Barrel distortion is usually associated with images that are photographed with extreme wide-angle lenses. The characteristics of barrel distortion are straight lines that appear near the edge of the frame are bent, the whole image appears to be spherical or curved outward and objects that are close to the camera appear grossly distorted. The opposite effect is pincushion distortion, which can be created with some telephoto lenses. Rather than bulging the image seems to recede into the background and straight lines that appear near the edge of the frame are bent inwards.

Correcting distortion and perspective

The example image was photographed with a wide-angle auxiliary lens attached to a digital camera. It displays both barrel distortion and converging verticals that are in need of correction.

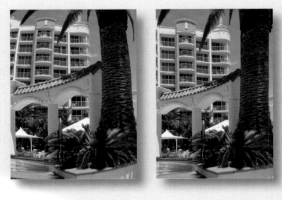

1. With the example open select Filter > Distort > Lens Correction. Zoom in or out using the Zoom control at the bottom left of the dialog and drag the grid with the Move Grid Tool, to a position where it can be easily used to line up a straight edge in the photo.

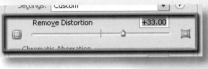

2. Adjust the Remove Distortion slider to the right to correct the barrel effects in the picture. Your aim is to straighten the curve edges of what should be straight picture parts.

3. Now concentrate on correcting the converging verticals. Move the Vertical Perspective option to the left to stretch the details at the top of the photo apart and condense the lower sections. Again aim to align straight and parallel picture parts with the grid lines.

4. If necessary, lighten the edges of the image by moving the Amount slider to the right and adjust the percentage of the picture that this control affects with the Midpoint control.

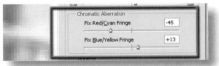

5. Zoom in to at least 600% to check for chromatic aberration problems and use the Fix Red/Cyan Fringe or Fix Blue/Yellow Fringe controls to reduce the appearance of color edges. Click OK to apply the correction settings. Crop the 'fish tail' edges of the corrected photo to complete.

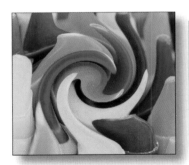

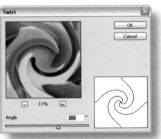

Twirl

Filter > Distort > Twirl

Effect: Spins and stretches image to look as if it is being sucked down a drain hole.

Variables: Angle

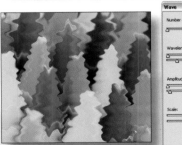

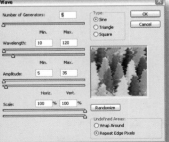

Wave

Filter > Distort > Wave

Effect: Image is rippled in a wave-like motion.

Variables: Number of Generators, Type, Wavelength, Amplitude, Scale, Undefined Areas, Randomize

NOISE FILTERS

The Noise filters group contains tools that are used for either adding noise (randomly colored pixels) to, or reducing the existing noise in, a photo. Dust & Scratches is designed to automatically hide picture defaults such as hairs or scratches in scanned photos. Despeckle, Median and the new Reduce Noise filter remove or hide the noise associated with high ISO pictures and the Add Noise filter is used to create and add noise to photos.

All the filters in this group, except Despeckle, are applied via their own filter dialog.

Add Noise...
Despeckle
Dust & Scratches...
Median...
Reduce Noise...

The new Reduce Noise filter

The feature includes a preview window, a Strength slider, a Preserve Details control and a Reduce Color Noise slider. As with the Dust & Scratches filter you need to be careful when using this filter to ensure that you balance removing noise whilst also retaining detail.

The best way to guarantee this is to set your Strength setting first, ensuring that you check the results in highlights, midtone and shadow areas. Next gradually increase the Preserve Details value until you reach the point where the level of noise that is being reintroduced into

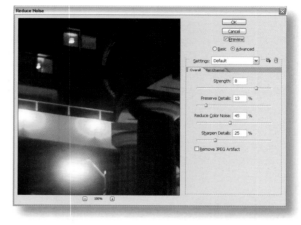

the picture is noticeable and then back off the control slightly (make the setting a lower number). For photographs with a high level of color noise (random speckles of color in an area that should be a smooth flat tone) you will need to adjust this slider at the same time as you are playing with the Strength control.

When the Advanced mode is selected the noise reduction effect can be applied to each channel (Red, Green, Blue) individually. This new for CS2 filter also works in 16-bit mode, contains saveable/loadable settings and a special option for removal of JPEG artifacts.

PIXELATE FILTERS

The Pixelate filters break up the image surface in a variety of ways. Some replicate the effect of printing processes such as Color Halftone and Mezzotint, others fracture the picture into smaller picture components of a regular size and shape. All the filters in this group, except Facet, are applied via their own filter dialog.

Color Halftone...
Crystallize...
Facet
Fragment
Mezzotint...
Mosaic...
Pointillize...

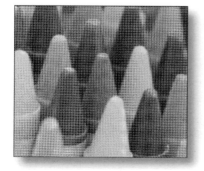

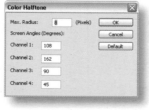

Color Halftone

Filter > Pixelate > Color Halftone

Effect: Similar to a close-up of a printed color magazine image.

Variables: Maximum Radius, Screen Angles for Channels 1–4

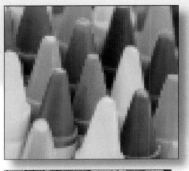

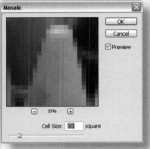

Mosaic

Filter > Pixelate > Mosaic

Effect: The image is broken into pixel-like blocks of flat color.

Variables: Cell Size

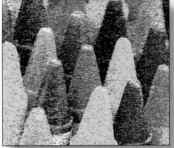

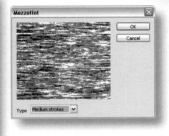

Mezzotint

Filter > Pixelate > Mezzotint

Effect: Adjustable stroke types are used to give tone to the image.

Variables: Type

RENDER FILTERS

The Render filters produce a range of different effects on the surface of your photo, including the creation of random clouds and fibers, the application of a flare highlight and the projection of a light source, or sources, onto the photo, creating areas of light and dark.

> Clouds
> Difference Clouds
> Fibers...
> Lens Flare...
> Lighting Effects...

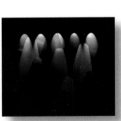

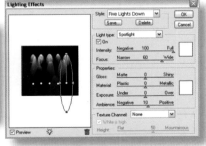

Lighting Effects

Filter > Render > Lighting Effects

Effect: Projects a variety of light sources onto the surface of the picture, creating areas of highlight and shade.

Variables: Style, Light Type, Properties, Texture Channel

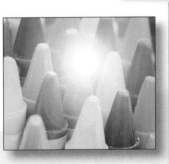

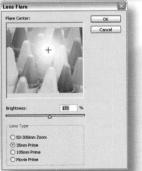

Lens Flare

Filter > Render > Lens Flare

Effect: Creation of a lens flare effect that is then superimposed on the original image.

Variables: Brightness, Lens Type

SHARPEN FILTERS

Photoshop provides a variety of sharpening filters designed to increase the clarity of digital photographs. The options are listed in the Filter > Sharpen menu and include the Sharpen, Sharpen Edges, Sharpen More, Unsharp Mask filters as well as the new Smart Sharpen option.

Sharpen
Sharpen Edges
Sharpen More
Smart Sharpen...
Unsharp Mask...

Digital sharpening techniques are based on increasing the contrast between adjacent pixels in the image. When viewed from a distance, this change makes the picture appear sharper. These Sharpen and Sharpen More filters are designed to apply basic sharpening to the whole of the image and the only difference between the two is that Sharpen More increases the strength of the sharpening effect.

One of the problems with sharpening is that sometimes the effect is detrimental to the image, causing areas of subtle color or tonal change to become coarse and pixelated. These problems are most noticeable in image parts such as skin tones and smoothly graded skies. To help solve this issue, Adobe included the Sharpen Edges filter, which concentrates the sharpening effects on the edges of objects only. Use this filter when you want to stop the effect being applied to smooth image parts.

Customizing your sharpening

Out of all the sharpening options in Photoshop CS2 the Smart Sharpen and Unsharp Mask filters provide the greatest control over the sharpening process by giving the user a variety of slider controls that alter the way the effect is applied to their pictures. Both filters contain Amount and Radius controls. The Unsharp Mask filter includes a Threshold slider and the Smart filter contains controls for adjusting sharpness in Shadows and Highlights independently (in Advanced mode) as well as a Removal option for ridding images or specific blur types (Gaussian, Motion or Lens Blur).

Sharpening controls

The **Amount slider** controls the strength of the sharpening effect. Larger numbers will produce more pronounced results, whereas smaller values will create more subtle effects.

The **Radius slider** value determines the number of pixels around the edge that are affected by the sharpening. A low value only sharpens edge pixels. High settings can produce noticeable halo effects around your picture so start with a low value first.

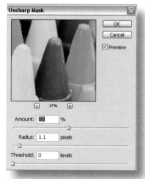

The **Threshold slider** is used to determine how different the pixels must be before they are considered an edge and therefore sharpened.

The **Remove** setting locates and attempts to neutralize different blur types.

The **Shadow and Highlight** tabs contain options for adjusting the sharpening effects in these tonal areas.

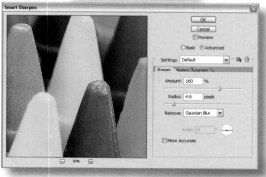

STYLIZE FILTERS

The Stylize filters produce very graphic and often colorful versions of your photos. The aim with this set of filters is not realism but the creation of striking designs that use the base photo as a reference. This is not the filter group to use if you are looking for subtle changes to add to your photos. Generally the filters in this group are not applied via the Filter Gallery dialog but rather have their own specific dialog containing both controls and preview.

Diffuse...
Emboss...
Extrude...
Find Edges
Glowing Edges...
Solarize
Tiles...
Trace Contour...
Wind...

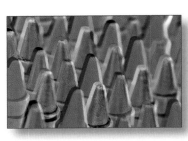
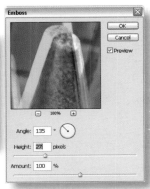

Emboss

Filter > Stylize > Emboss

Effect: Recreates the look of beaten or embossed metal with the raised edges outlined and colored.

Variables: Angle, Height, Amount

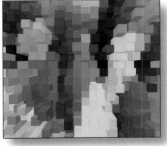
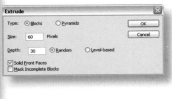

Extrude

Filter > Stylize > Extrude

Effect: The 'building block' filter creates colored and stacked three-dimensional blocks out of your original image.

Variables: Type, Size, Depth, Solid Front Faces, Mask Incomplete Blocks

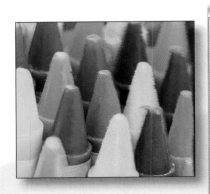
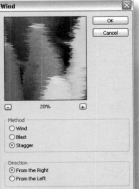

Wind

Filter > Stylize > Wind

Effect: Parts of the image are blurred in the direction of the prevailing wind.

Variables: Method, Direction

SKETCH FILTERS

The Sketch filters provide a range of generally monochrome fine art effects when applied to your photo. The controls included with each filter are used to alter the strength of the effect, sometimes the direction of the texture or the balance of light and dark changes. As many of the filters use the current foreground and background colors when applying their effects, changing these settings can provide drastically different results.

Generally the filters in this group are applied via the Filter Gallery dialog.

Bas Relief...
Chalk & Charcoal...
Charcoal...
Chrome...
Conté Crayon...
Graphic Pen...
Halftone Pattern...
Note Paper...
Photocopy...
Plaster...
Reticulation...
Stamp...
Torn Edges...
Water Paper...

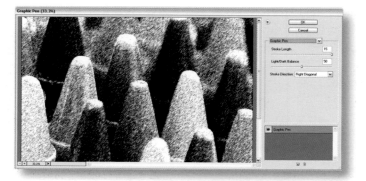

Graphic Pen

Filter > Sketch > Graphic Pen

Effect: Stylish black and white effect made with sharp-edged pen strokes.

Variables: Stroke Length, Light/Dark Balance, Stroke Direction

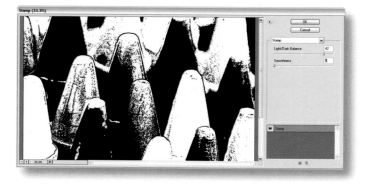

Stamp

Filter > Sketch > Stamp

Effect: Just broad flat areas of black and white.

Variables: Light/Dark Balance, Smoothness

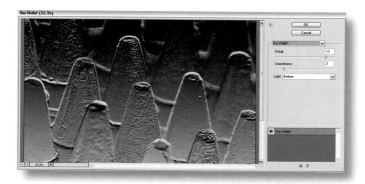

Bas Relief

Filter > Sketch > Bas Relief

Effect: Color reduced image with cross lighting that gives the appearance of a relief sculpture.

Variables: Detail, Smoothness, Light Direction

TEXTURE FILTERS

The Texture filter group provides a range of ways of adding texture to your photos. Most of the filters apply a single texture type and include controls for varying the strength and style of the effect, but the Texturizer filter adds to these possibilities by allowing users to add textures they create themselves to a photo.

All filters in this group are applied via the Filter Gallery dialog.

Craquelure...
Grain...
Mosaic Tiles...
Patchwork...
Stained Glass...
Texturizer...

The Texturizer filter

When applying the Texturizer filter the picture is changed to give the appearance that the photo has been printed onto the surface of the texture. The Scaling and Relief sliders control the strength and visual dominance of the texture, whilst the Light Direction menu alters the highlight and shadow areas. Different surface types are available from the Texture drop-down menu. The feature also contains the option to add your own files and have these used as the texture that is applied by the filter to the image.

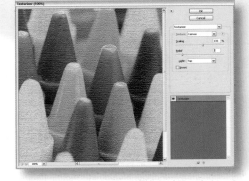

Making your own textures

Any Photoshop file (.PSD) can be loaded as a new texture via the Load Texture option in the side-arrow menu, top right of the Texturizer dialog. Simply shoot, scan or design a texture image and save as an Elements or Photoshop file (.PSD).

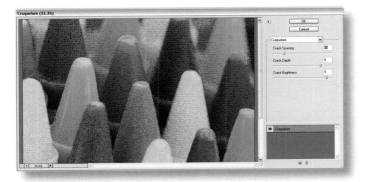

Craquelure

Filter > Texture > Craquelure

Effect: Cracks imposed on the surface of the original image.

Variables: Crack Spacing, Crack Depth, Crack Brightness

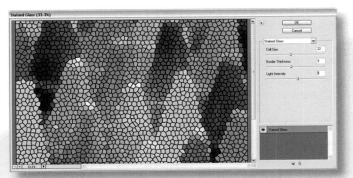

Stained Glass

Filter > Texture > Stained Glass

Effect: Image broken up into areas of color which are then bordered by a black line similar to stained glass.

Variables: Cell Size, Border Thickness, Light Intensity

VIDEO FILTERS

The Video filters deal specifically with problems associated with editing and enhancing still frames captured from video footage.

De-Interlace...
NTSC Colors

The De-Interlace filter

The De-Interlace filter is used to replace the missing picture detail that exists in captured video frames. It does this by either interpolating the pixels or duplicating the ones surrounding the area. Interpolation provides the smoothest results and Duplication the sharpest. The filter is not applied via the Filter Gallery dialog but rather has its own specific dialog that contains the Interpolation option.

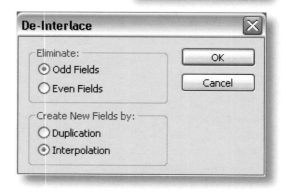

The NTSC Colors filter

The NTSC Colors filter ensures that the colors in the image will fit within the range of hues available for the NTSC television format. This sometimes means that the color gamut of the original image is compressed to ensure that no single hue is over-saturated when displayed via the television system.

OTHER FILTERS

The filters grouped together under the Other heading include the Custom filter, which is used for creating you own filter effects (see opposite page), the edge-finding High Pass filter, the Offset filter that shifts picture pixels by a set amount, and the Maximum and Minimum filters, which are most often used for modifying masks.

Custom...
High Pass...
Maximum...
Minimum...
Offset...

Filters in this group are not applied via the Filter Gallery dialog but rather have their own specific dialog containing both controls and preview.

Contrast and sharpening changes using the High Pass filter

The High Pass filter isolates the edges in a picture and then converts the rest of the picture to mid gray. The filter locates the edge areas by searching for areas of high contrast or color change. The filter can be used to add contrast and sharpening to a photo.

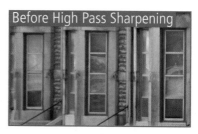

1. To start, make a copy of the picture layer that you want to sharpen, then filter the copied layer with the High Pass filter.
2. Next select the filtered layer and switch the blend mode to Hard Light.
3. Finally, adjust the opacity of this layer to govern the level of sharpening and contrast being applied to the picture layer.

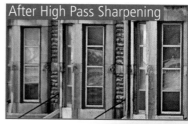

THE TEN COMMANDMENTS FOR FILTER USAGE

1. *Subtlety is everything.* The effect should support your image not overpower it.

2. *Try one filter at a time.* Applying multiple filters to an image can be confusing.

3. *View at full size.* Make sure that you view the effect at full size (100%) when deciding on filter settings.

4. *Filter a channel.* For a change try applying a filter to one channel only – Red, Green or Blue.

5. *Print to check effect.* If the image is to be viewed as a print, double check the effect when printed before making final decisions about filter variables.

6. *Fade strong effects.* If the effect is too strong try fading it. Use the 'Fade' selection under the 'Filter' menu.

7. *Experiment.* Try a range of settings before making your final selection.

8. *Mask then filter.* Apply a gradient mask to an image and then use the filter. In this way you can control what parts of the image are affected.

9. *Try different effects on different layers.* If you want to combine the effects of different filters try copying the base image to different layers and applying a different filter to each. Combine effects by adjusting the opacity of each layer.

10. *Did I say that subtlety is everything?*

Filter DIY

Can't find exactly what you are looking for in the hundreds of filters that are either supplied with Photoshop or are available for download from the Net? I could say that you're not really trying, but then again some people have a compulsion to 'do it for themselves'. Well, all is not lost. Photoshop provides you with the opportunity to create your own filtration effects by using its Filter > Other > Custom option.

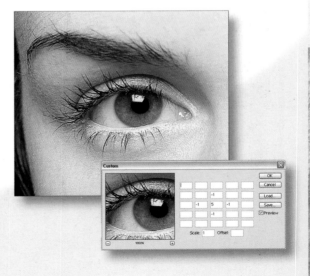

By adding a sequence of positive/negative numbers into the 25 variable boxes provided you can construct your own filter effect. Add to this the options of playing with the 'Scale' and 'Offset' of the results and I can guarantee hours of fun. Best of all your labors can be saved to use again when your specialist customized touch is needed.

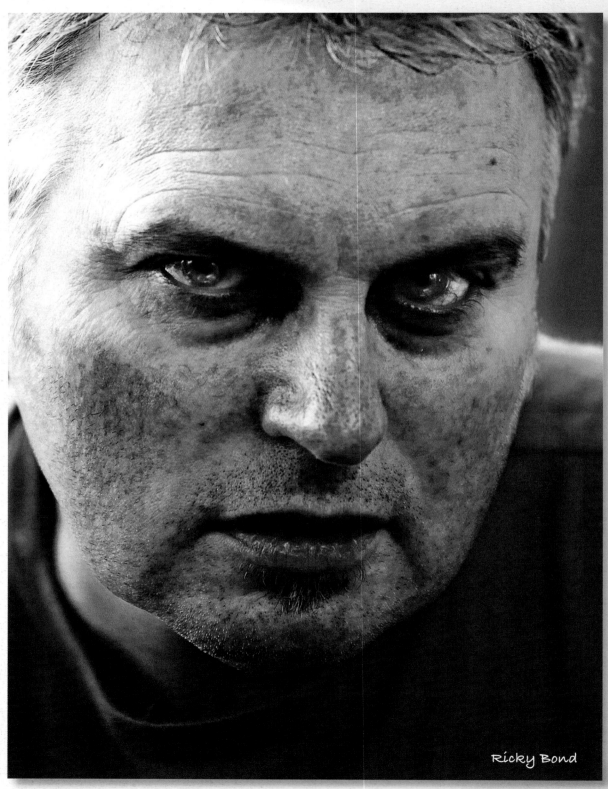

Ricky Bond

retouching projects

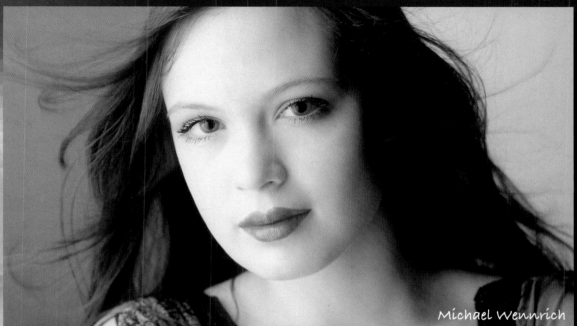

Michael Wennrich

essential skills

~ Develop skills using layers, adjustment layers, channels and layer masks.

~ Retouch and enhance images using the following techniques and tools:

- 16-bit/channel mode

- Adjustment layers and layer masks

- History and Healing Brushes

- Dust & Scratches and Liquify filters

- Unsharp mask

- Channel mixing

- Luminosity masks and layers.

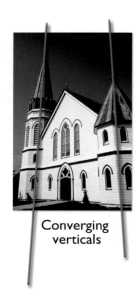

Converging
verticals

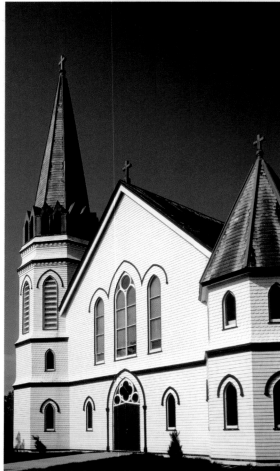

Perspective
corrected

Image courtesy of www.ablestock.com

Correcting perspective – *Project 1*

You know the story, you're visiting a wonderful city on holiday wanting to capture as much of the local scenes and architecture as possible. You enter the local square and point your camera towards an impressive three-spired building on the other side of the road only to find that you must tilt your camera upwards to get the peaks into the picture. At the time you think nothing of it and you move onto the next location. It is only when you are back at home about to print your photograph that you realize that the innocent 'tilt' has caused the edges of the building to lean inwards.

Now to a certain extent this isn't a problem; even though it is not strictly accurate, we all know that most buildings have parallel walls and the majority of people who look at your picture will take this into account – won't they?

Apart from a return trip and a reshoot is there any way to correct these converging verticals? Well, I'm glad you asked. Armed with nothing except Photoshop and the few steps detailed here, you can now straighten all those leaning architectural shots without the cost of the return journey.

PHOTOSHOP CS2 >>>

essential skills >>>

Lens Correction (50%)

Place mouse over control for help

OK

Cancel

Settings: Custom

Remove Distortion   0.00

Chromatic Aberration

Fix Red/Cyan Fringe   0

Fix Blue/Yellow Fringe   0

Vignette

Amount   0

darken   lighten

Midpoint   +50

Set Lens Default

Transform

Vertical Perspective   -35

Horizontal Perspective   0

Angle: 0.00   °

Edge: Transparency

Scale   100   %

50%

☑ Preview ☑ Show Grid Size: 16 Color:

Using the Lens Correction filter

1. Start by opening the example image in Photoshop and then select Filter > Distort > Lens Correction. Check the Preview and Show Grid options and adjust the magnification (zoom) setting so that the picture sits within the boundaries of the preview window.

2. Click the Move Grid Tool and click and drag the grid so that it aligns with a part of the picture that is meant to be vertical. In the example the center of each of the towers was used as the reference point. If needed, change the size of the grid to ensure that the spacing suits the example picture.

3. Drag the Vertical Perspective slider in the Transform section of the filter dialog to the left to broaden the top part of the picture and shrink the bottom. Fine-tune the adjustment so that the verticals in the building align with the grid. Click OK to apply the adjustment.

4. Once the filter dialog closes and the corrected image is passed back to the main Photoshop work space select the Crop Tool and drag a cropping marquee around the picture area to be retained. Hit the Enter/Return key to apply the crop.

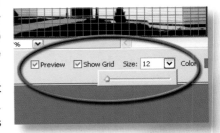

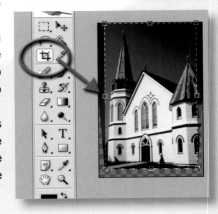

Manual control – technique 2

Feel like taking back the reins yourself? With the following steps you can achieve the same results possible with the Lens Correction filter.

1. After opening the offending image turn on the display grid (View > Grid). This will place a non-printing grid over the surface of the picture and will act as a guide for your adjustments. In most cases we need to move the two upper corners of the picture further apart to make them parallel. To achieve this we will use the Perspective feature built into the Photoshop Crop Tool.

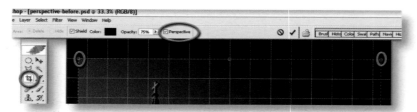

2. Select the Crop Tool from the toolbox. Click and drag a rough cropping marquee around the picture. Tick the Perspective option in the tool's Option bar. This option changes the way that the tool functions. It is now possible to use the corner handles of the crop marquee to manipulate the photograph's perspective.

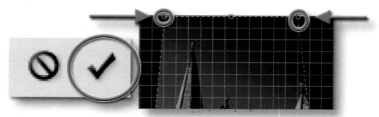

3. In our case we need to select both the top left and right handles and drag them inwards. Continue dragging until the crop marquee edges align with the building sides, or a part of the picture that is meant to be vertical. Double-click on the picture, or select the Tick button in the tool's Option bar, to apply the perspective transformation. Check to see that the building's edges now align with the grid lines. If this isn't the case, undo the perspective change (Edit > Undo Crop) and then reapply the crop with slightly different settings.

4. To complete the correction we need to make the building a little taller as the tilted camera has artificially shortened the spires. The picture needs to be a layer before we can apply the height transformation, so double-click onto the background layer in the Layers palette.

5. If we stretch the picture upwards without providing some canvas space for the extra height then the top or bottom of the building will be cropped. So before extending the height we need to increase the vertical size of the canvas. Choose Canvas Size from the Resize menu (Image > Resize > Canvas Size) and input a new value into the height box. Here I have used a value of 130% and anchored the bottom part of the picture so that the extra canvas is added to the top.

6. Now we can select the Scale feature from the Resize section of the Image menu (Edit > Transform > Scale) and click and drag the top handles to stretch the picture bigger. As a final step use the Crop Tool to trim the unused sections of the canvas away from the corrected image.

PHOTOSHOP CS2 >>>

Adjustment layers – *Project 2*

A localized adjustment can be created using the 'Fill' command. Selecting a layer mask and filling an active selection with either the foreground or background color will create a mask that limits adjustments or visibility in a localized area of the image. This allows the Selection Tools to be used in addition to the Paint Tools for the creation of masks. The fill shortcuts 'Command/Ctrl + Delete' (to fill with the foreground color) and 'Option/Alt + Delete' (to fill with the background color) speed up the masking process.

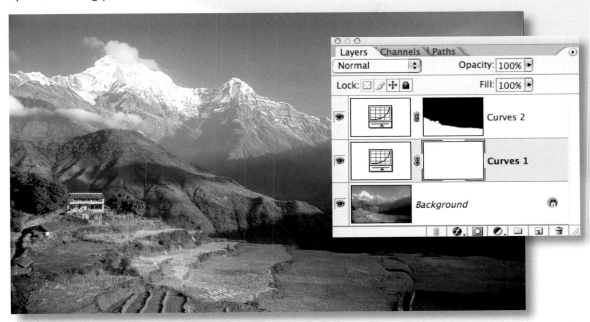

The Himalayas image demonstrates how an adjustment layer can be used to effect global changes to tonality and color whilst a second adjustment layer affects only the foreground due to the presence of a layer mask limiting its effect.

>>> essential skills >>>

1. Open the image file 'Himalayas.jpg'.

2. In the Layers palette click on the 'New fill or adjustment layer' icon and select a 'Curves' adjustment layer from the fly-out menu.

3. From the 'Channel' menu select the 'Red' channel. Click on the line in the center of the Curves box. Drag upwards until the line becomes a curve. Observe the changes to the color in the image window. Increase the level of the red in the image until you feel that the overall color has been corrected.

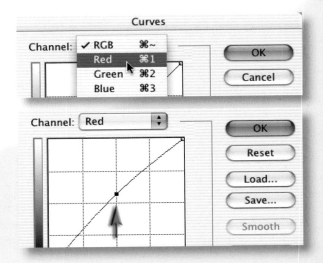

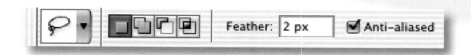

4. Using the 'Lasso Tool' (with a 2-pixel feather entered in the Options bar) select the fields in the foreground of the landscape.

Note > Feather selections to soften the transition between the adjusted and non-adjusted pixels. If you create a mask with a hard edge it can be softened by applying a small amount of 'Gaussian Blur' (Filter > Blur > Gaussian Blur).

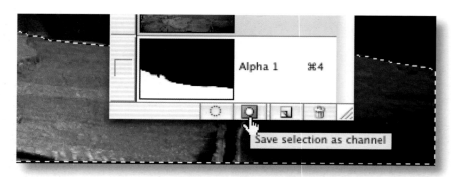

5. Click on the Channels palette (grouped with the Layers palette) and then click on the 'Save selection as channel' icon to save the selection as an alpha channel. This will ensure the selection is saved when the file is closed.

6. Return to the Layers palette. With the selection active create another new adjustment layer. Choose 'Curves' from the menu. The selection automatically limits the adjustment to the selected area by filling the rest of the layer mask with black.

7. In the Curves dialog box select the 'Green' channel. Pull the curve down to reduce the level of green in the foreground of the image and click OK to complete the tonal and color adjustments. Double-click the thumbnail on either adjustment layer to reopen the Curves dialog box in order to further modify the color or tonality.

Note > Drag an adjustment layer to the 'Delete layer' icon (trash can) to discard the adjustment.

8. To retain the adjustment layers when saving the image it is important to save the document as a Photoshop file (PSD) or a TIFF file with layers.

Note > The PDF and PSB file formats also support layers.

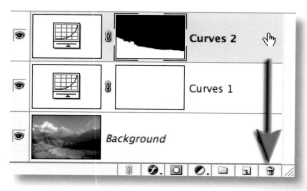

Target tones – *Project 3*

In this activity specific highlight, shadow and midtone values are targeted on an adjustment curve. The color cast is corrected using the 'Set Gray Point' eyedropper in the Curves dialog box and the color of the man's turban is selectively altered.

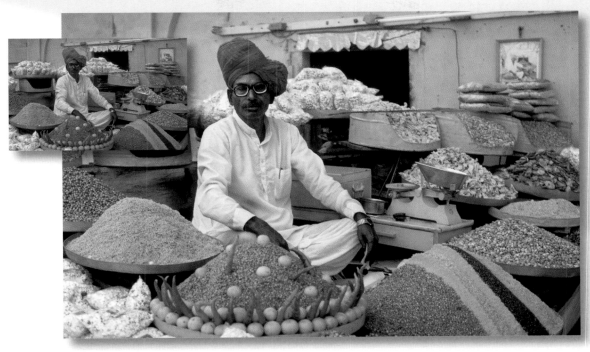

1. Open the file '**Market.jpg**' and select the 'eyedropper tool' in the Tools palette. Set the sample size of the eyedropper to a 5 by 5 Average in the Options bar to ensure general tonal values are sampled rather than individual pixel values.

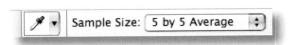

2. Create a Curves adjustment layer by clicking on the 'Create new fill or adjustment layer' icon at the foot of the Layers palette.

3. Move the mouse cursor outside of the Curves dialog box into the image window. The cursor will change to an eyedropper tool whatever tool was selected previously. Hold the mouse clicker down as you move around the image and note the 'Input' readout in the Curves dialog box. Move to a bright highlight in the image (a bright section of the shirt).

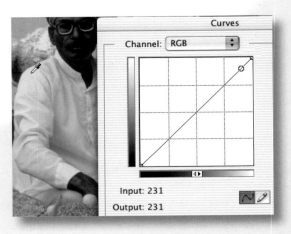

193

4. Select a tone that registers an input level that is approximately 235. Command/Ctrl-click whilst the pointer is over the image area to set an adjustment point on the curve.

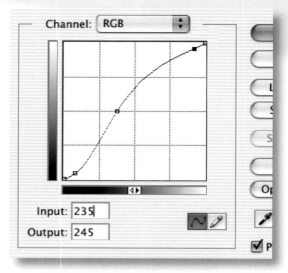

5. Move the cursor to an object with a dark tone (the rim of the man's spectacles). Select a tone that registers an input level that is approximately 15 to 20. Set an adjustment point as before.

6. Move the cursor to a part of the image that you would like to adjust to a midtone (the skin on the back of the man's hand would be ideal). Select a tone that registers an input level that is approximately 95. Set an adjustment point as before.

7. In the Curves dialog box drag the highlight adjustment point until the output value reads 245. Select and drag the shadow adjustment point until the output value reads 10. Select and drag the midtone adjustment point until the output value reads 127.

8. Select the 'Set Gray Point' eyedropper in the Curves dialog box (between the black and white point eyedroppers). Click on a suitable tone you wish to desaturate in an attempt to remove the color cast present in the image (the metal tray holding produce to the left of the man's shoulder would be ideal). The neutral tone selected to be the 'Gray Point' can be a dark or light tone within the image. If the tone selected is not representative of a neutral tone the color cast cannot be rectified effectively.

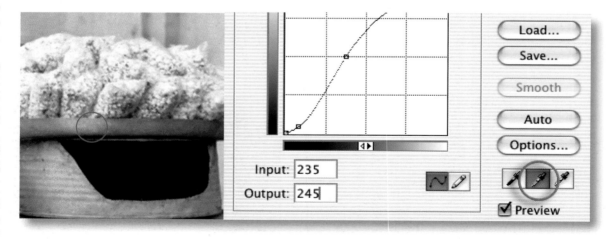

9. Fine-tune any color correction by selecting an individual channel from the pull-down menu in the Curves dialog box. Create an adjustment point or use the adjustment point created by the Gray Point eyedropper to perfect the color adjustment. Select OK to apply the Curves adjustment.

10. Create a 'Hue/Saturation' adjustment layer. Move the 'Hue' slider until the man's turban shifts to an orange/red hue. Decrease the saturation slightly.

Note > All colors will be modified towards red as the adjustments are made at this stage.

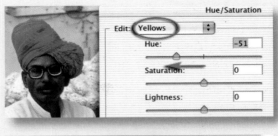

11. Fill the layer mask that accompanies the Hue/Saturation adjustment layer with black (Edit > Fill).

Note > If the default colors are set in the Tools palette the keyboard shortcuts 'Command/Ctrl + Delete' and 'Option/Alt + Delete' can be used to fill or clear a layer mask quickly.

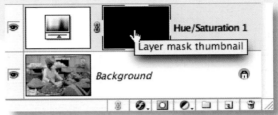

12. Select the 'Brush Tool' and make the foreground color white. In the Options bar set the opacity to between 80 and 100%. Select an appropriate brush size and paint the turban in the image to reveal the hue adjustment. If you paint over the edge simply switch the foreground color to black and paint to remove the previous adjustment. Save the image as a PSD file.

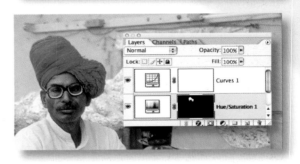

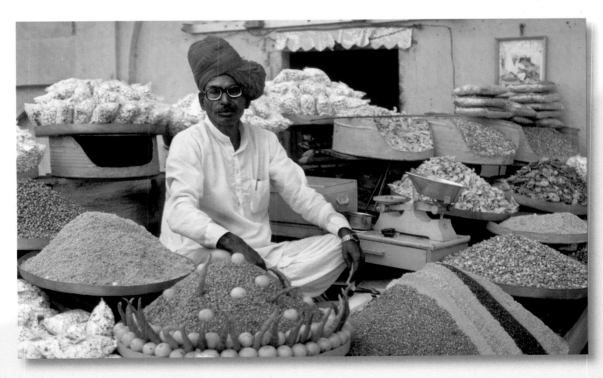

Crop, clean and color-correct – *Project 4*

This activity takes you through the complete series of steps required to retouch a digital file of poor quality. It is dirty, crooked and the color and tone are a long way from being correct. The process includes sharpening, which is the last step prior to printing.

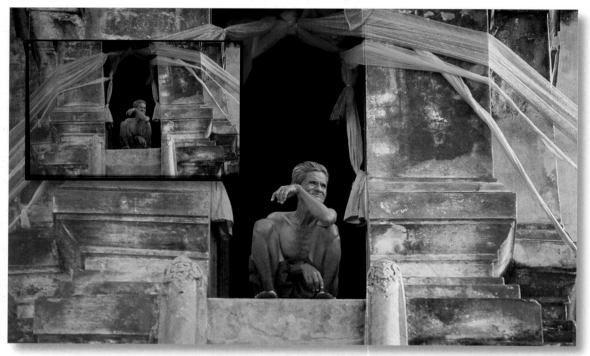

1. Open the file 'Temple.jpg'.

2. Select the 'Measure Tool' from the Tools palette (behind the 'Eyedropper Tool'). Click and drag along the edge of the step beneath the man's feet to draw a line parallel with the step.

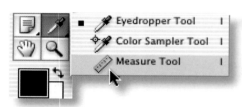

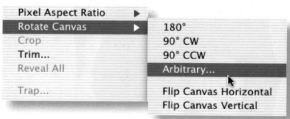

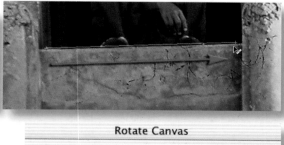

3. Go to Image > Rotate Canvas > Arbitrary. The angle of rotation required to straighten the image will automatically be entered in the 'Angle' text field. Click OK to rotate the canvas.

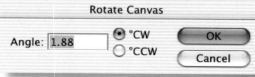

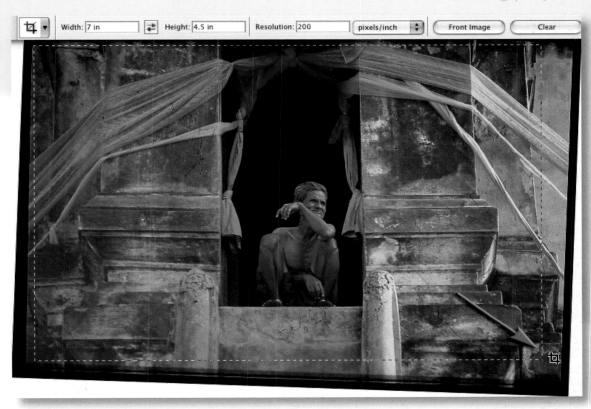

4. Set the output dimensions and resolution in the 'Options' bar (7in × 4.5in @ 200ppi). Drag the cropping marquee over the image to select an area that removes the black border and shaded lines at the base of the image.

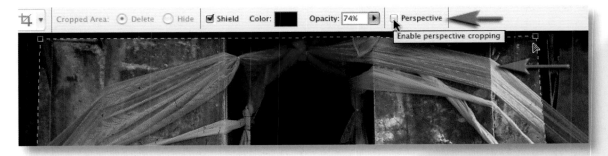

5. Check the 'Enable perspective cropping' box in the Options bar. Drag the top two corner handles of the bounding box inwards until the edges of the bounding box align with the verticals of the image. Press the tick or 'Commit current crop option' icon in the Options bar to crop the image to the required specifications.

Note > The keyboard shortcuts for cropping are 'Return/Enter' to commit the crop and 'Esc' to cancel the crop. Alternatively you can double-click inside the cropping marquee to commit the crop.

6. The Spot Healing Brush can be used to remove much of the damage in this image but a more advanced technique is required to remove some of the damage that lies close to saurated colors or fine detail. The technique is called the history brush technique. Start the process by creating a new 'snapshot' of the cropped image in the History palette. This snapshot will enable the use of the History Brush in the selective removal of the dust and scratches that cover much of the image.

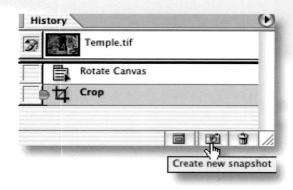

Note > The 'Dust & Scratches' filter cannot normally be applied globally to the whole image without removing excessive amounts of detail.

7. From the 'Filters' menu apply the 'Dust & Scratches' filter ('Filters > Noise > Dust & Scratches'). Use the smallest 'Radius' and 'Threshold' settings possible to remove the large majority of the damage.

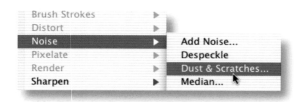

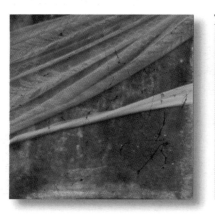
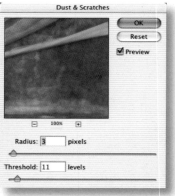
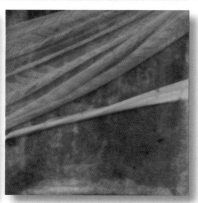

Note > Do not worry if the Dust & Scratches filter removes important detail as well as the dust and scratches. You will revert to a previous 'history state' and use the 'History Brush' for selectively cleaning the image.

8. Create another new snapshot and set the source for the History Brush on this latest snapshot by clicking in the window next to the snapshot thumbnail. Snapshots can be named by double-clicking on the snapshot name and typing in something more memorable than the default name.

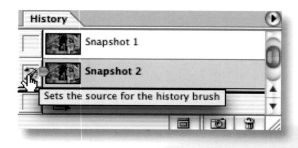

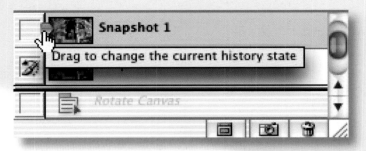

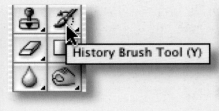

9. Change the current history state to the previous snapshot ('Snapshot 1') by clicking on it.

Note > The History Brush will be used to paint from the future state (minus dust and scratches) to the current state. The filter is limited to a localized adjustment.

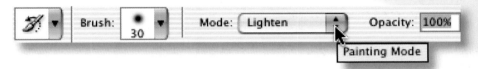

10. Select the 'History Brush' from the Tools palette. Select the 'Lighten' paint mode in the History Brush options.

Note > Set the paint mode to Darken if the marks or blemishes are lighter than the surrounding image.

11. Paint out the damage using an appropriate brush size (just larger than the damage being retouched). Zoom in on the image when required and navigate by pressing the spacebar (to access the Hand Tool) and dragging to move the image within the window.

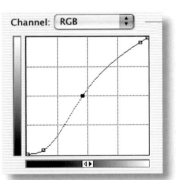 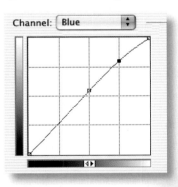 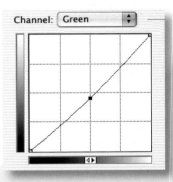

12. Create a new adjustment layer and select 'Curves' from the menu. Use the RGB curve to adjust the tonality of the image. Select a sample highlight from the sunlight striking the stonework to the right of the step and move it to a value of 245. Select a midtone from the shadow side of the man's forehead and move it to a value of 127. Select a dark tone above the man's head and move it to a value below 10. Remove the color cast by moving the curves in the individual Red, Green and Blue channels. Alternatively use the 'Set Gray Point' eyedropper and select the neutral gray from the man's hair.

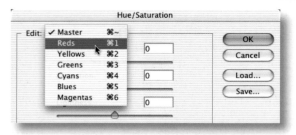 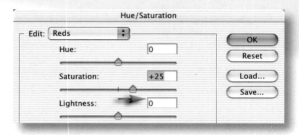

13. Create a 'Hue/Saturation' adjustment layer. Select 'Reds' from the pull-down menu. Increase the saturation by dragging the 'Saturation' slider to the right. As the warm tones in the image are restricted to the red scarves emerging from the temple and the man's skin, the rest of the image remains relatively unaffected. Click OK to apply the adjustment.

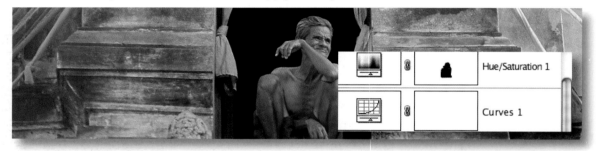

14. To limit the adjustment to just the scarves, paint into the adjustment layer's layer mask with black (set to 100% opacity) to conceal the increase in saturation to the man's skin. Alternatively fill the mask with black and paint with white to reveal the saturation adjustment to the scarves.

15. Create a copy merged layer (Select All > Copy Merged > Paste) and ensure this layer is on top of the layers stack. Set the blend mode to Luminosity.

16. View image at 100% (View > Actual Pixels). From the 'Filters' menu select the 'Unsharp Mask' or 'Smart Sharpen' from the Sharpen group of filters. Average settings are Amount 80 to 180, Radius 1.0, Threshold 3 (Unsharp Mask) or Remove Gaussian Blur (Smart Sharpen) if the image is to be printed via an inkjet printer. Be generous with the amount as this can be lowered later.

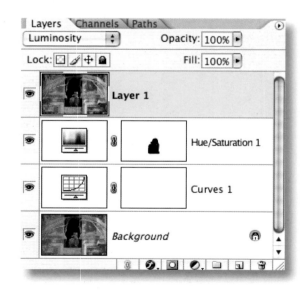

17. Print a test strip of the image and lower the opacity of the sharpen layer if less sharpening is required.

Note > See 'Capture and Enhance – Sharpening an image – Step 6' (page 67) for sharpening basics and 'Retouching Projects – Project 6' for advanced sharpening techniques.

Shadows and highlights – *Project 5*

Perhaps one of the most impressive new retouching features introduced with Photoshop CS was the Shadow/Highlight adjustment. The Shadow/Highlight adjustment feature allows users to work on the shadows or highlights in isolation to the rest of the tones in the image without using advanced masking and selection techniques using Curves. With the introduction of the Shadow/Highlight adjustment feature users should no longer feel frustrated with the shortcomings of the Levels adjustment feature, which does an excellent job of managing the overall spread of tones but is unable to focus or limit its attention without resorting to time-consuming selections.

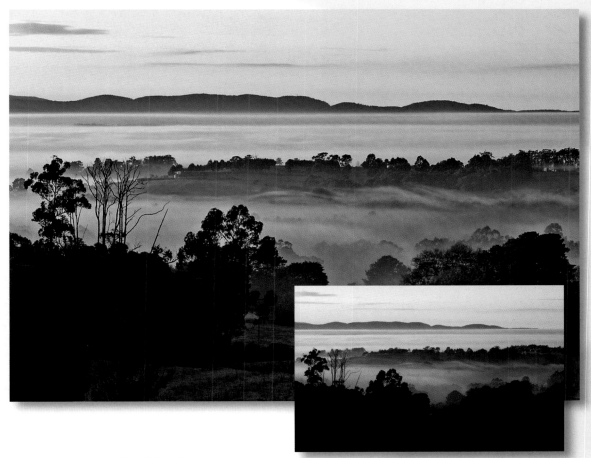

A new kid on the block

The Shadow/Highlight adjustment feature first appeared in Photoshop CS in 2003 and was almost overlooked by many experienced image editors who were used to manipulating tonality through the advanced adjustment feature called 'Curves'. The strength of the new adjustment feature for Elements 3 and Photoshop CS users (even for users of Curves), is its handling of midtone contrast and saturation and its user-friendly interface (its even kind to the histograms of bit impoverished 8-bit files). The only downside to this adjustment feature is that it is not available as an adjustment layer.

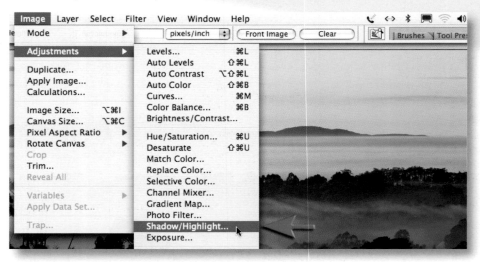

1. Locating the adjustment feature – The Shadow/Highlight adjustment feature is available from Image > Adjustments. It is not available as an adjustment layer. It is therefore recommended that you duplicate the background layer before using this adjustment feature.

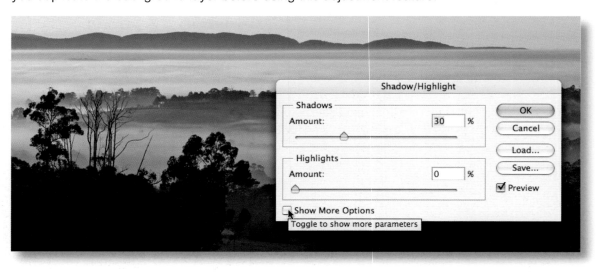

2. Modifying the tonality – The Shadow/Highlight dialog box in CS has a 'Show More Options' feature to allow the meticulous control freak to tweak the adjustment to their own liking (heaps more sliders). For most users, however, this is where the 'quick and easy' becomes the 'slow and slightly complex'. For most images with overly dark shadows, moving the Lighten Shadow slider or the Amount slider up to 30% or so will reveal the detail in the dark areas of the image that was previously hiding. Using higher values in CS without resorting to the extra options will often start to degrade rather than enhance the overall quality of the image.

Warning > Do not use this adjustment feature to compensate for a poorly calibrated monitor. There is not much value in optimizing the images for your own screen when they will look entirely different in print or on a correctly calibrated monitor.

3. Comparing the technique – Photoshop users who may have previously resorted to Curves to fix a shadow problem (raising the shadow values and lowering the midtone and highlight values) should be aware of the plateau that this creates in the midtone section, which often leads to low contrast in this area of the image. Note how the same adjustment using Shadow/Highlight gives you independent control over this value. There are advanced workarounds for CS users but all involve a great deal more time and energy than Shadow/Highlight demands.

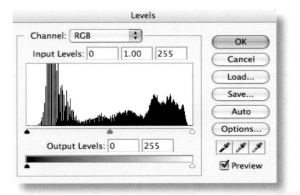
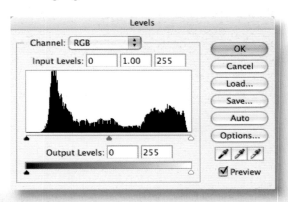

Note > Perhaps the icing on the cake for users considering whether to use the Shadow/Highlight in preference to other, more traditional techniques is to observe the histograms of files that have been modified. The illustration shows the sacrifices that have been made using Curves to open up the shadow tones (more experienced CS users will, however, be aware that spikes in histograms can mysteriously disappear when a file is resampled).

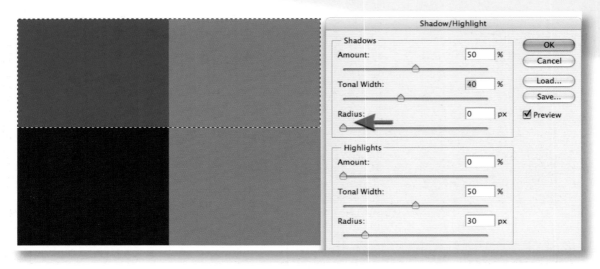

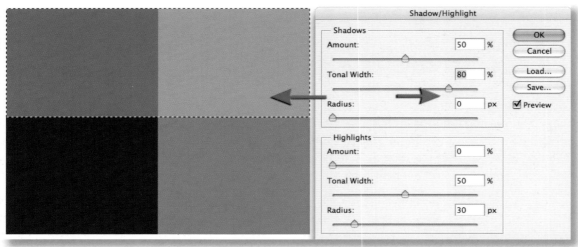

Options, options and more options

For CS2 users many of the 'Option' sliders such as Color Correction and Midtone Contrast make perfect sense – but what about Tonal Width and Radius? Let me illuminate – the Tonal Width slider controls which tones get affected by the Amount slider. Raise the Tonal Width slider and midtones start to come under the influence of the Amount slider. Take the radius to 0 to experiment with the relationship of the top two sliders. The illustration uses two tones placed side by side. The top half of these tones have been selected, so the bottom section remains unaffected by the Shadow/Highlight adjustments. With the Tonal Width slider set low, the lighter of the two tones remains unaffected by the adjustment. As the Tonal Width slider is raised the lighter tone is also affected by the adjustment.

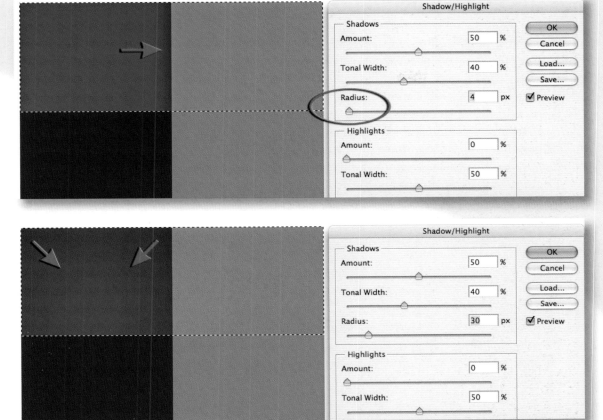

Raising the Radius amount will create localized contrast in the shadow areas. This is a very useful feature, but is perhaps the most difficult to come to terms with. The optimum value is dependent on both the resolution of the image and the size of the shadow areas in the image. I recommend obtaining an appropriate setting for the top two sliders and then zooming into the shadows to gain an idea of the optimum setting required for the Radius slider. The demonstration file shows the effects of raising the Radius slider by only a few pixels (magnified view). This sets up an edge contrast effect similar to the effects of the Unsharp Mask. Raising the slider softens the effect on smaller tonal differences within the shadow areas and pushes, or limits, the effect to the boundaries of the larger shadow areas. There is no right or wrong with this slider, just different visual outcomes.If you understand the principles of the Shadow adjustment then the Highlight adjustment won't come as any surprise. The adjustment capability of this Shadow/Highlight feature is so powerful that an image can be rendered either entirely flat or appear as if it has become a negative version of itself!

With this knowledge firmly in place open the project image and begin to massage the tonality and color into a shape that pleases your own subjective eye. The tonal manipulations on offer are not new, but the speed and ease of access are a breath of fresh air. This truly is Adobe's best quick fix to date.

Advanced sharpening techniques – *Project 6*

Most if not all digital images require sharpening – even if shot on a state-of-the-art digital mega-resolution SLR with pin-sharp focusing. Most cameras or scanners can sharpen as the image is captured but the highest quality sharpening is to be found in the image-editing software. Sharpening in the image-editing software will allow you to select the precise amount of sharpening and the areas of the image that require sharpening most. If sharpening for screen it is very much a case of 'what you see is what you get'. For images destined for print, however, the monitor preview is just that – a preview. The actual amount of sharpening required for optimum image quality is usually a little more than looks comfortable on screen – especially when using a TFT monitor (flat panel).

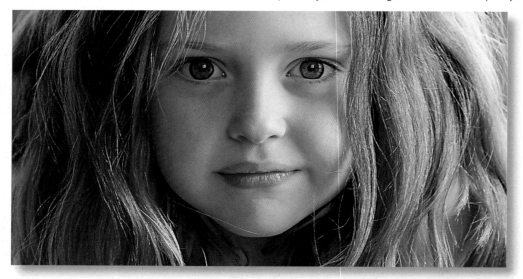

The basic concept of sharpening is to send the Unsharp Mask filter or Smart Sharpen filter on a 'seek and manipulate' mission. These filters are programmed to make the pixels on the lighter side of any edge they find lighter still, and the pixels on the darker side of the edge darker. Think of it as a localized contrast control. Too much and people in your images start to look radioactive (they glow), not enough and the viewers of your images start reaching for the reading glasses they don't own. The best sharpening techniques are those that prioritize the important areas for sharpening and leave the smoother areas of the image well alone, e.g. sharpening the eyes of a portrait but avoiding the skin texture. These advanced techniques are essential when sharpening images that have been scanned from film or have excessive noise, neither of which needs accentuating by the Unsharp Mask. So let the project begin.

Note > If you have any sharpening options in your capture device it is important to switch them off or set them to minimum or low (if using camera RAW set the sharpening amount to 0). The sharpening features found in most capture devices are often very crude when compared to the following technique. It is also not advisable to sharpen images that have been saved as JPEG files using high compression/low quality settings. The sharpening process that follows should also come at the end of the editing process, i.e. adjust the color and tonality of the image before starting this advanced sharpening technique. Reduce the levels of sharpening later if it proves too much.

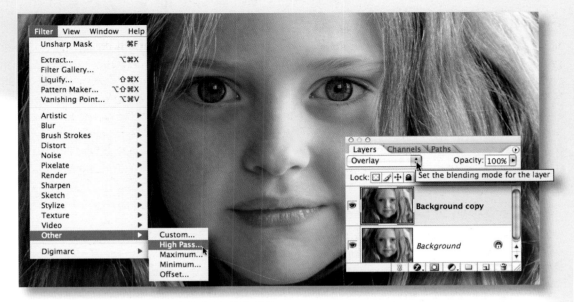

TECHNIQUE ONE – HIGH PASS

1. Duplicate the background layer and set the blend mode to Overlay. Select 'Overlay' from the blend modes menu in the Layers palette.

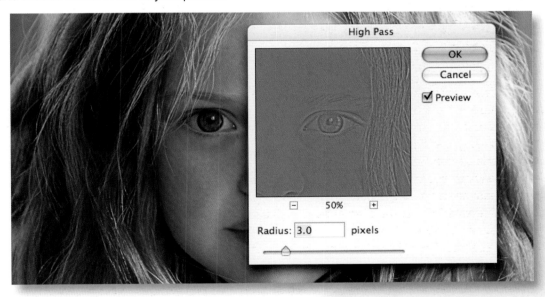

2. Go to 'Filter > Other > High Pass'. Increase the pixel radius until you achieve the correct amount of sharpening. A pixel radius of 1.0 if printing to Gloss paper and 3.0 if printing to Matte paper would be about normal.

Note > To adjust the level of sharpening later you can either adjust the opacity of the High Pass layer or set the blend mode of the 'High Pass' layer to 'Soft Light' or 'Hard Light' to increase or decrease the level of sharpening.

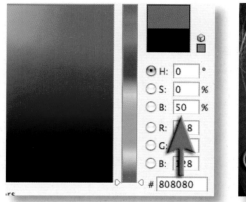 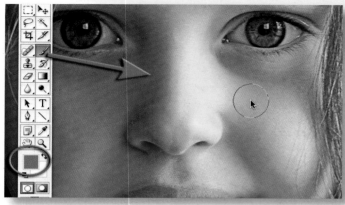

3. Click on the foreground color swatch in the Tools palette to open the Color Picker. Enter 0 in the Hue and Saturation fields and 50% in the Brightness field to choose a midtone gray. Select OK. Paint the High Pass layer to remove any sharpening that is not required, e.g. skin tones, skies, etc. This technique is especially useful for limiting the visual appearance of noise or film grain.

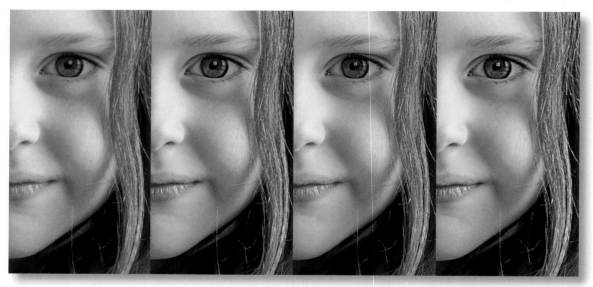

Detail from a portrait captured on a Nikon D1x. The RAW image was processed with 15% sharpening. First test has no subsequent sharpening. Second test uses a High Pass layer (3 pixel radius) in Soft Light mode. Third test has had the blend mode of the High Pass layer changed to Overlay mode. Fourth test has sharpening via a localized Unsharp Mask (100%) in Luminosity mode. The opacity slider could be used to fine-tune the preferred sharpening routine

4. Remember at this point the settings you have selected are being viewed on a monitor as a preview of the actual print. To complete the process it is important to print the image and then decide whether the image could stand additional sharpening or whether the amount used was excessive. If the settings are excessive you can choose to lower the opacity of the 'High Pass' layer. You can alternatively switch the blend mode of the 'High Pass' layer to 'Soft Light' to reduce the sharpness or 'Hard Light' to increase the sharpness.

SATURATION AND SHARPENING

Most techniques to increase the contrast of an image will also have a knock-on effect of increasing color saturation. As the High Pass and Unsharp Mask filters both increase local contrast there is an extended technique if this increased color saturation becomes problematic. You may not notice this in general image editing, but if you become aware of color fringing after applying the High Pass technique you should consider the following technique to limit its effects.

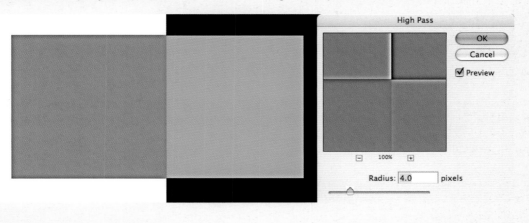

TECHNIQUE TWO – UNSHARP MASK/SMART SHARPEN

The second technique is a continuation of the first technique and is intended to address the issues of increased saturation leading to the effect of color fringing. If a merged layer is used as the sharpening layer (as in Project 3) and this layer is then changed to Luminosity blend mode the effects of saturation are removed from the contrast equation. This second technique looks how the benefits of localized sharpening and Luminosity sharpening can be combined.

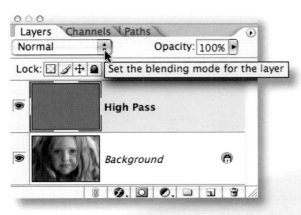

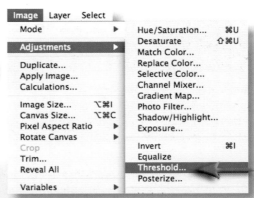

5. Change the blend mode of the High Pass layer back to Normal mode. Then apply a Threshold adjustment to the High Pass layer. Go to Image > Adjustments > Threshold.

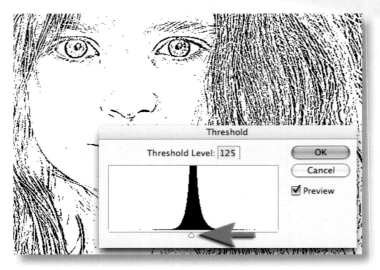
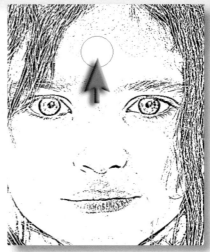

6. Drag the slider just below the histogram to isolate the edges that require sharpening. The aim of moving these sliders is to render all of those areas you do not want to sharpen white. Select 'OK' when you are done. Paint out any areas that were not rendered white by the Threshold adjustment that you do not what to be sharpened, e.g. in the portrait used in this example any pixels remaining in the skin away from the eyes, mouth and nose were painted over using the Paintbrush Tool with white selected as the foreground color.

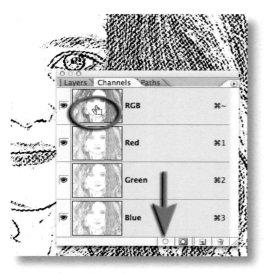
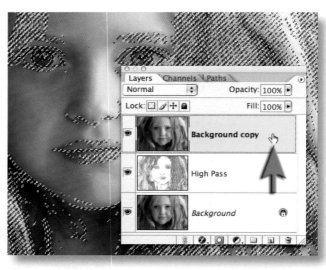

7. Go to the Channels palette and either Ctrl-click (PC) or Command-click (Mac) the RGB thumbnail or click on the 'Load channel as selection' icon from the base of the Channels palette to load the edge detail as a selection. Return to the Layers palette and drag the background layer to the new layer icon to make a background copy layer. Drag this background copy layer to the top of the layers stack.

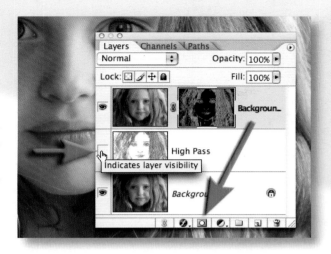
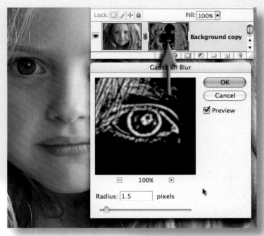

8. Switch off the visibility of the High Pass layer. Hold down the Alt or Option key and click on the 'Add layer mask' icon in the Layers palette. Make sure the layer mask thumbnail is the active part of the layer and then go to Filter > Blur > Gaussian Blur. Apply a 1.5 pixel radius blue to the mask.

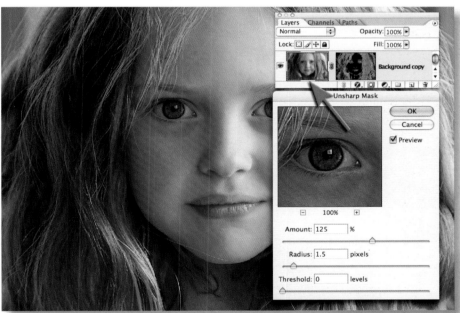

9. Now click on the image thumbnail on the background copy layer. Ensure the image is zoomed in to 100% for a small image or 50% for a larger print resolution image (200–300 ppi). Go to 'Filter > Sharpen > Smart Sharpen or Unsharp Mask'. Adjust the 'Amount' slider to between 80 and 150%. This controls how much darker or lighter the pixels at the edges are rendered. Choose an amount slightly more than looks comfortable on screen if the image is destined for print rather than screen.

Note > See Capture and Enhance for basic settings of the Unsharp Mask filter. The exact Threshold and Radius settings are not so critical for this advanced technique.

essential skills >>>   >>>   PHOTOSHOP CS2

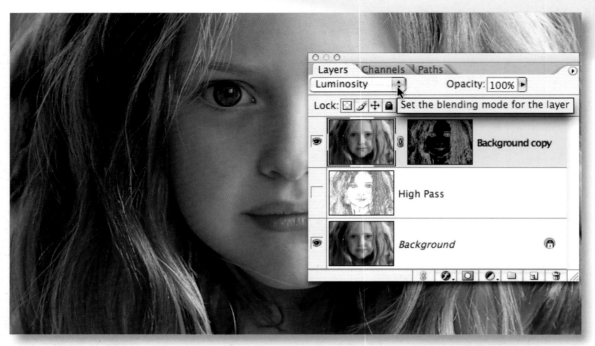

10. Change the blend mode of the sharpening layer (the uppermost layer) to Luminosity mode. Luminosity mode will restrict the contrast changes to brightness only, and will remove any changes in saturation that have occurred due to the use of the Unsharp Mask. The changes are often very subtle so this technique is only recommended when you become aware of the problems of color fringing due to increased saturation.

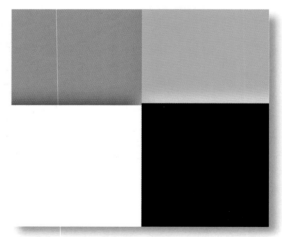

Before and after the Luminosity mode change

The illustration above is a maginified view of the effects of changing the blend to Luminosity. These two cutting-edge techniques are capable of producing razor sharp images that will really put the finishing touches to a folio quality image.

Glamor makeover – *Project 7*

The glamor portrait offers an excellent opportunity to test the effectiveness of a variety of image-editing skills. The portrait is an unforgiving canvas that will show any heavy-handed or poor technique that may be applied. Start with a color portrait that has been captured using a soft diffused light source.

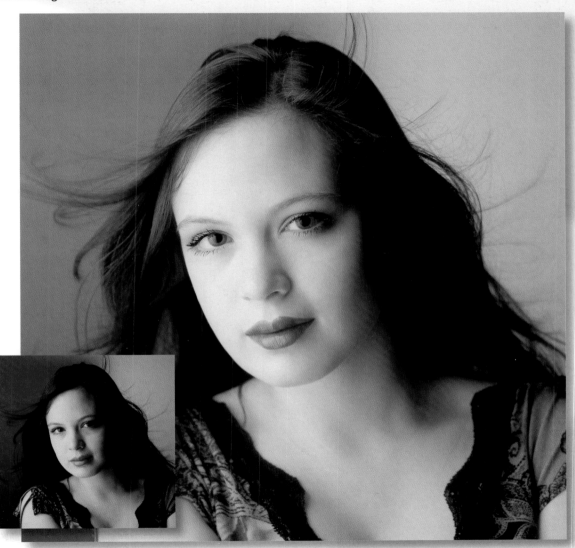

Photography by Michael Wennrich

Start with a 20 megabyte 16 bits per channel image file that has a good histogram and that has been color corrected. The objective of this project is to perfect various characteristics and not to make such changes that the character of the sitter is lost to the technique. Care should be taken not to excessively smooth skin texture and thereby create an artificial or plastic appearance. Fading filters and reducing opacity of brushes will help to smooth imperfections and not totally eliminate them.

213

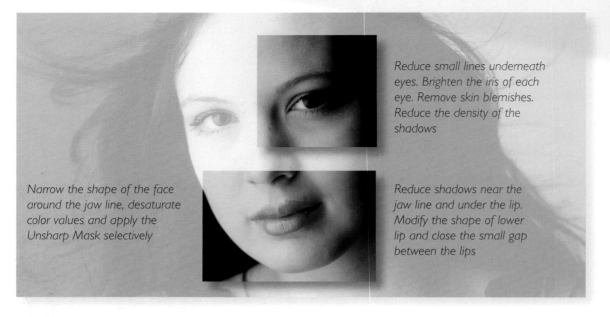

Reduce small lines underneath eyes. Brighten the iris of each eye. Remove skin blemishes. Reduce the density of the shadows

Narrow the shape of the face around the jaw line, desaturate color values and apply the Unsharp Mask selectively

Reduce shadows near the jaw line and under the lip. Modify the shape of lower lip and close the small gap between the lips

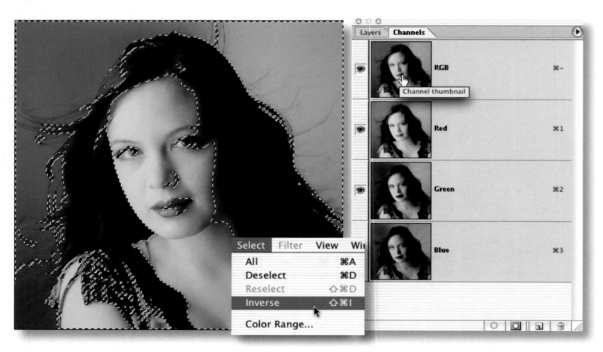

Adjust the tonality

1. To brighten the dark shadows use the Shadow/Highlight adjustment feature outlined in Project 5 or create a luminosity mask for an adjustment layer. A luminosity mask will help to isolate the shadows for adjustment and leave the highlights relatively unaffected. To select the luminosity from the Channels Command/Ctrl-click the master RGB channel. The resulting selection must be inverted before creating a Curves adjustment layer in the Layers palette.

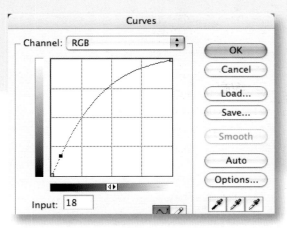

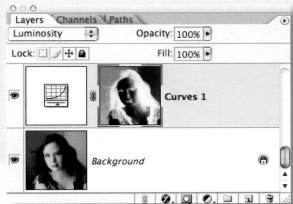

2. With the Luminosity selection active create a Curves adjustment layer and open the shadows by raising the curve to reveal any detail present. It is not necessary to peg the highlights as these values are being masked. The mask can be further enhanced to limit the adjustment layer's impact on the midtones and shadows by increasing its contrast (click on the layer mask thumbnail and use an adjustment from the 'Image' menu).

Remove blemishes from the skin

3. Always duplicate the background layer before starting to work directly on the pixels. Use the Spot Healing Brush to remove fine lines from underneath the eyes. Care must be taken when selecting the size and hardness of the brush. If an overly large soft-edged brush is used it can draw in color values from the eyelashes or eyelids that can contaminate the skin tone. If the repair area becomes contaminated with unwanted detail or color, switch to the Healing Brush Tool and make a selection to isolate the healing area from the different colors or tones prior to using the brush. If the brush is too hard the edges of the healing area will be visible. Sometimes it is better to use a smaller brush and make several passes rather than trying to complete the section with a single pass. The Healing Brush, with its protection of surface texture, is a superior alternative to using the Clone Stamp Tool at a reduced opacity.

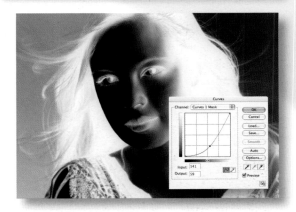

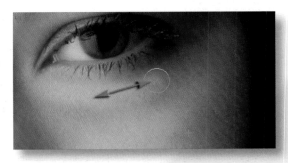

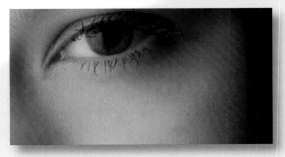

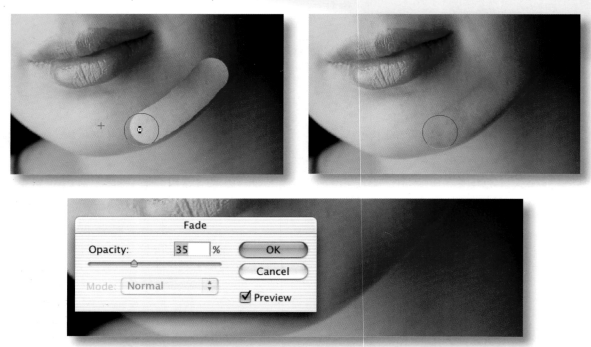

The Healing Brush in some respects behaves like a filter, and as such can be 'faded' from the Edit menu. The ability to fade the Healing Brush using the Fade command from the Edit menu can often disguise and blend the edges to create an undetectable patch.

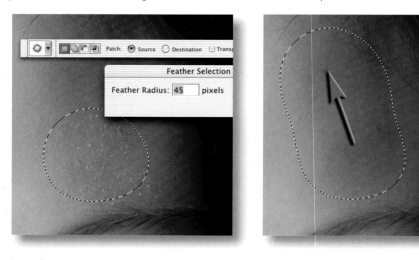

The Patch Tool can occasionally be used as a quick-fix solution to repairing a large area where the surrounding tone is similar and large enough to support the patch. The Feather Radius is critical to the success of the patch technique. If 'Source' is selected in the Patch options the damaged area must first be selected and then dragged to an area with a similar texture value that is undamaged. Small blemishes can be removed by either spotting with the Healing Brush or using the History Brush technique as described earlier.

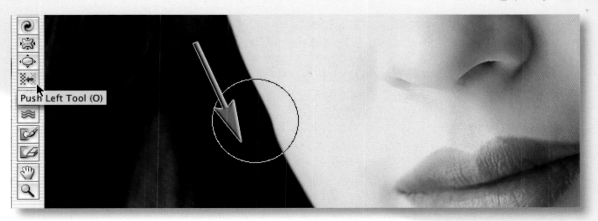

Push Left Tool (O)

Liquify

4. Ensure the 'Background copy' layer is selected before experimenting with the 'Liquify' filter. The Liquify filter can be used to modify the shape or line of various features. The 'Pucker Tool' is used to contract an area of the lip that is asymmetrical whilst the 'Push Left Tool' with the brush pressure set to 10% is used to move the edge of the face inwards. Using a graphics tablet instead of a mouse may also be helpful when using the Push Left Tool. It is important to exercise great restraint when using these tools, as the face can quickly become a cartoon caricature of itself when taken too far.

Note > The Liquify tools will soften detail which becomes obvious when overdone.

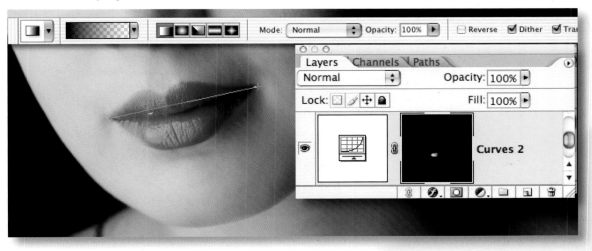

Selective color adjustment

5. The lips have been selected using a Lasso Tool and the selection feathered. A Curves adjustment layer is then applied to increase the depth of tone on the lighter side of the lips. A gradient mask is then applied (foreground to transparent) to hide the adjustment from the darker side of the lips. This evens out the lip color.

Note > The lips were later retouched again using the Clone Stamp Tool at a reduced opacity to close the small gap and lighten the lines and irregularities in the lip surface.

Eye highlighter

6. The focal point of any portrait is the eyes and some time can be spent making the most of this important feature. The whites of the eyes can be cleaned using the Healing Brush whilst a new layer filled with 50% gray can be used to dodge the eyes to brighten them. The iris of each eye can be selected using the Ellipse Tool. A second ellipse with the 'Subtract from selection' icon selected can be used to remove the pupil from the selection. Create a Hue/Saturation adjustment layer either to adjust the saturation and lightness or to 'Colorize' the eyes with a different color.

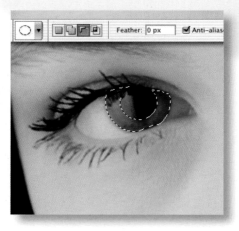

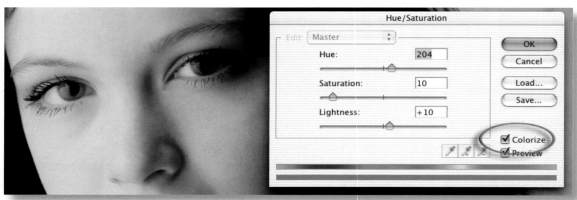

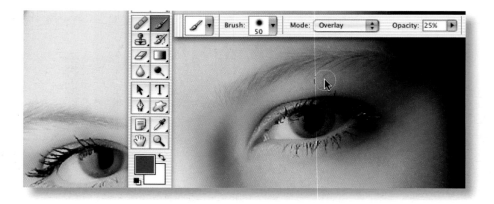

The 'makeover'

7. Make-up can by applied by brushing color onto a new layer set to an appropriate blend mode. Use a soft-edged brush set to a reduced opacity and build up the color slowly to obtain a subtle effect. The layer opacity can be reduced if necessary and a small amount of 'Gaussian Blur' can help to soften any edges that are noticeable.

PHOTOSHOP CS2

essential skills >>>

Channel mixing

8. A desaturated layer with a reduced opacity can be used to reduce the overall color saturation of this portrait image to create a different mood. This effect can be created by using the 'Channel Mixer'. The Channel Mixer can be placed on an adjustment layer and can selectively draw its grayscale information in differing amounts from the three channels. Viewing the red channel of a portrait image you will usually find that the skin texture is smoother than in the green or blue channels.

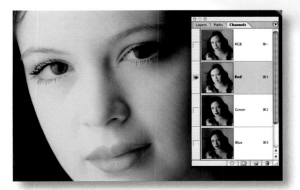 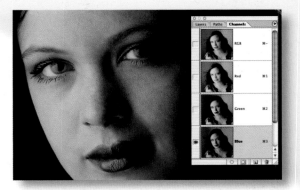

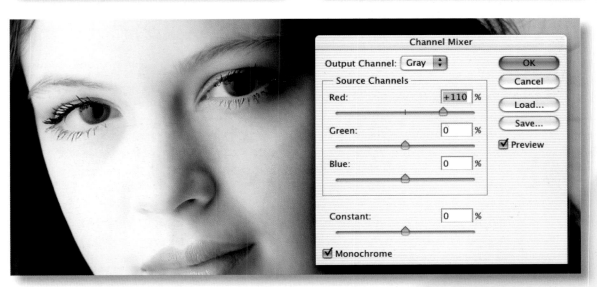

In the 'Channel Mixer' dialog box choose 'Gray' as the output channel and check the 'Monochrome' box. Adjust the red, green and blue channel sliders until you achieve the tonality and contrast you are looking for. Favoring the red channel over the green and blue will usually render a smoother appearance. The total amount in the three fields should add up to approximately 100% if the image is to retain its overall brightness level.

Sharpening

Smooth skin tones can be unduly sensitive to the application of the Unsharp Mask or Smart Sharpen filters. It is usual to raise the threshold slider sufficiently so that areas of smooth tonal gradation are left unaffected when using the Unsharp Mask. Film grain, image sensor noise and minor skin defects all come in for the sharpening treatment if the threshold is left too low. If the sharpening process is proving problematic a selective sharpening process should be considered (see Project 6).

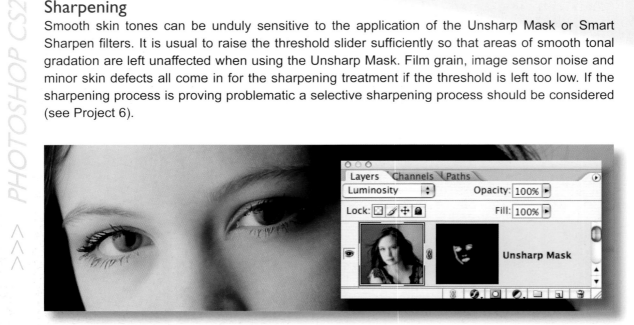

9. Create a sharpening layer by merging all the visible components off all of the other layers and pasting this information to a new layer on top of the layers stack. Create a layer mask as in 'Project 6' to shield the skin tones from the effects of the Unsharp Mask.

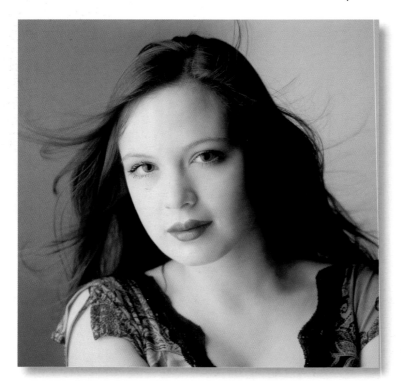

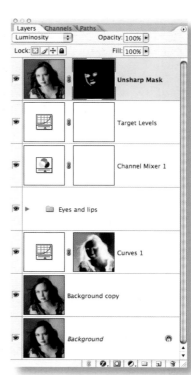

Tonal contraction – *Project 8*

Contrary to popular opinion – what you see is not what you always get. You may be able to see the detail in those dark shadows and bright highlights when the sun is shining – but can your CCD or CMOS sensor? Contrast in a scene is often a photographer's worst enemy. Contrast is a sneak thief that steals away the detail in the highlights or shadows (sometimes both). A wedding photographer will deal with the problem by using fill-flash to lower the subject contrast; commercial photographers diffuse their own light source or use additional fill lighting and check for missing detail using the 'Histogram' or a 'Polaroid'.

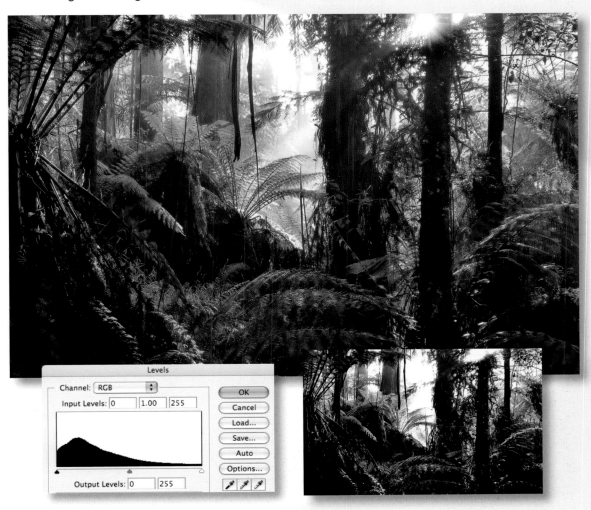

Landscape photographers, however, have drawn the short straw when it comes to solving the contrast problem. For the landscape photographer there is no 'quick fix'. A reflector that can fill the shadows of the Grand Canyon has yet to be made and diffusing the sun's light is only going to happen if the clouds are prepared to play ball.

Ansel Adams (the famous landscape photographer) developed 'The Zone System' to deal with the high contrast vistas he encountered in California. By careful exposure and processing he found he could extend the film's ability to record high contrast landscapes and create a black-and-white print with full detail. Unlike film, however, the latitude of a digital imaging sensor (its ability to record a subject brightness range) is fixed. In this respect the sensor is a strait-jacket for our aims to create tonally rich images when the sun is shining – or is it? Here is a post-production 'tone system' that will enrich you and your images.

Note > It is recommended to capture in RAW mode to exploit the full dynamic range that your image sensor is capable of as JPEG or TIFF processing in-camera may clip the shadow and highlight detail (see Digital Negatives).

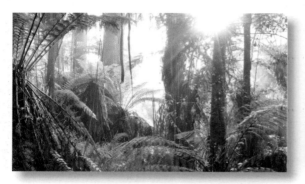 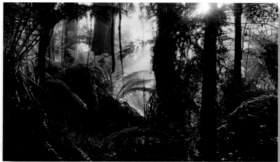

1. The first step to tonal riches is all in-camera. If we can't fit all the goodies in one exposure – then we'll just have to take two. The idea is to montage, or blend, the best of both worlds (the light and dark side of the camera's not quite all-seeing eye). To make the post-production easier we need to take a little care in the pre-production, i.e. mount the camera securely on a sturdy tripod. Take two exposures, one overexposing from the auto reading and the other underexposing from the auto reading. One or two stops either side of the meter indicated exposure should cover most high contrast situations.

Note > If you intend to use the new 'Automate > Merge to HDR' (High Dynamic Range) feature Adobe recommends that you use the shutter speed to bracket the exposures.

BRACKETING EXPOSURES

Setting your camera to 'auto bracket exposure mode' means that you don't have to touch the camera between the two exposures, thereby ensuring the first and second exposures can be exactly aligned with the minimum of fuss. Unfortunately for me, the little Fuji FinePix s7000 I was using for this image has auto bracket exposure but it is not operational in RAW capture mode – the only respectable format for self-respecting landscape photographers. This is where you dig out your trusty cable release and, if you are really lucky – have somewhere to screw it into! The only other movement to be aware of is something beyond your control. If there is a gale blowing (or even a moderate gust) you are not going to get the leaves on the trees to align perfectly in post-production. This also goes for fast-moving clouds and anything else that is likely to be zooming around in the fraction of a second between the first and second exposures.

Merge to HDR

New to CS2 is the Merge to HDR (High Dynamic Range) automated feature. A series of bracketed exposures can be selected and the Merge to HDR feature then aligns the images automatically. The Merge to HDR dialog box then opens and the user is invited to select a bit depth and a white point. It is recommended to save the file as a 32-bit image. This allows the exposure and gamma to be fine-tuned after the image is opened into Photoshop by going to Image > Adjustments > Exposure. As editing in 32 Bits/Channel is exceptionally limited the user will inevitably want to drop the bit depth to 16 or 8 Bits/Channel at some stage to make use of the full range of adjustment features.

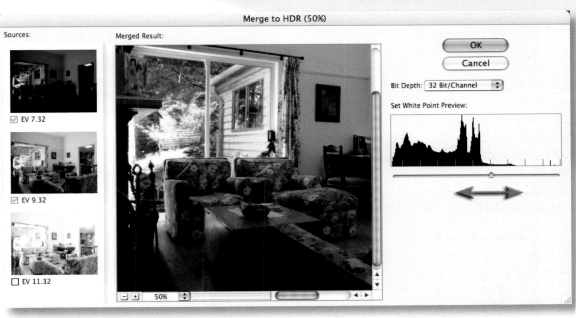

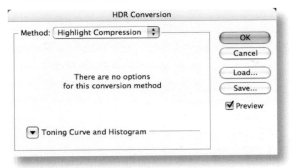

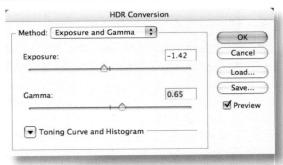

When the Photoshop user converts a HDR 32-bit image to 16 or 8 Bits/Channel the user can choose a conversion method that allows the best tonal conversion for the job in hand. With very precise working methods HDR images can provide the professional photographer with a useful workflow to combat extreme contrast working environments. For the casual user who encounters the occasional high contrast situation manual blending techniques can offer a simpler and faster solution to the contrast problem. Two of the most common manual techniques for blending exposures are outlined in the following pages.

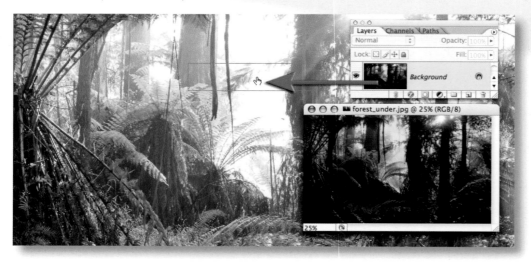

2. To merge the exposures manually you should select the Move Tool in the Tools palette and drag the dark underexposed image into the window of the lighter overexposed image (alternatively just drag the thumbnail from the Layers palette with any tool selected). Holding down the 'Shift' key as you let go of the image will align the two layers (but not necessarily the two images).

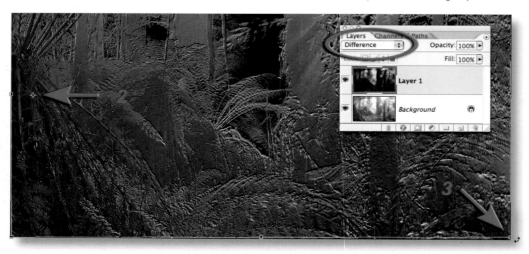

3. In the Layers palette set the blend mode of the top layer to 'Difference' to check the alignment of the two images. If they align – no white edges will be apparent (usually the case If the tripod was sturdy and the two exposures were made via an auto feature or cable release). If you had to resort to a friend's right shoulder you will now spend the time you thought you had saved earlier. To make a perfect alignment you need to select 'Free Transform' from the 'Edit' menu and either nudge the underexposed layer into position using the arrow keys on the keyboard and/or rotate the layer into position. This is achieved by moving the mouse cursor to a position just outside the corner handle of the 'Free Transform' bounding box and then rotating the layer into position. It may help if the axis of rotation is moved before rotating the layer in order to get a precise match.

Note > Two alternative approaches are now outlined on the following pages.

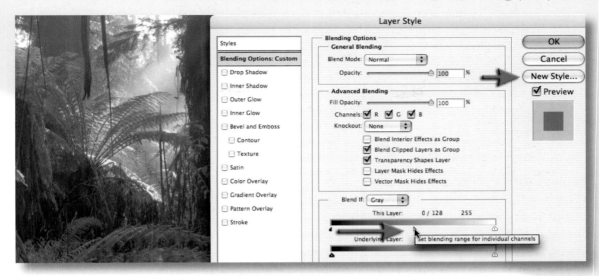

Advanced blending – *approach one*

4. Using the advanced blending options it is possible to reduce the opacity of the shadow tones on the top layer to reveal the shadow tones beneath. The effect can be faded in gradually, creating a blend of the optimum highlights from the top layer and the optimum shadow tones of the background layer.

Note > The second approach uses a layer mask instead of advanced blending techniques.

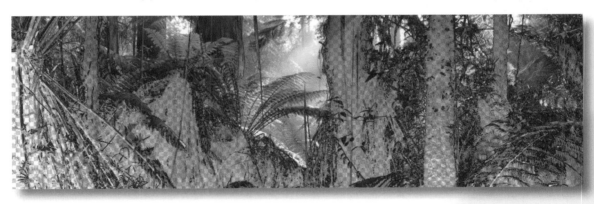

Access the advanced blending options by clicking on the 'Add a layer style' icon in the Layers palette and then choosing Blending Options or by simply double-clicking the layer in the Layers palette (be sure to click the layer and not the layer thumbnail or layer name). In the 'Blend if' section of this dialog box go to the 'This Layer' gray ramp. Split the black slider by holding down the Alt or Option key and dragging the right-hand side of the slider towards the higher levels. Observe the changes in the image when the slider is moved to 64, 128, 196 and all the way to 256. Click OK to exit this dialog box and apply the effect. Alternatively you can click on the 'New Style' button and save this setting in the Layer Style palette for use on subsequent projects.

225

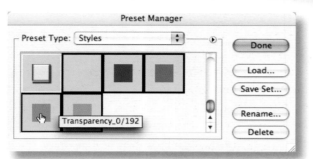
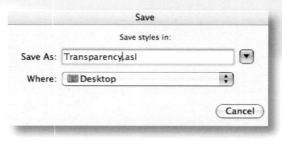

You can save these presets to enable a 'one-click' procedure by going to the Preset Manager (Edit menu). The style presets are saved as an 'asl' file. The presets can then be loaded into other copies of Photoshop on different computers by placing the file in the preset folder or by simply double-clicking the file. The transparency styles used in this project are also available on the supporting CD. To apply a transparency preset select the layer in the Layers palette and then click on each of the four presets in turn (located in the Styles palette) and choose the one that renders the best tonality.

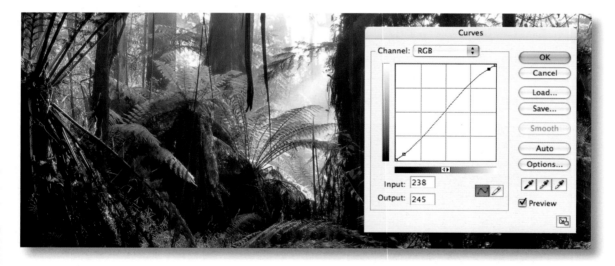

5. Create an adjustment layer by clicking on the 'Create new fill or adjustment layer' icon and choose 'Curves' from the submenu. The final step in the process is to target the deepest shadows and brightest highlights to the values best suited to your chosen output device. My own Epson inkjet paper handles the highlights really well and tones of 250 are easily distinguishable from the paper white (255). The precise targeting of the shadow tones are dependent on the inks and paper being used and can be anywhere between 10 and 20. Do not rely on your monitor at this stage if your final output is print – if in doubt print a test strip and readjust the target points if required. To target a tone refer to the 'Capture and Enhance' chapter or Project 3 in this chapter. Select OK when you are satisfied your image is looking fabulous.

Note > Finding the optimum values for your printer and media can be achieved by printing a tonal step wedge with known values to plot the capabilities of your printer.

Layer masks – *approach two*

4. Select the dark underexposed layer and click on the 'Add layer mask' icon in the Layers palette. From the 'Select' menu choose 'Select All'. Hold down the 'Alt' key (Option key on a Mac) and click on the layer mask. This allows you to view the empty contents of the layer mask rather than viewing the layer itself. If the layer mask is not selected in this way the contents of the clipboard will be pasted into a new layer. The image window should appear white prior to selecting the paste command. Apply a small amount of Gaussian blur to this mask.

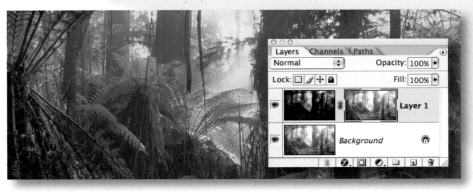

5. Alt/Option click the layer mask thumbnail a second time to view the effects of the combined layers. At this stage the midtone contrast is likely to be flat and there is no guarantee you will have a full spread of tones across the entire histogram after adding the layer mask. It will usually be necessary to manipulate and stretch the tonal range back to complete the process.

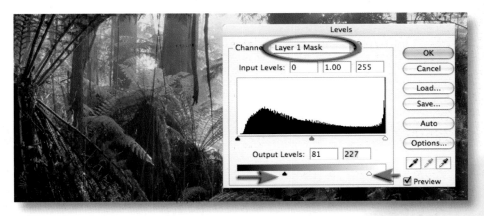

6. Adjust the contrast of the layer mask to change the contrast of the image. This can be achieved by using a 'Curves' or 'Levels' adjustment. The adjustment must be taken from the 'Image > Adjustments' submenu. It is important to ensure the layer mask thumbnail is still the selected item on the layer before applying the adjustment. The adjustment dialog box will indicate that it is the mask that is being adjusted and not the pixels on the layer. Lowering the contrast of the mask will increase the contrast of the image. This can be achieved in the Levels adjustment dialog box by sliding the output sliders towards the center of the histogram. Make sure the 'Preview' box is checked so that you can monitor the effects of the adjustment on the image itself.

227

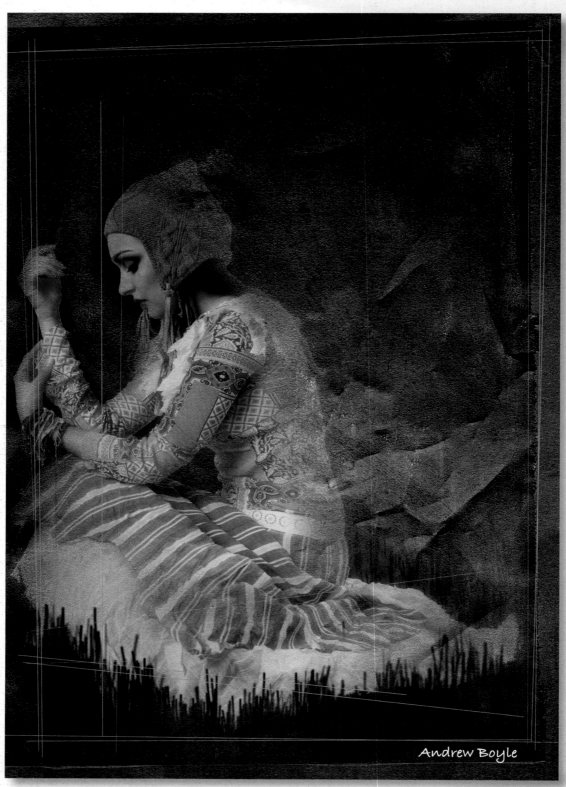

Andrew Boyle

toning projects

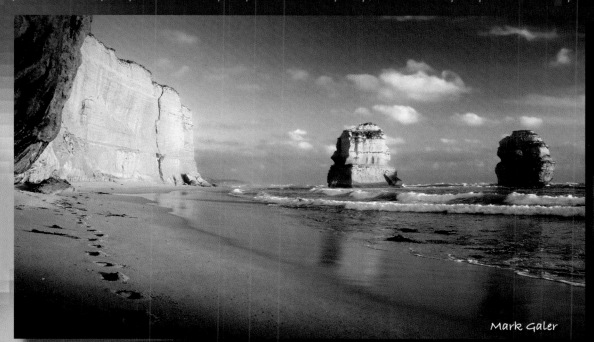

Mark Galer

essential skills

- ~ Create a monochrome or black and white image from an RGB master.
- ~ Create a toned image using a 'Gradient Map'.
- ~ Create a cross-processed effect using 'Curves' and 'Hue/Saturation' adjustment layers.
- ~ Create images that emulate lith prints, split-toned prints and duotones.

Black and white – *Project 1*

When color film arrived over half a century ago the pundits who presumed that black and white film would die a quick death were surprisingly mistaken. Color is all very nice but sometimes the rich tonal qualities that we can see in the work of the photographic artists are something certainly to be savored. Can you imagine an Ansel Adams masterpiece in color? If you can – read no further.

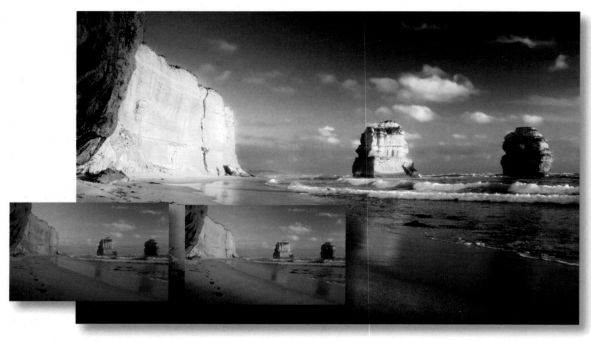

Creating fabulous black and white photographs from your color images is a little more complicated than hitting the 'Convert to Grayscale mode' or 'Desaturate' buttons in your image-editing software (or worse still, your camera). Ask any professional photographer who has been raised on the medium and you will discover that crafting tonally rich images requires both a carefully chosen color filter during the capture stage and some dodging and burning in the darkroom.

Color filters for black and white? Now there is an interesting concept! Well as strange as it may seem, screwing on a color filter for capturing images on black and white film has traditionally been an essential ingredient to the recipe for success. The most popular color filter in the black and white photographer's kit bag, that is used for the most dramatic effect, is the 'red filter'. The effect of the red filter is to lighten all things that are red and darken all things that are not red in the original scene. The result is a print with considerable tonal differences compared to an image shot without a filter. Is this a big deal? Well yes it is – blue skies are darkened and skin blemishes are lightened. That's a winning combination for most landscape and portrait photographers wanting to create black and white masterpieces.

Note > The more conservative photographers of old (those not big on drama) would typically invest in a yellow or orange filter rather than the 'full-on' effects that the red filter offers.

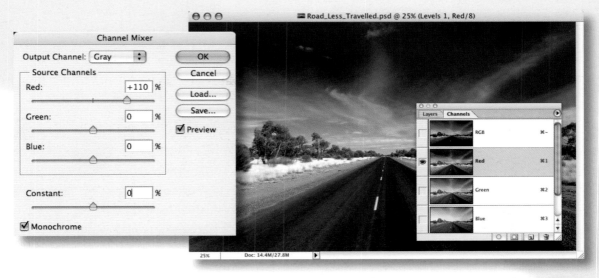

Now just before you run out to purchase your red filter and 'Grayscale image sensor' you should be reminded that neither is required by the digital shooter with access to image-editing software. Shooting digitally in RGB (red, green, blue) means that you have already shot the same image using the three different filters. If you were to selectively favor the goodies in the red channel, above those to be found in the mundane green and the notoriously noisy blue channels, when you convert your RGB image to Grayscale, you would, in effect, be creating a Grayscale image that would appear as if it had been shot using the red filter from the 'good old days'. You can see the different tonal information in the individual channels by using the 'Channels palette', and can then selectively combine the information using the 'Channel Mixer'. The use of the Channel Mixer can be a complex procedure for those who wish to create a monochrome version. This adjustment feature can easily clip tonal information unless you keep a careful eye on the histogram palette as you draw information from the three channels and try to balnce the overall brightness of the image at the same time. As luck would have it the famous digital guru 'Russell Preston Brown' has come up with a work-around that many image editors find easier to use than the Channel Mixer.

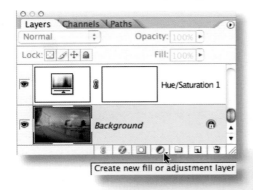
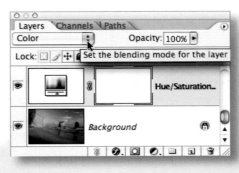

1. Click on the Adjustment Layer icon in the Layers palette and scroll down the list to select and create a 'Hue/Saturation' adjustment layer. You will make no adjustments for the time being but simply select OK to close the dialog box. Set the blend mode of this adjustment layer to 'Color'.

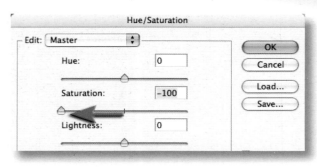
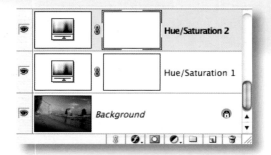

2. Create a second Hue/Saturation adjustment layer. Slide the Saturation slider all the way to the left (−100) to desaturate the image. Select OK. The image will now appear as if you had performed a simple Convert to Grayscale or Desaturate (remove color) command.

Note > This second adjustment layer should be sitting on top of the layers stack.

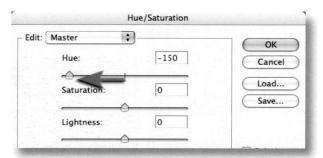
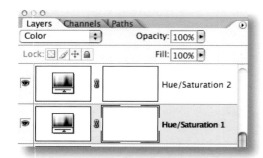

3. Select the first Hue/Saturation layer that you created and double-click the layer thumbnail to reopen the Hue/Saturation dialog box. Move the 'Hue' slider in this dialog box to the left. Observe the changes to the tonality of the image as you move the slider. Blues will be darkest when the slider is moved to a position around −150. Select OK. The drama of the image will probably have been improved quite dramatically already but we can take this further with some dodging and burning.

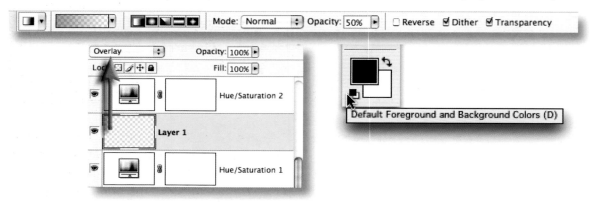

4. Click on the 'New Layer' icon in the Layers palette. Set the blend mode of the layer to 'Overlay'. Set the default 'Foreground and Background' colors in the Tools palette and then select the 'Gradient' tool. In the Options bar select the 'Foreground (black) to Transparent' and 'Linear' gradient options and then lower the opacity to 50%.

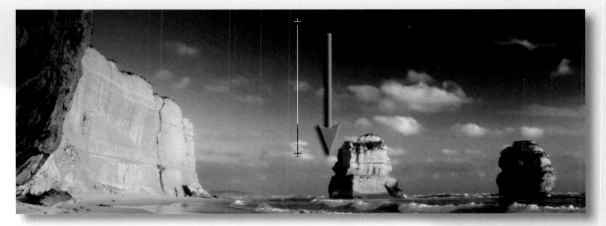

5. Drag one gradient from the base of the image to the horizon line, and a second from the top of the image window to the horizon line. This will have the effect of drawing the viewer into the image and create an increased sense of drama. Lower the opacity of the layer if the effect is too strong.

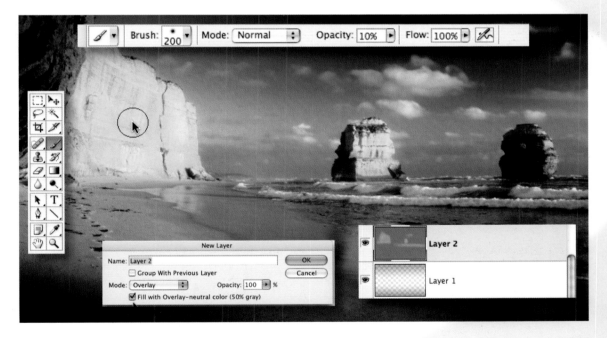

6. Press the 'Alt/Option' key and click on the 'New Layer' icon. In the New Layer dialog box set the blend mode to 'Overlay' and select the 'Fill with Overlay-neutral color' option. Select the Paintbrush Tool and select a soft-edged brush from the Options bar and lower the opacity to 10%. A layer that is 50% Gray in Overlay mode is invisible. This Gray layer will be used to dodge and burn your image non-destructively, i.e. you are not working on the actual pixels of your image. If any mistakes are made they can either be corrected or the layer can be discarded. Paint onto the Gray layer with Black selected as the foreground color to burn (darken) the image in localized areas or switch to White to dodge (lighten) localized areas. In the project image the cliffs and the surf were dodged to highlight them.

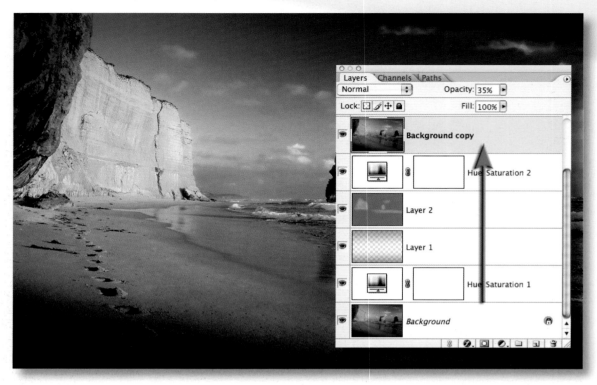

7. Try experimenting with the introduction of some of the original color. Duplicate the background layer by dragging it to the New Layer icon. Then drag the background copy further up the layers stack to a position just below the Levels adjustment layer. Reduce the opacity of this layer to let the black and white version introduce the drama once more.

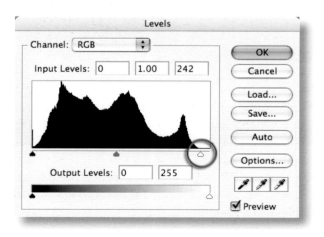

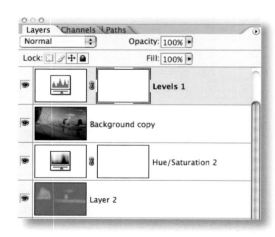

8. Select the top layer and then create a 'Levels' adjustment layer (one adjustment layer to rule them all) to sit above all of the other layers. Make sure the histogram extends all the way between the black and white sliders. Move the sliders in to meet the histogram if this is not the case.

Gradient maps – *Project 2*

Burning, toning, split-grade printing and printing through your mother's silk stockings are just some of the wonderful, weird and positively wacky techniques used by the traditional masters of the darkroom waiting to be exposed (or ripped off) in this tantalizing digital tutorial designed to pump up the mood and ambience of the flat and downright dull.

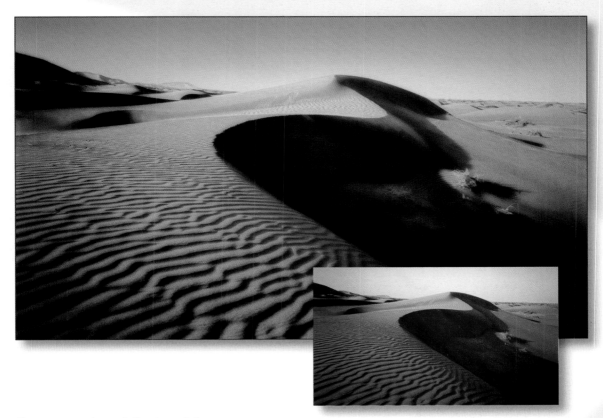

Seeing red and feeling blue

It probably comes as no small surprise that 'color' injects images with mood and emotional impact. Photographers, however, frequently work on images that are devoid of color because of the tonal control they are able to achieve in traditional processing and printing techniques. Toning the resulting 'black and white' images keeps the emphasis on the play of light and shade but lets the introduced colors influence the final mood. With the increased sophistication and control that digital image-editing software affords us, we can now explore the 'twilight zone' between color and black and white as never before. The original image has the potential to be more dramatic and carry greater emotional impact through the controlled use of tone and color.

The tonality of the tutorial image destined for the toning table will be given a split personality. The shadows will be gently blurred to add depth and character whilst the highlights will be lifted and left with full detail for emphasis and focus. Selected colors will then be mapped to the new tonality to establish the final mood.

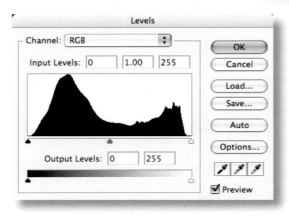

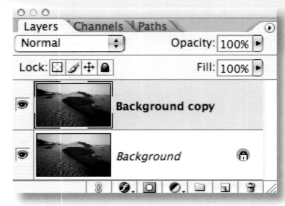

1. For the best results choose an image where the directional lighting (low sunlight or window light) has created interesting highlights and shadows that gently model the three-dimensional form within the image. Adjust the levels if necessary so that the tonal range extends between the shadow and highlight sliders. In the Layers palette drag the background layer to the New Layer icon to create a background copy.

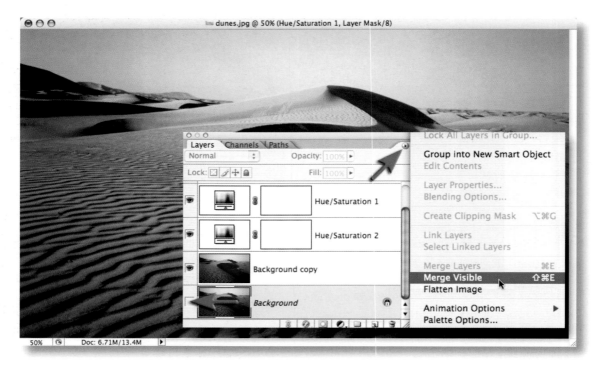

2. Convert this background copy to a black and white layer. Go to Image > Adjustments > Desaturate or create a higher contrast version using the techniques outlined in Project 1. If you have followed the techniques outlined in Project 1 you can switch off the visibility of the Background layer and select Merge Visible from the palette options. This step is optional but recommended when working with images in 16 Bits/Channel mode.

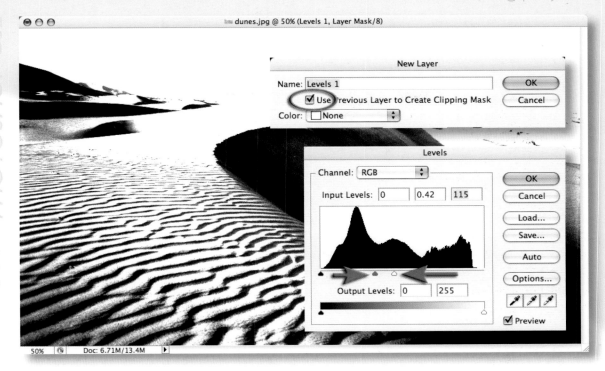

3. Use an 'adjustment layer' to adjust the tonality of this layer. Hold down the Alt/Option key on the keyboard and click on the 'Create new fill or adjustment layer' icon. In the 'New Layer' dialog box check the 'Group With Previous Layer' option. Click 'OK' to open the 'Levels' dialog box. Drag the highlight slider to the left until the highlights disappear. Move the 'Gamma' slider (the one in the middle) until you achieve good contrast in the shadows of the image. Select 'OK' to apply the levels adjustment.

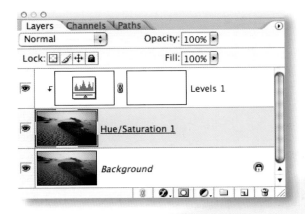
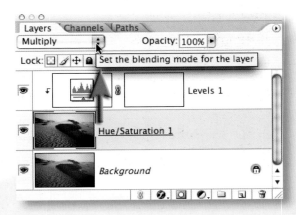

4. In the Layers palette switch the 'mode' of this black and white layer to 'Multiply' to blend these modified shadow tones back into the color image. The image will appear excessively dark but will be corrected in steps 6 to 8.

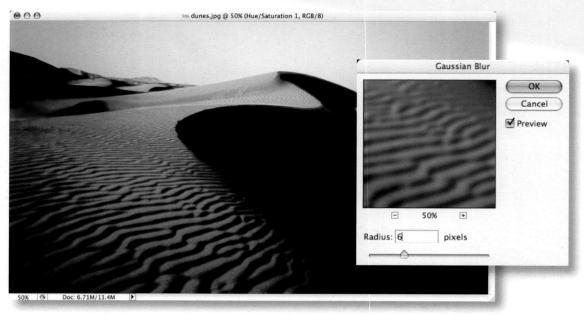

5. Go to 'Filter > Blur > Gaussian Blur' and increase the 'Radius' to spread and soften the shadow tones. With the Preview on you will be able to see the effect as you raise the amount of blur. Go to 'View > Zoom In' to take a closer look at the effect you are creating.

Note > This effect emulates the silk-stocking technique when it is applied to only the high contrast part of the split-grade printing technique made famous by Max Ferguson and digitally remastered in his book _Digital Darkroom Masterclass_ (Focal Press).

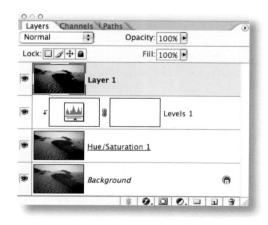

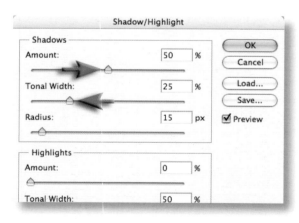

6. Lighten the shadows using the technique outlined in Project 7 of the Retouching Projects chapter or alternatively create a Merged layer (Select All > Copy Merged > Paste) and move to the top of the layers stack. Then use the Shadow/Highlight adjustment feature to lighten the overly dark shadows (see Retouching Projects > Project 5 for more information about this adjustment feature).

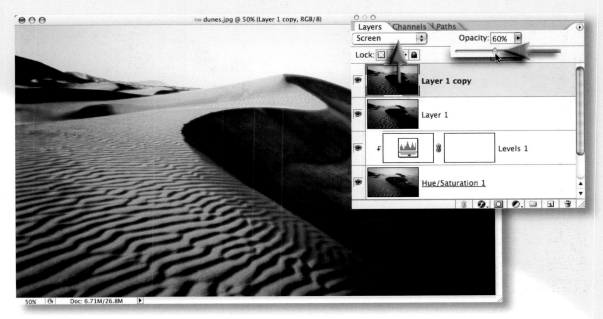

7. Another way of lightening the shadows independently of the highlights is to copy the layer from the previous step and adjust the layer blend mode to Screen. Adjust the opacity of the layer to fine-tune the shadow values. At this stage the brighter tones of the image will aslo be adjusted brighter. This can be corrected using the Advanced Blending options.

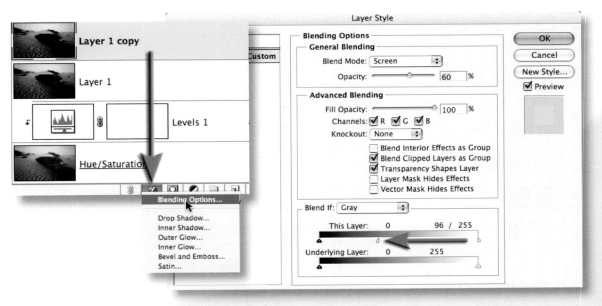

8. Double-click the layer or select 'Blending Options' from the 'Layer Style' menu. Hold down the Alt/Option key and drag the left side of the highlight slider to the left to render the highlight tones on this layer transparent (see Retouching Projects > Project 8 for more information about this technique).

PHOTOSHOP CS2 >>> >>>

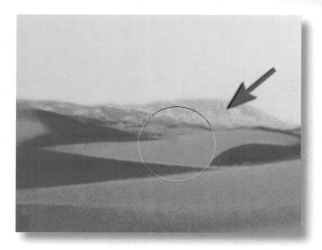

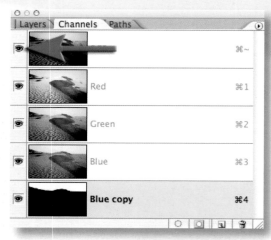

9. Bright areas of tone within the image can be distracting if they are not part of the main subject matter. It is common practice when working in a black and white darkroom to 'burn' the sky darker so that it does not detract the viewer's attention from the main focal point of the image. In the project image the overly bright sky detracts from the beautiful sweep of the dominant sand dune.

To darken the sky create a selection using the Channel Masking technique outlined in the Selections chapter (duplicating the blue channel and increasing the contrast using a Levels adjustment). Fine-tune the mask by switching on the visibility of the alpha channel and the RGB master channel. Use a hard-edged paint brush with the foreground color set to black and paint any areas missed by the channel masking process. Apply a 1.5 pixel Gaussian Blur to the finished mask.

essential skills >>> >>>

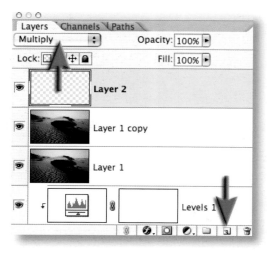

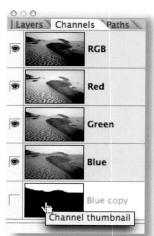

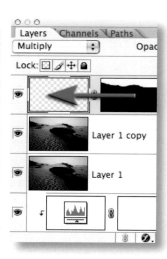

10. Create a new layer for the gradient sky and switch the blend mode to Multiply. Load the channel mask you created in the previous step as a selection (this will help shield the foreground from the gradient). With the selection active click on the Add Layer Mask icon in the Layers palette. Then click on the empty layer thumbnail to make this the active component of the layer.

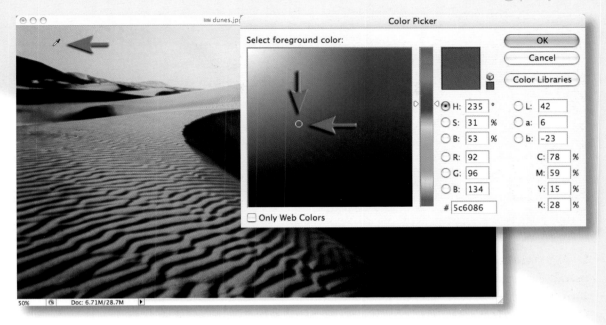

11. To create the gradient sky start by clicking on the foreground color swatch in the Tools palette to open the 'Color Picker'. Select a deep blue and select 'OK'. You can select a hue from the image and then make it darker and less saturated by moving the sample circle in the Color Picker lower and to the left.

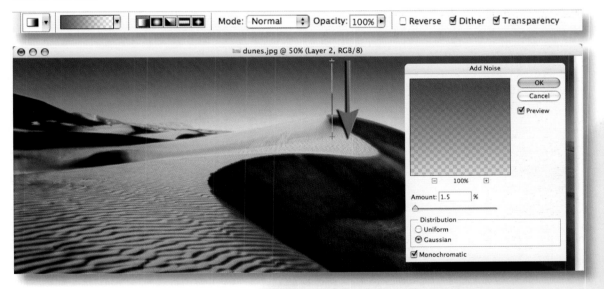

12. Select the Gradient Tool in the Tools palette. In the Options bar select the 'Foreground to Transparent' and 'Linear Gradient' options. Drag a gradient from the top of the image to just below the horizon line to darken the sky. Holding down the Shift key as you drag constrains the gradient, keeping it absolutely vertical. Go to Filter > Noise > Add Noise. Adding a small amount of noise will help to reduce any banding that may occur as a result of using the Gradient Tool.

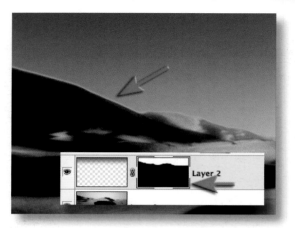
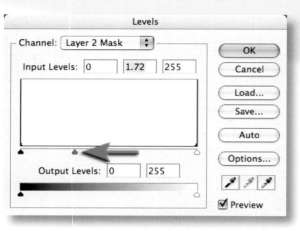

13. Zoom in and take a look at the edge where the sky meets the sand dunes. If you notice a small halo this can be corrected by making adjustments to the layer mask. Click on the layer mask thumbnail and from the Image > Adjustments menu choose 'Levels'. Moving the gamma slider will realign the edge precisely with the edge of the sand dunes. Moving the shadow and highlight sliders in the Levels dialog box will render the edge of the mask less soft.

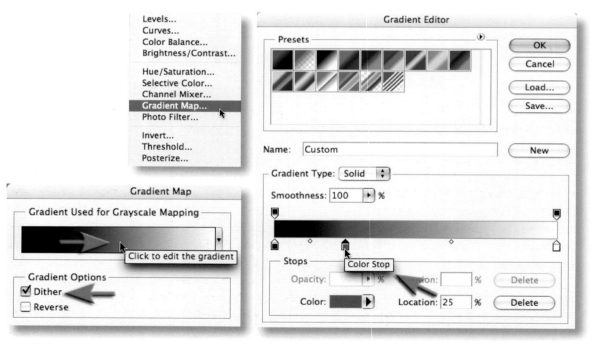

14. To introduce alternative colors into the image we can use a Gradient Map adjustment layer. Check the Dither option in the Gradient Map dialog box (to help to reduce banding) and then click on the gradient to open the 'Gradient Editor' dialog box. Click on the Foreground/background preset swatch to start the process. This will automatically remap the colors to a full tonal range black and white image. Click underneath the gray ramp to add a color stop. Move the stop to a location of 25%. Click on the color swatch to open the Color Picker.

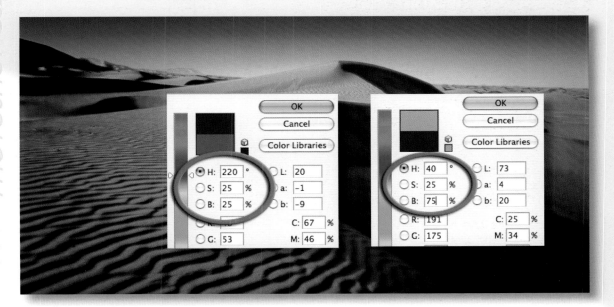

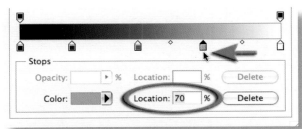

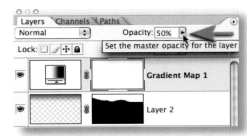

15. Choose a cool color with a brightness value of 25% to give character to the shadow tones. Create another stop and move it to a location that reads approximately 75%. This time try choosing a bright warm color with a brightness value of 75% to contrast with the blue chosen previously. Choosing desaturated colors from the Color Picker (less than 35%) will help to keep the effects subtle. Add a third midtone color stop if required. Drag these color sliders and observe the changes that occur to the tonality of your image. Be careful not to drag the sliders too close together as this will cause banding in the image. Once you have created the perfect gradient you can give it a name and save it by clicking on the 'New' button. This gradient will now appear in the gradient presets for quick access. Click OK in the Gradient Editor and Gradient Map dialog boxes to commit the gradient. Try lowering the opacity of the Gradient Map adjustment layer to introduce some of the original color into the image. Now all you need to do is lock yourself in the bathroom for half a day, dip your hands in some really toxic chemicals and you will have the full sensory experience of the good old days of traditional darkroom toning.

Note > The gradient map used in this toning activity can be downloaded from the supporting web site and loaded into the 'presets' by double-clicking the gradients preset file or clicking on the Load button in either the Gradient Editor or the Preset Manager.

Cross-process effect – *Project 3*

This technique is derived from an effect that was first established by processing color negative film in E-6 chemicals (normally used to process color transparency film). The technique is popular in the fashion photography industry and when applied to film processing is quite destructive to highlight and shadow tones. The same 'look' can be applied to digital files in a non-destructive way using adjustment layers.

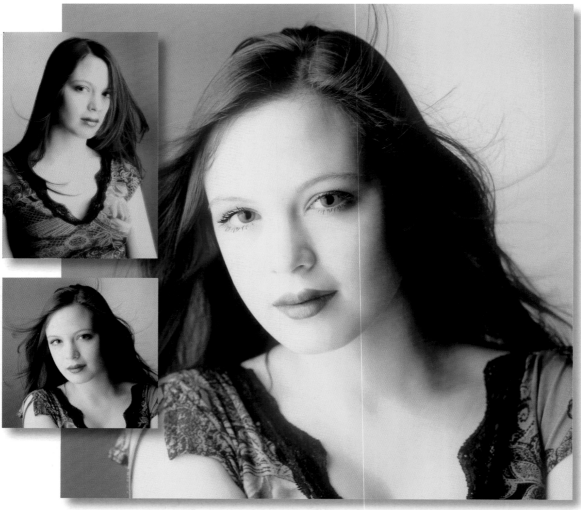

Photography by Michael Wennrich

The image top left is a straight scan from a cross-processed piece of film, whilst the enlarged portrait is a digital copy of the effect that has been achieved by using a Curves adjustment layer. The colors present in the film are simulated by shifting the color values and then increasing the color saturation using a Hue/Saturation adjustment layer. The precise color signature of cross-processed film varies depending on the type of film emulsion used but the characteristics are pinky-orange highlights with blue–cyan shadows. Detail is often lost in both shadows and highlights.

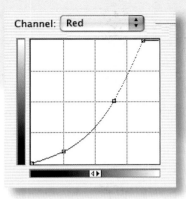 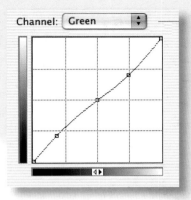 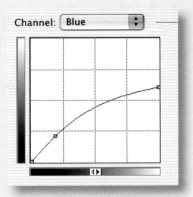

1. Start with the 'glamor portrait' image from the activity in the 'Retouching Projects' chapter. Create a 'Curves' adjustment layer and use the channel information above as a starting point to modify and manipulate the color values.

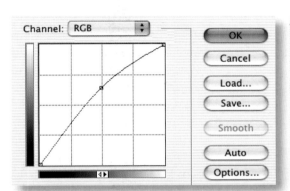 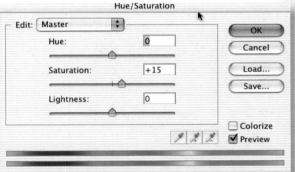

2. With the color values moved modify the tonality using the master 'RGB' channel and then use a Hue/Saturation adjustment layer to increase the saturation to match the cross-processed look. The settings for both of these adjustment layers can be saved for future use by clicking on the 'Save' button in the adjustment layer dialog boxes.

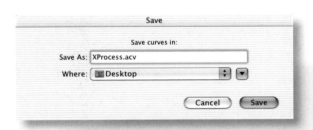 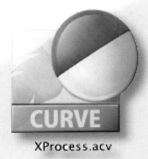

XProcess.acv

Note > The curves setting used in this cross-process activity can be downloaded from the supporting web site and loaded into the Curves dialog box by clicking on the Load button.

Lith printing – *Project 4*

There is no doubt that a well-crafted lith print is, to borrow an oft-used phrase from my father-in-law, 'a thing of beauty is (therefore) a joy forever'. The trick, for the experienced and occasional darkroom users alike, is the production of such a print. Even with frequent reference to publications penned by lith guru Tim Rudman, I have always had difficulty getting consistency with the production of my prints. Despite this frustration my love affair with the process still continues. There is something quite magical about the quality of images created using this technique and it is this magic that I hanker after. They are distinctly textured and richly colored and their origins are unmistakable.

The process, full of quirky variables like age and strength of developer and the amount of overexposure received by the paper, is unpredictable and almost always unrepeatable. In this regard at least, most printers, myself included, found the whole lith printing process both fascinating and infuriating. This said, it's almost a decade since lith printing started to become more commonplace and there is no sign of people's interest declining.

'Long live lith!' I hear you say, 'but I shoot digital'. Well, good news: the digital worker with basic skills, a copy of Photoshop CS2 and a reasonable color printer can reproduce the characteristics of lith printing without the smelly hands, or the dank darkroom.

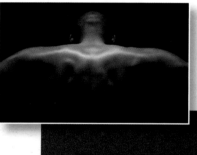

A digitally produced lith print can exhibit similar color and grain characteristics to those typically found in chemically produced originals

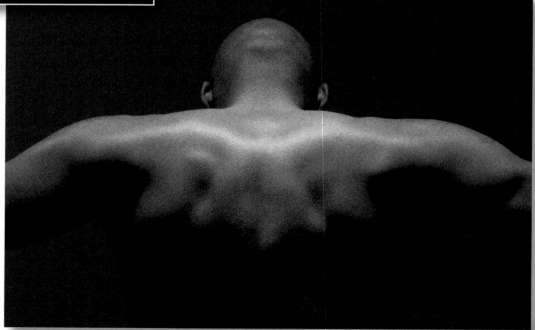

Image courtesy of www.ablestock.com

1. If you ask most photographers what makes a lith print special the majority will tell you it's the amazing grain and the rich colors. Most prints have strong, distinctive and quite atmospheric grain that is a direct result of the way in which the image is processed. This is coupled with colors that are seldom seen in a black and white print. They range from a deep chocolate, through warm browns, to oranges and sometimes even pink tones. If our digital version is to seem convincing then the final print will need to contain all of these elements. Whether you source your image from a camera or a scanner, make sure that the subject matter is conducive to making a lith-type print. The composition should be strong and the image should contain a full range of tones, especially in the highlights and shadows. Delicate details may be lost during the manipulation process, so select an image that still works when the fine details are obscured by coarse grain. Good contrast will also help make a more striking print.

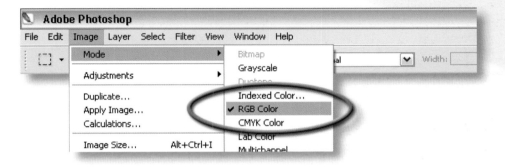

2. Now that you have selected a picture with a strong composition, let's add some color. Photoshop provides a couple of options for adding the distinctive lith colors. The simplest approach uses the Hue/Saturation control as a way of changing a full color picture into a tinted monochrome, but keep in mind that the duotone techniques described later in this chapter can also be used for this purpose. If your original is in Grayscale mode the first step is to change the file to a mode that is capable of displaying color. For our purposes a switch to RGB Color will suffice (Image > Mode > RGB Color).

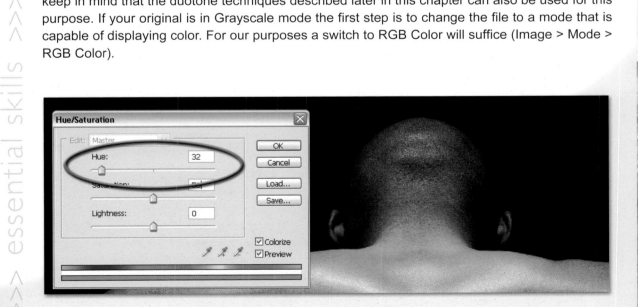

3. Now open the Hue/Saturation feature (Image > Adjustments > Hue/Saturation). With the Colorize box ticked you can select the color of the tint via the Hue slider. Moving the slider along this scale will gradually change the overall color of the picture whilst retaining the white and black parts of the picture.

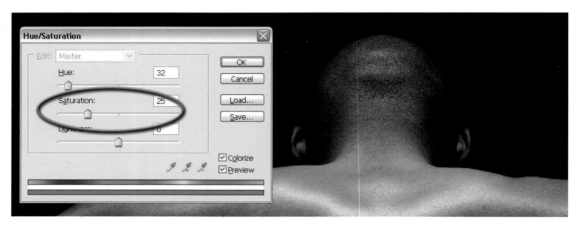

4. Now adjust the strength or vividness of the color using the Saturation slider. Low values will produce subtle coloring whereas higher settings create more dramatic results. Selecting a value of 0% produces a picture devoid of any color, just containing black, white and gray.

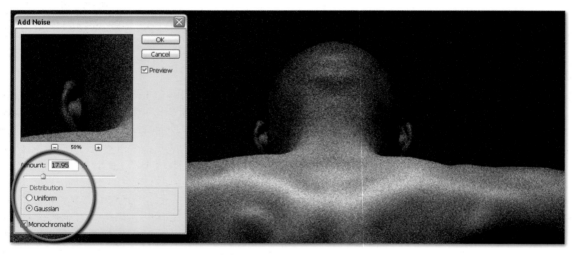

5. To simulate the texture of the lith print, filter the image using either the Grain (Filter > Texture > Grain) or Noise (Filter > Noise > Add Noise) filter. Most of these types of filters have slider controls that adjust the size of the grain, its strength and how it is applied to various parts of the image. The settings you use will depend on the resolution of your picture as well as the amount of detail it contains. The stronger the filter effects the more details will be obscured by the resultant texture. Be sure to preview the filter settings with the image magnification set at 100% so that you can more accurately predict the results. Here I have the used the 'Noise' filter with both the Gaussian and Monochrome options set.

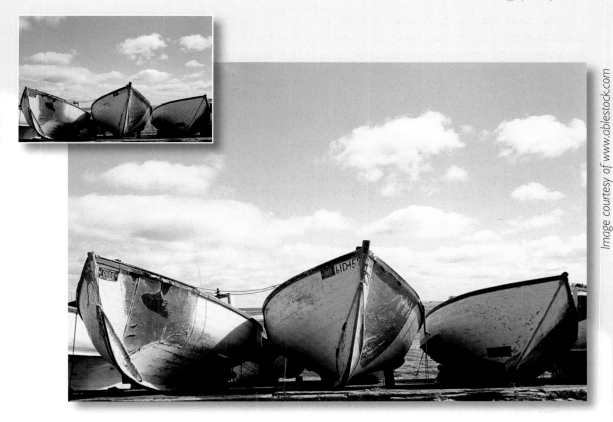

Image courtesy of www.ablestock.com

PHOTOSHOP CS2

>>> essential skills >>>

Split toning – *Project 5*

Traditional darkroom workers have prided themselves over the years with their ability to produce beautifully toned black and white prints. The famous sepia colored pictures of our past are wonderful examples of toning. Advanced practitioners have even delved into complex two- or three-toner methods that enabled highlights, midtones and shadows to be colored separately. This technique, which is often called split toning, required the use of several toning and bleaching baths as well as carefully planning the toning sequences if it was to be successful.

As we have already seen in the lith printing technique the digital version of the chemical toning process is not nearly so difficult. Toning a digital black and white print is a comparatively easy process, drawing on the Colorize option of the Photoshop's Hue/Saturation command (Image > Adjustments > Hue/Saturation). With straight toning being this easy surely there must be a way to use these ideas to selectively color highlights, midtones and shadows (split toning). Well, Photoshop provides the means with its Color Balance feature (Image > Adjustments > Color Balance), which can selectively tone shadows, midtones and highlights.

Making the Color Balance changes via adjustment layers means that it is possible to introduce a tint, non-destructively, into your black and white images whilst at the same time limiting the color to the tonal range that you have selected.

249

1. If your original is a color image then you will need to 'desaturate' the file first. Create a new Hue/Saturation adjustment layer (Layer > New Adjustment Layer > Hue/Saturation) and drag the Saturation slider all the way to the left. This creates a grayscale image, but in RGB mode. This means that the picture can be colored. If you are using a grayscale picture then convert it to RGB Color first via Image > Mode > RGB Color.

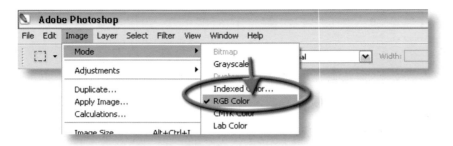

2. Creating a grayscale in this manner often produces flat or low contrast results. Use a Curves or Levels adjustment layer (Layer > New Adjustment Layer > Levels or Curves) to improve any contrast or brightness problems resulting from the conversion.

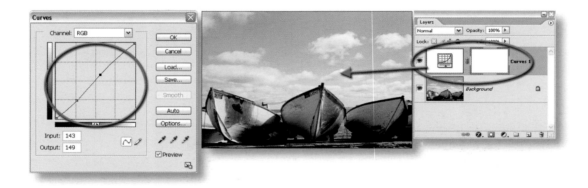

3. Next, to selectively tint the shadows of the picture we will use a Color Balance adjustment layer (Layer > New Adjustment Layer > Color Balance). Select the Shadows option, move the cyan–red slider to the right and the magenta–green setting to the left. This adds a warm tint to the shadow tones in the picture. Click OK.

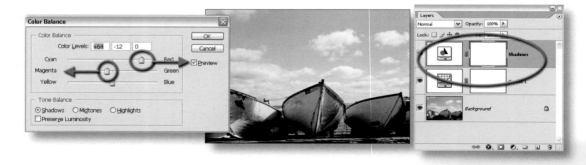

4. To tone the highlights a different color create another Color Balance adjustment layer and select the Highlights option. Move the yellow–blue color slider to the left and the other two settings equally to the right. Click OK. This introduces a yellowing of the highlight tones.

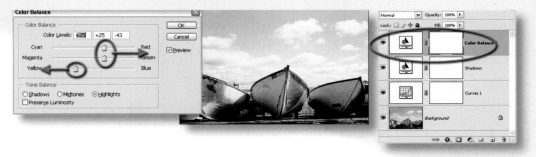

Selective toning – *Project 6*

An extension to this technique is to apply your toning methods to a specific area of your image. Using one of the Selection Tools available in Photoshop, isolate a portion of your image. With the selection still active tone the area using either the Colorize option with the Hue/Saturation control or the Color Balance feature. For even more dramatic results the selection can then be inversed (Select > Inverse) and a different tint can be applied to the rest of the image.

Image courtesy of www.able stock.com

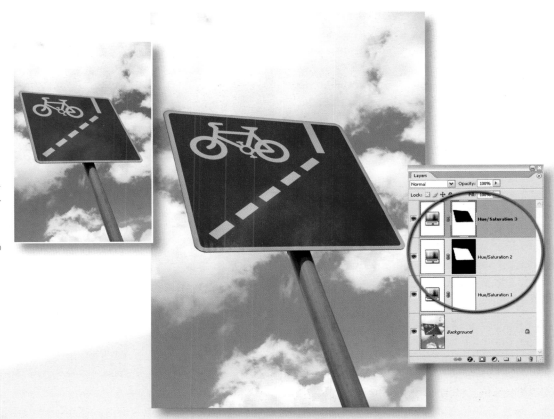

Duotones, tritones and quadtones – *Project 7*

For those readers with a lithographic printing background the idea of toning a black and white image using a duotone process will be quite familiar. To best understand the technique, keep in mind that ink is used to form the image on the printed page. In a straight black and white halftone, the photograph is printed with black ink only. A duotone image, by contrast, is made using two inks instead of one. By controlling which part of the image is printed with which color it is possible to print images that look like split-tone photographic prints.

Photoshop has a sophisticated duotone editor that makes it possible to take advantage of this creative technique. The editor allows the user to select the two colors that will be present in the final image as well as edit which parts of the tonal curve each particular ink will be applied to. Adjusting the shape of the curve can restrict the first color to just the shadow areas, letting the second color be used for printing the rest of the picture. Unlike the other techniques we have looked at, if you want to try making a duotone you will need to start the process with a grayscale image.

Tri- and quadtones extend your creative possibilities even more by adding extra inks into the equation. If this all seems a little too complex then try the duotone presets that come bundled with Photoshop. Here the colors and curve shapes have been designed to provide images with smooth and even transitions between tones and hues. You can usually find these digital toning presets in the goodies folder in your Photoshop directory.

The qualities and colors present in a well-crafted duotone can also be printed using standard desktop printers by ouputting from Photoshop directly or changing the file to RGB mode before printing normally.

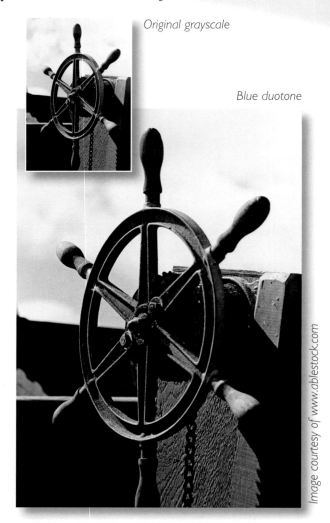

Original grayscale

Blue duotone

Image courtesy of www.ablestock.com

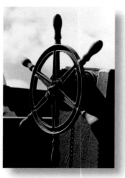

Rose duotone

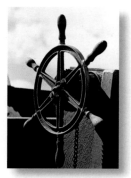

Brown duotone

PHOTOSHOP CS2

>>>

1. Start by converting a color picture to grayscale using the Image > Mode > Grayscale function. Apply any contrast and brightness adjustments necessary to redistribute the picture's tones. Switch the picture's mode to Duotone (Image > Mode > Duotone).

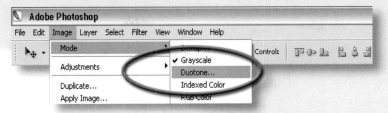

2. Once inside the Duotone Options dialog change the Type setting from Monotone to Duotone. This automatically adds the possibility of a second ink color to the document. The Tritone option uses three inks and the Quadtone setting four.

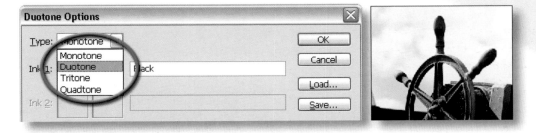

3. To select the second ink color, double-click in the Ink 2 color area of the dialog. This will open the color palette, from which you can select the other color to be mixed with black.

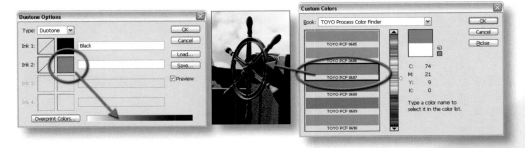

4. By double-clicking the Curve thumbnail in the Duotone dialog, you can adjust the prominence of each ink color across the tonal scale.

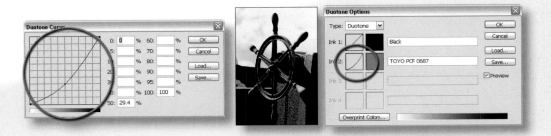

essential skills >>>

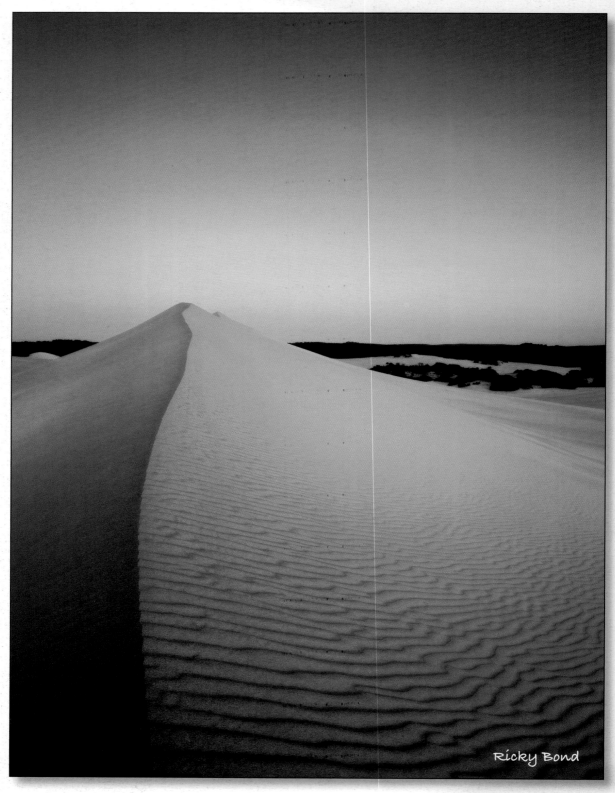

Ricky Bond

montage projects

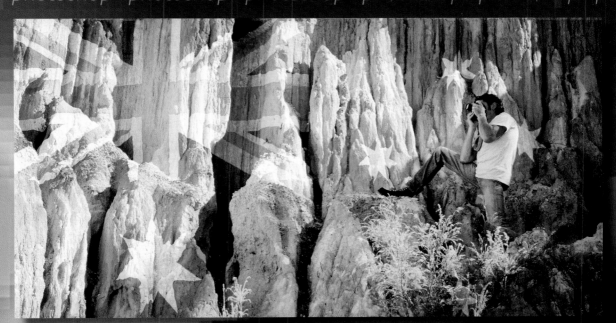

Mark Galer

essential skills

~ Use Quick Mask mode, alpha channels and layer masks to create a simple montage.
~ Create a simple montage using layer blend modes.
~ Use clipping masks, layer masks and layer styles to create a montage with graphics.
~ Use advanced blending techniques to render selective pixels transparent.
~ Use displacement maps to mould a graphic to a three-dimensional form.
~ Use the Pen Tool and the Extract filter to aid the extraction process.
~ Create and preserve shadows for convincing montage work.
~ Use layer styles, blend modes and layer comps in advanced montage work.
~ Create a panoramic image using the Photomerge filter.

Magic Wands and Quick Masks – *Project 1*

A common task in digital image editing is to strip out the subject and place it against a new background – the simplest form of montage. The effectiveness of such a montage is often determined by whether the image looks authentic (not manipulated).

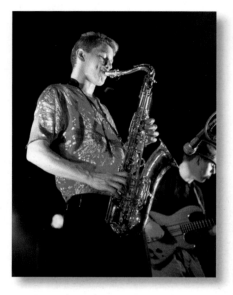

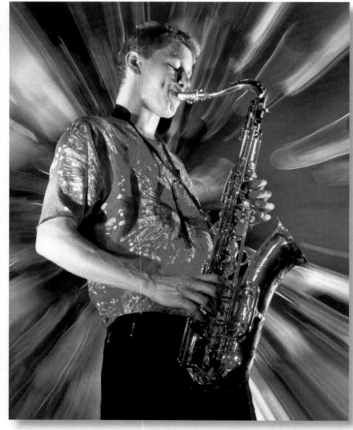

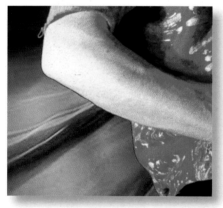

In order to achieve this the digital photographer needs to modify the edge of any selection so that it is seamless against the new background. A crude or inappropriate selection technique will make the subject appear as if it has been cut out with the garden shears and is floating above the new background. A few essential masking skills can turn the proverbial sow's ear into the silk purse.

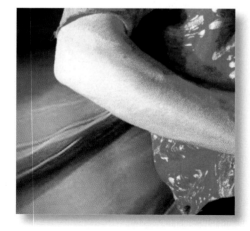

Open the stock images for this tutorial (Montage > Project1.jpg' and 'Project1b.jpg') from the supporting CD. As with any montage work it is advisable to check that the pixel dimensions of each image are similar and the image modes (RGB or Grayscale) are the same. For a quick check depress the Alt/Option key and click the document size box at the base of the image window.

Note > The resolution and image mode of an image pasted into another image will automatically be adjusted to match the resolution and mode of the new host file. The 'Transform' command can be used to adjust the scale of the imported image using 'Interpolation' but excessive scaling can lower the overall quality of the image. It is better to 'downsample' the larger image (decrease the total number of pixels) rather than sample up the smaller one. Exceptions can be made for background images where there is little fine detail, e.g. water, sky, fire, etc.

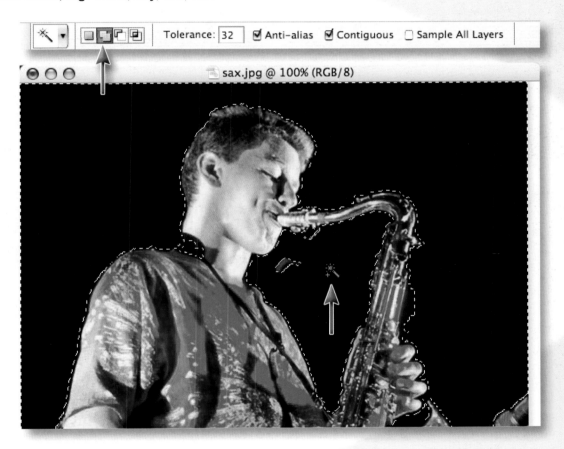

1. Start by selecting the majority of the sax image's background using a combination of the Magic Wand and Lasso Tools. Start with the default tolerance of 32 for the Magic Wand Tool but you may like to experiment with varying the setting. Increase the setting to select more of the background. Lower the tolerance if the selection invades the subject. Keep the Shift key depressed to build on, or add to, each successive selection. Areas around the saxophone player's trousers will be difficult to select using these tools due to the tonal similarities. Use the '**Quick Mask Mode**' to complete the selection work.

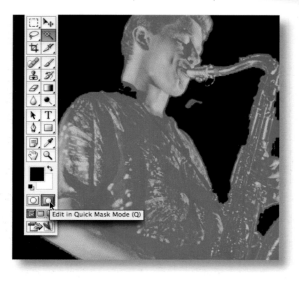

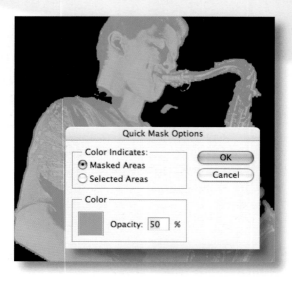

2. Set the foreground and background colors to their default setting in the Tools palette and then click on the 'Edit in Quick Mask Mode' icon in the Tools palette. Double-clicking the icon will open up the 'Quick Mask Options'. Choose either 'Masked Areas' or 'Selected Areas' depending on your preference. Click the color swatch to open the 'Color Picker' and select a contrasting color to that found in the image you are working on. Set the color to a saturated green with 50% opacity.

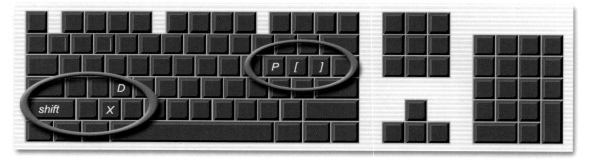

Useful shortcuts for masking work

Brush size and hardness: Using the square bracket keys to the right of the letter P on the keyboard will increase or decrease the size of the brush. Holding down the Shift key whilst depressing these keys will increase or decrease the hardness of the brush.

Foreground and background colors: Pressing the letter D on the keyboard will return the foreground and background colors to their default settings (black and white). Pressing the letter X will switch the foreground and background colors.

Zoom and Hand Tools: Use the Command/Ctrl + Spacebar shortcut to access the Zoom Tool and the Spacebar by itself to drag the image around in its window. The combination of these shortcuts will make shorter work of creating accurate selections.

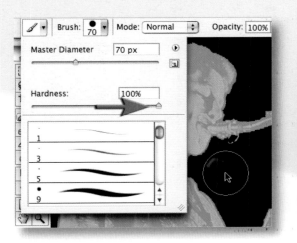
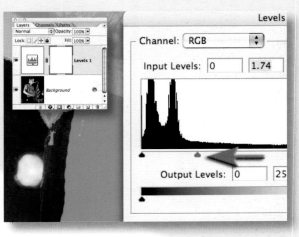

3.   Select the Paintbrush Tool from the Tools Palette and an appropriate hard-edged brush from the Options bar. Painting or removing a mask with the brush will result in a modified selection when the edit mode is returned to normal (the icon next to the 'Quick Mask Mode' icon). The foreground and background colors can be switched when painting to subtract or add to the mask. Zoom in on areas of fine detail and reduce the size of the brush when accuracy is called for. Adding an adjustment layer to temporarily brighten the image may help you to paint an accurate mask against some of the dark edges. Click on 'Edit in Standard Mode' when the painted mask is complete.

Note > If you select the 'Move' Tool in the Tools palette and drag the saxophone player a short distance you will notice that the selection has a fringe of dark pixels surrounding it. There is no way of gaining accurate previews using selections so we will continue to modify the edge quality using masks. Undo the move (Command/Ctrl + Z) or go back in the 'Histories' to the point prior to the move.

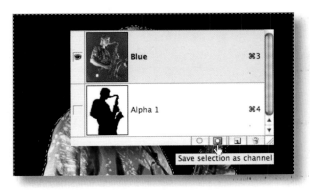
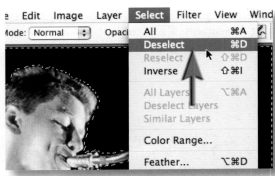

4. Save the selection as an alpha channel by going to the Channels palette and clicking on the 'Save selection as channel' icon. Now that the selection is stored, save your work in progress and go to 'Select > Deselect'.

Note > Change the name of the original file and save as a TIFF or PSD (the JPEG file format does not support additional channels). The alpha channel contains a record of your selection. This selection can be recalled if the selection is lost or the file is closed and reopened.

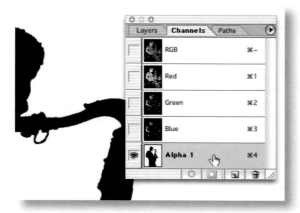 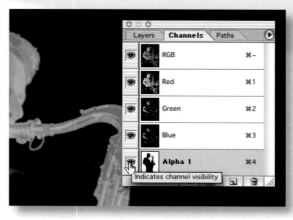

5. Click on the Alpha 1 channel to view the mask by itself or the 'visibility' or 'eye' icon to view the mask and image together. Before returning to the Layers palette, switch off the alpha channel visibility and select the master RGB channels view at the top of the Channels palette.

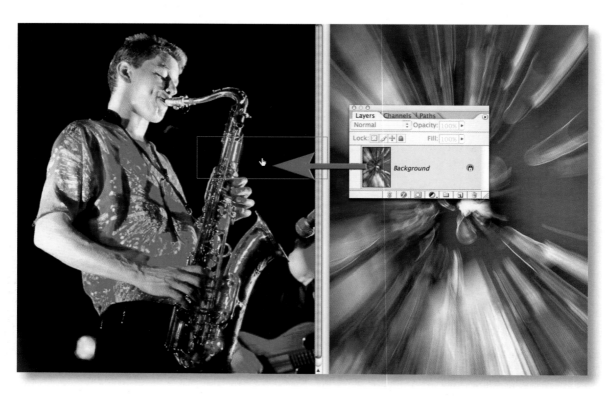

6. Position the new background image (zoom) alongside the saxophone image. Click on the background layer in the Layers palette and drag it to the saxophone image. A border will appear momentarily around the saxophone image to indicate that it will accept the new layer. Depress the Shift key as you let go of the zoom layer to center the zoom image in the canvas area.

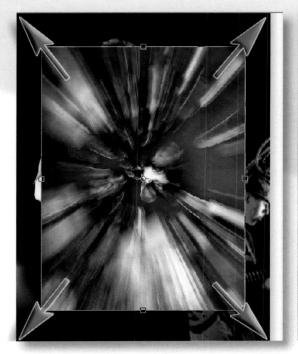
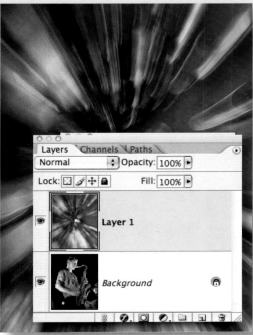

7. The image now comprises two individual layers. The background layer is concealed by the zoom layer. Select the top layer (the zoom image) and then go to 'Edit > Free Transform' (Command/Ctrl + T). Drag a corner handle to resize the image to fit the background. Holding down the Shift key whilst you drag will constrain the proportions whilst dragging inside the bounding box will move the image. Press the 'Commit' icon in the Options bar or press the Return/Enter key to apply the transformation.

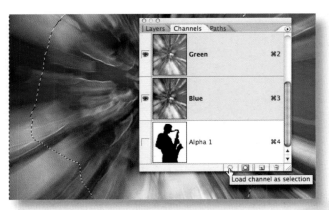
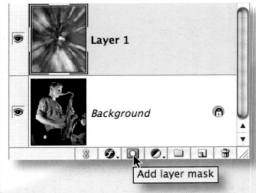

8. To reload your selection go to the alpha channel in the Channels palette. Drag the channel to the 'Load channel as selection' icon at the base of the Channels palette or Command/Ctrl-click the alpha channel. Return to the Layers palette and with the zoom layer as the active layer click on the 'Add layer mask' icon. The layer mask will conceal the portion of the zoom image to reveal the saxophone player. It is important to note that the section of the zoom image that is no longer visible has been masked and not removed permanently.

Note > The 'masked' and 'selected' areas are the reverse of each other. Areas that were not part of the original selection become the masked areas. Holding down the Option key as you select 'Add layer mask' reverses the layer mask so that the selection becomes the mask.

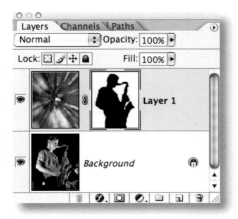
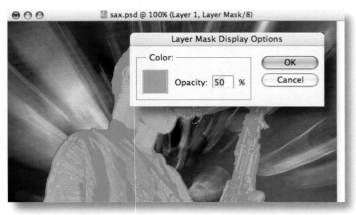

9. The edge of the mask at the moment has a sharp, well-defined edge that is not consistent with the edge quality in the original image. This will be modified so that the edge quality does not stand out now that the saxophone player is viewed against a lighter background color. Double-click the 'Layer 1 Mask' channel to open the 'Display Options'. Select the same options that you used for the 'Quick Mask Mode' earlier. Hold down the Alt/Option and Shift keys and click on the layer mask to view the mask and image at the same time. Click on the image thumbnail when you would like to return to the normal view.

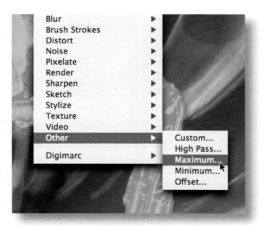
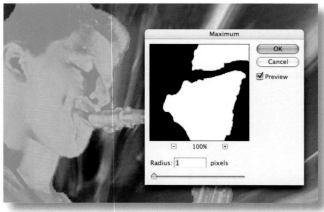

10. Contract the mask by going to 'Filters > Other > Maximum'. Increasing the pixel radius will move the edge of the mask to conceal any fringe pixels that are being displayed from the background layer.

Note > As well as moving the edge of the mask one pixel at a time the mask also becomes more 'rounded' and this can have a detrimental effect on any fine detail present at the edge of the subject.

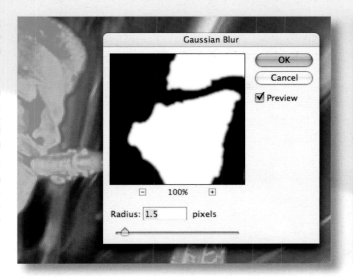

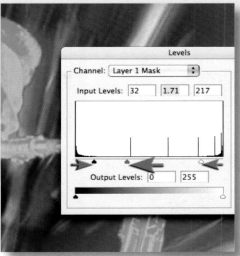

11. With the Layer 1 Mask active go to 'Filters > Blur > Gaussian Blur'. Soften the edge by increasing the pixel radius in this dialog box. One or two pixels will usually do the trick. Click the Layer 1 image thumbnail to review the edge quality of the saxophone player. The Gaussian Blur softens the edge of the mask but may reveal some of the background as a dark halo around the lighter edges. If this occurs return to the Maximum filter once again and shrink the mask by a further pixel or alternatively use a Levels adjustment technique as outlined in the Selections chapter.

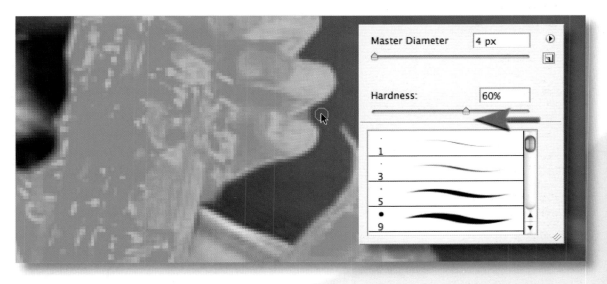

12. Any imperfections still evident can be corrected by clicking on the mask thumbnail in the Layers palette and then painting with black to increase the mask or painting with white to remove sections of the mask. You will need to match brush hardness with the slightly soft edge of the mask if your work is to go unnoticed. Test the brush hardness is appropriate by viewing the layer mask thumbnail (Alt/Option + Shift-click the mask thumbnail).

Creating a simple blend – *Project 2*

Blending two images in the computer is similar to creating a double exposure in the camera or sandwiching negatives in the darkroom. Photoshop allows a greater degree of control over the final outcome. This is achieved by controlling the specific blend mode, position and opacity of each layer. The use of '**layer masks**' can shield any area of the image that needs to be protected from the blend mode. The blending technique enables the texture or pattern from one image to be modeled by the form of a selected subject in another image.

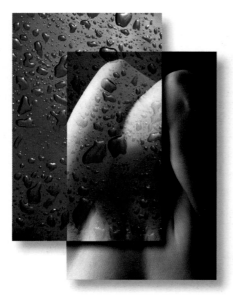

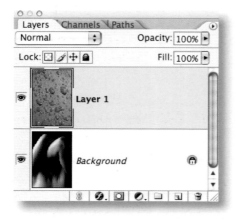

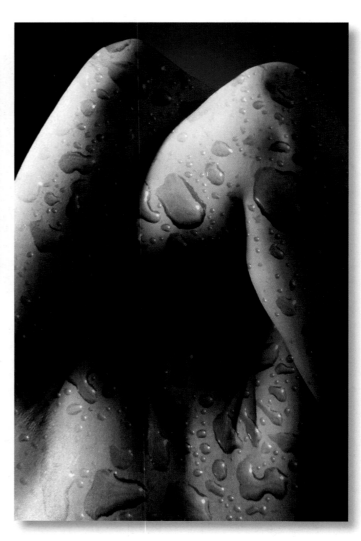

Note > In the montage above the image of the body has been blended with an image of raindrops on a car bonnet. The texture blended takes on the shadows and highlights of the underlying form but does not wrap itself around the contours or shape of the three-dimensional form.

264

Download the images from the supporting web site or use your own images to complete this simple blend. The secret to success is in the selection of appropriate imagery to complete the task as outlined in the first two steps of the process.

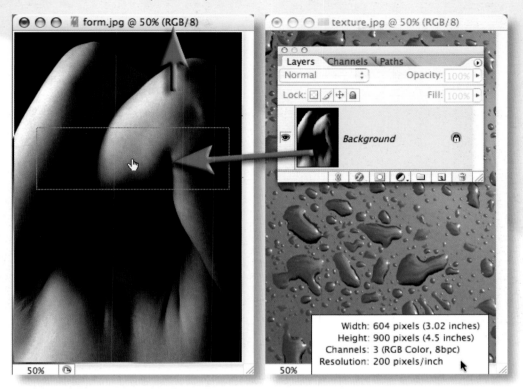

1. Select or create one image where a three-dimensional subject is modeled by light. Try photographing a part of the human body using a large or diffused light source at right angles to the camera. The image should ideally contain bright highlights, midtones and dark shadows. Scan the image and save as 'Form'. Alternatively use the image titled 'form.jpg' provided on the web site to support this study guide.

2. Select or create another image where the subject has an interesting texture or pattern. Scan the image and save as 'Texture'. Try using a bold texture with an irregular pattern. The texture should ideally have a full tonal range with good contrast. A subtle or low contrast texture may not be obvious when blended. Alternatively use the image provided to support this study guide that is titled 'texture.jpg'.

3. Alt/Option-click the document sizes in the bottom left-hand corner of each image window to check that the image pixel dimensions (width and height) are similar. It is possible to blend a colored texture with a grayscale image. If the color of the texture is to be retained the grayscale image containing the form must first be converted to RGB by going to 'Image > Mode > RGB'.

4. Click and drag the layer thumbnail of the texture image into the form image. Hold down the Shift key as you let go of the texture thumbnail to center the image in the new window. Use the Move Tool to reposition the texture if required.

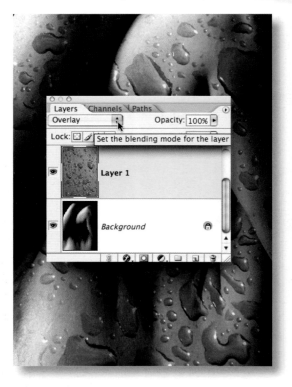
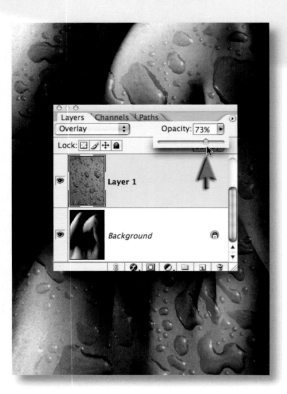

5. Set the blend mode of the top layer to Overlay. Experiment with adjusting the opacity of the top layer using the opacity slider in the Layers palette.

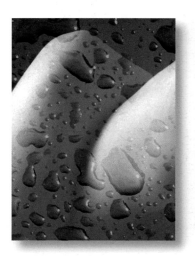
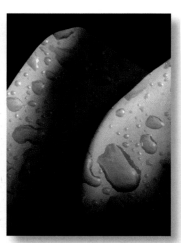
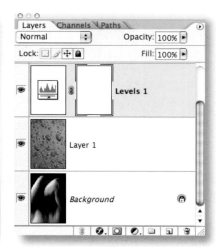

6. Experiment with adjusting the blend mode to either Screen or Multiply. Observe the changes that take place in the image and pay particular attention to the information that can be seen in the shadows and highlights. Also try adding a Levels adjustment layer and making corrections to either the shadow or highlight slider and the gamma slider.

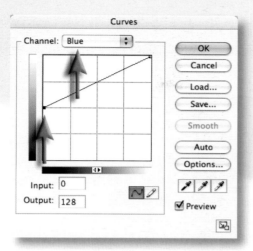

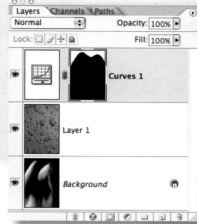

7. Make a selection of the black background. Adjust the softness and position of the edge of the selection using the techniques outlined in Project 1. With the active selection create a Curves adjustment layer. Adjust the color of the background by moving the 0 anchor point to an ouput value of 128 in one or more of the color channels. Select OK when you have created a background color to your liking.

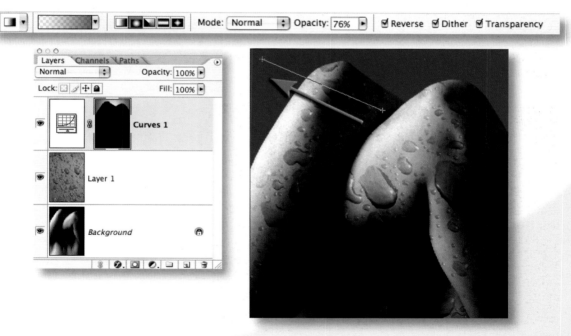

8. Select the Gradient Tool in the Tools palette. Select the Foreground to Transparent and Radial Gradient options. Set the opacity to approximately 75% and select the Reverse, Dither and Transparency options. Click and drag from a position just behind the top of the arms out towards the top corner of the image window to create a backlight effect. Sharpen the image using techniques outlined in Project 6 of the Retouching Projects chapter.

Clipping groups and layer styles – *Project 3*

Using a variety of techniques outlined in the preceding pages it is possible to construct an elaborate montage that demonstrates the creative applications of layers and masks.

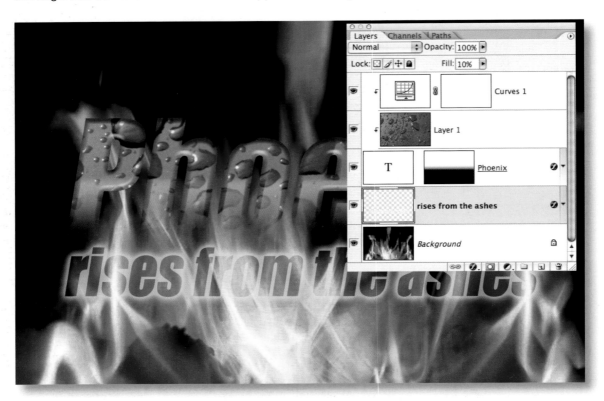

This project makes use of a layer mask which is filled using the Gradient Tool. This graduated layer mask allows the typography to appear gradually as if from the fire. A '**clipping group**' is used to assign the texture 'raindrops' to the typographic form (creating a layer mask would have given the same effect). The three-dimensional look of the typography is created by applying a layer effect called '**Bevel and Emboss**' to the typographic layer. The finishing touches were created by using an adjustment layer clipped to the texture to increase its contrast.

1. Open the image '**Montage > Project3a.jpg**'. Select the Type Tool in the Tools palette and open the Character palette from the Options bar. Specify the font, style and size of the text (with the characters selected, typing minus or plus values in the tracking box will move letters closer or further apart).

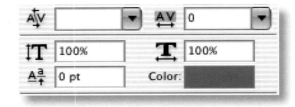

Note > Color is normally selected by clicking the color swatch. Color is not important for this exercise as the type will be filled with another image. Ensure that anti-alias is selected (crisp, strong or smooth) and then click OK.

2. Stretch or distort the type layer by applying the '**Free Transform**' command (Command/Ctrl + T). The type in the example has been stretched vertically by dragging the top-center handle upwards. Press the Return/Enter key to apply the transformation.

Note > Transform alters the shape and/or size of the subject matter on a single selected layer. Holding the Shift key down whilst dragging a corner handle will constrain the proportions. Holding down the Ctrl/Command key will allow you to skew the text.

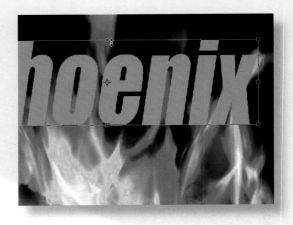

3. Apply an effect or '**Layer Style**' to this typographic layer, 'Layer > Layer Style > Bevel and Emboss' or choose it from the 'Add a layer style' menu in the Layers palette.

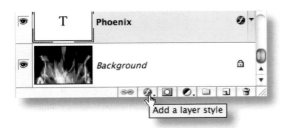

Ensure that an 'Inner Bevel' is selected from the Style menu, adjust the look of the bevel and click OK. The effect can be adjusted later by double-clicking on the effects layer.

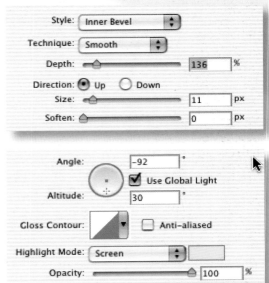

4. With the type layer still selected add a layer mask by clicking the '**Add a mask**' icon at the foot of the Layers palette. An empty layer mask will appear in the Layers palette beside the typography thumbnail. With this thumbnail selected you can use any of the paint tools to paint a layer mask. A layer mask will conceal information on its own layer. The darker the color that you use to paint with, the more information on this layer will be concealed. If black is selected, the pixels in the location of the mask will be completely concealed. If a middle tone is used the opacity of the information will be reduced.

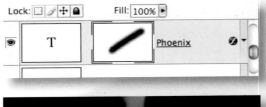

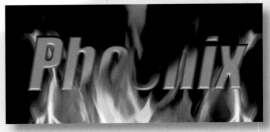

5. Set the default foreground and background colors in the toolbox (black and white). Click on the layer mask in the Layers palette to select it rather than the type. Select the Linear Gradient Tool in the Tools palette. Select Foreground to Background or Foreground to Transparent and 100% opacity. Move the cursor to the bottom of the typography in the main image window. Click and drag the gradient cursor from the base of the letters to the top of the letters. A linear gradient will appear in the layer mask and the typography should be half hidden behind this layer mask. Experiment with dragging shorter and longer gradients.

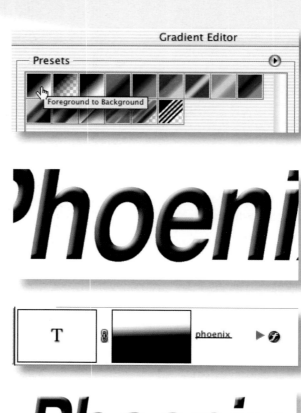

6. The layer mask can be moved by selecting the Move Tool and dragging inside the main image window. To move the typography and not the mask you must first click on the typography thumbnail in the Layers palette. To move both the layer mask and the typography at the same time you must first click between the layer mask and typography windows in the Layers palette. This action creates a link between both elements. The link can be broken by clicking on the icon.

7. Select the Type Tool again and click beneath the word you have just created. Select a smaller point size and type the additional copy. Highlight the text and adjust the size if necessary. Reposition the copy by dragging the type and then click OK.

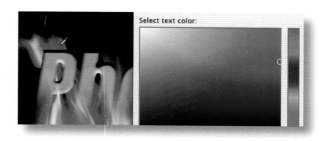

8. Click the 'Color Swatch' in the type options to open the Color Picker. To choose a color from the image move the cursor onto the image window. The cursor appears as an eyedropper and can sample a color by clicking on it. This color will then be assigned to the typography.

Layer Style

Styles	Outer Glow

Styles

Blending Options: Custom

☐ Drop Shadow

☐ Inner Shadow

☑ Outer Glow

☐ Inner Glow

☐ Bevel and Emboss

   ☐ Contour

   ☐ Texture

☐ Satin

☐ Color Overlay

☐ Gradient Overlay

☐ Pattern Overlay

☐ Stroke

Outer Glow

Structure

Blend Mode: Screen

Opacity: 100 %

Noise: 0 %

Elements

Technique: Softer

Spread: 23 %

Size: 32 px

Quality

Contour: ☐ Anti-aliased

Range: 100 %

Jitter: 0 %

OK

Cancel

New Style...

☑ Preview

9. Apply an 'Outer Glow' layer style to this typographic layer. Adjust the opacity, spread and size to create the desired effect surrounding the typography. Click the color box to open the Color Picker and choose a yellow color from the image.

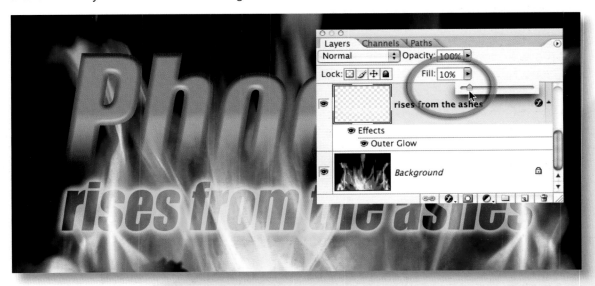

Note > It is possible to control the opacity of the 'fill color' and the layer opacity separately. By reducing the fill color the typography can made transparent whilst the layer style remains at 100% opacity.

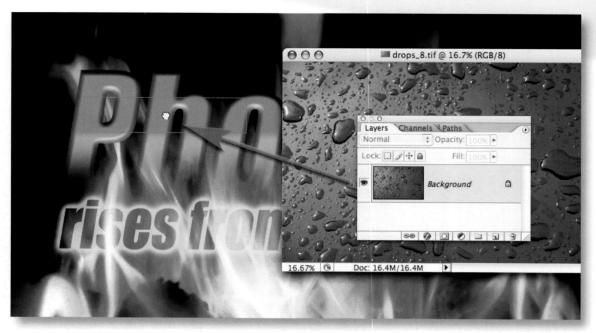

10. Open the image containing the texture you wish to paste into the typographic form (the image '**Project3b.jpg**' was used in this example). Ensure the image is of a similar size and resolution to that required. The size can be modified later using the 'Free Transform' command but the digital photographer must be careful not to increase the size of any image excessively ('interpolation' will lower the overall quality). Drag the thumbnail of the drops in the Layers palette into the image window containing the fire and text. The texture will be placed on a layer above the other layers, completely concealing both the typography and the background.

11. A clipping group is required in order to fill the typography with the image of the raindrops. Go to 'Layer > Create Clipping Mask' or move the mouse cursor to the line that divides the two layers in the Layers palette. By holding down the Option/Alt key the clipping icon should appear (two overlapping circles). Clicking whilst holding down the Option/Alt key will group the layers together. The layer thumbnail is indented and the name of the base layer in the clipping group is underlined. The typography acts as a mask.

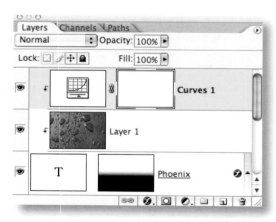

12. Finally an adjustment layer is applied to the top layer. Increase the contrast and/or change the color of the raindrops. It too is clipped to the typography layer to limit its effects to the raindrops only.

Note > Adjustment layers will affect all layers beneath them unless clipped.

Advanced blending – *Project 4*

This project utilizes the advanced blending via the blending or layer options dialog box and the use of filters to create special effects. The project also makes use of the '**Transform**' commands to modify layer content.

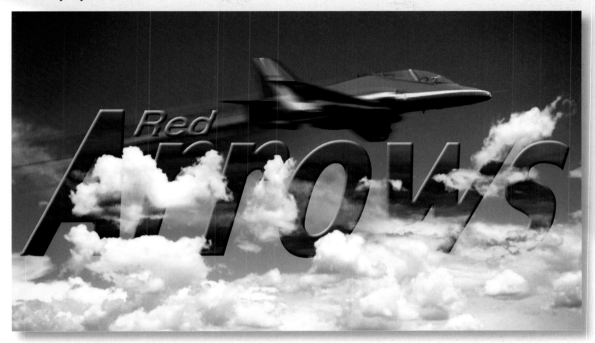

The technique of making the typography disappear amongst the cloud cover is created by a sandwiching technique and a selective blend mode applied to the top layer.

The sky is duplicated and the copy moved to the top of the layers stack. The darker levels (the blue sky) are blended or made transparent whilst the lighter levels (the clouds) are kept opaque. The typography now appears where the sky is darker and is obscured by the lighter clouds.

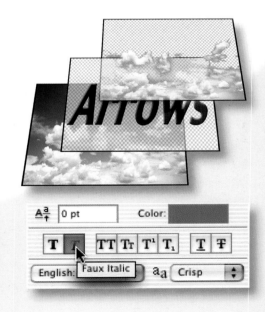

1. Open the image '**Montage > Project4a.jpg**'. Click on the Type Tool in the Tools palette and create the desired typography. The example uses a Charcoal font, '**Faux Bold**' and '**Faux Italic**' (a Photoshop feature that allows any font to be made italic or bold). Any bold italic font would be suitable for this project.

273

2. The layer effect 'Bevel and Emboss' is applied to this type layer. Select 'Inner Bevel' from the Style menu and select an appropriate 'Angle' that is consistent with the light source in the rest of the image. Choose a blend mode, opacity and color for both the highlights and shadows. In the example both the highlight and shadow were set to 100% and the angle was set to 120°.

3. Duplicate the background layer 'Sky' by dragging the layer in the Layers palette to the 'New Layers' icon at the base of the Layers palette. Move the background copy to the top of the layers stack above the type layer (this action will temporarily obscure the type layer).

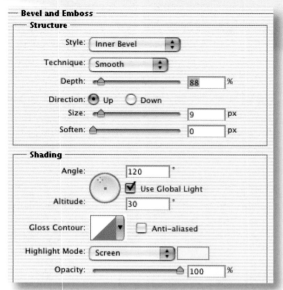

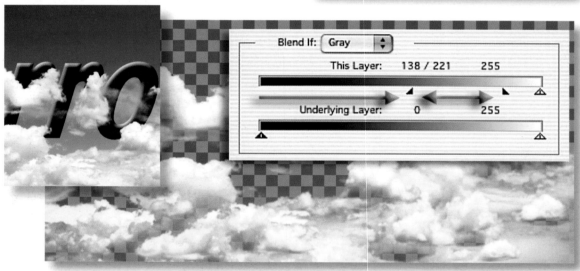

4. Double-click the background copy layer. The 'Blending Options' dialog box will open. This dialog box allows the user to change the opacity and blend mode of the layer. The bottom half of the box allows the user to control the range of levels that may be blended. Dragging the left-hand slider on the top ramp to a position of 150 allows all of the darker tones, or levels, to be made transparent. The typography on the layer below is now visible in all areas where the pixels are 0 to 150. The effect at present is abrupt. The type disappears suddenly into the clouds rather than gradually. A more gradual transition can be achieved by fading the effect over a range of pixels rather than selecting a single layer value at which 100% transparency takes place. By holding down the Option/Alt key and dragging the slider it is possible to split the black slider. Drag the right half of the slider to a value of around 200. This action creates the desired effect of the type fading slowly into the cloud cover.

5. Apply a fill to the typography using the technique used in the last project. Open the image that will be used to fill the type '**Montage > Project4b.jpg**'. The image is opened and dragged (using the Move Tool) or copied and pasted into the sky image. The image is moved to a position directly above the type layer in the Layers palette and is '**clipped**' to the type layer (see 'Project 3').

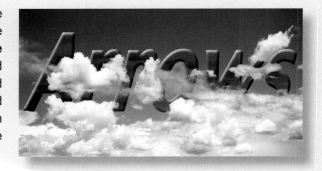

6. An adjustment layer is then added and clipped with the storm clouds and typography (see 'Project 3'). The adjustment layer is used to shift the colors of the storm cloud towards blue. This can be achieved by using either a Color Balance or a Curves adjustment layer.

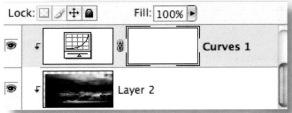

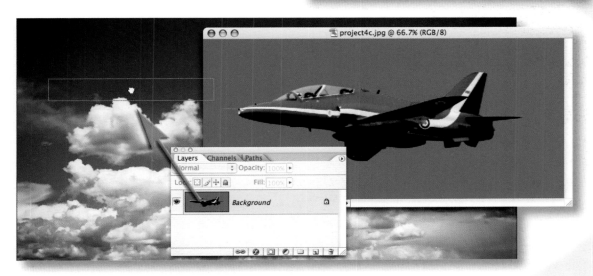

7. Open the image '**Montage > Project4c.jpg**'. Drag the layer thumbnail of the jet from the Layers palette into the canvas area of the sky image.

8. Click on the 'Add layer mask' icon in the Layers palette. Mask the sky on this layer using selection and painting tools (see 'Montage > Project 1'). Remember to apply a small amount of Gaussian Blur to this layer mask.

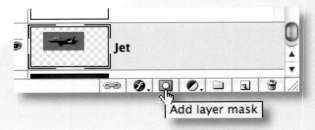

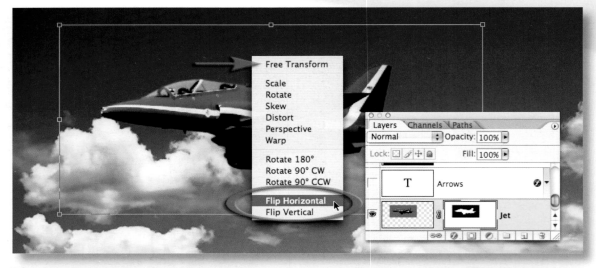

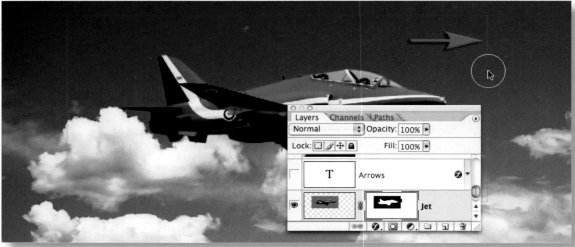

9. Go to the Edit menu and choose 'Transform > Flip Horizontal'. Then select the layer mask and paint out any edges that may have appeared as a result of blurring or contracting the layer mask. To create the movement effect duplicate the aircraft layer twice (drag the layer to the 'Create new layer' icon). Choose Blur > Motion Blur from the Filters menu to apply a 15-pixel blur to the uppermost jet layer. Apply a 300-pixel Motion Blur to the bottom jet layer. Ensure that the 'Angle' is appropriate for the direction of travel or movement. If you need to see a preview of the effect drag inside the preview window until part of the aircraft appears.

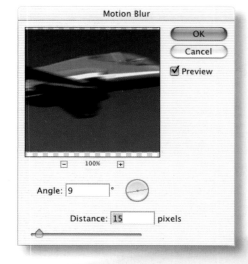

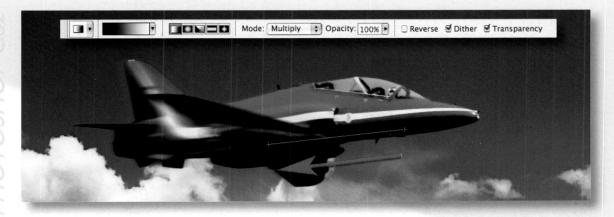

10. Position the 15-pixel blur above and the 300-pixel blur beneath the original. Select the 'Gradient' Tool from the Tools palette. Select the 'Linear Gradient', 'Foreground to Background' and 'Multiply' mode options in the Options bar. Drag the Gradient Tool to conceal the front half of the blurred aircraft. With the 300-pixel blur layer selected choose Transform > Rotate from the Image menu and move the streak into position.

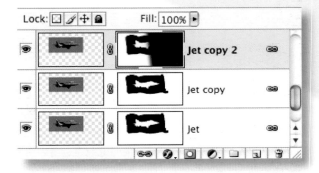

11. Create an additional type layer to add the word 'Red'. Select a red from the aircraft using the eyedropper tool. This color will be placed in the foreground color swatch in the Tools palette and become the default color for the typography. Click and drag the new type layer into position. From the Edit menu choose Transform > Skew to increase the angle of lean of the typography. From the Filters menu choose Stylize > Wind and select 'From the Right' to give the appropriate direction of travel.

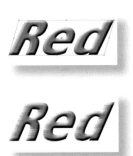

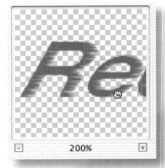

Note > To apply a filter to a type layer the type must first be rendered (into pixels). If type is rendered it is no longer editable.

Save a PSD version of the image. Choose 'Save a Copy' from the 'Save As' dialog box. Select Photoshop from the pull-down menu.

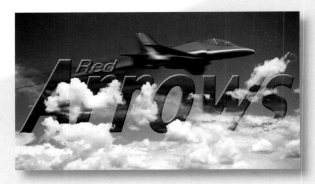

277

Displacement maps – *Project 5*

The layer '**blend**' modes are an effective, but limited, way of merging or blending a pattern or graphic with a three-dimensional form. By using the blend modes the pattern or graphic can be modified to respect the color and tonality of the 3D form beneath it. The highlights and shadows that give the 3D form its shape can, however, be further utilized to wrap or bend the pattern or graphic so that it obeys the form's perspective and sense of volume. This can be achieved by using the 'Displace' filter in conjunction with a 'displacement map'. The 'map' defines the contours to which the graphic or pattern must conform. The final effect can be likened to 'shrink-wrapping' the graphic or pattern to the 3D form.

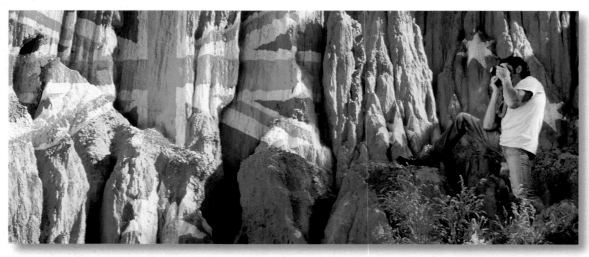

Displacement requires the use of a PSD image file or 'displacement map' created from the layer containing the 3D form. This is used as the contour map to displace pixels of another layer (the pattern or graphic). The brightness level of each pixel in the map directs the filter to shift the corresponding pixel of the selected layer in a horizontal or vertical plane. The principle on which this technique works is that of 'mountains and valleys'. Dark pixels in the map shift the graphic pixels down into the shaded valleys of the 3D form whilst the light pixels of the map raise the graphic pixels onto the illuminated peaks of the 3D form.

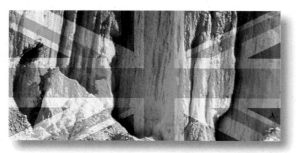 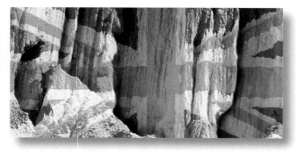

Note how the straight lines of the Union Jack are distorted after the Displace filter has been applied. The first image looks as though the flag has been projected onto the rock surface, whilst in the second image it appears as though it has been painted or shrink-wrapped onto the rock surface.

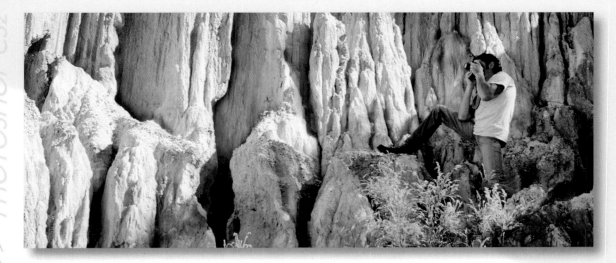

The limitation of the displacement technique is that the filter reads dark pixels in the image as being shaded and light pixels as being illuminated. This of course is not always the case. With this in mind the range of images that lend themselves to this technique is limited. A zebra would be a poor choice on which to wrap a flag whilst a nude illuminated with soft directional lighting would be a good choice. The image chosen for this project lends itself to the displacement technique. Directional light models the rock face. Tonal differences due to hue are limited.

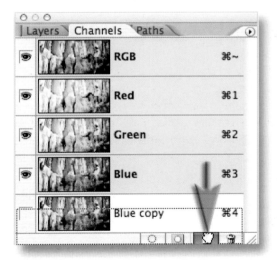

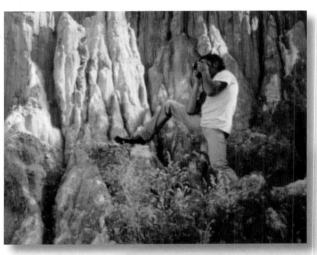

1. In order to apply the Displace filter you must first create a grayscale image to become the displacement map. Open the image '**Montage > Project5a.jpg**'. In the Channels palette locate the channel with the best tonal contrast between the shadows and the highlights. Duplicate this channel by dragging it to the New Layer icon at the base of the palette.

2. Apply a small amount of 'Gaussian Blur' from the Filters menu and adjust the levels so that the contrast range extends from black to white.

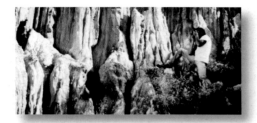
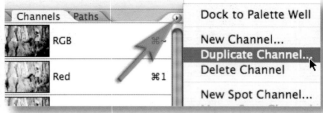

3. Export this channel to become the displacement map by choosing '**Duplicate Channel**' from the Channels menu and then '**Document > New**' from the Destination menu. Save the exported PSD file. This will be your displacement map.

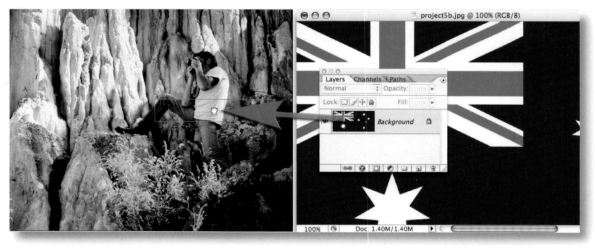

4. A small paper flag was scanned so that it could be used as a flat two-dimensional graphic or pattern (**Montage > Project5b.jpg**). Drag the flag into the rock ace image. Apply the 'Free Transform' from the Edit menu to obtain a 'good fit' if necessary.

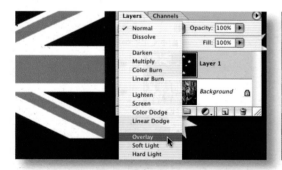
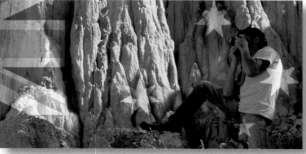

5. From the blend modes choose an appropriate blend mode and layer opacity for the desired effect you would like to achieve. The 'Overlay' or 'Soft Light' blend modes are a good place to start, although 'Color Burn' proved effective in this instance.

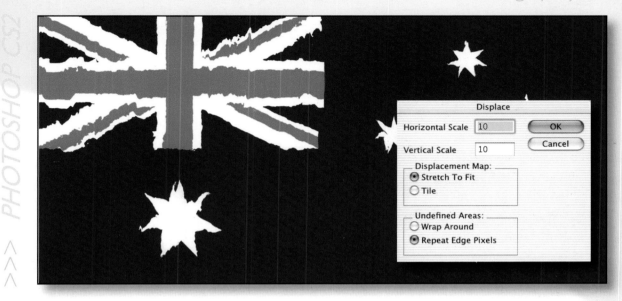

6. Choose 'Filter > Distort > Displace' and enter the amount of the displacement. Select OK and then select the displacement map you created earlier. The distortion is applied to the layer. The Displace filter shifts the pixels on the selected layer using a pixel value from the displacement map. Levels 0 and 255 are the maximum negative and positive shifts whilst level 128 produces no displacement.

Note > The amount of Gaussian Blur applied to the displacement map will help smooth an excessively jagged displacement. Increase the blur of the displacement mask to smooth the displacement further.

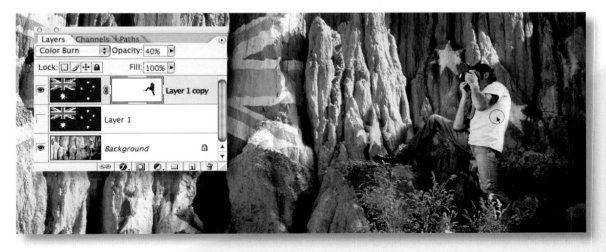

7. To complete the wrap select the map layer in the Layers palette and click the 'Add layer mask' icon in the Layers palette. Use a soft-edged brush and paint into the layer mask using black as the foreground color. This action will shield the man from the blend.

Alternative approach using the 'Liquify' filter

An alternative approach to distorting the graphic using the Displacement filter in '**Project 5**' would be to use the '**Liquify**' filter. Instead of using the '**Blue copy**' channel to create a displacement map it can be used to '**freeze**' an area of the image prior to selectively displacing the unfrozen pixels using the '**Warp Tool**'. This alternative method of displacing pixels on one layer, to reflect the contours of another layer, is made possible in the Liquify filter due to the option to see the visibility of additional layers other than the one you are working on.

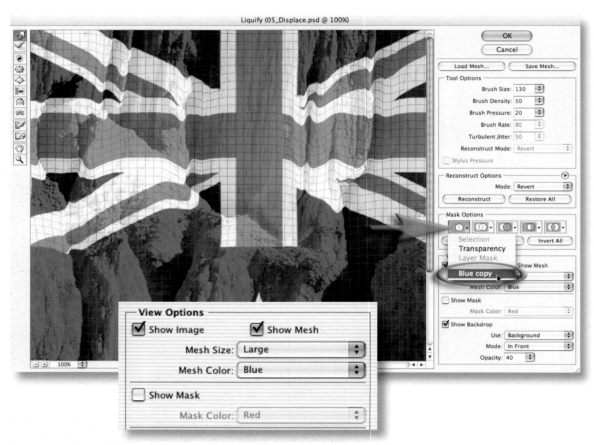

To try this alternative approach complete the first five steps of 'Project 5', skipping step 3. When you reach step 6, instead of creating a displacement map, click on the graphic layer and go to Filter > Liquify. Check the 'Show Backdrop' option in the dialog box and select 'background layer' from the menu. Adjust the opacity to create the optimum environment for displacing the pixels. To selectively freeze the darker pixels in the image load the 'Blue copy' channel in the 'Mask Options'. Check 'Show Mesh' in the 'View Options'. Select a brush size and pressure and then stroke the graphic upwards whilst observing the contours of the rock wall to displace the lighter pixels. Select 'Invert All' in the 'Mask Options' so that you can displace the darker pixels in the opposite direction.

Paths and selections – *Project 6*

With the basic drawing skills covered in the previous section we are ready to create a path that can be converted into a selection and then used as a layer mask. To become a Path Master (for the pen is sometimes mightier than the light sabre or magic wand) this project will seek to mask part of an image that can be quite difficult to isolate using techniques outlined at the start of the chapter.

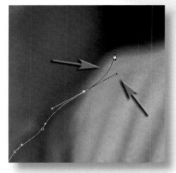

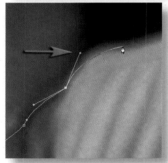

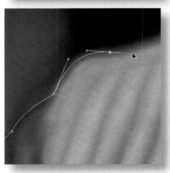

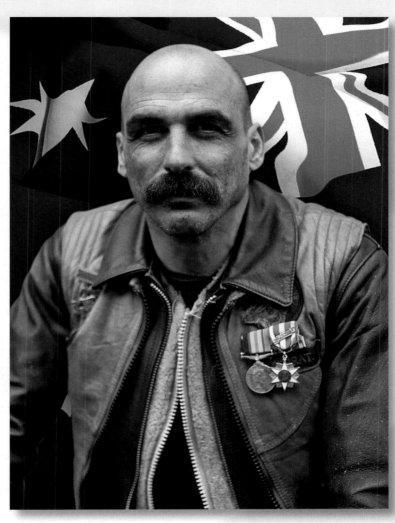

1. To select the man from the background, start on the left side of the project image 'Vet.jpg' (where the arm meets the side of the frame) and use as few anchor points as possible to reach the side of the man's head (see Selections > Basic steps 1 to 4). Remember you can choose to cancel or move a direction line by holding down the Alt/Option key and clicking on either the last anchor point or its direction point before creating a new segment of the path. As the edge of the man's jacket is slightly blurry, due to the shallow depth of field, draw an edge that eliminates some of the blur.

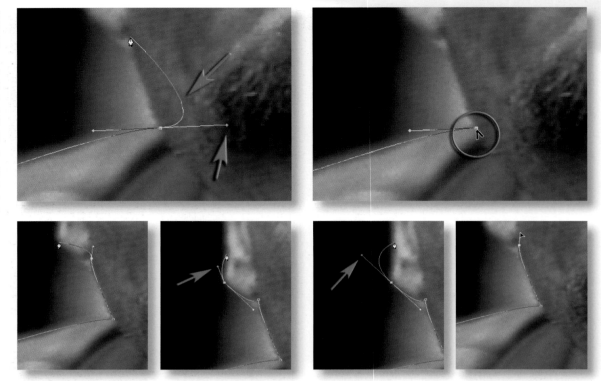

2. Continue to work your way around the neck and ear. Zoom in using the keyboard shortcut Ctrl + Spacebar (PC) or Command + Spacebar (Mac) and work close. Drag the image around in the image window using the Spacebar key to access the Hand Tool.

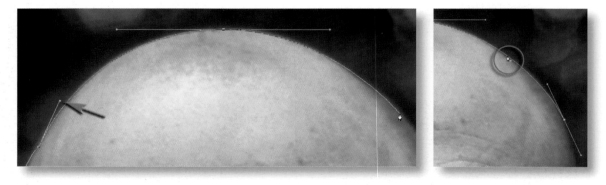

3. When you select the top of the head you will be able to work more quickly as fewer anchor points are required. Moving the Pen Tool over a segment of the path already completed will give you the option to click and add an anchor point to the path. Moving the Pen Tool over a previous anchor point will enable you to click to delete an anchor point.

Note > Check that you have the 'Auto Add/Delete' option checked in the Options bar if the above is not happening for you.

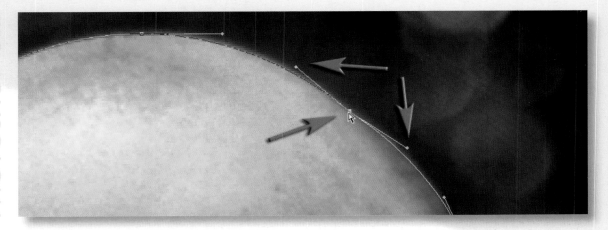

Holding down the Ctrl key (PC) or Command key (Mac) will momentarily change the Pen Tool to the Direct Selection Tool (a white arrow). The Direct Selection Tool enables you to move an anchor point (or its associated direction lines) by dragging it to a new location. Hold down the Shift key whilst the Direct Selection Tool is active to click on more than one anchor point and move multiple segments of the path. Note how an active anchor point is solid rather than hollow after it has been selected.

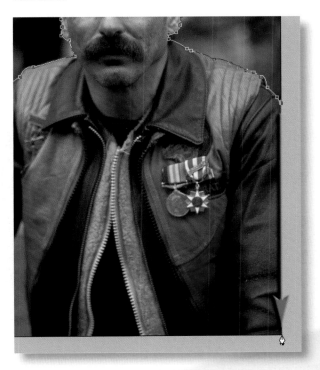

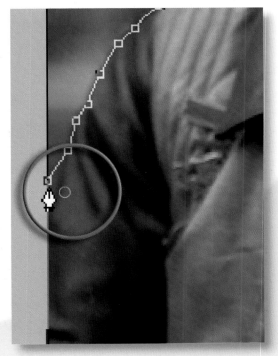

4. Continue creating anchor points until you reach the right side of the image window. Then place an anchor point in the bottom two corners of the image. Return to the start point and click on it to close the path.

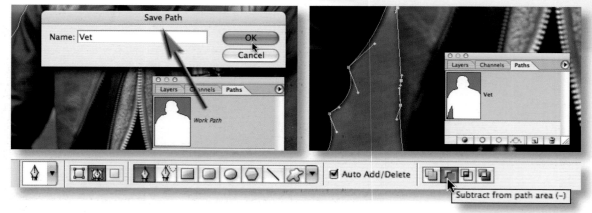

5. In the Paths palette double-click the Work Path. This will bring up the option to save the Work Path and ensure that it cannot be deleted accidentally. A saved path can be modified by first clicking on the path in the Paths palette, selecting the Pen Tool in the Tools palette and then selecting the 'Add to' or 'Subtract from path area' icon in the options bar. Select the Subtract from path area icon' and proceed to remove the area of background under the man's arm using the same pen techniques as before. The path is now complete so we must now prepare the file prior to loading the path as a selection.

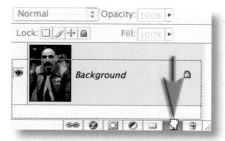

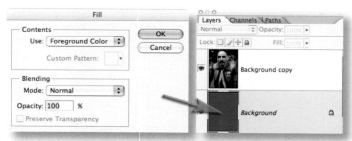

6. To test the effectiveness of the path it is best to view the subject that will be masked against a flat tone. In this example the background has been duplicated and the old background has been filled with a color (Edit > Fill).

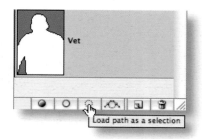

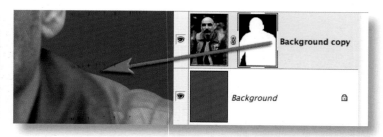

7. Load the path as a selection by clicking on the icon in the Paths palette and then, with the Vet layer selected in the Layers palette, click on the 'Add layer mask' icon. If you zoom in you will see just how smooth and crisp those edges really are. Although smooth and accurate they are in fact a little too sharp for most photographic masking. This can be rectified by applying a small amount of Gaussian Blur.

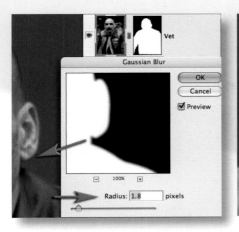

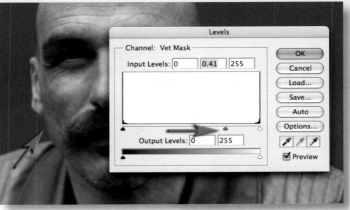

8. Apply a small amount of Gaussian Blur to the layer mask (Filter > Blur > Gaussian Blur). The radius of the Gaussian Blur should match the edge quality of the original subject. A 1 or 2 pixel radius will often be appropriate for most subjects. The alignment of the mask can be further modified (if required) by using a Levels adjustment (Image > Adjustments > Levels). This realignment is required only if a small halo is visible around any part of the subject. This will depend on the accuracy of your path and the tone and color of both the subject and the new background. In the Levels dialog box move the central gamma slider to the right to remove any visible halo. Moving the black and/or white point sliders will remove some of the blur previously applied using the Gaussian Blur filter.

Note > If a halo is present in only an isolated section of the subject then you should first proceed to make a selection of this area using a Lasso or Marquee Tool using a small amount of feather and then proceed to use the Levels adjustment technique outlined above.

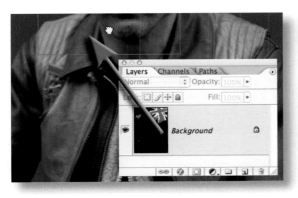

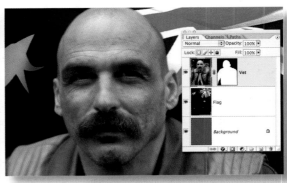

9. Open the file containing the new background '**Montage > Project6b.jpg**' and then drag the layer thumbnail into the Vet image. Hold down the Shift key as you let go of the thumbnail to center the flag in the Vet file. Project complete! Now if you put your hand on your heart, you will probably admit to this taking far longer than any other selection process you have ever used previously. With practice however comes speed, and although the pen is never going to replace the other selection tools there are times when, if you put your hand on the same heart, you will have to admit that this is sometimes the hands down winner when smooth edges are paramount.

Extract filter – *Project 7*

The Extract filter can effectively work with a soft or blurred edge, but when this edge is viewed against a very different tone, the edge looks out of place. These 'soft edges' can, however, be 'worked' so that they can be blended into the new background.

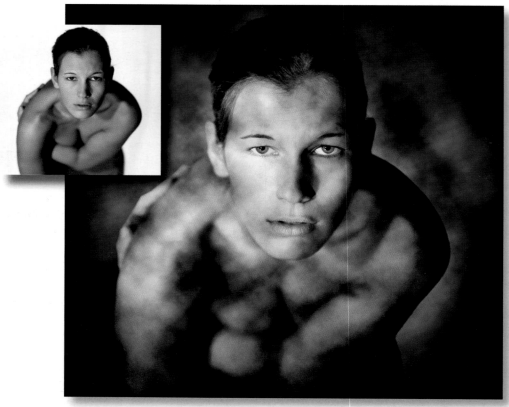

Photography by Benedikt Partenheimer

1. If you are starting with a grayscale image and would like to introduce color you must first convert the image mode to RGB (Image > Mode > RGB). The next step is to import or create a new background. It is possible to create a background using the 'Clouds' filter that resembles the brushed canvas backdrops used by many portrait photographers. To achieve this effect click on the 'New Layer' icon in the Layers palette. In the Tools palette set the foreground color to black and the background color to a light shade of gray (double-click the color swatch and then choose a color from the 'Color Picker'). To apply the clouds effect go to 'Filter > Render > Clouds'.

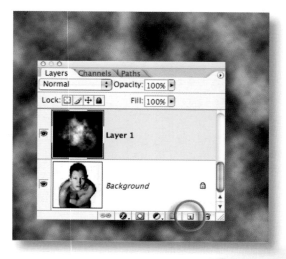

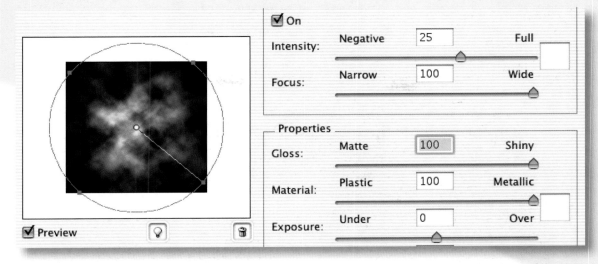

2. To create the illusion of an effects light on the backdrop the 'Lighting Effects filter' was used (Filters > Render > Lighting Effects). By clicking and dragging on the handles in the preview box the circle, or spread, of light can be controlled. Select an intensity value that keeps the highlights from 'blowing out' or becoming white and the shadows from 'filling in' or becoming black.

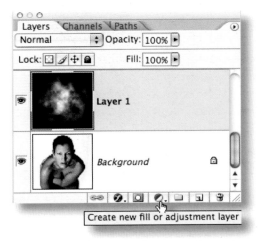

3. Create a Curves adjustment layer to color the clouds layer by clicking on the 'Create new fill or adjustment layer' icon. From the pull-down menu in the Curves dialog box select a color channel and create a curve to color the layers beneath.

4. Duplicate the background layer containing the subject to be extracted (Layer > Duplicate Layer) and move it to the top of the layers stack (Layer > Arrange > Bring to Front).

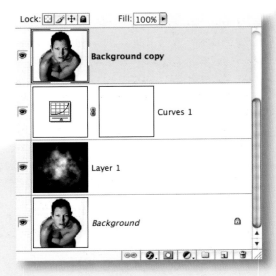

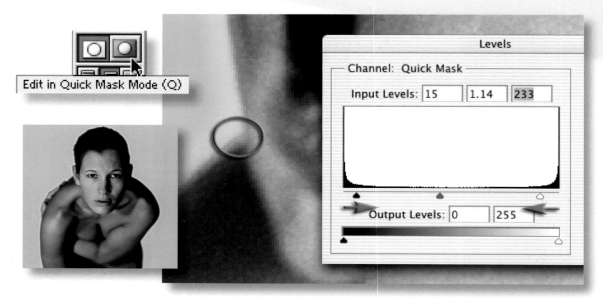

5. The following steps in the process prepare the way for, and speed up the selection process when using, the Extract filter. The 'Magic Wand' is used to make a rough selection of the white background on the background copy layer. This initial selection may fall short of some of the 'soft edges' because of the slow transition between dark and light, which may repel the wand's attempts to make an effective selection. The Magic Wand selection by itself is usually imprecise at selecting a typical background. This can be rectified in a controlled way by first feathering the selection and then using a Levels adjustment in 'Quick Mask Mode'. Slide either the highlight slider or the shadow slider to expand or contract the selection so that it falls closer to the edge of the figure. Zoom in on a soft edge to get a clear idea of the effects of moving the sliders. Once the edge of the mask has been modified exit the Quick Mask Mode (press Q) to return to a selection.

Note > It is important to either feather the selection (Select > Feather) or blur the mask for this technique to work. The precise amount of feathering is, however, dependent on both the resolution of the image and the edge quality of the subject being extracted.

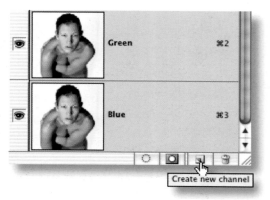
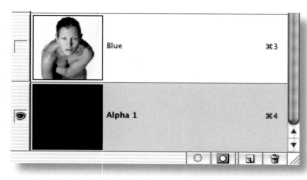

6. With the selection active click on the 'Create new channel' icon to create a new empty alpha channel (filled with black).

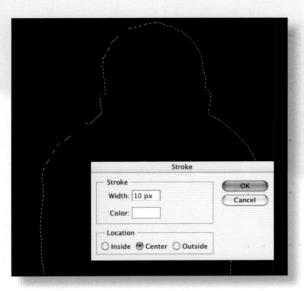

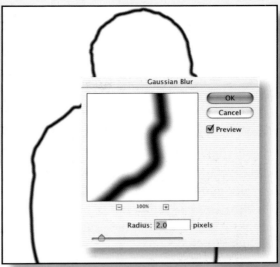

7. Stroke the selection (Edit > Stroke). Click on the 'Color' swatch and choose white from the Color Picker. The stroke width you choose should cover the soft edges of the subject you are extracting. Deselect to remove the selection.

8. Apply a small amount of Gaussian Blur (Filter > Blur > Gaussian Blur) to the channel and then invert the channel (Image > Adjustments > Invert). Return to the Layers palette and ensure the background copy layer is selected.

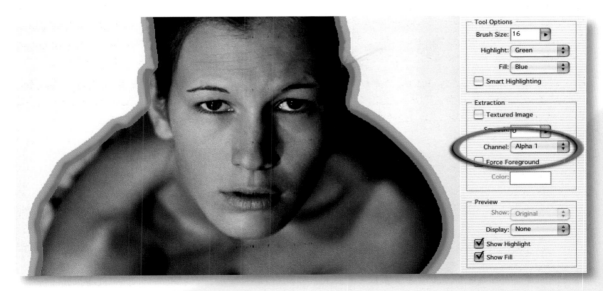

9. Select 'Extract' from the 'Filter' menu and 'Alpha 1' from the Channel pull-down menu. The outline of the subject will be automatically loaded for you, thus saving a lot of painstaking work with the Highlighter Tool.

10. Use the 'Edge Highlighter Tool' to include any areas missed by the alpha channel selection. This may include fine detail that extends from the border or very soft edges that exceed the width of the edge highlight. Zoom in to get a close look at the edge and avoid painting too deeply into the subject itself. Use the Spacebar to access the Hand Tool so that you can drag the magnified edge through the preview window.

Note > When using the 'Edge Highlighter Tool' you can paint generously into the background but care must be taken not to paint too deeply into the subject as this may result in a loss of subject detail.

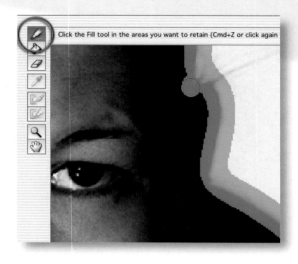

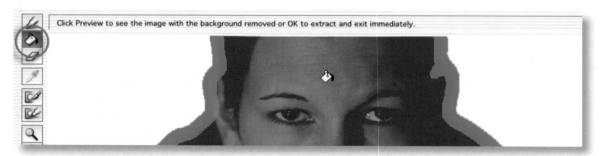

11. Fill the area you wish to retain using the 'Fill Tool' or bucket. The fill color denotes the area to be retained by the extraction process.

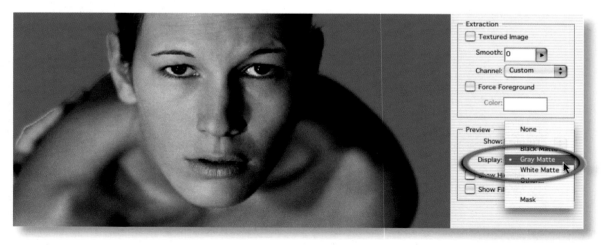

12. Select a 'matte' color from the 'Display' pull-down menu that is closer in tone to the new background. This will help you identify any unwanted edge detail left over from the old background.

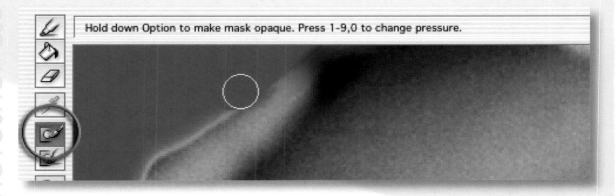

Hold down Option to make mask opaque. Press 1-9,0 to change pressure.

13. Use the 'Cleanup Tool' to remove any unwanted pixels. Select a low pressure (by pressing a lower number key on your keyboard) to reduce the opacity of the edge pixels gradually. Pressing the Option/Alt key on the keyboard can restore full opacity to the edge pixels. Any ragged edges produced by the extraction process (usually created where edge contrast is low) can be smoothed out or made sharper using the 'Edge Touchup Tool'. Click 'OK' when the edge has been modified to look good against the preview matte.

Note > Many find the 'Edge Touchup Tool' a little unwieldy to use, as it is able to move the location of the edge as well as replace and remove pixels in its attempt to smooth the edge. It takes a lot of practice to use effectively. If your subject/background contrast is sufficient you can often avoid using this tool altogether. A little extra time spent when capturing the image to ensure sufficient contrast will save time during this stage of the process.

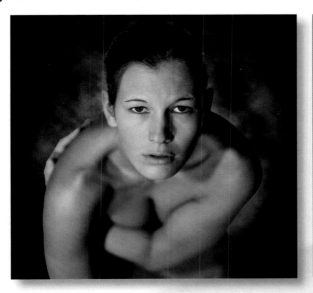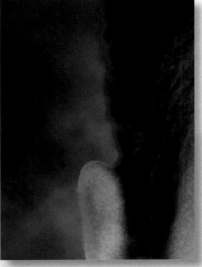

14. The edge pixels that were modified in the last step using the 'Cleanup Tool' were adjusted to look good against a matte color. The edge pixels may not look so good against the exact tone and color of the new background now that the extraction has been performed. If the edge pixels are now too dark or too light, burning or dodging selectively can modify them further.

293

PHOTOSHOP CS2 >>>

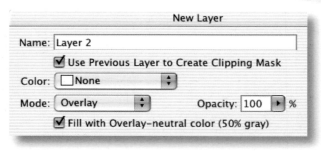
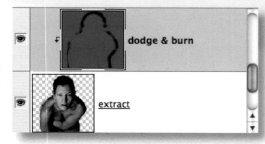

15. It is possible to burn or dodge the offending pixels on the background copy layer itself (choose a low brush pressure and set the 'Range' of the Burn and Dodge Tools, located in the Options bar, to highlight or shadow to limit the effects). An alternative option is to burn or dodge the pixels on a '50% gray' layer set to 'Overlay' blend mode that has been grouped with the background copy layer. Adjustments made to this layer modify the pixel values on the layer below, whilst areas that are left as 50% gray leave the pixels below unaffected.

Note > The advantage of working on a separate layer is that it offers an extremely flexible way of editing an image. Working on a separate layer allows you to repeatedly change your mind regarding the level of adjustment required. Fifty percent gray overlay layers, together with adjustment layers and layer masks, offer the least destructive method of image editing. Pixel values, rather than being changed repeatedly, are changed only once when the image is flattened prior to printing.

16. Once the pixels have been modified to a more suitable tone for the new background, the edge can be softened further if required. A softer edge can be achieved by using a layer mask. Make a selection by holding down the Command/Ctrl key when clicking the 'Background copy' thumbnail.

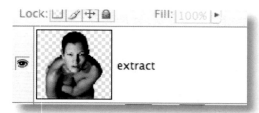

Note > The completed layers that form the new background have been placed in a 'Layer Set' to help prevent the Layers palette becoming unduly crowded.

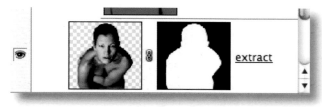

17. Click on the 'Add layer mask' icon to create a layer mask using the selection.

18. Apply a small amount of 'Gaussian Blur' to this mask (Filters > Blur > Gaussian Blur). This will soften any hard edges remaining from the extraction process. The edges should now look very comfortable against the new background.

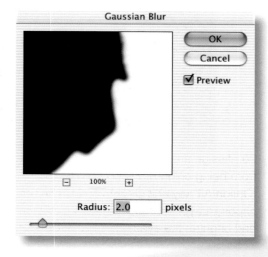

>>> essential skills >>>

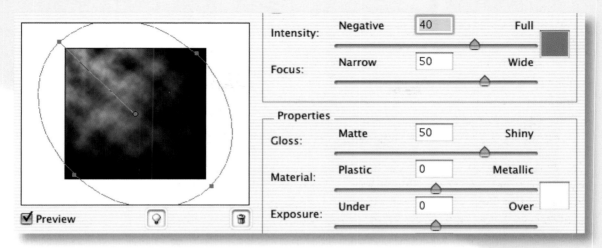

19. Create a new layer and apply the Clouds filter again. A 'Spotlight' lighting effect is used to reflect the lighting used on the model. Click on the top color swatch to pick an appropriate color for the effect.

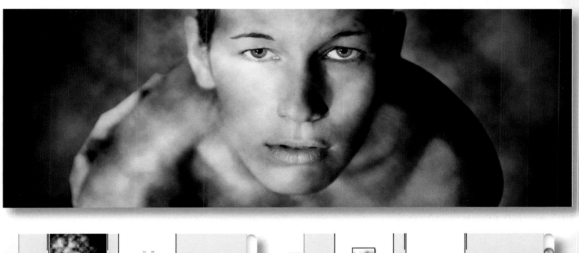

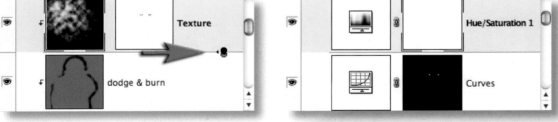

20. Assign an Overlay blend mode to the new layer. Add a layer mask to protect the whites of the eyes from being colored. Finally the layer is grouped with the background copy layer by holding down the 'Option/Alt' key and clicking on the dividing line between this layer and the previous layer (alternatively choose 'Layer > Group with Previous' from the menu). Use adjustment layers with layer masks to color and brighten the eyes (the focal point of the image) and refine the overall image.

Layer comps – *Project 8*

The flatbed scanner is surprisingly good at capturing objects and artifacts that aren't absolutely flat. Forty-eight-bit export scanners are now an affordable reality for most imaging students and enthusiasts. This project will demonstrate how a range of compositing or montage skills can be used to construct artwork from a range of flatly lit source material.

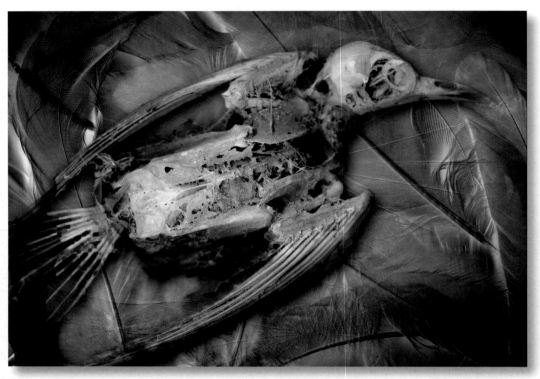

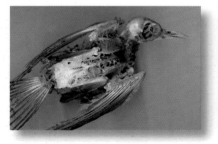 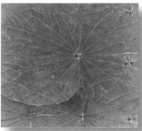 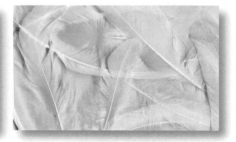

The source material – a mummified bird together with a few feathers and a book cover made from dried leaves

Choose one or two objects and some interesting textures that are visually interesting – watercolor paper, scrunched-up plastic bags, etc. If the outcome is to be a full-page print you should aim to scan around 10 megabytes of pixels per file (double that if you are scanning in 48-bit mode). Ensure the histogram for each component piece is optimized prior to starting the montage.

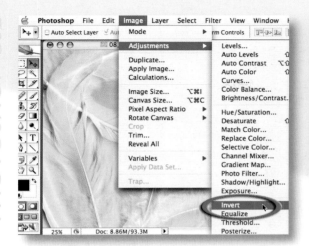 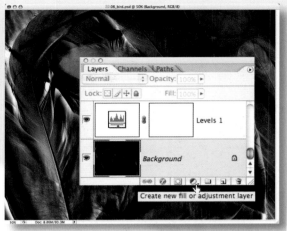

1. Choose the image that will become the background layer. The feathers image in this project was 'inverted' (Image > Adjustments > Invert) to provide a darker background for the mummified bird. The tonal qualities were optimized using an adjustment layer before importing the second texture layer.

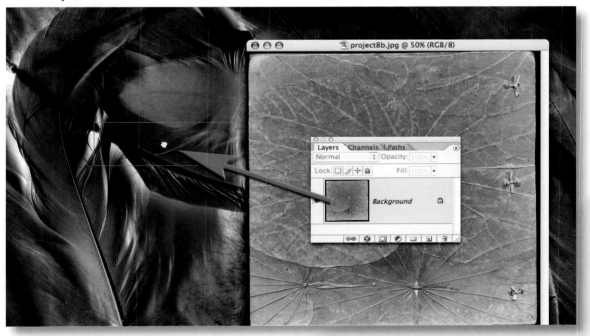

2. Position the second texture image (the leaves) alongside the feathers image. Click on the background layer in the Layers palette and drag it into the feathers image window. A border will appear momentarily around the feathers image to indicate that it will accept the new layer. Depress the Shift key as you let go of the leaves layer to center it in the canvas area. Free Transform the image to fit the new canvas ('Edit > Free Transform'). Click on the 'Add layer mask' icon at the base of the Layers palette.

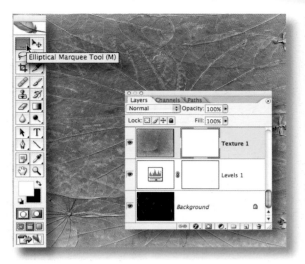
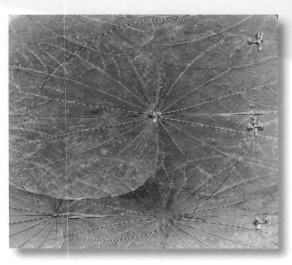

3. Click on the 'Elliptical Marquee Tool' and draw a large ellipse in the canvas area just large enough to accommodate the main subject matter. To angle the selection to suit the angle of the subject matter select 'Transform Selection' from the Select menu. Move to just outside one of the corner handles and position the cursor until a double-headed arrow appears. Drag the selection to rotate it to a new position. Using the Free Transform command from the Edit menu will rotate the pixels if the layer mask is not selected. When you are happy with the new angle of the ellipse press the Return/Enter key to commit the transformation.

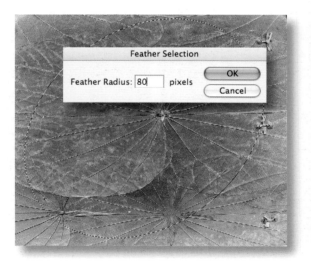
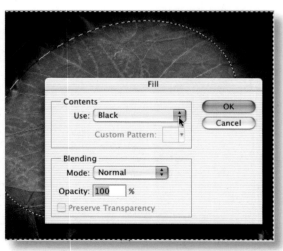

4. From the Select menu choose Feather ('Command/Ctrl + Option + D') and select a very generous feather radius (80+ pixels for a full-page image). Go to 'Select > Inverse' and then 'Edit > Fill'. Fill the selection with black. If black is already the foreground color you could use the keyboard shortcut 'Option/Alt + Delete'.

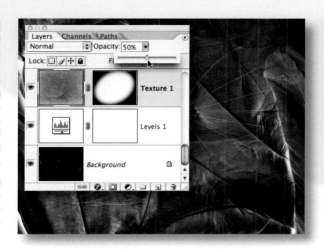

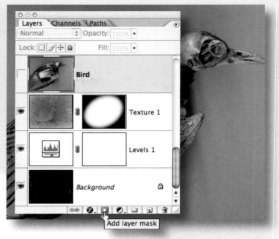

5. Lower the opacity of this layer and/or experiment with the blend modes until you get a pleasing balance between the two layers.

6. Bring in the third component to this montage and create a selection (using all of your favorite techniques) to separate the bird from its background. When the selection is complete (don't forget to feather it by one or two pixels – no pun intended) hit the 'Add layer mask' icon once again.

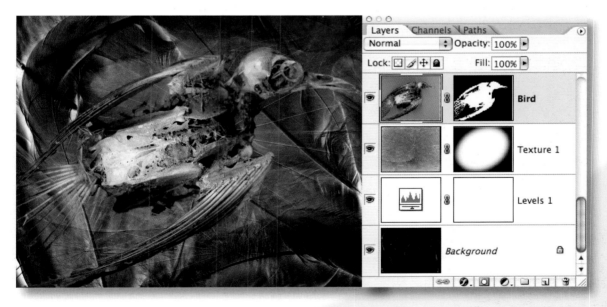

7. With the bird now transplanted to its new background all of the elements are in place but are not 'at one with each other'. What we need are some shadows to give the subject a sense of three-dimensional form that was removed by the flat light of the scanner. This, together with the addition of a drop shadow, will unite the bird with its new background. Time to save the work in progress and put the kettle on for a cup of tea because we are nearly there.

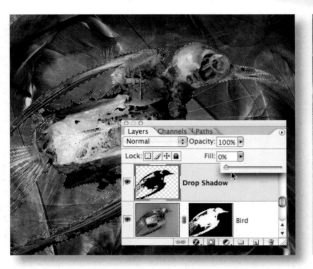 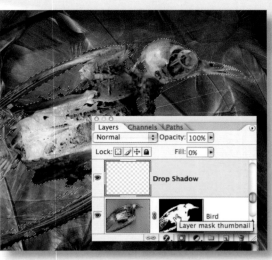

8. Click on the 'New Layer icon' at the base of the Layers palette and then hold down the Command/ Ctrl key whilst clicking the layer mask thumbnail on the bird layer to reload your selection. When the selection reappears click on the new layer in the Layers palette and fill the selection with black. The next step may seem a bit strange but we are going to hide the black bird (or should that read magpie) by setting the 'Fill' opacity of the layer to 0%. If you are using an older version of Photoshop you can find the 'Fill opacity slider' in the 'Blending Options' by double-clicking the layer. To this invisible bird we will now add the shadows. Strange but true!

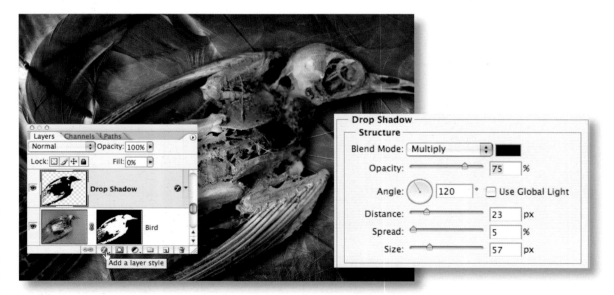

9. From the 'Add a layer style' icon at the base of the Layers palette choose 'Drop Shadow'. Choose settings that appear as if the object were now sitting on the background.

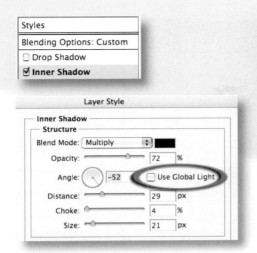

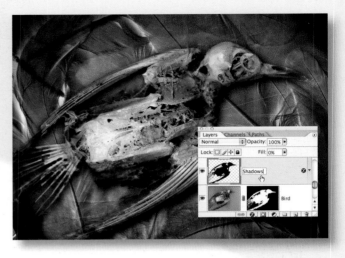

10. From the Styles palette choose 'Inner Shadow' and reverse the lighting direction. The mixture of Inner Shadow and Drop Shadow should give your subject the depth you may be looking for. Before you start patting yourself on the back and rushing off to get that cup of tea I asked you to make you will need to check the accuracy of your masking skills. Set the screen view to 'Actual pixels' (double-click the magnifying glass in the Tools palette or use the keyboard shortcut 'Command/Ctrl + Zero') and then drag the image around to inspect your handiwork. Any haloes or fringes can usually be corrected by working directly on the layer you applied the layer styles to.

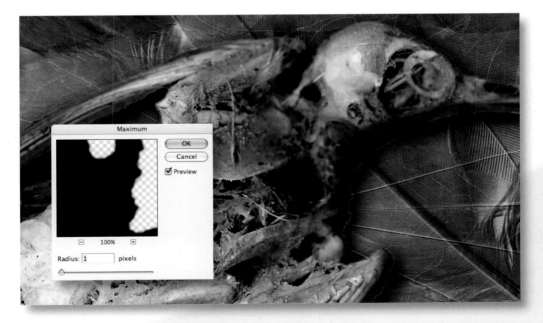

11. To remove any unsightly ghosting or fringes that may appear around your main subject try applying the 'Maximum' or 'Minimum' filter to your layer styles layer. Go to 'Filters > Other > Maximum/Minimum'. This should shrink or expand your mask to conceal those unsightly lines you have been trying to get rid of for years.

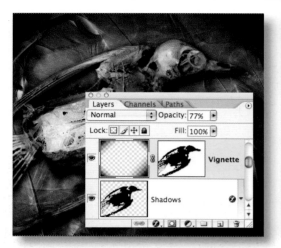

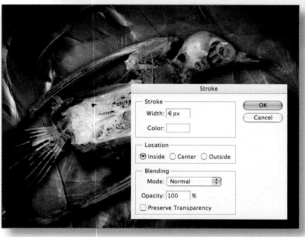

12. The image can be 'tarted up' for good measure with the application of a subtle vignette (Gradient Tool with the Foreground to Transparent option) to further darken the edges and a thin contrasting border color ('Select > Select All' and then 'Edit > Stroke').

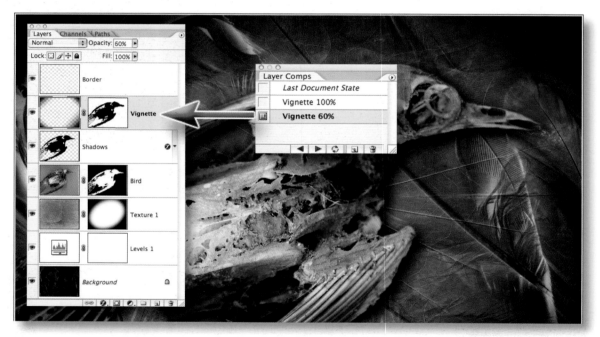

Layer Comps

As you move through the infinite number of variables that can be selected for layer visibility, position and layer styles to achieve a visual outcome it is possible to record each variable as a 'Layer Comp'. It is similar in practice to creating a 'snapshot' in the Histories palette or using the non-linear histories to explore a variety of compositing options. The advantage to Layer Comps is that, unlike histories and snapshots, they are saved with the image file and therefore available when the file is reopened.

Cast shadows – *Project 9*

Cast shadows, instead of drop shadows, are often an essential feature in montage work. In order to create the illusion that an object or subject belongs in the environment the shadow that is cast must respect the source of light, lighting quality and perspective. Shadows can sometimes be extracted from the original image but sometimes the shadows must be created from scratch.

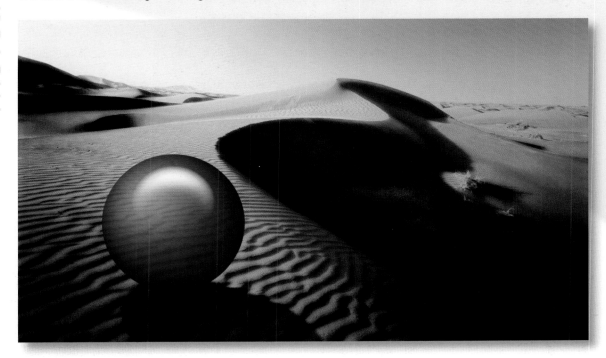

1. Use the Ellipse Tool to create a sphere in the landscape prepared for the previous project. Holding down the Shift key as you drag will constrain the ellipse to a circle. Pressing the Spacebar whilst drawing the circle will allow you to reposition the graphic.

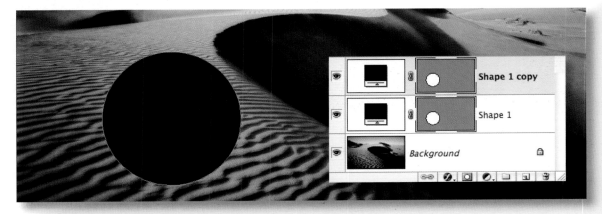

2. Duplicate this vector layer by dragging the layer to the 'New Layer' icon in the Layers palette.

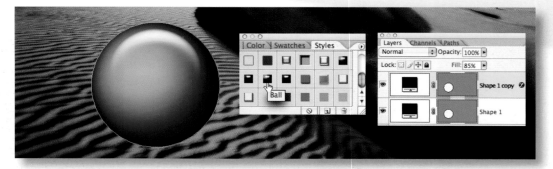

3. Add a layer style to the top shape layer. Select the layer and then click on the layer style in the Styles palette or drag the layer style from the palette to the required layer.

Note > You can download the style for this shape from the supporting web site. The style can then be loaded by double-clicking the preset, via the 'Preset Manager' from the 'Edit' menu or via the Styles palette options.

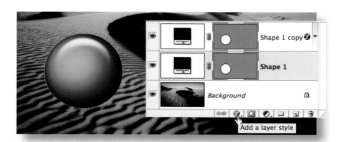
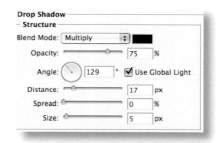

4. Add a drop shadow to the 'Shape 1' layer by clicking on the 'Add a layer style' icon in the Layers palette. Set the blend mode to 'Multiply', the opacity to 75% and keep the size and spread values small. Precise settings of the shadow can be modified later.

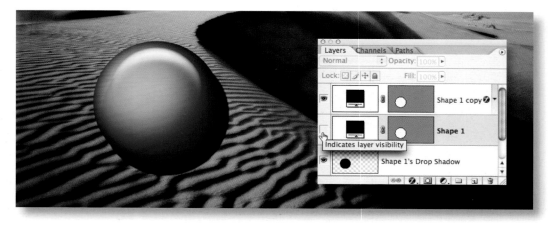

5. Go to 'Layer > Layer Style > Create Layer' to place the Shape 1 drop shadow on its own layer. Switch off the visibility of the 'Shape 1' layer.

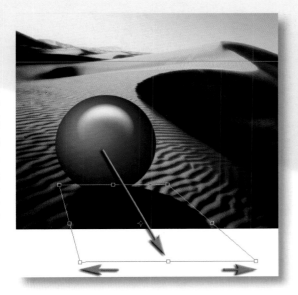 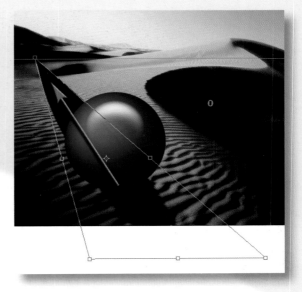

6. Use a guide dragged from a ruler or the 'Line Tool' to mark the horizon line within the image.

7. Select the 'Shape 1's Drop Shadow' layer and apply the 'Free Transform' command from the 'Edit' menu. Drag the top center handle of the Free Transform bounding box down so that the shadow is cast forwards from the strong backlight present in the image. Press the Ctrl/Command key and reposition each corner handle to create some perspective. The perspective can be checked for accuracy by dragging the top center handle of the Free Transform bounding box to the horizon line – if the points meet at the horizon line the perspective is correct.

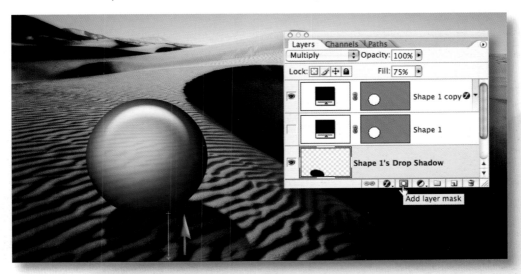

8. Add a layer mask to the shadow layer and use the Gradient Tool with a low opacity to fade the shadow as it moves further away from the sphere.

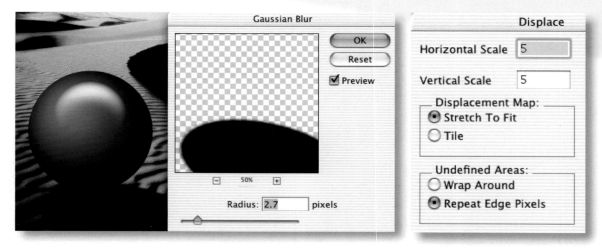

9. The shadow can be softened using the 'Gaussian Blur' filter and by adjusting the opacity of the shadow layer. The shadow can also be made to undulate over an uneven surface by using either the 'Liquify' filter or the 'Displace' filter as described in the 'Layer Blends' chapter.

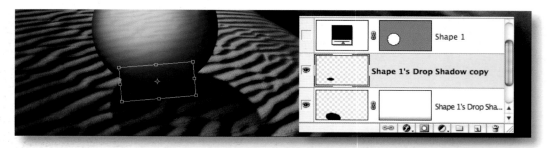

10. A second shadow can be added directly beneath where the object touches the surface. This secondary shadow helps the object appear 'grounded'. The original shadow layer can be duplicated and the Free Transform command used to resize and reposition this smaller shadow.

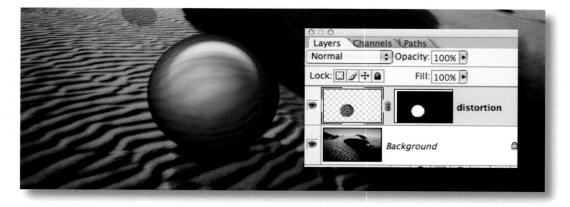

11. To complete the illusion the 'Bloat Tool' in the 'Liquify' filter was used to distort the ripples in the sand visible through the sphere.

Preserving shadows – *Project 10*

The shadow of a subject quite often bears little resemblance to the front view of the subject in the image and therefore cannot be recreated easily or convincingly. In these instances it may be preferable to preserve the shadow from the original image rather than recreating it in Photoshop. If the light source is diffused the edge of the shadow is very difficult to select. The following technique aids this process.

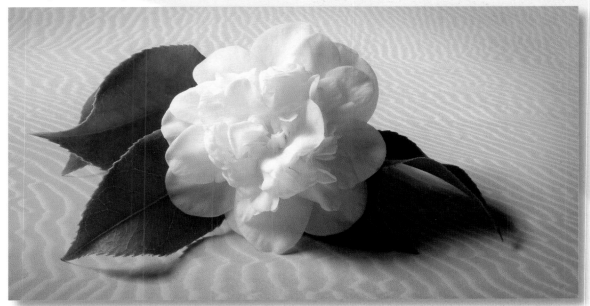

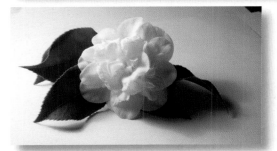

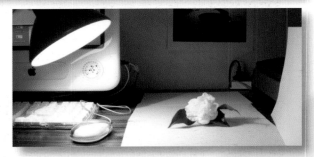

The flower for this tutorial was photographed (using a Fuji FinePix) on a cold winter's morning in Victoria whilst the sand (shot on Kodachrome film) hails from the Great Indian Desert in Rajasthan. Unlikely bedfellows, but with a little craft the two can lie together comfortably within the same frame – but only if the subtle shadow (created by a not-so-subtle 75-watt globe and a couple of pieces of white paper) is captured with all of its subtlety and delicately transplanted to its new home in the desert.

Botanical Health Warning: The delicate petals of the flower can be cooked, frazzled or fried by the heat of a tungsten lamp in just a few minutes. Be prepared to work quickly or use soft window light as a low-temperature alternative.

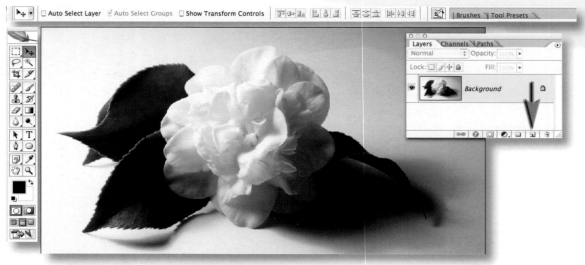

1. Duplicate the background layer by dragging the layer to the 'New Layer' icon in the Layers palette. Don't worry if the edges of your white paper are in the frame. Just be sure to capture the subject and its shadow.

Note > The surface used does not have to be white, but should be relatively texture-free. This will avoid mismatched textures when the shadow is transported to its new home.

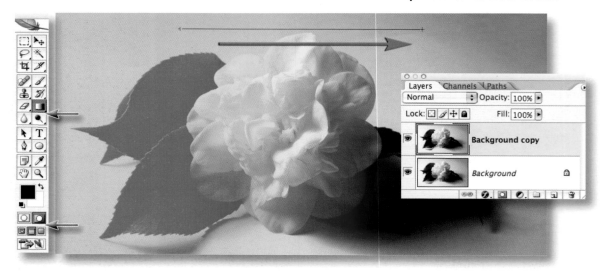

2. The initial steps in this project aim to reduce the background tone to white and leave the shadows intact. The fall-off of light from the directional light source (the white background gradually becoming gray on the side furthest from the light) can be balanced using an adjustment layer. Select the 'Default Foreground and Background Colors', 'Quick Mask Mode' and the 'Gradient Tool' in the 'Tools palette'. Select the 'Linear Gradient' and the 'Foreground to Transparent', or 'Foreground to Background' option in the 'Options' bar. Drag a gradient from the brighter side of the image to the darker side of the image. A gradient in the default masking color will appear. Exit Quick Mask Mode to reveal the resulting selection.

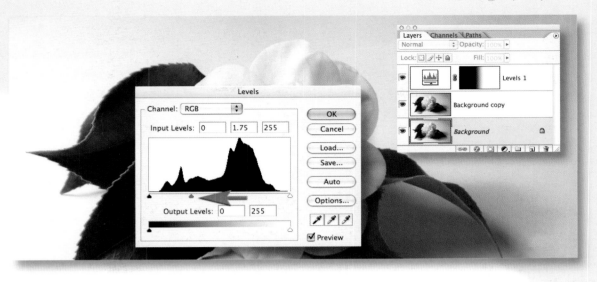

3. From the base of the Layers palette select a 'Levels' adjustment layer. The active selection will create a layer mask for the adjustment layer. Move the central 'Gamma' slider and/or highlight slider to the left to brighten the background so that both sides of the background are of a similar tone. Be careful not to lose the shadows in this process. Select 'OK' when a satisfactory balance has been achieved.

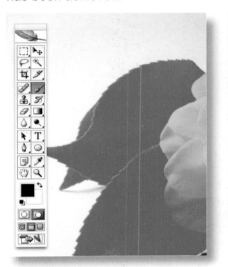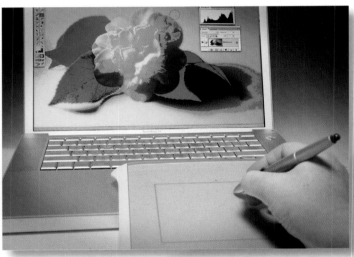

4. Use the painting tools in 'Quick Mask Mode' to make a selection of the flower on the background layer. Remember to feather the selection appropriately or apply a small amount of 'Gaussian Blur' to the mask. Click on the layer mask icon in the Layers palette to apply a layer mask to the background copy layer.

Note > A graphics tablet can be used to make light work of tricky selections such as the one performed in this project.

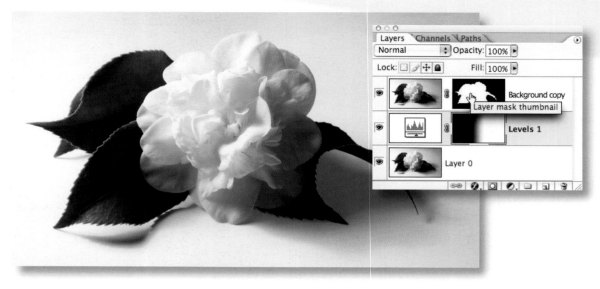

5. Drag the background copy layer to a position above the Levels adjustment layer. This will ensure the adjustment layer created in the previous step does not affect your subject.

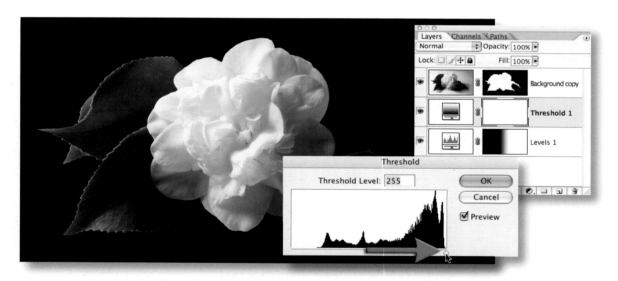

6. From the 'Create new fill or adjustment layer' menu in the Layers palette select 'Threshold'. This Threshold adjustment layer will help in the process of isolating the subtle shadows and enable us to drop the remainder of the background to pure white (255). Drag the threshold slider all the way to the right – a threshold level of 255. All of the pixels outside of the mask will now appear black. Select 'OK' to exit the Threshold dialog box.

Note > Check the positioning of the layers in the Layers palette if your own result does not match that achieved in the illustration above.

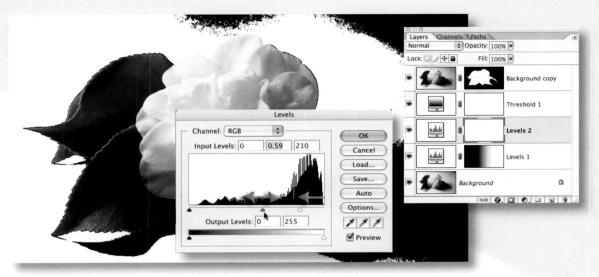

7. Create a Levels adjustment layer below the Threshold adjustment layer. Move the 'Gamma' and 'Highlight' sliders until you can isolate the shadows of your subject from the surrounding surface. The shadows should now appear clearly defined. Not all of the background surrounding the shadows will be rendered white by this step. Have no fear, the whitewash step follows.

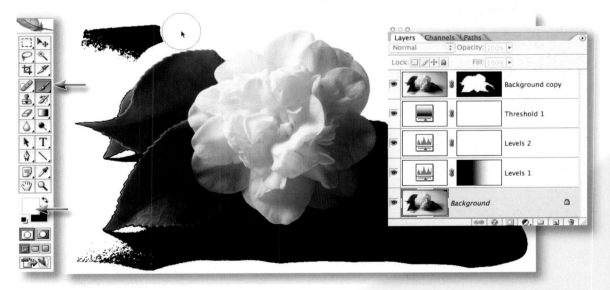

8. Select the 'Paintbrush' in the 'Tools palette' and click on the 'Switch Foreground and Background Colors' icon so that white is now the foreground colour. Now paint out anything that is not a shadow.

Note > If the thought of painting directly onto the background layer is not something you are comfortable with, then either duplicate the background layer again or take comfort in the fact that you already have an unadjusted background copy layer as your insurance policy.

PHOTOSHOP CS2

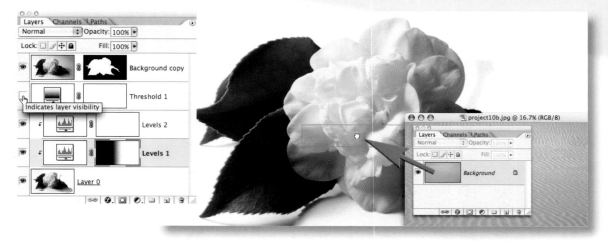

9. The threshold layer has now served its purpose and its visibility can be switched off, or the layer deleted by dragging it to the trash icon in the Layers palette. When the threshold is removed from the equation the background will appear white and the subtlety of the shadows will reappear. The coast is now clear for the introduction of the new background. Open the new background file and drag its thumbnail from the Layers palette into the window of your work-in-progress file. Hold down the Shift key as you let go of the file to center it in the host canvas. The new background will appear above the modified background layer for the moment.

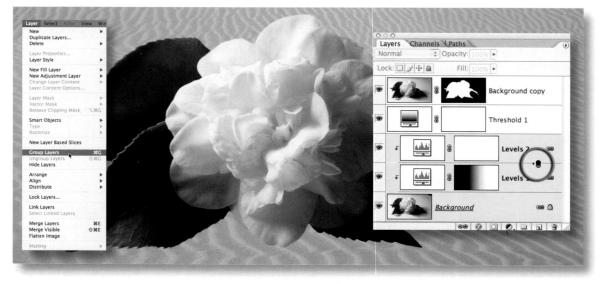

10. The next step involves moving the old background to a position above the new background (the sand dunes). Group or link the background layer with its associated adjustment layers. Then create a clipping mask with the adjustment layers and the background layer (hold down the Alt/Option key and click on the dividing line between each of the layers). This action will ensure the new background remains unaffected when the adjustment layers are moved up in the Layers palette in the next step.

essential skills >>>

PHOTOSHOP CS2

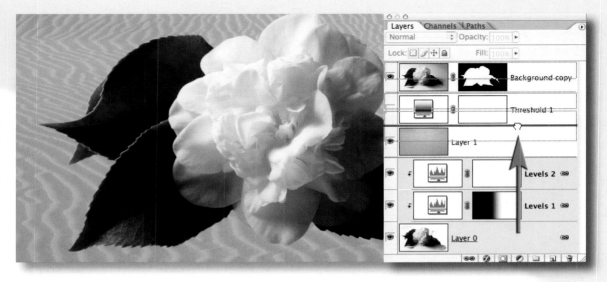

11. Double-click the background layer to change its name. When the layer no longer carries the name 'background' it can be moved up the layers stack by clicking and dragging it to position the new background. The linked layers should accompany it on its travels. The new background will momentarily be replaced with the old white background once again.

essential skills

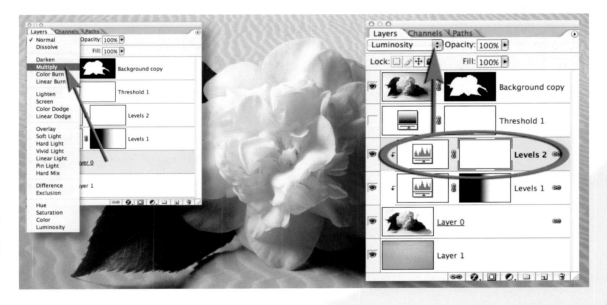

12. The final step merges or blends the subtle shadows into their new home. Select the old background layer and change its blend mode to Multiply (click on the blend mode menu in the Layers palette next to the opacity control). Set the adjustment layers to Luminosity mode if you need to reduce any color that has been introduced from the old background. Add a further Hue/Adjustment layer to this clipping group if additional desaturation is required.

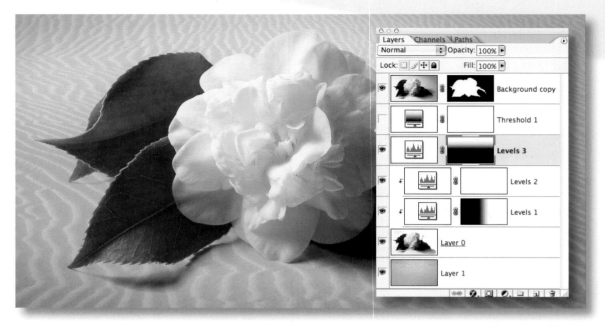

13. Finishing touches to this project could include the addition of a very subtle vignette, making the background lighter as it fades into the distance and the usual sharpening process prior to printing. If an additional adjustment layer gets accidentally grouped with the Clipping group go to the Layer menu and select the 'Release Clipping Mask' command.

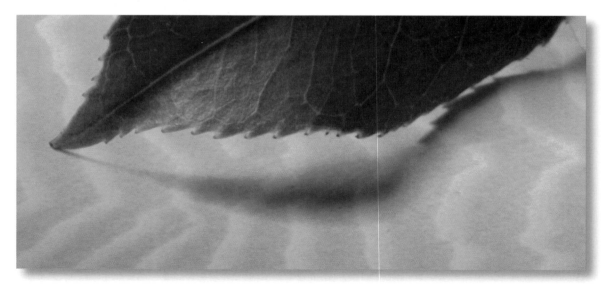

This technique provides those photographers burdened with a meticulous eye a useful way of retaining and transplanting the subtle and complex shadows from the original image to create sophisticated and professional montages.

Creating a panorama – *Project 11*

In recent years shooting multiple pictures of a scene and then stitching them to form a panoramic picture has become a popular project with digital photographers. This is the first time that Photoshop has shipped with Photomerge. The stitching program that first found its feet in Photoshop Elements has been included as a standard feature in Photoshop. This tool combines a series of photographs into a single picture by ensuring that the edge details of each successive image are matched and blended so that the join is not detectable. Once all the individual photographs have been combined the result is a picture that shows a scene of any angle up to a full 360°.

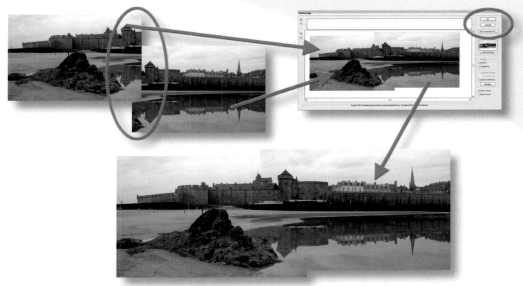

The feature can be started from the File menu (File > Automate > Photomerge) or via the Tools > Photoshop > Photomerge option in the Bridge file browser. The latter approach allows the user to select suitable source pictures from within the browser before activating the feature. At this point Photoshop attempts to automatically arrange and match the edge details of successive pictures.

In most circumstances Photomerge will easily position and stitch your pictures but there will be occasions where one or more images will not be stitched. These pictures are stored in the light box area (top) of the Photomerge dialog, where you can click-drag them to the correct position in the composition.

Individual pieces of the panorama can be moved or rotated at any time using the tools from the toolbar on the left-hand side of the dialog. Advanced Blending and Perspective options are set using the controls on the right. Photoshop constructs the panorama when the OK button is clicked.

Ensuring accurate stitching

To ensure accurate stitching successive images need to be shot with a consistent overlap of between 15 and 30%. The camera should be kept level throughout the shooting sequence and should be rotated around the nodal point of the lens wherever possible. The focal length, white balance, exposure and aperture need to remain constant whilst shooting all the source pictures.

1. Select Photomerge from the File menu (File > Automate > Photomerge) to start a new panorama. Click the Browse button in the dialog box. Search through the thumbnails of your files to locate the pictures for your panorama. Click the Open button to add files to the Source Files section of the dialog.

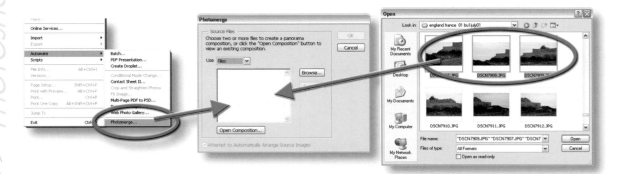

2. Select OK to open the Photomerge dialog box and start to edit the layout of your source images. To change the view of the images use the Move View Tool or change the scale and the position of the whole composition with the Navigator. Images can be dragged to and from the light box to the work area with the Select Image Tool.

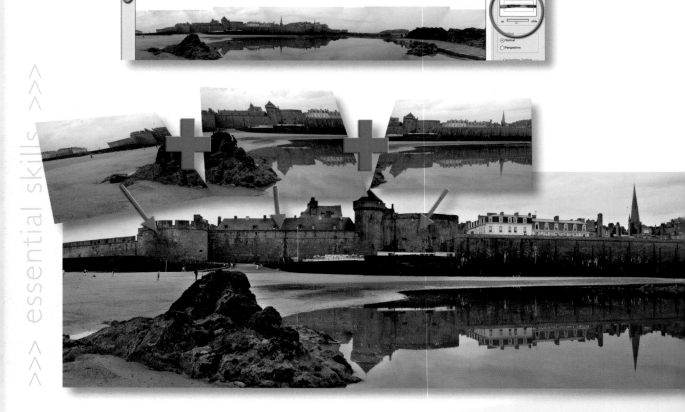

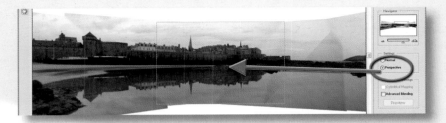

3. With the Snap to Image function turned on, Photomerge will match like details of different images when they are dragged over each other. Ticking the Use Perspective box will instruct Elements to use the first image placed into the layout area as the base for the composition of the whole panorama. Images placed into the composition later will be adjusted to fit the perspective of the base picture.

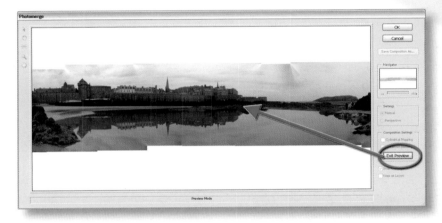

4. The Cylindrical Mapping option adjusts a perspective corrected image so that it is more rectangular in shape. The Advanced Blending option will try to smooth out uneven exposure or tonal differences between stitched pictures. The effects of Cylindrical Mapping as well as Advanced Blending can be viewed by clicking the Preview button. The final panorama file is produced by clicking the OK button.

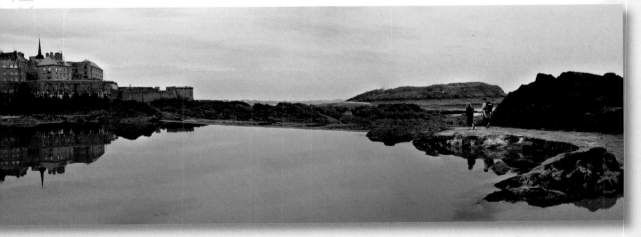

Solutions to common stitching problems

Moving subjects

One of the banes of the panoramic photographer's life is the subject that moves during a shooting sequence. The source of the problem may be people, cars or even clouds, but no matter how carefully you capture and stitch your source photos, the final panorama often features half a person, or object, as a result of Photomerge trying to match the edges of dissimilar pictures.

These problems can be fixed in one of two ways – either remove or repair the problem area.

Remove – To remove the problem you can use the Healing Brush, Patch or Clone Stamp Tools to sample background parts of the scene and paint over stitching errors. The success of this type of work is largely based on how well you can select suitable areas to sample. Color, texture and tone need to be matched carefully if the changes are to be disguised in the final panorama.

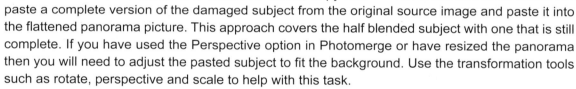

Be careful though, as repeated application of these tools can cause noticeable patterns or smoothing in the final picture.

Repair – In some instances it is easier to select, copy and paste a complete version of the damaged subject from the original source image and paste it into the flattened panorama picture. This approach covers the half blended subject with one that is still complete. If you have used the Perspective option in Photomerge or have resized the panorama then you will need to adjust the pasted subject to fit the background. Use the transformation tools such as rotate, perspective and scale to help with this task.

Adjusting the opacity of the pasted subject while you are transforming will help you match its details with those beneath. When complete the opacity is changed back to 100%. Finishing touches can be applied to the edges of the pasted images to ensure precise blending with the background using the Eraser Tool.

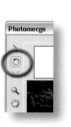
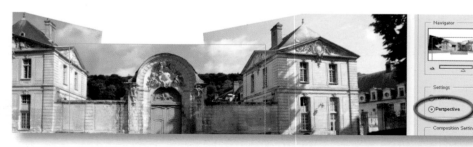

Misaligned picture parts

Shooting your source sequence by hand may be your only option when you have forgotten your tripod or you are purposely traveling light, but the inaccuracies of this method can produce panoramas with serious problems. One such problem is ghosting or misalignment. It is a phenomenon that occurs when edge elements of consecutive source pictures don't quite match. When Photomerge tries to merge the unmatched areas of one frame into another the mismatched sections are left as semi-transparent, ghosted or misaligned.

You may be able to alleviate the problem by carefully rotating difficult source images using the Rotate Image Tool and then selecting the Perspective option from the settings on the right of the dialog. If all else fails then the only option may be to repair the affected areas using the Clone Stamp or Healing Brush Tools but by far the best solution and certainly the most time-efficient one is to ensure that the camera and lens nodal point are situated over the pivot of the tripod at the time of capture. A little extra time spent in setting up will save many minutes editing later.

Extreme brightness range

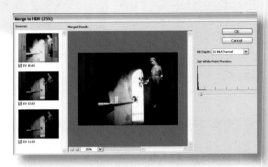

Digital cameras have a limit of the range of brightness that they can capture before details in shadow and highlight areas are lost. For most shooting scenarios the abilities of the average sensor are up to the job, but in certain extreme circumstances such as when a panorama encompasses both a view of a sunlight outdoors scene as well as a dimly lit interior the range of tones is beyond the abilities of these devices.

Rather than accept blown highlights or clogged shadows the clever panorama photographer can combine several exposures of the same scene to extend the range of brightnesses depicted in the image. The process involves shooting three images of the one scene using different exposures. The difference in exposure should be great enough to encompass the contrast in the scene. The different images are then combined using the new Merge to HDR feature (File > Automate > Merge to HDR) and saved as a single picture to be used as part of a stitched sequence.

Changes in color and density

Changes in color and density from one source image to the next can occur for a variety of reasons – the sun went behind a cloud during your capture sequence or the camera was left on auto exposure or auto white balance and changed settings during the shooting of the source sequence. When these images are blended the differences are noticeable at the stitch point in large areas of similar color and detail such as sky.

Auto fix – The 'Advanced Blending' feature in Photomerge will account for slight changes from one frame to the next by extending the graduation between one source image and the next. This 'auto' technique will disguise small variations in exposure/color and generally produce a balanced panorama, but for situations with large density discrepancies the source images may need to be edited individually.

Manual fix – The simple approach to balancing the density of your source images is to open two or more of the pictures and visually adjust contrast and brightness using tools like the Levels feature. For a more precise approach use the Info palette (Window > Info) to display the RGB values of specific common areas in pictures whilst adjusting their color and density using the Levels feature.

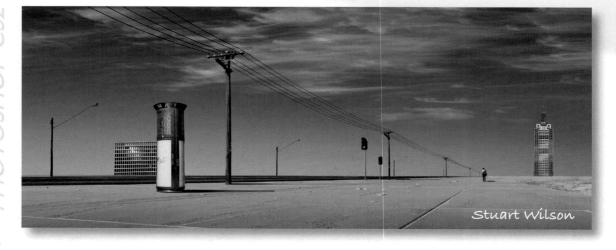

Stuart Wilson

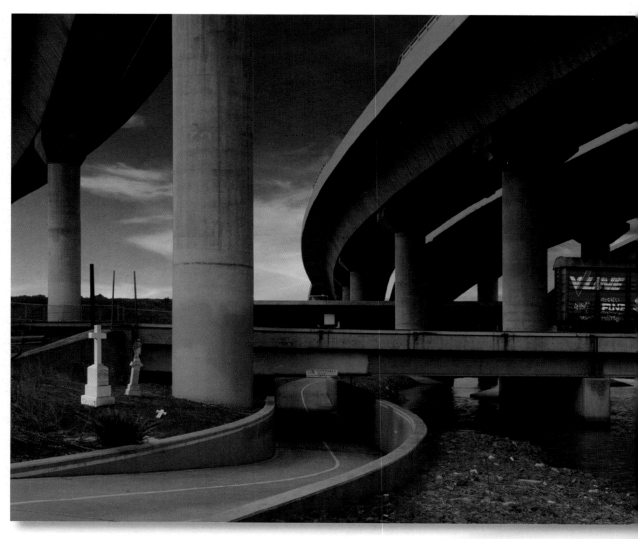

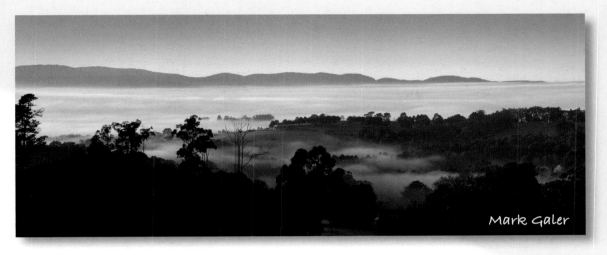

Mark Galer

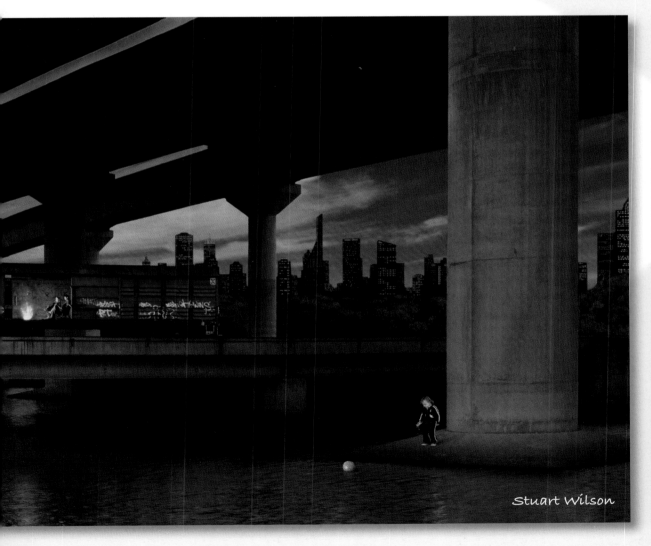

Stuart Wilson

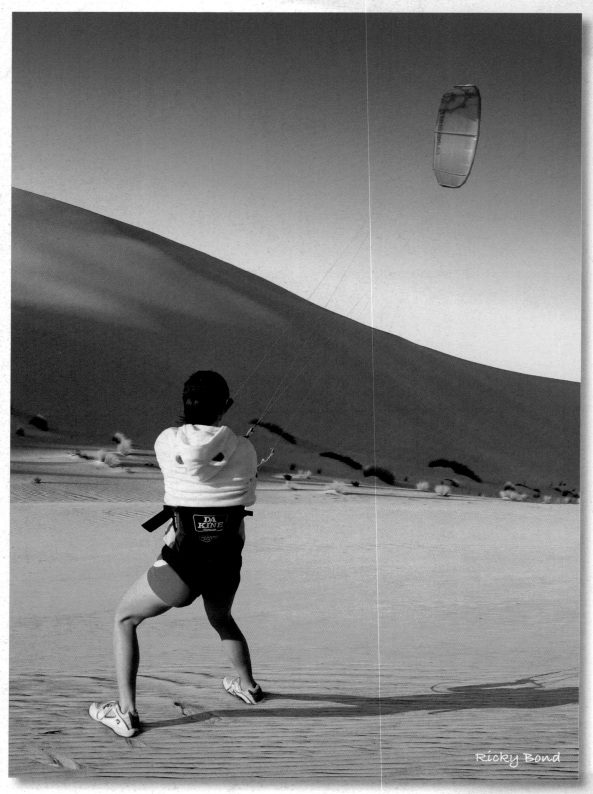

Ricky Bond

special effects

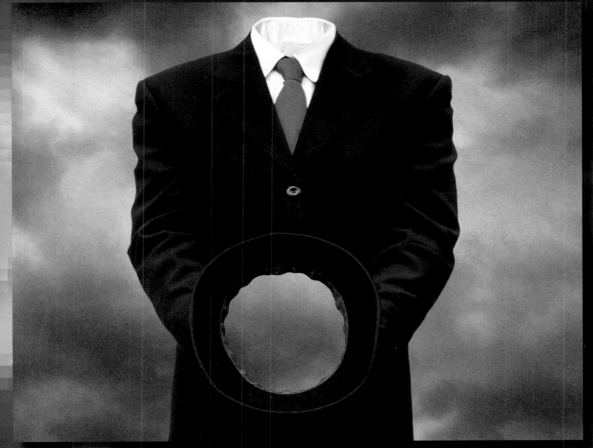

Anica Meehan

essential skills

~ Create a posterized image using the 'Posterize' and 'Gradient Map' adjustment layers.

~ Explore the creative potential of digital diffusion.

~ Selectively decrease the depth of field.

~ Create an image that emulates the polaroid transfer effect.

~ Explore the creative potential of selective filtering.

Posterization – *Project 1*

Sometimes the difference between a good portrait and a great portrait is simply the quality of light used to illuminate the subject. Soft directional light is usually great for creating a flattering or glamorous portrait, but if the light is too flat, the drama or impact of a character portrait can be lost. In this activity the Posterize command comes to the rescue to enhance the character and create a little drama!

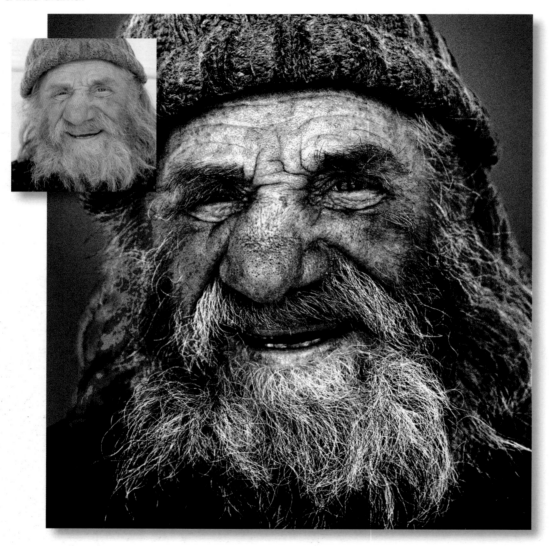

Using the Posterize command in Photoshop (Image > Adjustments > Posterize) is as simple as selecting the command and typing in the number of levels required. You will find the Posterize command can be very effective for dividing grayscale images into large flat areas of tone to create a dramatic graphic impact. The effects of posterization, however, are often far less successful if the command is applied directly to an RGB color image. The aim of this activity is to create a successful and dramatic posterized color image.

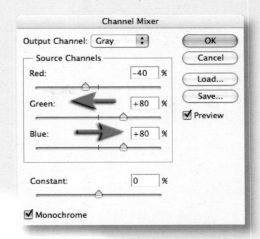

1. Open the 'Special Effects > Project1.jpg' portrait image from the supporting CD. Duplicate the background layer by dragging it to the 'New Layer' icon in the Layers palette. Although the final image will be color you need to convert this background copy layer using either the Channel Mixer or the technique outlined in the Toning chapter. If using a Channel Mixer adjustment layer be sure to clip the adjustment layer to the background copy and check the Monochrome box.

Note > The preview in the Channel Mixer dialog box will remain monochrome even when the Monochrome box is unchecked.

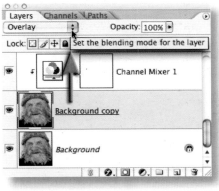

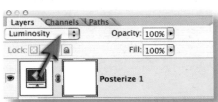

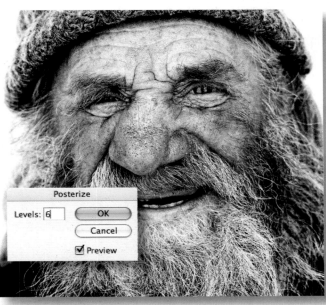

2. Set the background copy layer to Overlay mode. Hold down the Alt/Option key and choose 'Posterize' from the adjustment layer options. Set the blend mode to 'Luminosity'. From the Posterize dialog box select 6 levels (this will give you white, black and four intermediate tones). The Posterize command at this stage offers no control over the exact placement of these tonal values. This control can be achieved by using a gradient map and a Curves adjustment layer.

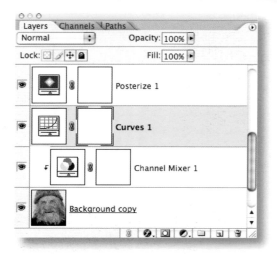

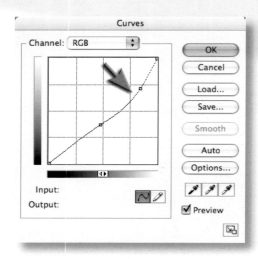

3. Add a Curves adjustment layer immediately below the Posterize adjustment layer and then create a tone curve that places or realigns the six tonal steps for maximum graphic impact.

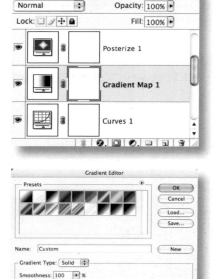

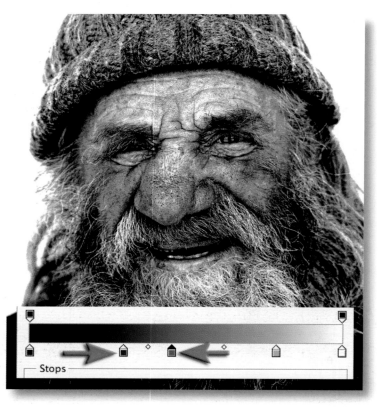

4. Add a Gradient Map adjustment layer directly below the Posterize adjustment layer. Choose a 'black to white' gradient and then create additional stops for shadows, midtones and highlights. See 'Toning Projects > Gradient Maps – Project 2' for more information on creating color stops. Move the color stops to fine-tune the posterize effect.

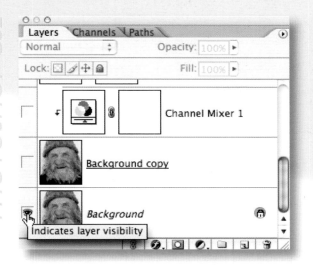

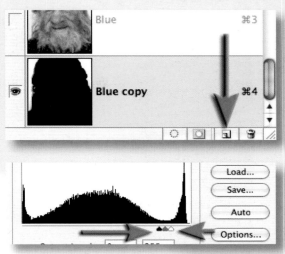

5. Hold down the Alt or Option key and click the visibility icon on the background layer to switch off the visibility of all layers except the background layer. Create a channel mask (see Selections) by duplicating the blue channel and increasing the contrast using a Levels adjustment. Click on the master RGB channel and return to the Layers palette. Alt/Option-click the visibility icon on the background layer to switch on the visibility of all layers again.

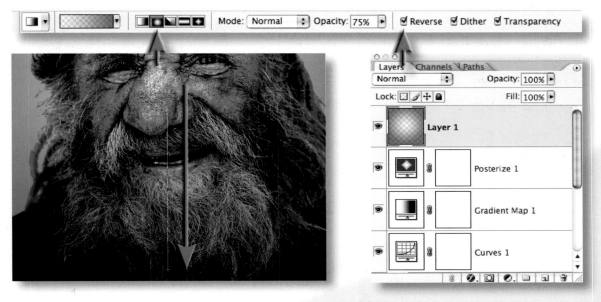

6. By adding a vignette it is possible to remove the bright distracting background. Click on the 'New Layer' icon to create a new empty layer and then click on the Foreground color swatch and select a deep blue from the Color Picker. Select the Gradient Tool from the Tools palette and the Foreground to Transparent, Radial, Reverse, Dither and Transparency options with an opacity of approximately 75%. Drag a gradient from the center of the image to the bottom edge of the image.

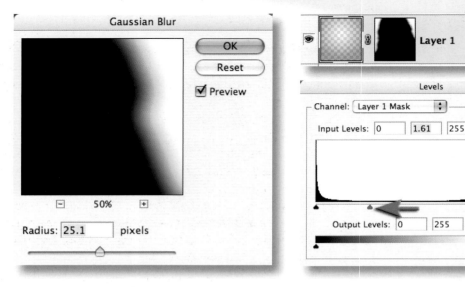

7. Load the 'Blue Copy' alpha channel as a selection and then add a layer mask to the gradient layer. Apply a generous Gaussian Blur filter to the layer mask and then adjust the 'choke' or amount of halo using a Levels adjustment (Image > Adjustments > Levels).

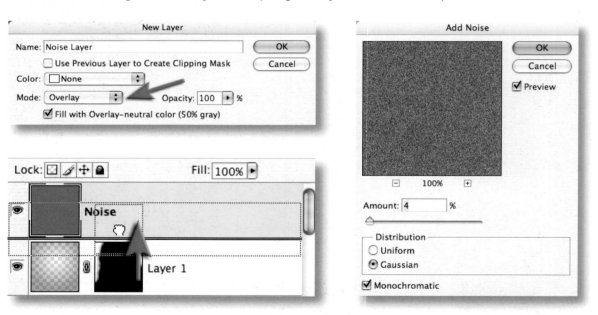

8. Add another new layer and from the layer options choose 'Overlay' and 'Fill with Overlay-neutral color'. Go to Filter > Noise > Add Noise to add texture to the liquid smooth tone of the background. Hold down the Option key and drag the layer mask from the gradient layer to the noise layer (CS2 only). This will duplicate the layer mask and limit the noise to the background only. This project demonstrates how tonality and color can have a huge impact on the mood and impact, and how, with a little digital dexterity, the extraordinary can be released from the ordinary.

Digital diffusion – *Project 2*

Most photographers have an obsession with sharpness. It seems that we are all striving for the ultimate quality in our images. We carefully select good lenses and always double check our focusing before making that final exposure. All this so that we can have sharp, well-focused images that we can be proud of.

It almost seems like a mortal sin then for me to be describing a technique on how to make your images 'blurry', but like it or not, these days the photographic world is full of diffused or blurred imagery. From the color food supplements in our weekend papers to the latest in portraiture or wedding photography, subtle (and sometimes not all that subtle) use of diffusion in contemporary images can be easily found.

Traditionally, adding such an effect meant placing a 'mist' or 'fog' filter in front of the camera lens at the time of shooting or positioning diffusion filters below enlarging lenses when printing. The digital version of these techniques allows much more creativity and variation in the process and relies mainly on the use of layers, blending modes and the 'Gaussian Blur' filter.

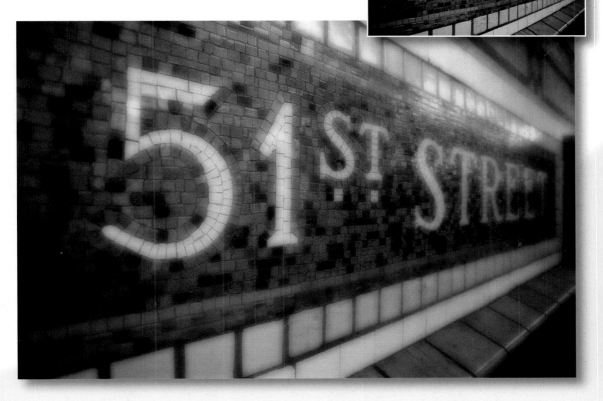

Diffused image made by combining a sharp and a blurred layer with the Luminosity blend mode

The Gaussian Blur filter that can be found in most image-editing packages effectively softens the sharp elements of the picture when it is applied. Used by itself, this results in an image that is, as expected, quite blurry, and let's be frank, not that attractive. It is only when this image is carefully combined with the original sharp picture that we can achieve results that contain sharpness and diffusion at the same time and are somewhat more desirable. So essentially we are talking about a technique that contains three distinct steps.

1. First, make a copy of the background layer by selecting Layer > Duplicate. Title the copy 'Blur Layer' using the Duplicate Layer dialog.

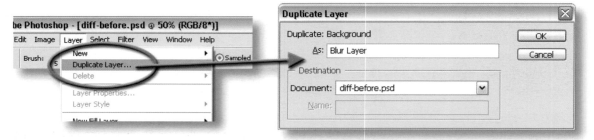

2. With this layer selected, apply the Gaussian Blur filter. You should now have a diffused or blurred layer sitting above the sharp original. If you don't like the look of the Gaussian diffusion then you can choose another effect such as the Diffuse filter instead. This filter is not as controllable as Gaussian Blur but does achieve a different effect.

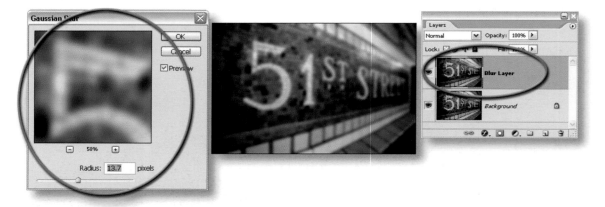

3. Finally, change the layer 'blending mode' using the drop-down menu in the top left of the Layers palette. As we have already seen, Photoshop contains many different blending modes that control how any layer interacts with any other. The Normal, Soft Light, Multiply and Luminosity modes all work well for this picture. Of course other modes might work better on your own images so make sure that you experiment. Additionally, you can change the 'opacity' (top right of the dialog) of the blurred layer as well. Adjusting this setting changes the transparency of the blurred layer, which in turn determines how much of the layer below can be seen. More opacity means less of the sharp layer characteristics are obvious. By carefully combining the choice of blending mode and the amount of opacity, the user can create infinite adjustments to the diffusion effect.

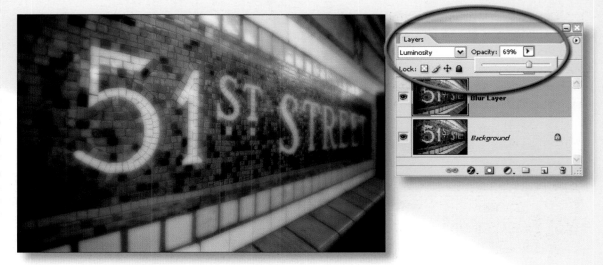

One step further

In some instances it might be preferable to keep one section of the image totally free of blur. This can be achieved by applying the Gaussian filter via a graded selection to your original image. This way some of the picture remains sharp whilst the rest is diffused.

1. Open the base image and make a copy layer of the background using the Layer > Duplicate Layer command. Make sure that the Gradient Tool options are set to 'Foreground to Transparent' and 'Radial Gradient'. Switch to Quick Mask mode and create a mask from the center of the '51' to the outer right-hand edge of the image.

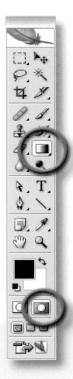

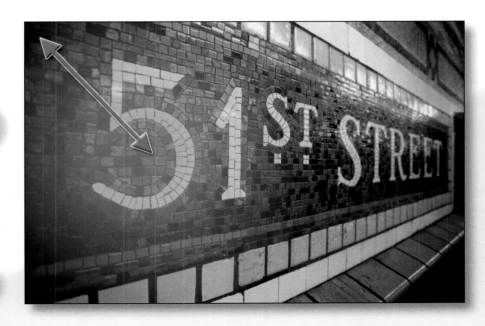

2. Switch back to the Selection mode to reveal the graded circular selection. Depending on the Quick Mask settings, the selection may enclose the parts of the picture that were masked or may isolate the opposite areas in the picture. To change between these two different selections use the Select > Inverse command. Apply the Gaussian Blur filter to the copied layer with the selection still active. By applying this extra step to the duplicate of the original picture (on a separate layer) it is possible to use blending modes and opacity to further refine the strength and character of the diffusion effect.

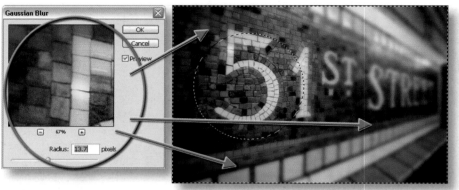
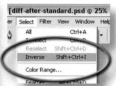

3. To complete the technique and disguise the areas of the picture that have been smoothed with the action of the Gaussian Blur filter you need to try to match the texture of the non-diffused and diffused areas. Do this by adding a very small amount of noise to the picture. The Add Noise filter (Filter > Noise > Add Noise) can be applied to the whole image or via the selection that was used to blur the layer originally. In either case apply only the minimum amount necessary to disguise the changes.

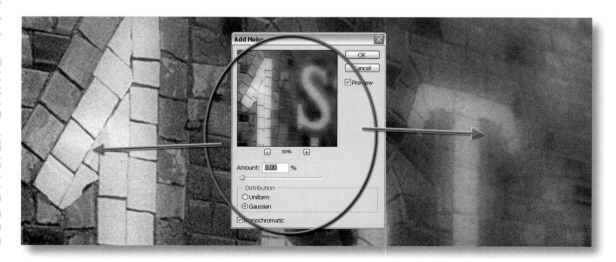

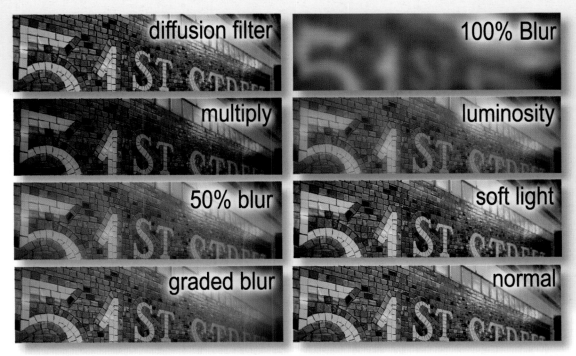

Examples of different diffusion techniques and blending modes

Even more control

You can refine your control over the diffusion process even more by using the Eraser Tool to selectively remove sections of the blurred layer.

At its simplest level this will result in areas of blur contrasted against areas of sharpness; however, if you vary the opacity of the Eraser then you can carefully feather the transition points.

The addition of the erasing step allows much more control over the resultant image. It is possible to select, and highlight, the focal points of the photograph whilst not losing the overall softness of the image.

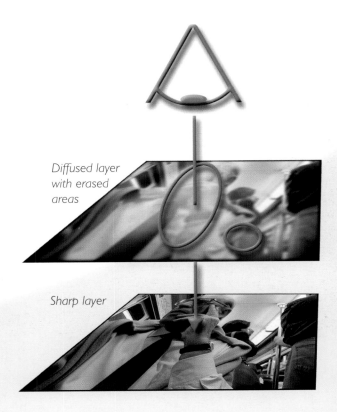

Diffused layer with erased areas

Sharp layer

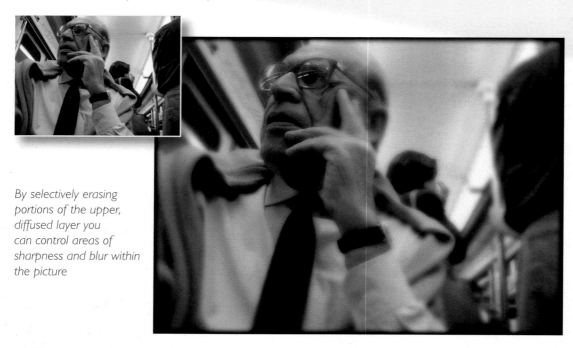

By selectively erasing portions of the upper, diffused layer you can control areas of sharpness and blur within the picture

1. Start with a picture that contains the duplicated blurred layer sitting above the sharp original picture. Select the Eraser Tool and set it to a soft-edged brush with an opacity of 20%.

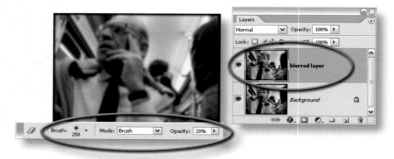

2. With the upper blurred layer selected, start to erase the parts of the blurred layer to reveal the sharpness beneath. Repeat the erasing action for areas that you want sharpest whilst leaving non-essential sections with no changes. It may be easier to think of the erasing action as 'painting back the sharpness' of the picture.

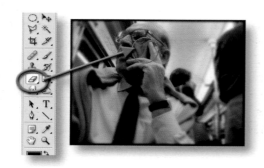

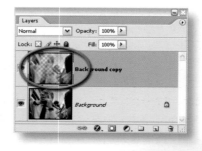

Creative depth of field – *Project 3*

The Gaussian Blur filter or Lens Blur filter can be used creatively to blur distracting backgrounds. Most digital cameras achieve greater depth of field (more in focus) at the same aperture when compared to their 35mm film cousins due to their comparatively small sensor size. This is great in some instances but introduces unwelcome detail and distractions when the attention needs to be firmly fixed on the subject – and not the woman in the background picking her nose!

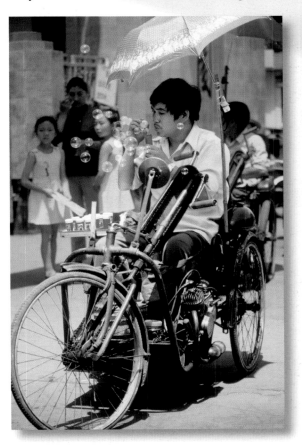 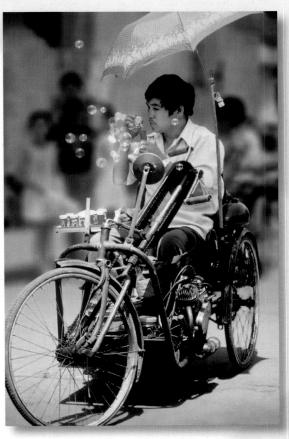

There is often a lot to think about during the capture of an image and the time required to consider the appropriate aperture and shutter speed combination for the desired visual outcome often gets the elbow. Photoshop can, however, come to the rescue and drop a distracting background into a murky sea of out-of-focus oblivion. A careful selection to isolate the subject from the background and the application of either the 'Gaussian Blur' filter or 'Lens Blur' filter usually does the trick. Problems with this technique arise when the resulting image, all too often, looks manipulated rather than realistic. A straight application of the Gaussain Blur filter will have a tendency to 'bleed' strong tonal differences and saturated colors into the background fog, making the background in the image look more like a watercolor painting rather than a photograph. The Gaussian Blur filter will usually require some additional work if the post-production technique is not to become too obvious. A more realistic shallow depth of field effect is created by using the 'Lens Blur filter'.

PHOTOSHOP CS2

>>>

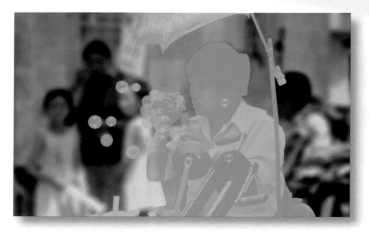
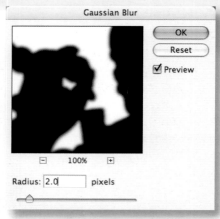

1. Whichever Blur filter you decide to use you will first need to make a selection of the main subject. Duplicate the background layer and then make a selection of the foreground subject (or alternatively load the saved selection in the project PSD file on the supporting CD). This selection will isolate the foreground subject from the blurring technique that will follow. If you intend to use a mixture of selection tools, adjust the feather setting in the Options bar to 0. Perfect the selection using a hard-edged brush in 'Quick Mask mode'. Apply a Gaussian Blur filter (Filter > Blur > Gaussian Blur) to the mask to replicate the edge quality of the main subject. Exit Quick Mask mode when the selection is finished.

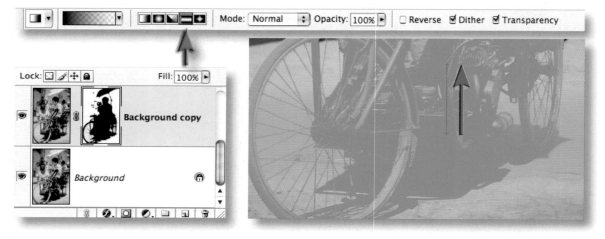

2. Use the selection to create a layer mask. The mask will require further work in order to create an area of sharp focus in the background for positioning or anchoring the subject realistically in its environment. The subject will need to be planted firmly on an area of ground that is in sharp focus so that it will not appear to float. A simple gradient that includes part of the background in the selection will anchor the subject and allow the background to fade gradually from focus to out of focus. Select the Default Colors in the Tools palette and then select the Gradient Tool. Choose the 'Foreground to Transparent', 'Reflected Gradient' and 'Multiply' options in the Options bar at 100% opacity. Drag the Gradient Tool from the center of the wheel on the left-hand side of the image a short way towards the top of the wheel.

essential skills >>> >>>

Lens Blur filter

3. The Lens Blur filter was new to Photoshop CS and will now work on 16 Bit/Channel files in CS2. The filter is extremely sophisticated, allowing you to choose different styles of aperture and control over the specular highlights to create a more realistic camera effect. The filter introduces none of the bleed that is associated with the Gaussian Blur technique. Click on the image thumbnail in the Layers palette to make sure this is the active part of the layer rather than the layer mask. From the 'Blur' submenu in the 'Filter' menu, select the Lens Blur filter. From the 'Depth Map' section of this dialog box choose 'Layer Mask'.

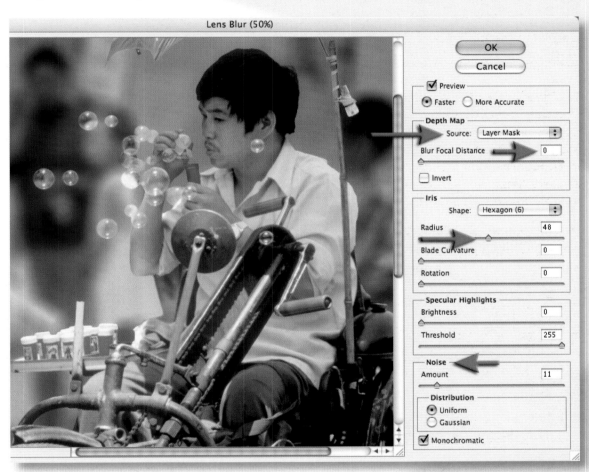

Set the focal point (region of sharp focus) if the foreground subject is not already sharp. This can be set using the 'Blur Focal Distance' slider or by simply clicking on the foreground subject in the preview window. Choose the depth of field required by moving the Radius slider. The Blade Curvature, Rotation, Brightness and Threshold sliders fine-tune the effect. Finally apply a small amount of noise to replicate the textural quality (noise or film grain) of the rest of the image that will remain in focus. Click OK when the blur quality has been achieved. Steps 4 and 5 in this project may also help the user fine-tune the layer mask after the Lens Blur filter has been applied.

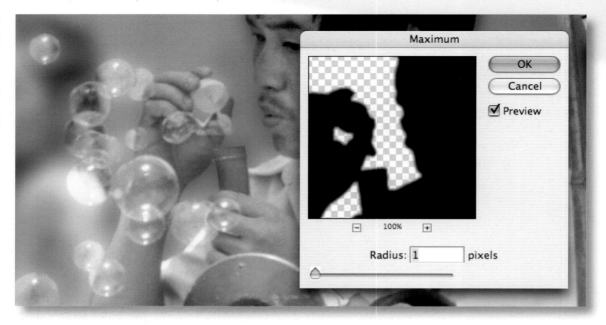

4. Further refinement of the edge can be achieved after the Lens Blur filter has been applied by moving the edge of the layer mask to align with your subject using the Maximum or Minimum filters from the 'Filter > Other' submenu. A one or two pixel radius is often sufficient to remove any tell-tale halo. If a halo is present around a localized area of the subject only, you can first make a selection with the Lasso Tool prior to using the Maximum or Minimum filter.

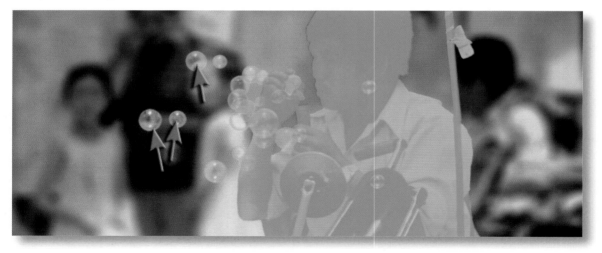

5. To retrieve areas of focus that were blurred accidentally select black as the foreground color and a soft-edged Paintbrush with an opacity of 50%. Select the mask layer and paint any areas of the subject that appear too blurry to increase the detail present. Several passes of the brush set at 50% opacity will gradually increase the detail and leave a subtle edge. Hold down the Alt or Option key and the Shift key and click on the layer mask thumbnail to view the layer mask and image together if this helps the process.

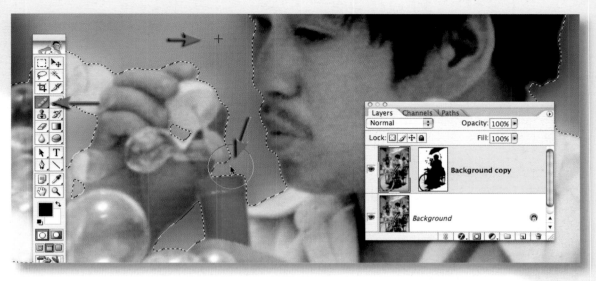

Note > When the Gaussian Blur filter is used to blur a background, saturated colors or contrasting tones bleed into the background from the edge of the subject . This can be removed by using the Clone Tool or Healing Brush Tool and a selection. Press the 'Alt' key (PC) or Option key (Mac) to sample an area that is free from the color or tonal bleed and paint these pixels to mask the unwelcome effect. If using the Clone Stamp Tool use a brush at a reduced opacity and make several passes (choosing a different source for each subsequent pass).

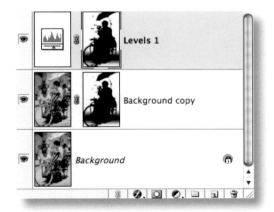

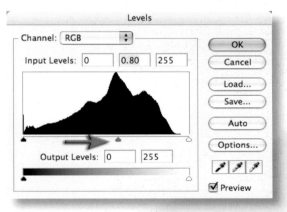

6. Use the selection to create a localized 'Levels' adjustment layer to lower the overall brightness of the background to further draw attention to the foreground subject matter.

FUTURE DEVELOPMENTS – SHIFTING FOCUS

If digital cameras are eventually able to record distance information at the time of capture this could be used in the creation of an automatic depth map for the Lens Blur filter. Choosing the most appropriate depth of field could be relegated to post-production image editing in a similar way to how the white balance is set in camera RAW.

Digital Polaroid transfer effect – *Project 4*

Most readers will probably be familiar with Polaroid instant picture products – you push the button and the print is ejected and develops right before your eyes. For many years professional image-makers have been using the unique features of this technology to create wonderfully textured images. The process involved substituting watercolor paper for the printing surface supplied by Polaroid. As a result the image is transferred onto the roughly surfaced paper and takes on a distinctly different look and feel to a standard Polaroid print.

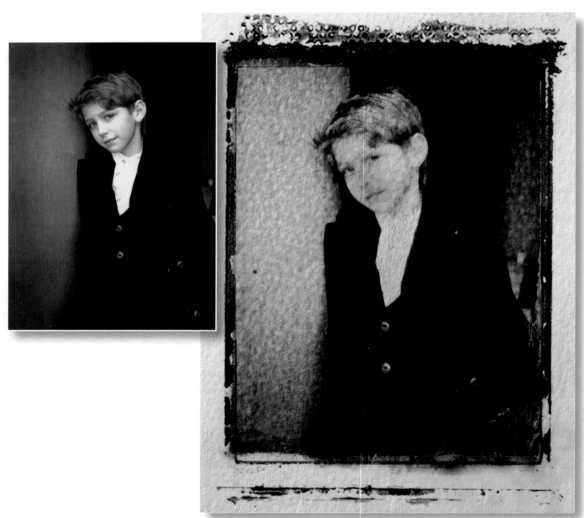

Much acclaimed for its artistic appeal, the technique was not always predictable and, much to the frustration of a lot of photographers, it was often difficult to repeat the success of previous results. There were three main problems – dark areas of an image often didn't transfer to the new surface, colors and image detail would bleed unpredictably, and it was difficult to control how dark or light the final print would be. I know these problems intimately as it once took me 16 sheets of expensive instant film to produce a couple of acceptable prints.

PHOTOSHOP CS2

>>> essential skills >>> >>>

A digital solution

This success ratio is not one that my budget or my temperament can afford. So I started to play with a digital version of the popular technique. I wanted to find a process that was more predictable, controllable and repeatable. My first step was to list the characteristics of the Polaroid transfer print so that I could simulate them digitally. To me it seemed that there were four main elements:

~   Desaturated colors
~   Mottled ink
~   Distinct paper texture and color
~   The Polaroid film frame.

To duplicate these characteristics on the desktop would mean that I could capture the essence of the Polaroid process.

1. The Polaroid technique requires the watercolor paper to be slightly wet at the time of transfer. The moisture, whilst helping the image movement from paper to paper, tends to desaturate the colors and cause fine detail to be lost. These characteristics are also the result of the coarse surface of the donor paper.

So the first step of the digital version of the process is to desaturate the color of our example image. In Photoshop this can be achieved by using the Image > Adjustments > Hue/Saturation. With the dialog open carefully move the Saturation slider to the left. This action will decrease the intensity of the colors in your image.

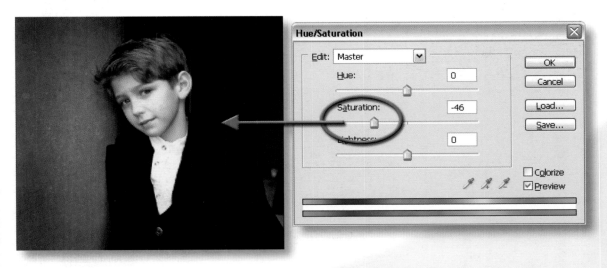

2. The distinct surface and image qualities of Polaroid transfer prints combine both sharpness and image break-up in the one picture. To reproduce this effect digitally, I copied the original image onto a second layer. My idea was to manipulate one version so that it displayed the mottled effect of the transfer print whilst leaving the second version untouched. Then using the blending modes or opacity features of Photoshop's layers I could adjust how much sharpness or mottle was contained in the final result.

In practice, I started by duplicating the image layer. This can be achieved by selecting the layer to be copied and then using the Duplicate Layer command located under the Layers menu. Alternatively you can drag the layer to the New Layer button at the bottom of the Layers palette.

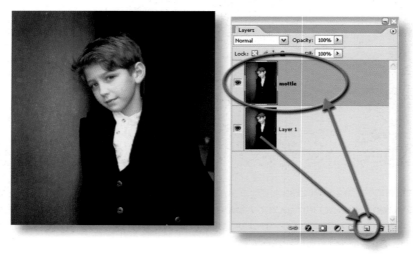

3. With the uppermost layer selected, I then needed to find a method to simulate the mottle of the transfer print. Though not exactly right, I found that by combining the effects of the Paint Daubs and Palette Knife filters I could produce reasonable results. When using these filters yourself keep in mind that the settings used will vary with the style and size of your image. Use the ones in the example as a starting point only. This part of the process is not an exact science. Play and experimentation is the name of the game. You might also want to try other options in the Artistic, Sketch or Texture selections of the Filter menu.

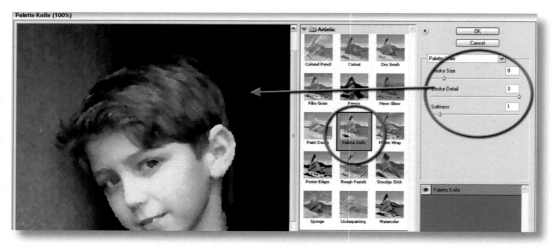

4. The last step in this texture stage is to combine the characteristics of the two layers. This can be achieved by either changing the blending mode of the uppermost layer or by adjusting its opacity, or both. For the example image a simple opacity change was all that was needed, but don't be afraid to try a few different blend/opacity combinations with your own work.

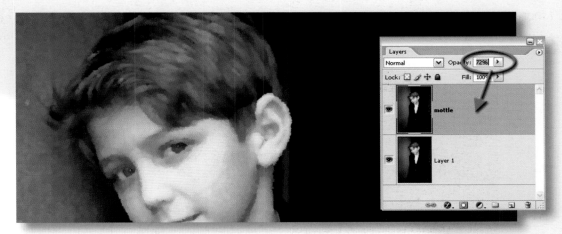

5. The paper color and texture are critical parts of the appeal of the transfer print. These two characteristics extend throughout the image itself and into the area that surrounds the picture. For this to occur in a digital facsimile it is necessary to provide some space around the image using Photoshop's Canvas Size feature (Image > Canvas Size).

Unlike Image Size, this option allows the user to increase the size of the canvas that all image layers (including the background layer) are sitting upon without changing the image itself. In the example the canvas width was increased by 120% and the height by 140%.

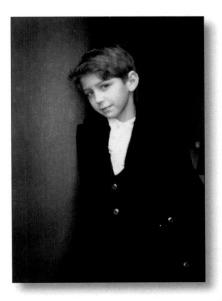

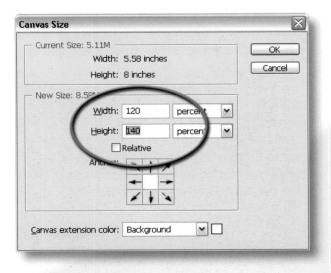

6. To add the texture to both image and surround I flattened (Layer > Flatten Image) the two image layers and the white background into a single layer. Next, I photographed a section of watercolor paper to use as a customized texture with the Texturizer filter (Filter > Texture > Texturizer). You can download and use this very file from the book's web site or pick one of the other options from the Texture pop-up list.

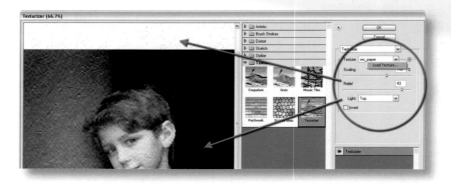

7. With the texture complete, I played with the overall color of the image using the Levels feature (Image > Adjustments > Levels). I altered the blue and red channels independently and concentrated on the lighter tones of the image so that rather than the paper being stark white it took on a creamy appearance.

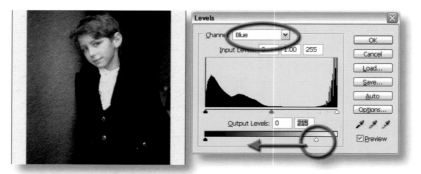

8. The last part of the process involves combining the final image with a scan of a Polaroid film edge. You can make your own by scanning a Polaroid print and then removing the image or you can download the edge I used for the example from the book's web site. Open the edge file as a separate document. Click onto the edge picture and drag it onto your picture. The edge will automatically become a new layer on top of the existing image layer. With the edge layer selected change the layer's blend mode to Multiply. Notice that the white areas of the layer are now transparent allowing the picture beneath to show through. Finally use the Scale command to adjust the size of the edge to fit the image.

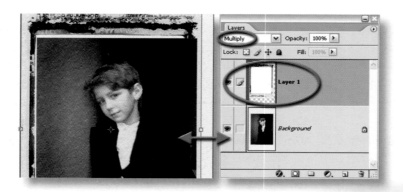

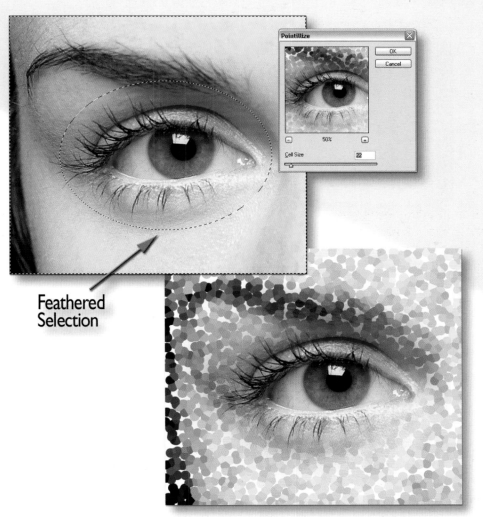

Feathered
Selection

Creative filtering – *Project 5*

One way of controlling the way that a filter changes your image is to restrict its effect with the use of a selection. This can be achieved by creating a feathered selection or a soft-edged mask.

Feathered selection

1. Before selecting the filter make a selection of the area that you don't want to be altered. In this example the eye was isolated with the Ellipse marquee. Next invert the selection (Select > Inverse) so that the rest of the picture is then selected and then add some feathering (Select > Feather) so that there is a gradual change between the filter effect and the unfiltered parts of the picture. Now select the filter and apply the effect to the selected area.

Soft-edged mask

A faster approach would be paint a mask over the area in Quick Mask mode with a soft-edged brush and then switch back to Standard Edit mode to reveal the selection.

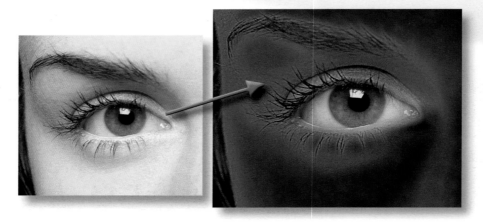

You can obtain a more painterly approach to applying filter effects with the aid of the History Brush.

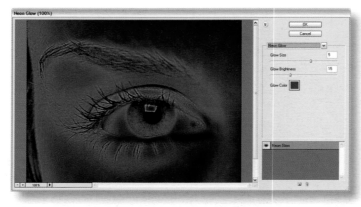

1. Start by filtering the picture with the effect you want to apply. Adjust the filter settings to suit the image and click OK. Here the Neon Glow filter is used to provide graphic contrast with the model's skin tone.

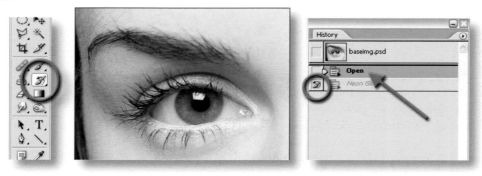

2. Next open the History palette (Window > History) and click the step before the filter application. Select the History Brush from the toolbox and click into the box on the left of the filter history state.

A small icon of the History Brush will appear, signifying that you are now painting using this state as your source.

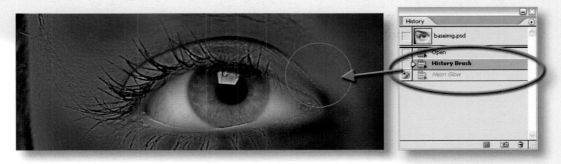

3. Now you can brush over the picture, painting the filter effect as you go. Altering the opacity of the brush will change the transparency of the effect.

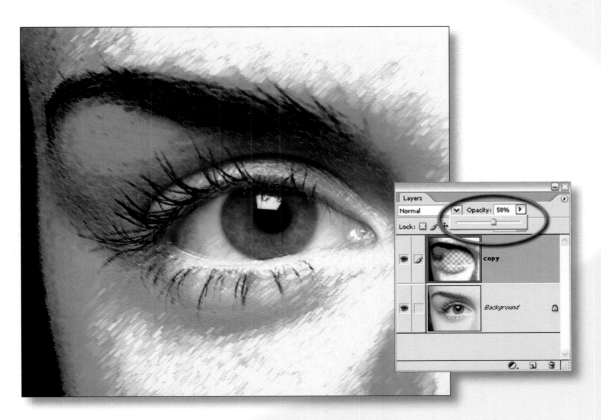

Yet another approach is to apply the filter to a copy of the picture that has been stored on a separate layer above the original. The Eraser Tool can then be used to remove sections of the filtered layer to reveal the unaltered picture beneath. In addition the opacity of the filtered layer can be adjusted so that the whole effect becomes semi-transparent

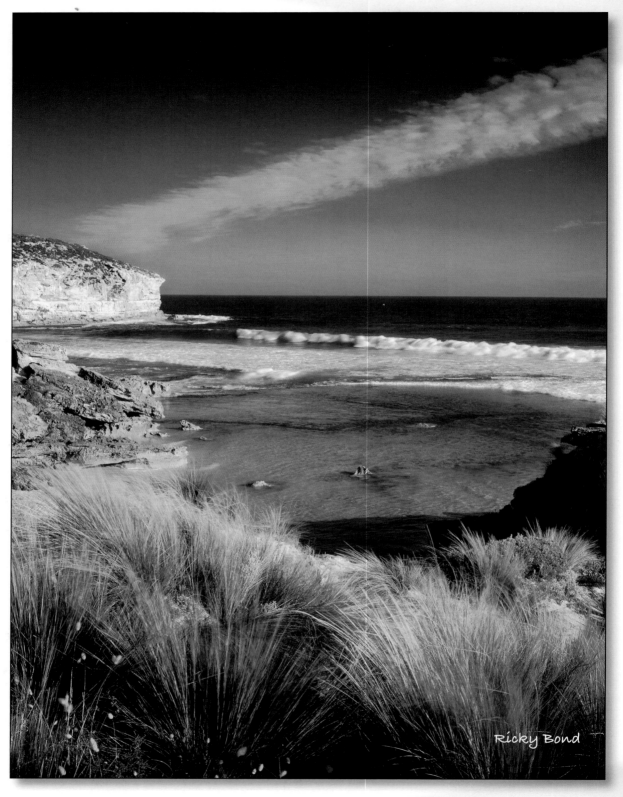

Ricky Bond

Glossary

Additive color	A color system where the primaries of red, green and blue mix to form the other colors.
Adjustment layer	Image adjustment placed on a layer.
Adobe gamma	A calibration and profiling utility supplied with Photoshop.
Algorithm	A sequence of mathematical operations.
Aliasing	The display of a digital image where a curved line appears jagged due to the square pixels.
Alpha channel	Additional channel used for storing masks and selections.
Analyse/Analysis	To examine in detail.
Anti-aliasing	The process of smoothing the appearance of a curved line in a digital image.
Aperture	A circular opening in the lens that controls light reaching the film.
Area array	A rectangular pattern of light-sensitive sensors alternately receptive to red, green or blue light.
Artifacts	Pixels that are significantly incorrect in their brightness or color values.
Aspect ratio	The ratio of height to width. Usually in reference to the light-sensitive area or format of the camera.
Bit	Short for binary digit, the basic unit of the binary language.
Bit depth	Number of bits (memory) assigned to recording color or tonal information.
Bitmap	A one-bit image, i.e. black and white (no shades of gray).
Blend mode	The formula used for defining the mixing of a layer with those beneath it.
Brightness	The value assigned to a pixel in the HSB model to define the relative lightness of a pixel.
Byte	Eight bits. The standard unit of binary data storage containing a value between 0 and 255.
Captured	A record of an image.
CCD	Charge Coupled Device. A solid state image pick-up device used in digital image capture.
Channels	The divisions of color data within a digital image. Data is separated into primary or secondary colors.
Charge Coupled Device	See CCD.
CIS	Contact image sensor. A single row of sensors used in scanner mechanisms.
Clipboard	The temporary storage of something that has been cut or copied.

Clipping group	Two or more layers that have been linked. The base layer acts as a mask, limiting the effect or visibility of those layers clipped to it.
Cloning Tool	A tool used for replicating pixels in digital photography.
CMOS	Complementary Metal Oxide Semiconductor. A chip used widely within the computer industry, now also frequently used as an image sensor in digital cameras.
CMYK	Cyan, Magenta, Yellow and black (K). The inks used in four-color printing.
Color Picker	Dialog box used for the selection of colors.
Color fringes	Bands of color on the edges of lines within an image.
Color fringing	See *Color fringes*.
Color gamut	The range of colors provided by a hardware device, or a set of pigments.
Color space	An accurately defined set of colors that can be translated for use as a profile.
ColorSync	System level software developed by Apple, designed to work together with hardware devices to facilitate predictable color.
Complementary metal oxide semiconductor	See *CMOS*.
Composition	The arrangement of shape, tone, line and color within the boundaries of the image area.
Compression	A method for reducing the file size of a digital image.
Constrain proportions	Retains the proportional dimensions of an image when changing the image size.
Contact image sensor	See *CIS*.
Context	The circumstances relevant to something under consideration.
Continuous tone	An image containing the illusion of smooth gradations between highlights and shadows.
Contrast	The difference in brightness between the darkest and lightest areas of the image or subject.
CPU	Central Processing Unit, used to compute exposure.
Crash	The sudden operational failure of a computer.
Crop	Reduce image size to enhance composition or limit information.
Curves	Control for adjusting tonality and color in a digital image.
DAT	Digital Audio Tape. Tape format used to store computer data.
Default	The settings of a device as chosen by the manufacturer.
Defringe	The action of removing the edge pixels of a selection.
Density	The measure of opacity of tone on a negative.

Depth of field	The zone of sharpness variable by aperture, focal length or subject distance.
Descreen	The removal of half-tone lines or patterns during scanning.
Device	An item of computer hardware.
Device dependent	Dependent on a particular item of hardware. For example, referring to a color result unique to a particular printer.
Device independent	Not dependent on a particular item of hardware. For example, a color result that can be replicated on any hardware device.
Digital audio tape	See *DAT*.
Digital image	A computer-generated photograph composed of pixels (picture elements) rather than film grain.
Download	To copy digital files (usually from the Internet).
Dpi	Dots per inch. A measurement of resolution.
Dummy file	To go through the motions of creating a new file in Photoshop for the purpose of determining the file size required during the scanning process.
Dye sublimation print	A high quality print created using thermal dyes.
Dyes	Types of pigment.
Edit	Select images from a larger collection to form a sequence or theme.
Editable text	Text that has not been rendered into pixels.
Eight-bit image	A single-channel image capable of storing 256 different colors or levels.
Evaluate	Assess the value or quality of a piece of work.
Exposure	Combined effect of intensity and duration of light on a light-sensitive material or device.
Exposure compensation	To increase or decrease the exposure from a meter-indicated exposure to obtain an appropriate exposure.
Feather	The action of softening the edge of a digital selection.
File format	The code used to store digital data, e.g. TIFF or JPEG.
File size	The memory required to store digital data in a file.
Film grain	See *Grain*.
Film speed	A precise number or ISO rating given to a film or device indicating its degree of light sensitivity.
F-numbers (f-stops)	A sequence of numbers given to the relative sizes of aperture opening. F-numbers are standard on all lenses. The largest number corresponds to the smallest aperture and vice versa.
Format	The size of the camera or the orientation/shape of the image.
Frame	The act of composing an image. See *Composition*.
Freeze	Software that fails to interact with new information.

FTP software	File Transfer Protocol software is used for uploading and downloading files over the Internet.
Galleries	A managed collection of images displayed in a conveniently accessible form.
Gaussian Blur	A filter used for defocusing a digital image.
GIF	Graphics Interchange Format. An 8-bit format (256 colors) that supports animation and partial transparency.
Gigabyte	A unit of measurement for digital files, 1024 megabytes.
Grain	Tiny particles of silver metal or dye that make up the final image. Fast films give larger grain than slow films. Focus finders are used to magnify the projected image so that the grain can be seen and an accurate focus obtained.
Gray card	Card that reflects 18% of incident light. The resulting tone is used by light meters as a standardized midtone.
Grayscale	An 8-bit image with a single channel used to describe monochrome (black and white) images.
Half-tone	A system of reproducing the continuous tone of a photographic print by a pattern of dots printed by offset litho.
Hard copy	A print.
Hard drive	Memory facility that is capable of retaining information after the computer is switched off.
Highlight	Area of subject receiving highest exposure value.
Histogram	A graphical representation of a digital image indicating the pixels allocated to each level.
Histories	The memory of previous image states in Photoshop.
History Brush	A tool in Photoshop with which a previous state or history can be painted.
HTML	Hypertext markup language. The code that is used to describe the contents and appearance of a web page.
Hue	The name of a color, e.g. red, green or blue.
Hyperlink	A link that allows the viewer of a page to navigate or 'jump' to another location on the same page or on a different page.
ICC	International Color Consortium. A collection of manufacturers including Adobe, Microsoft, Agfa, Kodak, SGI, Fogra, Sun and Taligent who came together to create an open, cross-platform standard for color management.
ICM	Image Color Management. Windows-based software designed to work together with hardware devices to facilitate predictable color.

Image Color Management	See *ICM*.
Image setter	A device used to print CMYK film separations used in the printing industry.
Image size	The pixel dimensions, output dimensions and resolution used to define a digital image.
Infrared film	A film that is sensitive to the wavelengths of light longer than 720nm, which are invisible to the human eye.
Instant capture	An exposure that is fast enough to result in a relatively sharp image free of significant blur.
International Color Consortium	See *ICC*.
Interpolated resolution	Final resolution of an image arrived at by means of interpolation.
Interpolation	Increasing the pixel dimensions of an image by inserting new pixels between existing pixels within the image.
ISO	International Standards Organization. A numerical system for rating the speed or relative light sensitivity of a film or device.
ISP	Internet Service Provider, allows individuals access to a web server.
Jaz	A storage disk capable of storing slightly less than 2GB, manufactured by Iomega.
JPEG (.jpg)	Joint Photographic Experts Group. Popular image compression file format.
Jump	To open a file in another application.
Juxtapose	Placing objects or subjects within a frame to allow comparison.
Kilobyte	1024 bytes.
Lab mode	A device-independent color model created in 1931 as an international standard for measuring color.
Lasso Tool	Selection Tool used in digital editing.
Latent image	An image created by exposure onto light-sensitive silver halide ions, which until amplified by chemical development is invisible to the eye.
Latitude	Ability of the film or device to record the brightness range of the subject.
Layer	A feature in digital editing software that allows a composite digital image where each element is on a separate layer or level.

Layer mask	A mask attached to a layer that is used to define the visibility of pixels on that layer.
LCD	Liquid Crystal Display.
LED	Light-Emitting Diode. Used in the viewfinder to inform the photographer of exposure settings.
Lens	An optical device usually made from glass that focuses light rays to form an image on a surface.
Levels	Shades of lightness or brightness assigned to pixels.
Light cyan	A pale shade of the subtractive color cyan.
Light magenta	A pale shade of the subtractive color magenta.
LiOn	Lithium ion. Rechargeable battery type.
Lithium Ion	See *LiOn*.
LZW compression	A lossless form of image compression used in the TIFF format.
Magic Wand Tool	Selection Tool used in digital editing.
Magnesium lithium	See MnLi.
Marching ants	A moving broken line indicating a digital selection of pixels.
Marquee Tool	Selection Tool used in digital editing.
Maximum aperture	Largest lens opening.
Megabyte	A unit of measurement for digital files, 1024 kilobytes.
Megapixels	More than a million pixels.
Memory card	A removable storage device about the size of a small card. Many technologies available result in various sizes and formats. Often found in digital cameras.
Metallic silver	Metal created during the development of film, giving rise to the appearance of grain. See *Grain*.
Minimum aperture	Smallest lens opening.
MnLi	Magnesium lithium. Rechargeable battery type.
Mode (digital image)	RGB, CMYK, etc. The mode describes the tonal and color range of the captured or scanned image.
Moiré	A repetitive pattern usually caused by interference of overlapping symmetrical dots or lines.
Motherboard	An electronic board containing the main functional elements of a computer upon which other components can be connected.
Multiple exposure	Several exposures made onto the same frame of film or piece of paper.
Negative	An image on film or paper where the tones are reversed, e.g. dark tones are recorded as light tones and vice versa.
NiCd	Nickel cadmium. Rechargeable battery type.

Nickel cadmium	See *NiCd*.
Nickel metal hydride	See *NiMH*.
NiMH	Nickel metal hydride. Rechargeable battery type.
Noise	Electronic interference producing white speckles in the image.
Non-imaging	To not assist in the formation of an image. When related to light it is often known as flare.
Objective	A factual and non-subjective analysis of information.
ODR	Output device resolution. The number of ink dots per inch of paper produced by the printer.
Opacity	The degree of non-transparency.
Opaque	Not transmitting light.
Optimize	The process of fine-tuning the file size and display quality of an image or image slice destined for the web.
Out of gamut	Beyond the scope of colors that a particular device can create.
Output device resolution	See *ODR*.
Path	The outline of a vector shape.
PDF	Portable Document Format. Data format created using Adobe software.
Pegging	The action of fixing tonal or color values to prevent them from being altered when using Curves image adjustment.
Photo multiplier tube	See *PMT*.
Piezoelectric	Crystal that will accurately change dimension with a change of applied voltage. Often used in inkjet printers to supply microscopic dots of ink.
Pixel	The smallest square picture element in a digital image.
Pixelated	An image where the pixels are visible to the human eye and curved lines appear jagged or stepped.
PMT	Photo multiplier tube. Light sensing device generally used in drum scanners.
Portable Document Format	See *PDF*.
Pre-press	Stage where digital information is translated into output suitable for the printing process.
Primary colors	The three colors of light (red, green and blue) from which all other colors can be created.
Processor speed	The capability of the computer's CPU measured in megahertz.

Quick Mask mode	Temporary alpha channel used for refining or making selections.
RAID	Redundant array of independent disks. A type of hard disk assembly that allows data to be simultaneously written.
RAM	Random access memory. The computer's short-term or working memory.
Redundant array of independent disks	See *RAID*.
Reflector	A surface used to reflect light in order to fill shadows.
Refraction	The change in direction of light as it passes through a transparent surface at an angle.
Resample	To alter the total number of pixels describing a digital image.
Resolution	A measure of the degree of definition, also called sharpness.
RGB	Red, green and blue. The three primary colors used to display images on a color monitor.
Rollover	A web effect in which a different image state appears when the viewer performs a mouse action.
Rubber Stamp	A tool used for replicating pixels in digital imaging.
Sample	To select a color value for analysis or use.
Saturation (color)	Intensity or richness of color hue.
Save a Copy	An option that allows the user to create a digital replica of an image file but without layers or additional channels.
Save As	An option that allows the user to create a duplicate of a digital file but with an alternative name, thereby protecting the original document from any changes that have been made since it was opened.
Scale	A ratio of size.
Scratch disk memory	Portion of hard disk allocated to software such as Photoshop to be used as a working space.
Screen real estate	Area of monitor available for image display that is not taken up by palettes and toolbars.
Screen redraws	Time taken to render information being depicted on the monitor as changes are being made through the application software.
Secondary colors	The colors cyan, magenta and yellow, created when two primary colors are mixed.
Sharp	In focus. Not blurred.
Silver halide	Compound of silver often used as a light-sensitive speck on film.
Single lens reflex	See *SLR camera*.

Slice	Divides an image into rectangular areas for selective optimization or to create functional areas for a web page.
Slider	A sliding control in digital editing software used to adjust color, tone, opacity, etc.
SLR camera	Single lens reflex camera. The image in the viewfinder is essentially the same image that the film will see. This image, prior to taking the shot, is viewed via a mirror that moves out of the way when the shutter release is pressed.
Snapshot	A record of a history state that is held until the file is closed.
Soft proof	The depiction of a digital image on a computer monitor used to check output accuracy.
Software	A computer program.
Subjective analysis	Personal opinions or views concerning the perceived communication and aesthetic value of an image.
Subtractive color	A color system where the primaries of yellow, magenta and cyan mix to form all other colors.
System software	Computer operating program, e.g. Windows or Mac OS.
Tagging	System whereby a profile is included within the image data of a file for the purpose of helping describe its particular color characteristics.
Thematic images	A set of images with a unifying idea or concept.
TIFF	Tagged Image File Format. Popular image file format for desktop publishing applications.
Tone	A tint of color or shade of gray.
Transparent	Allowing light to pass through.
Tri-color	A filter taking the hue of either one of the additive primaries, red, green or blue.
True resolution	The resolution of an image file created by the hardware device, either camera or scanner, without any interpolation.
TTL meter	Through-the-lens reflective light meter. This is a convenient way to measure the brightness of a scene as the meter is behind the camera lens.
Tweening	Derived from the words in betweening – an automated process of creating additional frames between two existing frames in an animation.
UCR	Under color removal. A method of replacing a portion of the yellow, magenta and cyan ink, within the shadows and neutral areas of an image, with black ink.
Under color removal	See *UCR*.
Unsharp Mask	See *USM*.

Unsharp Mask filter	A filter for increasing apparent sharpness of a digital image.
URL	Uniform resource locator. The unique web address given to every web page.
USM	Unsharp Mask. A process used to sharpen images.
Vector graphic	A resolution-independent image described by its geometric characteristics rather than by pixels.
Video card	A circuit board containing the hardware required to drive the monitor of a computer.
Video memory	Memory required for the monitor to be able to render an image.
Virtual memory	Hard drive memory allocated to function as RAM.
Visualize	To imagine how something will look once it has been completed.
Workflow	Series of repeatable steps required to achieve a particular result within a digital imaging environment.
Zip	A storage disk manufactured by Iomega, available in either 100MB or 250MB capacity.
Zoom Tool	A tool used for magnifying a digital image on the monitor.

Keyboard Shortcuts

⌥ = Option ⇧ = Shift ⌘ = Command

Action	Keyboard Shortcut
Navigate and view	
Fit image on screen	Double-click Hand Tool or ⌘/Ctrl + 0 '(zero)'
View image at 100%	Double-click Zoom Tool or ⌥/Alt + ⌘/Ctrl + 0 '(zero)'
Zoom Tool (magnify)	⌘/Ctrl + Spacebar + Click image
Zoom Tool (reduce)	⌥/Alt + ⌘/Ctrl + Click image
Full/standard screen mode	F
Show/hide rulers	⌘/Ctrl + R
Show/hide guides	⌘/Ctrl + ;
Hide palettes	Tab key
File commands	
Open	⌘/Ctrl + O
Close	⌘/Ctrl + W
Save	⌘/Ctrl + S
Save As	⇧ + ⌘/Ctrl + S
Undo/Redo	⌘/Ctrl + Z
Step Backward	⌥/Alt + ⌘/Ctrl + Z
Step Forward	⌘/Ctrl + ⇧ + Z
Selections	
Add to selection	Hold ⇧ key and select again
Subtract from selection	Hold ⌥/Alt key and select again
Copy	⌘/Ctrl + C
Cut	⌘/Ctrl + C
Paste	⌘/Ctrl + V
Paste Into	⌘/Ctrl ⇧ + V
Free Transform	⌘/Ctrl + ⇧ + T (Shift key new to CS2)
Distort image in Free Transform	Hold ⌘ key + Move handle
Feather	⌘/Ctrl ⌥/Alt + D
Select All	⌘/Ctrl + A
Deselect	⌘/Ctrl + D
Inverse selection	⌘/Ctrl + I
Edit in Quick Mask Mode	Q

Painting

Set default foreground and background colors	D
Switch between foreground and background color	X
Enlarge brush size (with Paint tool selected)	]
Reduce brush size (with Paint tool selected)	[
Make brush softer	[+ Shift
Make brush harder	] + Shift
Change opacity of brush in 10% increments (with Paint tool selected)	Press number keys 0 – 9
Fill with foreground color	⌥/Alt ⌫
Fill with background color	⌘/Ctrl ⌫

Adjustments

Levels	⌘/Ctrl + L
Curves	⌘/Ctrl + M
Select next adjustment point in Curves	Ctrl + Tab

Layers and masks

Add new layer	⇧ ⌘/Ctrl + N
Load selection from layer mask or channel	⌘/Ctrl + Click thumbnail
Change opacity of active layer in 10% increments	Press number keys 0 – 9
Add layer mask – Hide All	⌥/Alt + Click 'Add layer mask' icon
Move layer down/up	⌘/Ctrl + [or]
Group selected layers	⌘/Ctrl + G
Create Clipping Mask	⌘/Ctrl + ⌥/Alt + G
Disable/enable layer mask	⇧ + Click layer mask thumbnail
Preview contents of layer mask	⌥/Alt + Click layer mask thumbnail
Preview layer mask and image	⌥/Alt + ⇧ + click layer mask thumbnail
Group or clip layer	⌘/Ctrl + G
Blend modes	⌥/Alt + ⇧ + (N, M, S, O, Y) **N**ormal, **M**ultiply, **S**creen, **O**verlay, **L**uminosity

Crop

Enter crop	Return key
Cancel crop	Esc key
Constrain proportions of crop marquee	Hold ⇧ key
Turn off magnetic guides when cropping	Hold ⌥/Alt ⇧ keys + Drag handle

Web Links

Resources

Essential Skills	http://www.photoshopessentialskills.com
RMIT Photography	http://www.rmit.edu.au/adc/photography
Adobe Digital Imaging	http://www.adobe.com/digitalimag/main.html
Martin Evening	http://www.martinevening.com
Luminous Landscape	http://www.luminous-landscape.com
Digital Photography Review	http://www.dpreview.com
Digital Dog	http://www.digitaldog.net
Epson	http://www.epson.com
Computer Darkroom	http://www.computer_darkroom.com
Inkjet Mall	http://www.inkjetmall.com

Tutorials

Adobe	http://www.adobe.com/products/tips/photoshop.html
Phong	http://www.phong.com
Russell Brown	http://www.russellbrown.com
Think Dan	http://www.thinkdan.com/tutorials/photoshop.html
Planet Photoshop	http://www.planetphotoshop.com
Ultimate Photoshop	http://www.ultimate-photoshop.com
Scan Tips	http://www.scantips.com

Photomedia illustrators

Paul Allister	obscur@hotpop.com
Ricky Bond	rbphoto@bigpond.net.au
Andrew Boyle	andrewb_photography@lycos.com
Catherine Dorsen	photoflare@hotmail.com
Andrew Elliot	aforandrew@hotmail.com
Samantha Everton	http://www.samanthaeverton.com
Orien Harvey	orien_harvey@ekit.com
Benedikt Partenheimer	benediktion@web.de
Raphael Ruz	http://endersan.com
Fabio Sarraff	http://www.fabiosarraff.com
Amber Williams	amber_williams@mail.com
Stuart Wilson	http://www.stuartwilson.com.au

Supporting CD

The CD is a veritable treasure trove of supporting files for the projects in this book. The CD uses a web browser interface to supply quick and easy access to many of the images. Many of the images in the Foundations and Advanced techniques sections of the books are to be found on the CD together with the images for the projects sections.

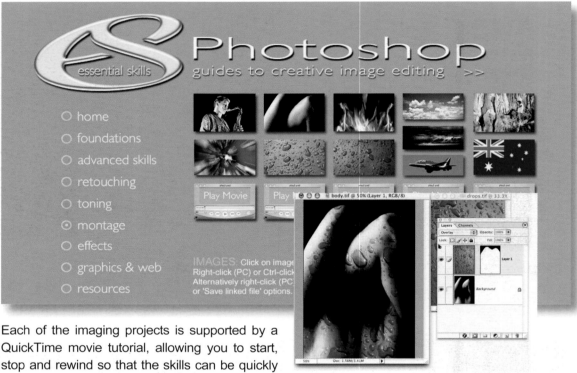

Each of the imaging projects is supported by a QuickTime movie tutorial, allowing you to start, stop and rewind so that the skills can be quickly and easily acquired.

Open the JPEG images and watch the supporting movies

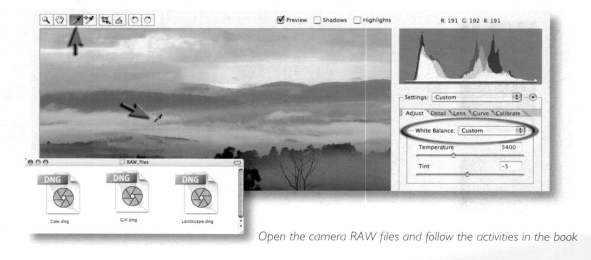

Open the camera RAW files and follow the activities in the book

PHOTOSHOP CS2 >>>

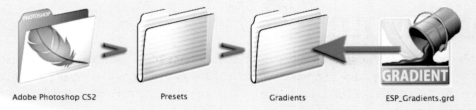

Load the Adobe presets to enhance your Adobe software

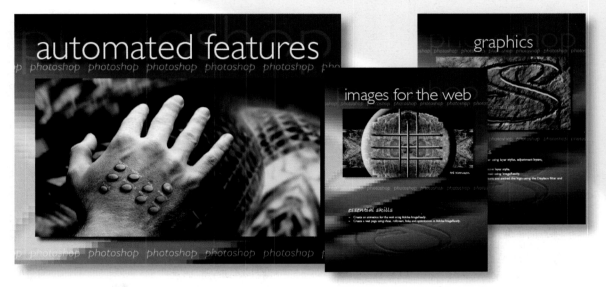

Open one of the three PDF chapters from the CD to further enhance your imaging skills

>>> essential skills >>>

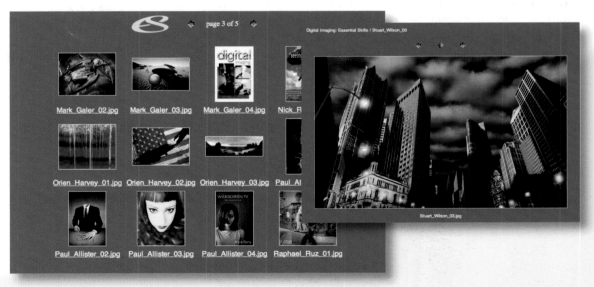

Access a comprehensive gallery of inspirational images

363

CD Contents *(see previous pages for overview)*

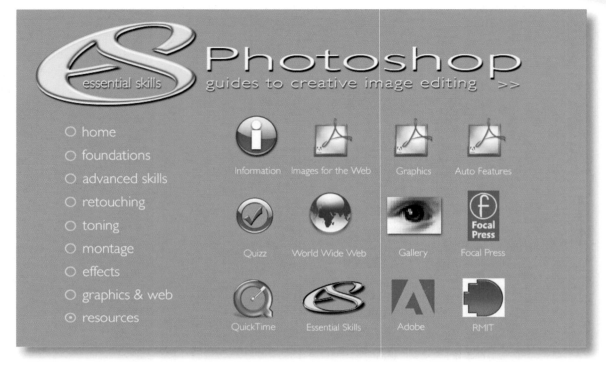

THE CD PROVIDES EXTENSIVE SUPPORT IN THE FORM OF:

- Four hours of movie tutorials.
- Over 70 high quality JPEG images to support imaging projects.
- Three camera RAW files used in the chapter 'Digital Negatives'.
- Four multi-layered PSD files for the graphics and web projects.
- Four Adobe presets to enhance perfomance capabilities of software.
- Printable PDF file of keyboard shortcuts to act as a quick and handy reference guide to speed up your image-editing tasks.
- A gallery of inspirational images.
- Quizzes to test your digital imaging knowledge (answers at end of file).
- Links to useful web sites and contacts for digital illustrators and photographers used in the creation of this book.
- Links to the Focal Press, Essential Skills, Adobe and RMIT University web sites.

Essential Skills supporting website

For all the latest support materials go to: http://www.photographyessentialskills.com

CD Index

As well as containing supporting images, presets and QuickTime movie tutorials, the CD also stores three additonal PDF chapters with supporting images for those users interested in graphics, web and automated features.

graphics, web & workflow

Index